DISCARD

THE
Street-Wise Spanish
SURVIVAL GUIDE

D0813606

DISCARD

THE
Street-Wise Spanish
SURVIVAL GUIDE

A Dictionary of Over 3,000 Slang Expressions, Proverbs, Idioms, and Other
Tricky English and Spanish Words and Phrases Translated and Explained

**Eleanor Hamer and
Fernando Díez de Urdanivia**

Skyhorse Publishing

Copyright © 2008 by Eleanor Hamer and Fernando Díez de Urdanivia

All Rights Reserved. No part of this book may be reproduced in any manner without the express written consent of the publisher, except in the case of brief excerpts in critical reviews or articles. All inquiries should be addressed to Skyhorse Publishing, 555 Eighth Avenue, Suite 903, New York, NY 10018.

Skyhorse Publishing books may be purchased in bulk at special discounts for sales promotion, corporate gifts, fund raising, or educational purposes. Special editions can also be created to specifications. For details, contact Special Sales Department, Skyhorse Publishing, 555 Eighth Avenue, Suite 903, New York, NY 10018 or info@skyhorsepublishing.com.

www.skyhorsepublishing.com

10 9 8 7 6 5 4 3 2 1

Library of Congress Cataloging-in-Publication Data
    Hamer, Eleanor.
    The street-wise Spanish survival guide : a dictionary of over 3,000 slang expressions, proverbs, idioms, and other tricky English and Spanish words and phrases translated and explained / Eleanor Hamer and Fernando Diez de Urdanivia.
        p.   cm.
    ISBN 978-1-60239-250-2 (alk. paper)
    1. Spanish language—Slang—Glossaries, vocabularies, etc.   2. Spanish language—Idioms—Glossaries, vocabularies, etc.   3. Spanish language—Dictionaries—English.   I. Díez de Urdanivia, Fernando.
II. Title.

PC4971.H36   2008
468.3'421—dc22

                                                                                        2008013023

Printed in China

Contents

About the Authors

About this Book

Born in Mexico to a British family, **Eleanor Hamer**'s professional life began in Lima, Peru where she taught English as a second language for four years at the **Instituto Peruano-Norteamericano** and the **Universidad de Lima.** She then moved back to Mexico, where she was made director of the Insurgentes branch of the **Berlitz School of Languages** in Mexico City. A short time later, she became co-owner and Director of **Pennington Cultural Center**, then Director of the language laboratory at **Ingenieros Civiles Asociados**.

During the next few years, she wrote her first course in English as a second language, and in 1975, she established **Hamersharp**, a school for English as a second language designed for business executives. There she developed the definitive and highly effective course used successfully at the **Hamersharp** schools to this date. She also wrote **Writing Business English** for the most advanced students. Her aversion to administrative work led her to give up running **Hamersharp**, and for the last 15 years, she has been the official translator for Price Waterhouse (now PricewaterhouseCoopers) in Mexico City.

Fernando Díez de Urdanivia is a graduate of the Carlos Septién García school of journalism in Mexico. The son of a prominent Mexican journalist, he has written for *Excélsior*, *Novedades*, *El Heraldo de México*, *El Día*, and *El Universal*. He founded *El Diario de la Tarde de Novedades* and for many years wrote for a wide variety of Mexican magazines (including *Hoy*, *Abside* and *Sembradores*). In 1998 he was awarded the National Journalism Prize for his interviews.

He has taught Spanish composition and literature at the **Escuela Carlos Septién García**, the **Universidad Motolinía**, the **Centro de Estudios of the University of California** in Mexico, the **Chicano Studies Center de Santa Barbara**, California in México, and the **Instituto Cultural Hispano** Mexicano, and was director of the **Centro de Estudios Periodísticos**. He has also taught many literary and creative writing workshops.

His published works include *Mi historia secreta de la música*, *Cómo hablan los que escriben* (interviews with famous writers), *Te doy mi Palabra de Amor*, *Sabiduría en pocas líneas*, *En el umbral del milenio* (50 interviews each with prominent Mexicans over the age of 70) and *Dichas y dichos de la comida insólita de México* (unknown food of Mexico), *Carlos del Castillo*, *Heraldo de Bach en México* (biography of the Mexican music teacher), *Al final del camino* and *Burocraterapia* (short stories), as well as *Cuento Modernista Hispanoamericano* (analysis of short stories during this period).

About this Book

This is not a text book, but a very efficient reference book aimed at filling the void that confronts people who already have a fairly good knowledge of Spanish but can't seem to progress beyond what they learned in the classroom.

One of the most interesting portions of the book is the chapter containing easy-to-understand details of words, phrases, expressions and sayings of real-life Spanish as it is actually spoken in Latin America. They are arranged in alphabetical order (according to the English alphabet) and translated into English, with real-life examples and explanations that help the reader grasp the true and complete meaning. That chapter has a counterpart, based on the most common expressions in English, with equivalents provided in Spanish.

The *pièce de résistance* of this book is the chapter on the dreaded false cognate, a source of so many embarrassing situations. There is even a section where bad words are explained.

Symbols are used to provide information in a variety of ways, including cautions such as ⌂ for "slang" and ✖ for "very vulgar". They save a lot of guessing and cross checking.

All these elements give the student with the equivalent of what they could otherwise gain only from years of living with knowledgeable, educated Spanish-speaking people.

Far from offering up the usual collection of tedious theories, the grammar chapter supplies useful clues, including an understanding of the subjunctive voice, and the use of problematic words such as *para, por, pero* and *sino*.

This book is concerned with other significant aspects of the Spanish-speaking world as well. It explains the ins and outs of customs, dress, food and other cultural differences that can make life frustrating for the uninitiated. It includes a chapter to involve the student in Mexican cultural peculiarities and explains Mexican food and specific dishes with which the foreign visitor is usually unfamiliar but which are found on practically all menus. It also contains a unique (though discrete) explanation of the Mexican "albur" (heretofore a mystery to non-native speakers of Spanish).

This book is the result of 30 years of experience and hard work. Both co-authors are extremely well qualified. One is a native speaker of English and the other a native speaker of Spanish. Both are lifelong teachers of English and Spanish. This fact sets the book apart and provides an unequalled assurance of its accuracy in identifying the nuances, overtones and subtle meanings of real-life Spanish.

Symbols

Author's Acknowledgements

Person   ☺

Thing   ☐

Person or Thing   ☺☐

Literally   📖

Used By Teenagers   ♛♛

Slang   🔔

Used Mainly in Mexico   ⚑

Mildly Vulgar   ⇩

Quite Vulgar   ↓

Very Vulgar   ✘

Authors' Acknowledgments

The authors wish to thank and acknowledge the help of Luisa Ma. Alvarez de Jaubert ✝, Dr. Richard Barrutia✝, Eleanor Merino-Hamer, María Martínez, Bárbara de los Reyes, Hilde Sotomayor, with very special thanks to Carmen Bermejo, without whose skills this book would never have become a reality.

I
EXPRESSIONS

A. Common Expressions in Spanish

It is a well-known fact that structures vary from language to language, sometimes to such an extent that the overall meaning of a sentence or phrase may be utterly different from its component parts. This is even more true of idiomatic expressions. It usually takes years of living in a foreign country to master the structures and idioms of its language. However, the following explanations will probably go a long way to shorten this difficult process and make it less painful.

Below are a few examples of normal Spanish construction which demonstrate the absurdity of analyzing word for word.

Acabar de . . .
— **Acabar** is "to finish" and **de** is "of", but **acabar de** + verb is "to have just finished ❑".
- **Marta acaba de comer (desayunar) (cenar).**
  Marta just had lunch (breakfast) (dinner).
- **Acaban de empezar.**
  They just got started.

Dar con . . .
— **Dar** is "to give" and **con** is "with", but **dar con** is "to find" or "to come up with ❑".
- **No damos con el hotel.**
  We can't find the hotel.
- **Finalmente dimos con la solución.**
  We finally came up with the solution.

Hacer el papel . . .
— This is literally "to make paper", but means to "play a role".
- **Él hace el papel del ciego.**
  He plays the role of the blind man.
- **No me gustó cómo hizo su papel.**
  I didn't like the way she played her role.

Por si acaso; por si + verb
— Literally "for if perhaps". It means "just in case".

- **Lleva dinero, por si acaso.**
  Take some money, just in case.
- **Traje paraguas, por si llueve.**
  I brought an umbrella, just in case it rains.

Following is an assortment of interesting idiomatic expressions. As can be seen, words don't usually give much of an idea as to the overall meaning. *Section 1* contains expressions listed as verbs, as they can be conjugated. *Section 2* groups expressions that do not stand alone but must be used as part of a sentence and *Section 3* groups self-contained expressions (that stand alone).

All expressions are in alphabetical order, according to the English language. Words in parentheses are not considered for alphabetical purpose.

When the *literal translation* of an expression is interesting, it is given, preceded by the symbol 📖. Expressions used only in Mexico have the ⏚ symbol. Expressions marked ✝✝ are sometimes used also by adults.

If you want to know the Spanish equivalent of an expression in English, see *Section B*.

1. VERBS

Abrir(se) de capa (📖 To open your cape)
— To speak frankly and sincerely
- **Se abrió de capa cuando le pregunté acerca de mi hijo.**
  He gave it to me straight when I asked him about my son.

Aguantar carros y carretas
— To have the capacity to take a lot of negative acts or nonsense from ☺
- **A veces tengo que aguantarles carros y carretas a los latosos de mis parientes.**
  Sometimes I have to take a lot of nonsense from my annoying relatives.

Alborotar el gallinero (📖 To get the chickens in a flap)
— To get everyone in an uproar
- **No vayas a decir nada de los despidos proyectados. No queremos alborotar el gallinero.**
  Don't say anything about the projected layoffs. We don't want to get everyone in an uproar.

Aliviar(se)
— To give birth
- **En este hospital se alivió Jimena.**
  Jimena gave birth in this hospital.

Andar
— To be after ☺ (when used with "**tras de ☺**")
- **Enrique anda tras Lucía.**
  Enrique is after Lucy.
— To be doing ☐
- **Ya me cansé de andar buscando trabajo.**
  I'm tired of looking for work.
— To go steady (when used with "**con ☺**")
- **¿Andas en serio con alguien?**
  Are you going steady with someone?

Note: **Andar** is often (incorrectly) used instead of **estar** in the present progressive, as in the second example above, or in **Ando cocinando unos huevos**, which should be **Estoy cocinando unos huevos** (*I am cooking some eggs*).

♫ Andar amolado(a)
— To be in a bad way (as concerns money or health)
- **He andado amolado de dinero.**
  I've been in a bad way as concerns money.

Andar con el Jesús en la boca
— To be distraught

- **La pobre Leonor anda con el Jesús en la boca.**
  Poor Leonor is distraught.

Andar(se) con rodeos
— To beat around the bush

- **No te andes con rodeos. ¡Dímelo claro!**
  Don't beat around the bush. Come right out with it!

Andar de boca en boca (📖 To go from mouth to mouth)
— To be on everyone's lips; to be the talk of the town.

- **Angélica anda de boca en boca.**
  Angelica is the talk of the town.

Andar de la ceca a la meca; Andar del tingo al tango
— To go to a lot of places

- **Anduve de la ceca a la meca para encontrar lo que quería.**
  I had to go to a million places to find what I wanted.

Andar del tingo al tango (see Andar de la ceca a la meca)

Andar de malas
— To have a run of bad luck

- **No quiero correr riesgos ahorita. He andado de malas.**
  I don't want to take any chances. I have had a run of bad luck.

Andar (estar) en las nubes (📖 To be in the clouds)
— To be on cloud nine; to be (mentally) somewhere else (daydreaming)

- **Desde que lo aceptó Adriana, José Luis anda en las nubes.**
  Jose Luis has been on cloud nine ever since Adriana agreed to go steady with him.
- **¡Muchacho! Atiende a la clase. ¡Estás en las nubes!**
  Hey kid! Pay attention in class! You are daydreaming!

Andar giro(a) (girito(a))
— To be still going strong

- **A sus ochenta y siete años, nuestra abuela todavía anda muy girita.**
  Our grandmother is still going strong at 87.

Andar norteado(a)
— To be disoriented

- **Todavía ando norteado. Apenas llevo dos días en esta ciudad.**
  I'm still disoriented. I've only been in this city for two days.

Armar(se) la gorda
— To start a fight

- **Se puso agresivo y armó la gorda en el bar.**
  He got nasty and started a fight in the bar.

Expressions

- **Si nos siguen provocando, aquí se va a armar la gorda.**
  If they keep picking on us, there's going to be a fight.

Barajar(la) (más) despacio (📖 To shuffle ❐ more slowly)
— To explain ❐ more slowly.

- **Perdón, no entiendo nada. Barájamela más despacio.**
  Sorry, I didn't get that. Explain it again more slowly.

Brillar por su ausencia (📖 To shine by your absence)
— To be very conspicuously absent

- **En la boda, Dolores brilló por su ausencia.**
  Everybody noticed that Dolores wasn't at the wedding.

Buscarle ruido al chicharrón (📖 To poke the **chicharrón** until it makes a noise); **Buscarle tres pies al gato**
— To ask for it; To burn the candle at both ends; To look for trouble

- **Si no sigues las reglas de esta casa, le estás buscando ruido al chicharrón (le estás buscando tres pies al gato).**
  If you don't follow the rules of the house, you are looking for trouble.

Caer al pelo
— To be just the thing; to be just what one wants or needs

- **El cinturón que me regalaste me cayó al pelo.**
  The belt you gave me was just what I wanted.

Caer bien (o mal)*
— To like ❐☺

- **Elisa me cae muy bien.**
  I really like Elisa.
- **Arturo no me cae bien (Arturo me cae mal).**
  I don't like Arturo.

— When one is speaking of food, this expression means "it goes down well." When **mal** is used instead of **bien**, the meaning is the opposite.

- **El chocolate me cae mal.**
  Chocolate doesn't agree with me.
- **El consomé le cae bien a uno cuando está enfermo.**
  Broth goes down well when one is sick.

Note: In English, the subject used with the verb "to like" is the person who experiences the feeling of liking or affection. In Spanish, the subject is the person who is the object of that liking or affection.

Caer como cubeta de agua fría (📖 To fall on ☺ like a bucket of cold water)
— To astonish; to stun

- **La noticia me cayó como cubeta de agua fría.**
  The news stunned me.

Calentar(le) la cabeza a ☺ (📖 To heat up ☺'s head)

— To prejudice ☺ against ☺ or ❐

- **Efrén le calentó la cabeza a Carlos para que acusara a José.**
  Efren got Carlos all worked up so he would accuse Jose.

Cargar con el muerto (📖 To carry the body)

— To be blamed for ❐

- **Arnulfo tuvo que cargar con el muerto por lo que pasó en la fiesta.**
  Arnulfo got all the blame for what happened at the party.

Chupar(se) el dedo (📖 To suck your thumb)

— To be born yesterday

- **No me vengas con ese cuento. No me chupo el dedo, ¿sabes?**
  Don't give me that story. I wasn't born yesterday, you know.

Colgar(se) de la lámpara (see Poner el grito en el cielo)

Comer ansias (📖 To eat anxiety)

— To be anxious or fidgety

- **No hay prisa. Tómalo con calma. No comas ansias.**
  There is no hurry. Take it easy. Calm down.
- **Por andar comiendo ansias, me salió todo mal.**
  Everything went wrong because I was in such a nervous state.

Comer(se) con los ojos a ☺

— To stare longingly at ☺

- **Juan se la estaba comiendo con los ojos.**
  Juan was staring at her longingly.

Correr como reguero de pólvora (📖 To spread like a trail of burning gun-powder)

— To spread like wildfire; to travel like lightning

- **La noticia corrió como reguero de pólvora.**
  The news spread like wildfire.

Correr por cuenta de ☺

— To be on ☺

- **Las siguientes copas corren por mi cuenta.**
  The next round is on me.

— To see to it that . . .

- **De mi cuenta corre que no lograrán embargarte.**
  I'll see to it that you're not sued.

Costar (mucho) trabajo (see Dar trabajo)

— To be very difficult

Expressions

- **Me costó mucho trabajo ser amable con Julio.**
  It was very difficult to speak to Julio politely.

Creer(se) la divina garza (📖 To consider yourself the divine stork)
— To think a lot of yourself; to be conceited
- **Elena se cree la divina garza porque la escogieron para hacer el comercial.**
  Elena thinks she's God's gift to this world because she was chosen to do the commercial.

Creer(se) la gran cosa
— To think a lot of oneself; to be conceited
- **Chucho se cree la gran cosa porque está en el equipo.**
  Chucho has a big head because he's on the team.

Dar a luz (📖 To give (a baby) the light)
— To give birth
- **Mi cuñada dio a luz unos mellizos preciosos.**
  My sister-in-law had darling twins.

Dar(le) al clavo
— To hit the nail on the head
- **Aurelio le dio al clavo con su respuesta.**
  Aurelio hit the nail on the head with his answer.

Dar(le) ánimo(s) a ☺
— To give ☺ moral support or courage.
- **El güisquito me dio ánimo para entrar a hablar con el director.**
  That whiskey gave me the courage to go in and talk to the director.
— To encourage ☺
- Speaker A: **¿Cómo puedes seguir manejando después del accidente?**
  How can you go on driving after the accident?
- Speaker B: **Gracias a Gloria, que siempre me da ánimos.**
  Thanks to Gloria. She always encourages me and makes me feel brave.
— In the negative **"dar ánimos"** is a sarcastic way of saying "I really appreciate your support".
- Speaker A: **Te noto muy demacrado.**
  You look very wan.
- Speaker B: **¡No me des ánimos!**
  Flattery will get you nowhere.

🏮 Dar(le) atole con el dedo a ☺ (📖 To feed ☺ gruel with your finger)
— To take advantage of ☺'s innocence
- **Sospecho que Carmen te está dando atole con el dedo.**
  I suspect Carmen is not playing fair with you.

⇩ Dar batería
— To give ☺ a good go; to put up a fight

- **Te gané muy fácilmente. No me diste batería.**
  I beat you hands down. You didn't really try.
— To satisfy ☺ sexually
- **¿Crees que ese viejito le da batería a su mujer?**
  Do you suppose that old man satisfies his wife in bed?

Dar(le) coba a ☺
— To butter up ☺
- **Esa muchacha siempre le está dando coba a la maestra.**
  That girl is always buttering up the teacher.

📖 Dar color
— To pay for ❒
- **Yo pagué la vez pasada; a ver si hoy das color.**
  I paid last time. It's your turn to pay.
— To take sides; to be clear
- **Ernesto no da color en el problema de la herencia.**
  Ernesto takes no sides in this business of the inheritance.
- **Lalo, eres muy aguado. Ni pintas, ni das color.**
  Lalo, you're so wishy-washy. You can't decide one way or the other.

Dar(le) con la puerta en las narices a ☺
— To slam the door in ☺'s face (literally or figuratively)
- **Se enojó mucho y me dio con la puerta en las narices.**
  He got really upset and slammed the door in my face.

Dar(se) cuenta de ❒; Dar(se) cuenta de que . . .
— To notice ❒ (that . . .)
- **Me di cuenta del error demasiado tarde.**
  I noticed the mistake too late.
— To realize ❒ (that . . .)
- **¿No te das cuenta de que estás haciendo una tontería?**
  Don't you realize that what you're doing is not very bright?

Dar(le) cuerda a ☺ (📖 To wind ☺ up)
— To egg ☺ on; to encourage ☺; to humor ☺
- **Rosendo siempre dice tonterías y Amalia siempre le da cuerda.**
  Rosendo always talks nonsense, and Amalia always eggs him on.
- **¡Por amor de Dios, no le des cuerda!**
  For God's sake, don't encourage him!

Dar(se) cuerda solo(a) (📖 To wind yourself up)
— To work yourself up, to get carried away
- **Desde que murió su mujer, Jorge se está dando cuerda solo.**
  Since his wife died, Jorge's been working himself into a real depression.

Expressions

Dar(selas) de □
— To pretend to be □ you are not
- **Manuel se las da de arquitecto.**
  Manuel always passes himself off as an architect.

Dar de alta
— To register; to sign up; to put on the payroll, etc. (except in a hospital, where **dar de alta** is to discharge a patient)
- **Si vas a trabajar, tienes que darte de alta en Hacienda.**
  If you're going to start working, you have to register as a taxpayer at the Treasury Department.
- **Estas dos muchachas aún no están dadas de alta en la nueva escuela.**
  These two girls still haven't been registered at the new school.
- **Ya llevo tres semanas trabajando aquí, y todavía no me dan de alta.**
  I've been working here for three weeks, and I still haven't been put on the payroll.
- **Hijo, hay que dar de alta el coche nuevo.**
  Son, we have to register the new car.
- **Doctor, ¿cuándo me dan de alta? Ya me quiero ir a casa.**
  Doctor, when will I be discharged from the hospital? I want to go home.

Dar de baja
— To take ☺ off the registry, list, payroll, etc.
- **Me dieron de baja en el club cuando renuncié a la compañía.**
  When I quit my job, they cancelled my club membership.

Dar de botana
— To put out □ to munch on
- **Nos dieron de botana aceitunas rellenas.**
  They gave us stuffed olives to munch on.

Dar de comer a ☺□
— To feed ☺□
- **¿Ya le diste de comer a los niños?**
  Have the children eaten (been fed)?
- **A esta hora siempre le da de comer al pollo.**
  She always feeds the chicken at this time.

Dar(se) el lujo de + verb (📖 To give yourself the luxury of + verb)
— To be able to afford to + verb (not always connected with money)
- **No puedo darme el lujo de pelearme con mi jefe.**
  I can't afford to quarrel with my boss.

Dar(le) en la torre a ☺ (📖 To hit ☺ on the tower)
— To do □ terrible to ☺

Expressions

- **Por confiado, ya te dieron en la torre.**
  You got taken because you're too trusting.

Dar(le) en qué pensar a ☺
— To give ☺ food for thought

- **Su actitud nos dio a todos mucho en qué pensar.**
  His attitude gave us all food for thought.

Dar ganas de (see Tener ganas)
— To be appealing; to feel like ☐

- **Con este calor dan ganas de meterse a nadar.**
  With this heat, you feel like getting into the pool.

Dar gato por liebre (📖 To give a purchaser a cat instead of a hare)
— To deceive ☺, especially when referring to a purchase at the market.

- **No estoy seguro, pero creo que me dieron gato por liebre.**
  I'm not sure, but I think I was taken for a ride (I was deceived).

Dar(se) ínfulas (see Ser presumido)
— To put on airs

- **Esa señora se da muchas ínfulas porque tiene título.**
  That woman puts on airs because she has a college degree.

Dar lástima (see Dar pena)

Dar lata
— To bother ☺; to be a pain

- **Este coche da mucha lata.**
  This car is giving me a lot of trouble.
- **La casera siempre está dando lata (es una latosa).**
  The landlady is always bugging me (she's a pain).

Dar mala espina (📖 To give a bad thorn)
— To give ☺ a nasty feeling; to make ☺ suspicious

- **Su tardanza en resolver me da mala espina.**
  His delay in replying to my request makes me suspicious.

Dar patadas de ahogado (📖 To thrash around uselessly in the water when you'll drown anyway)
— To fight a losing battle

- **Vicente, no pierdas el tiempo resistiéndote al divorcio. Son patadas de ahogado.**
  Vincent, don't waste your time trying to avoid the divorce. You're fighting a losing battle.

Dar pena; dar lástima
— To (make ☺) feel sorry for ☺

Expressions

- **Con tu modo de ser lograste que Irma te cortara; me das pena.** (This is offensive; said in sympathy, this would be **¡Qué lástima!** or **¡Qué pena!**)
  You are such a pain that Irma finally dropped you. I feel sorry for you.
— To feel embarrassed
  - **Me da pena pedirle dinero.**
    I feel embarrassed (I'm too timid) to ask her to lend me some money.

Dar(se) por ofendido(a)
— To take offense
  - **Hernán se dio por ofendido porque no aceptaron su propuesta.**
    Hernan took offense because his proposal was turned down.

Dar(le) por su lado a ☺ (see Seguirle la corriente a ☺)
— To humor ☺, to go along with ☺
  - **Tu abuelo ya está viejo. No discutas con él. Dale por su lado para que no se enoje.**
    Your grandfather is old. Don't argue with him. Humor him so he doesn't get upset.
  - **Gloria le da por su lado a su marido para conservar la armonía.**
    Gloria goes along with everything her husband says just to keep the peace.

Dar(se) por vencido(a)
— To give up
  - **No he logrado conseguir suficiente dinero para el proyecto, pero me doy por vencido.**
    I haven't been able to raise all the money for the project, but I'm not giving up.

Dar(le) sabor al caldo (📖 To give the broth some taste)
— To make things interesting
  - **Las peripecias del viaje fueron las que le dieron sabor al caldo.**
    The unexpected things that happened on the trip were what made it interesting.

Dar trabajo (see Con trabajo(s) and Costar (mucho) trabajo)
— To be difficult
  - **Da mucho trabajo limpiar este piso.**
    It's a pain getting this floor clean.

Dar(se) una vuelta (📖 To give yourself a turn)
— To visit; to drop in; to drop by
  - Speaker A: **¿Cuándo van a estar listos los zapatos?**
    When will the shoes be ready?
    Speaker B: **Dése una vuelta el martes.**
    Drop by on Tuesday.
  - **Me voy a dar una vuelta por casa de Lola esta noche.**
    I'm going to drop in on Lola tonight.

Dar(le) un norte a ☺
— To give ☺ directions to get somewhere or to do ❑

- **No sé por dónde llegar. Dame un norte.**
  I don't know how to get there. Give me a pointer (some help).

Dar un plantón a ☺ (📖 To plant ☺) (see **Dejar plantado**)
— To stand ☺ up or to keep ☺ waiting

- **A Cosme le dieron un plantón de dos horas.**
  Cosme was stood up for two hours (was made to wait for two hours).

Dar(le) vuelta a la tortilla (📖 To turn the **tortilla** over)
— To give ☐ a rest; to forget it

- **Chema, no sigas disgustado. Ya dale vuelta a la tortilla.**
  Chema, don't be upset anymore. Give it a rest.

Dar(le) vueltas (a una idea) (📖 To turn an idea over and over)
— To think ☐ over carefully; to consider a project

- **Mario le está dando muchas vueltas al plan.**
  Mario is really giving a lot of thought to the plan.

Decir(le) hasta la despedida a ☺
— To tell ☺ off in no uncertain terms; to let ☺ have it

- **Si lo sigues fastidiando, te va a decir hasta la despedida.**
  If you keep on bugging him, he's really going to let you have it.

Dejar ☺☐ a la buena de Dios
— To leave ☐ to chance; to neglect ☺☐

- **Estos irresponsables muchachos dejan todo a la buena de Dios.**
  These irresponsible kids just leave everything to chance (neglect their responsibilities).

Dejar con un palmo de narices a ☺ (see **Quedar(se) con un palmo de narices**)
— To thumb your nose at ☺; to give ☺ the brush off

- **Luisa dejó a Jaime con un palmo de narices.**
  Luisa gave Jaime the brush-off.

Dejar chiflando en la loma a ☺
— To pay no attention to ☺

- **No vino ninguno de mis amigos a ayudarme; me dejaron chiflando en la loma.**
  None of the friends I invited came to help me; they just left me to my own devices.

Dejar dicho
— To leave word

- **Deja dicho si quieres que te recoja.**
  Leave word if you want me to pick you up.
- **Dejó dicho que volvería a las 4:00.**
  He left word that he would be back at 4:00.

Expressions

Dejar plantado(a) a ☺ (see Dar un plantón a ☺)
— To stand ☺ up
- **Ya me cansé de que siempre me dejes plantado.**
  I'm tired of you standing me up.

Dejar vestida y alborotada a ☺ (📖 To leave ☺ all dressed up and excited)
— To leave ☺ all dressed up with nowhere to go; to stand ☺ up
- **Los muchachos que nos iban a llevar a la fiesta nunca llegaron. Nos dejaron vestidas y alborotadas.**
  The boys who were supposed to take us to the party never turned up. They left us all dressed up with nowhere to go.

Descubrir el hilo negro (📖 To discover black thread)
— To feel that you have made an important discovery, when it's actually nothing new
- **Speaker A: ¿Sabes qué? Me he fijado que la sábila es buenísima para los raspones.**
  Guess what? I've noticed that aloe is great for scrapes.
  Speaker B: ¡Hombre! Descubriste el hilo negro.
  Boy! What a discovery! What else is new?

Deshacer(se) de ☺□
— To get rid of ☺□
- **Voy a tener que deshacerme de estos muebles.**
  I'm going to have to get rid of this furniture.
- **¿Cómo diablos puedo deshacerme de este cobrador?**
  How on earth can I get rid of this collection agent?

Dominar(se)
— To control yourself; to get hold of yourself
- **Tuve que dominarme para no darle una trompada.**
  I had to control myself to keep from socking him.
- **Eres demasiado violento. ¡Domínate!**
  You're too violent. Get hold of yourself!

Dormir a pierna suelta (📖 To sleep with your legs all spread out)
— To sleep like a log
- **Después de varios insomnios, anoche dormí a pierna suelta.**
  After several nights of insomnia, I slept like a log last night.

Echar a perder ☺□ (see Echar(se) a perder)
— To spoil ☺□
- **Mi mamá echó a perder a mi hermano desde chiquito.**
  My mother spoiled my brother from the time he was born.
- **Le echaste a perder la velada a todos.**
  You spoiled the evening for everyone.

Expressions

Echar(se) a perder
— To spoil (go bad) (intransitive)
- **El jamón se echó a perder porque no lo pusiste en el refri.**
  The ham spoiled because you didn't put it in the fridge.

Echar de cabeza a ☺
— To make ☺ look bad by revealing a secret about him or her
- **Consuelo no sabe guardar secretos. Ya echó de cabeza a Luisa.**
  Consuelo doesn't know how to keep a secret. She spilled the beans about Luisa.

Echar de menos a ☺❑
— To miss ☺❑
- **De veras extraño a mis amigos.**
  I really miss my friends.
- **Echo de menos los dulces que hacía mi madre.**
  I miss the sweets my mother used to make.

Echar(se) de ver
— To be noticeable
- **Luego luego se le echan de ver los años cuando Sara no se maquilla.**
  With no make-up, Sara's age is immediately evident.

Echar en saco roto ❑ (📖 To put ❑ into a sack with a hole in it)
— To ignore advice; to let something go in one ear and out the other
- **No eches en saco roto lo que te dije de esa persona.**
  Don't forget what I said about that person.

Echar flores a ☺ (📖 To throw flowers at ☺)
— To flatter or compliment ☺
- **Todo el mundo me echó flores por mi vestido.**
  Everyone complimented me on my dress.

Echar(le) ganas a ❑ (see **Hacer con ganas ❑**)

Echar indirectas a ☺
— To hint at ❑
- **Ya . . . ya me voy. No me estén echando indirectas.**
  OK, OK, I'm leaving now. I got the hint (I know what you're hinting at).

Echar la casa por la ventana (📖 To throw the house out the window)
— To go the whole hog; to go all out
- **El día de su cumpleaños echaron la casa por la ventana.**
  On his birthday, they went the whole hog.

Echar las campanas al vuelo
— To celebrate
- **No eches las campanas al vuelo. Todavía no tienes el premio seguro.**
  Wait before you start celebrating, The prize isn't yours yet.

Expressions

Echar un ojo al gato y otro al garabato
— To be alert to two things at the same time
- **Tengo que hacer la comida y cuidar a los niños, así que aquí me tienes con un ojo al gato y otro al garabato.**
  I have to prepare lunch and take care of the kids, so here I am trying to juggle both jobs.

Encargar
— To get pregnant
- **Rita encargó al mes de casada.**
  Rita got pregnant a month after her wedding.
— To ask ☺ to do □ for you
- **Ahora que vas al mercado, ¿te puedo encargar unos cigarros?**
  Since you are going to the market, could you please buy some cigarettes for me?

Encargar(se) de □
— To take charge of □
- **Por favor, encárgate una hora de los alumnos.**
  Take charge of the students for an hour, please.

Enseñar el cobre (📖 To show the copper; from silver or gold-plated copper, when the plating wears thin, the copper shows through)
— To show ☺'s true colors
- **Tu amigo no tardó en enseñar el cobre.**
  It wasn't long before your friend showed his true colors.

Estar a gusto
— To be comfortable or at ease; to enjoy oneself
- **No gano mucho, pero estoy muy a gusto en este trabajo.**
  I don't make much, but I love this job.

Estar (andar) a la cuarta pregunta
— To be totally broke
- **El pobre de Alberto siempre está a la cuarta pregunta.**
  Poor Albert is always entirely broke.

Estar a punto de + verb; estar por +verb
— To be about to do □
- **Estaba a punto de irme cuando sonó el teléfono.**
  I was about to leave when the telephone rang.
- **Gloria ha estado por renunciar varias veces.**
  Gloria has been on the verge of quitting several times.

Estar al corriente (con or de) □ (see Estar al día con □)
— To be up to date with □
- **Luis no está al corriente de las noticias.**
  Luis is not up to date with the latest news.

Expressions

- **Jorge jamás está al corriente con sus pagos.**
  Jorge's never up to date with his payments.

Estar al día con ❑
— To be up to date on or with ❑

- **Es obvio que no estás al día con el chisme de Yvonne.**
  You're obviously not up to date on the gossip about Yvonne.

Estar al tanto de ❑
— To be up on ❑; to be informed about ❑

- **Acabo de llegar y todavía no estoy al tanto de lo que pasa.**
  I don't know what is going on; I arrived just now.

⌨ Estar amolado(a) (see **Andar amolado(a)**)

⌨ Estar apachurrado(a) (📖 To be squashed)
— To be sad, down in the mouth, down in the dumps, blue

- **Agustín ha estado muy apachurrado desde que terminó con Alma.**
  Agustin has been really blue since he broke up with Alma.

Estar como agua para (pa') chocolate (📖 To be as hot as the water needed to melt chocolate)
— To be absolutely furious

- **El Sr. Gómez quiere hablar contigo; está como agua pa' chocolate.**
  Mr. Gomez wants to speak to you; he's mad as hell.

Estar con el agua hasta el cuello (📖 To have the water level up to your neck)
— To be up to here with ❑; to be in hot water; to be at the breaking point

- **No puedo seguir gastando así; estoy con el agua hasta el cuello.**
  I can't spend another cent. I'm up to my eyeballs in debt.

Estar (andar) de capa caída (📖 To go around with your cape drooping)
— To be somewhat depressed, downhearted

- **Me parece que Roberto está (anda) de capa caída.**
  Roberto seems a bit depressed.

Estar (andar) de genio (see **Estar (andar) de malas**)

Estar (andar) de malas
— To be in a bad mood; to be in a funk (also means to have a run of bad luck)

- **Ahorita no le quiero pedir nada a papá. Anda de malas.**
  I don't want to ask Dad for anything right now. He's in a bad mood.

⌨ Estar en chino (📖 To be in Chinese)
— To be practically impossible; to be very difficult

- **¡Tengo que corregir 200 examenes para mañana! ¡Está en chino!**
  I've got to correct 200 examinations by tomorrow! How on earth am I ever going to get them done?

Estar en estado
— To be pregnant
- **Cuando está en estado, mi esposa tiene náuseas.**
  My wife always feels nauseated when she's pregnant.

Estar en las nubes (📖 To be in the clouds)
— To be thinking of 🔲 else
- **Ernesto no aprobó el examen porque siempre está en las nubes durante la clase.**
  Ernesto failed the test because he's always daydreaming in class.

Estar forrado(a) de (en) billetes (📖 To be upholstered with money)
— To be filthy rich; to be rolling in money; to have money coming out your ears
- **La novia de Gilberto no es muy bonita, pero está forrada en billetes.**
  Gilberto's girlfriend isn't that pretty, but she's filthy rich.

Estar harto(a) (📖 To be full of 🔲) (see **Tener harto(a)**)
— To be utterly fed up
- **Ya estoy harto (hasta el gorro, hasta la coronilla) con esta traducción interminable que tengo que hacer.**
  I've had it up to here with this endless translation I have to do.

Estar hasta el gorro (📖 To be up to your cap) (see **Estar harto(a)**)

Estar hecho(a) un brazo de mar
— To be enraged, in a state, fit to be tied
- **Ahí viene doña Lupe hecha un brazo de mar.**
  Here comes doña Lupe, fit to be tied.

Estar hasta la coronilla (📖 To be up to the crown of your head) (see **Estar harto(a)**)

Estar hinchado(a) de dinero (📖 To be swollen with money) (see **Estar forrado de billetes**)

Estar loco(a) de atar (📖 To be crazy enough to be tied up)
— To be stark, staring, raving mad; to be completely nuts
- **No le hagas caso. Está loco de atar.**
  Don't pay any attention to him. He's out of his mind.

Estar podrido(a) en dinero (📖 To be rotten with money) (see **Estar forrado de billetes**)

Estar por + verb 🔲 (see **Estar a punto de** + verb 🔲)

Estar que arde (📖 To be burning)
— To be hot; to sizzle
- **La situación política del país está que arde.**
  The political situation in the country is sizzling.

Estar tirado(a) a la calle
— To be down and out (physically or economically)
- **La pobre gorda de tu prima está tirada a la calle.**
  That poor fat cousin of yours is a sight!
- **Tu primo tiene bastante dinero. No está nada tirado a la calle.**
  Your cousin has a lot of money. He is by no means down and out (broke).

Faltar a su palabra
— To break your word
- **Me imaginé que Raúl iba a faltar a su palabra.**
  I suspected Raul was going to break his word.

Faltar(le) al respeto a ☺
— To be disrespectful to ☺; to offend ☺
- **Los alumnos de la Sra. Gómez nunca le faltan al respeto.**
  Mrs. Gómez's students are never rude to her.

Guardar cama
— To stay in bed
- **No creí que este resfriado me obligara a guardar cama.**
  I didn't think this cold would make me stay in bed.

Haber moros en la costa (📖 There are Moors on the coast)
— The walls have ears (said when there are eyes and ears that could see and hear things).
- **Después hablamos de eso, porque ahorita hay moros en la costa.**
  Let's talk about that later. The walls have ears.

Hablar de bulto
— To gesticulate while talking
- **Si sigues hablando de bulto mientras manejas, vamos a chocar.**
  If you keep on gesticulating while you're driving, we're going to have an accident.

Hablar hasta por los codos (📖 To speak from all parts of your body, including your elbows)
— To talk ☺'s ear off; to chatter; to talk too much
- **Ese tipo me cansó. Habla hasta por los codos.**
  That guy wore me out. He talks your ear off.

Hacer(se) a la idea
— To get used to the idea
- **No logro hacerme a la idea de que mi hermano está muerto.**
  I can't get used to the idea that my brother is dead.

Hacer(se) cargo de ☐
— To take charge of ☐; to take over
- **No te preocupes. Me haré cargo de todo en tu ausencia.**
  Don't worry. I'll take charge of everything while you are away.

Expressions

Hacer caso a ☺; hacer caso de ☐
— To heed or pay attention to ☺☐
- **Haz caso de lo que dice tu abuelo.**
  Pay attention to what your grandfather says (and act on it).
- **Te lo advertí, pero no me hiciste caso.**
  I warned you, but you ignored me.

Hacer cola
— To stand in line
- **Tú haz cola para los boletos, mientras yo estaciono el coche.**
  You stand in line for the tickets while I park the car.

Hacer como que . . . + verb (see **Hacer que** + verb)
— To pretend that . . .
- **Hago como que trabajo.**
  I pretend to be working.
- **Haz como que no te das cuenta.**
  Pretend you don't notice.

Hacer con ganas ☐; echar(le) ganas a ☐; meter(le) ganas a ☐
— To do ☐ with "gusto", with determination, with great effort, or to the nth degree
- **¡Mira! Esto lo hice con muchas ganas. ¿Cómo me salió?**
  Look! I put a lot of effort into this. How did it turn out?
- **¡Oye! Si no le vas a echar (a meter) ganas, ¡olvídalo!**
  Hey! If you're going to do it halfheartedly, forget it!

⚥ Hacer(se) cruces
— To wonder
- **Toda la noche me estuve haciendo cruces sobre el motivo de su actitud.**
  All night I was wondering why he acted the way he did.

⚥ Hacer de cuenta
— To imagine; to make believe or pretend
- **No te pongas nervioso. Haz de cuenta que no estoy aquí, y vuélvelo a intentar.**
  Don't get nervous. Pretend I'm not here, and try again.

Hacer de tripas corazón
— To get up the guts to do ☐
- **Hice de tripas corazón y le pedí un aumento al jefe.**
  I got up the guts to ask the boss for a raise.

Hacer el favor de + verb
— To do a favor
- **Hágame (hazme) el favor de mover su (tu) coche.**
  Do me the favor of moving your car.
— To take a girl to bed

- **A Rebeca le hizo el favor su novio.**
  Rebecca's boyfriend took her to bed (had sex with her).

Hacer falta
— To lack; to have need of; to be missing
- **Hace falta papel para la junta.**
  We're lacking paper for the meeting.
- **Hace falta un traductor.**
  We need a translator.
- **Aquí hace falta una silla.**
  There's a chair missing here.

Hacer(le) gracia a ☺
— To be amusing
- **Sus chistes no me hacen gracia. Son de mal gusto.**
  His jokes aren't funny. They're in bad taste.
- **Este perrito me hace mucha gracia.**
  This little dog is very amusing.

Hacer juego con □
— To match □
- **Tu blusa no hace juego con la falda.**
  Your blouse doesn't match your skirt.

⌂ Hacer puente
— To take the day(s) off between a weekend and a holiday (or vice versa) in order to make a long weekend of it
- **Como el día de las madres era martes, hicimos puente.**
  Since Mother's Day was on Tuesday, we stayed over and took Monday off.

Hacer que + verb (see Hacer como que + verb)
— To pretend you're doing □; to fake □
- **Juan hace que trabaja, pero en realidad no hace nada.**
  John pretends he's working, but he never gets anything done.

Hacer(se) (del) rogar
— To pretend to be reluctant, so that ☺ has to beg you to do □
- **¡Andale!, yo sé que quieres ir. No te hagas del rogar.**
  Come on! I know you'd like to go. Why do you make me beg you?

⌂ Hacer San Lunes (▦ To celebrate St. Monday)
— To take Monday off because the weekend was too exhausting.
- **Todos los que se fueron a Acapulco hicieron San Lunes.**
  All the people who went to Acapulco were absent on Monday.

Expressions

Hacer topillo (see **Ver(le) la cara a** ☺ under Slang in Mexico)

— To make a crooked deal; to pull a fast one

- **Cuídate de esos vendedores. Te quieren hacer topillo.**
  Careful with those salesmen; they're out to cheat you.

Hacer un drama; hacer un tango (📖 To make a drama or tango)

— To have a fit; to make a big stink about ❑

- **Hizo un drama porque usé su coche.**
  She had a fit because I used her car.
- **No sabes el tango que hice cuando se perdió Fifí.**
  You have no idea what a stink I made when Fifí got lost.

Hacer(sele) un nudo en la garganta a ☺

— To get a lump in your throat

- **Cuando me dijeron que había muerto, se me hizo un nudo en la garganta.**
  When they told me he had died, I got a lump in my throat.

Importar un bledo; 🐧 **Importar un (serenado) cacahuate**

— Not to care; not to give a damn (note that the expression is negative without the use of a negative word)

- **El fracaso de su compañía me importa un bledo (un serenado cacahuate).**
  I don't give a damn about his company's bankruptcy.

🐧 **Importar un (serenado) cacahuate** (📖 Not to care a peanut. **Serenado** means left out all night; this shrinks the peanut and makes it undesirable.) (see **Importar un bledo**)

🐧 **Ir(le) como en feria a** ☺

— To have ❑ very unpleasant happen to you . To have a bad experience, like when you go to a fair. In olden times, if you had a bit too much to drink at a fair, some pretty awful things could happen to you at the hands of all the slick operators, prostitutes, etc.

- Speaker A: **¿Cómo te fue en el viaje?**
  How was your trip?
- Speaker B: **Me fue como en feria. Me perdieron el equipaje, me robaron los cheques de viajero, y me intoxiqué con unos mariscos.**
  It was awful. The airline lost my baggage, my traveler's checks were stolen, and I got food poisoning from some seafood.

🐧 **Ir(se) con su música a otra parte** (📖 To take your music somewhere else)

— To go bother someone else; to stop being a nuisance; to stop getting in the way

- **Estás ocupada, mejor me voy con mi música a otra parte.**
  I can tell you are too busy. I better go away and stop bothering you.

Ir de compras

— To go shopping

> - **Se fue de compras con María.**
>   *She went shopping with María.*

Ir de parranda
— To go on a drinking and carousing spree

> - **Hace tiempo que mi marido no se va de parranda.**
>   *My husband hasn't gone on a binge for ages.*

Ir de paso
— To be in transit; to be just going through a place

> - **No necesitaré hotel, porque voy de paso.**
>   *I won't need a hotel because I'm just on my way through.*

Ir(se) de pinta
— To play hookey

> - **Los chicos se fueron de pinta dos veces el mes pasado.**
>   *The kids played hookey twice last month.*

Ir volando (📖 To go flying)
— To go in a great hurry, in a rush, in a flash

> - **Se fue volando, porque lo estaban esperando.**
>   *They were waiting for him so he left in a hurry.*

Jalar(le) las orejas a ☺ (📖 To pull ☺'s ears)
— To scold ☺; to bawl ☺ out

> - **Voy a tener que jalarle las orejas a Paquito por llevarse el coche sin permiso.**
>   *I'm going to have to scold Paquito for taking the car without permission.*

Levantar falsos
— To accuse ☺ falsely

> - **Sabes muy bien que Juan no es infiel; no levantes falsos.**
>   *You know very well that Juan is not unfaithful; don't accuse him falsely.*

Lucir(se)
— To do 🗆 beautifully, usually to impress ☺; to do a great job of 🗆

> - **Oye mamá . . . ¡qué pollo tan exquisito! Te luciste.**
>   *Hey, Mom . . . this chicken is out of this world! You outdid yourself.*
> - **¿Qué me pondré? Me quiero lucir en la fiesta porque va a estar Pepe.**
>   *What should I wear? I want to make a great impression because Pepe is going to be at the party.*

— To do something bad; to make an impression by doing 🗆 negative

> - **Llegaste una hora tarde, ¡de veras que te luciste!**
>   *You arrived an hour late. You really made an impression!*

Llegar a ser 🗆
— To become 🗆 (over an extended period of time)

> - **Pepito jamás llegará a ser cantante.**
>   *Pepito will never become a singer.*

Expressions

Llevar al baile a ☺ (📖 To take ☺ to the dance)
— To trick ☺
- **Creo que mis socios ya me llevaron al baile.**
  I think my partners have tricked me.

Llevar(se) bien (mal) con ☺
— To get along well (badly) with ☺
- **Ellos se llevan muy bien.**
  They get along very well.
- **Me llevo muy mal con mi esposa.**
  I don't get along with my wife.

Llevar(se) la palma
— To take the prize for ❑ bad
- **Se llevó la palma por su trajecito de mal gusto.**
  He took the prize for the worst outfit.

Llevar x tiempo (mucho tiempo) (poco tiempo) (x días)
— To take or to spend a certain length of time
- **Llevo tres días en este proyecto, y no he terminando aún.**
  I've been at this project for three days and still haven't finished.

Llover a cántaros
— To rain cats and dogs
- **Estaba lloviendo a cántaros.**
  It was raining cats and dogs.

℞ Llover en su milpita (📖 To rain in your cornfield)
— To have a great deal of (or repeated) bad (good) luck; to have something good happen to you
- **¡Pobre Jesús! Lo despidieron de su trabajo, su esposa está esperando el quinto hijo, y le robaron el coche. De veras que le está lloviendo en su milpita.**
  Poor Jesus! He was fired from his job, his wife is expecting their fifth child, and his car was stolen. What rotten luck!
- **¡Me saqué la lotería! Hasta que me llovió en mi milpita.**
  I won the lottery! I'm finally having some luck.

Llover sobre mojado (📖 To rain on wet ground)
— One thing after another; it doesn't rain, but it pours
- **No es que la cosa sea tan grave; es que al pobre Rubén le ha llovido sobre mojado.**
  No, it's not so awful really, but with Ruben it's just one thing after another.

Mantener(se) al corriente con ❑
— To keep up to date with ❑
- **No es fácil mantenerse al corriente con los pedidos.**
  It's not easy to keep up to date with the purchase orders.

Mantener al corriente de □ a ☺

— To keep ☺ informed regarding □

- **Manténgame al corriente sobre la salud de su papá.**
  Keep me informed about your Dad's health.

Mentar (mencionar) la soga en casa del ahorcado (📖 To mention the rope when you are in the house of the person who was hanged)

— To touch a sore spot

- **Sus papás acaban de divorciarse. Hablar de divorcios aquí es mentar la soga en casa del ahorcado.**
  Her parents just got divorced. Mentioning divorce here is touching a sore spot.

Meter(se) con ☺

— To look for trouble with ☺; to mess with ☺

- **Si se meten conmigo, les va a ir como en feria.**
  If they're looking for trouble with me, they're going to get it.

— To get involved with ☺

- **¿Cómo se le ocurre meterse con un hombre casado?**
  How could she get involved with a married man?

Meter(se) en camisa de once varas (📖 To wear a shirt eleven "**varas**" long; one **vara**, a measure no longer used, is equivalent to 0.835 meters)

— To bite off more than you can chew

- **Pablo se va a meter en camisa de once varas si acepta ese contrato.**
  Pablo is going to bite off more than he can chew if he accepts that contract.

Meter(le) ganas a □ (see **Hacer con ganas** □)

Meter la cuchara (📖 To stick in your spoon)

— To put your oar in; to butt in; to put in your two cents' worth

- **La imprudente de Hortensia tuvo que meter su cuchara.**
  Hortensia just had to put in her two cents' worth. She's so tactless!

Meter la mano al fuego por ☺

— To vouch for ☺

- **Yo no meto la mano al fuego por Arnoldo.**
  I won't vouch for Arnold.

Montar(se) en su macho

— To be (or get) stubborn

- **Cuando Vicente se monta en su macho, no escucha razones.**
  When Vincent sets his mind on something, he won't listen to reason.

Morder(se) la lengua (📖 To bite your tongue)

— To throw stones at glass houses; to accuse ☺ else of something you are guilty of yourself

- **¿Me dijiste flojo? ¿No te mordiste la lengua?**
  Did you accuse me of being lazy? Look who's talking!

No dar golpe
— To be jobless
- **¡Pobre Ana! Su marido tiene meses que no da golpe.**
  Poor Ana! Her husband hasn't worked for months.

🔄 No dar paso sin guarache (sin linterna)
— To be out for number one; to be very calculating (when your every move is calculated to benefit you)
- Speaker A: **Todo lo que hace Carlos es para que le aumenten el sueldo.**
  Everything Carlos does is aimed at getting a salary increase.
- Speaker B: **Sí, él no da paso sin guarache.**
  Yes, he's very calculating.

No dar pie con bola
— To make no headway; to be completely inept; to do everything wrong
- **No sé qué me pasa; hoy no doy pie con bola.**
  I don't know what's wrong with me; I can't get anything right today.

No dar una
— To make no headway at all; to be completely inept; to do everything wrong
- **No sé qué me pasa; hoy no doy una.**
  I don't know what's wrong with me; I can't get anything right today.

🔄 No dejar(se)
— Not to let people take advantage of you
- **Un tipo trató de quitarme mi lugar de estacionamiento, pero no me dejé.**
  Some guy tried to steal my parking place, but I didn't let him.
- **Si tu marido trata de darte un cochecito japonés en lugar de un Ford, ¡no te dejes, hijita!**
  If that husband of yours tries to give you a little Japanese car instead of a Ford, stand up for your rights!

No dejar ni a sol ni a sombra a ☺
— Not to let up
- **Mis acreedores no me dejan ni a sol ni a sombra.**
  My creditors just don't let up on me.

No importar(le) a ☺
— I don't care (you don't care, he doesn't care, etc.)
- Speaker A: **Juan se arrepintió de lo que te hizo.**
  Juan is sorry for what he did to you.
- Speaker B: **No me importa.**
  I don't care.

No llegar(le) ni a los talones a ☺
— To be nothing compared to ☺
- **Nora se cree mejor secretaria que Tere. La verdad es que no le llega ni a los talones.**
  Nora considers herself a better secretary than Tere. The fact is that she is nothing compared to Tere.

♫ No medir(se)
— To do a really extraordinary job of ☐; to go overboard
- **Le regaló un Ferrari a su novia. No se midió.**
  He gave his girlfriend a Ferrari. He really went overboard.

No poder ver ni en pintura a ☺ (📖 To hate seeing ☺ even in a picture)
— Not to be able to stand the sight of ☺; to dislike ☺ thoroughly
- **Mi mamá no puede ver a mi novio ni en pintura.**
  My mother can't stand the sight of my boyfriend.

No romper un plato (📖 To be incapable of breaking a plate)
— To seem innocuous; to appear incapable of doing anything wrong
- **Con su carita de inocente, parece que no rompe un plato.**
  She looks so innocuous with that innocent look of hers.

♫ No ser cosa de "enchílame otra" (📖 To not be just a question of cooking up another **enchilada**)
— To be no easy matter
- **No te creas que es cosa de enchílame otra.**
  Don't think it's easy.

No ser de mal ver (see **Ser de buen ver**)
— Not to be bad looking
- **Sarita no es de mal ver.**
  Susana isn't bad looking.

No soltar ni un quinto (📖 To not let go of even a nickel)
— To be a tightwad; to be stingy
- **El tacaño de Rafael no soltó ni un quinto para ayudar a Lupe.**
  Rafael is so stingy. He didn't contribute five cents to help Lupe.

No soltar prenda
— To be very discreet; to keep a secret; (not) to let the cat out of the bag
- **Camilo es muy discreto. No suelta prenda.**
  Camilo is very discreet. He won't let the cat out of the bag.

No tener dos dedos de frente (📖 To have a forehead that measures less than two fingers from eyebrows to hairline)
— To be very stupid
- **El pobre Tomás no tiene dos dedos de frente.**
  Poor Thomas is not too bright.

Expressions

No tener nombre (📖 To have no name)
— To be unspeakably awful
- **Lo que le hizo Eugenio a su hermano no tiene nombre.**
  What Eugenio did to his brother is simply unspeakable.

No tener oficio ni beneficio
— To be worthless or useless (people only)
- **El vago de tu cuñado no tiene oficio ni beneficio.**
  Your lazy brother-in-law is pretty useless.

No tener pelos en la lengua (📖 To have no hairs on your tongue)
— To be very outspoken
- **Leonor no tiene pelos en la lengua. Mandó a Pepe al demonio.**
  Leonor says exactly what she means. She simply told Pepe to go to hell.

No valer la pena (see **Valer la pena**)

No venir al caso (see **Venir al caso**)

No ver(le) ni el polvo a ☺ (📖 To see not even the dust kicked up in a fast getaway. Said when ☺ leaves in an enormous hurry)
— To beat it; to scram
- **Alicia arrancó su auto y no le vimos ni el polvo.**
  Alice started her car and she was gone in a flash.

Pagar el pato (📖 To pay for the dead duck); **Pagar los platos rotos**
— To be made the scapegoat; to be blamed (or take the blame) for ☺ else's mistake or wrongdoing
- **Yo sé quien va a pagar el pato (los platos rotos) por ese enredo.**
  I know who's going to be made the scapegoat for this mix-up.

Pagar los platos rotos (see **Pagar el pato**)

🔒 **Pasar(se) de tueste** (📖 To get too toasted); **Pasar(sele) la mano**
— To go too far; to go to extremes
- **Fue bueno que le dijeras sus verdades, pero te pasaste de tueste (se te pasó la mano).**
  It was OK for you to scold her, but you went too far.

Parar(se) de pestañas (see **Poner el grito en el cielo**)

Pasar(sele) la mano (see **Pasar(se) de tueste**)

Pasar la pena negra
— To have a terrible time of □
- **De regreso de la excursión pasamos la pena negra.**
  We had a really bad time on the way back from the outing.

Pasar las de Caín (📖 To experience what Cain went through)

— To go through hell
- **Mario perdió todo su dinero y está pasando las de Caín.**
  Mario lost all his money and he's going through hell now.

Pasar por alto
— To ignore; to disregard; to overlook; to pay no attention
- **No debemos pasar por alto las advertencias que nos hizo el profesor.**
  We shouldn't disregard the professor's advice.

Pedir(le) peras al olmo (📖 To expect an elm to bear pears)
— To ask the impossible
- **No esperes que lo haga. No hay que pedirle peras al olmo.**
  Don't expect him to do it. You mustn't ask the impossible.

Pegar(sele) las sábanas a ☺ (📖 To have the sheets stick to you)
— To oversleep
- **Como anoche me desvelé, hoy se me pegaron las sábanas.**
  I overslept today because I was up late last night.

Perder los estribos (📖 To loose your stirrups)
— To lose control of yourself
- **Perdónenme por insultarlos. Perdí los estribos.**
  Forgive me for insulting you. I got carried away.

Pescar(las) al vuelo (📖 To catch ☐ in flight)
— To catch ☐ like lightening
- **Nadie más supo de lo que estaba hablando Julia, pero Oscar se las pescó al vuelo.**
  No one else had any idea of what Julie was talking about, but Oscar caught on right away.

Poder(le) a ☺
— To be affected by ☐
- **Le pudo mucho la muerte de Leticia.**
  Leticia's death really affected him.

Poner(se) a peso el kilo
— To become extremely difficult
- **¡Me descubrieron! Ahora sí se me puso a peso el kilo.**
  I've been caught! Now I'm really in hot water.

Poner cara de palo (📖 To make a wooden face)
— To have a poker face
- **Ernesto, como siempre, puso su cara de palo.**
  As usual, Ernesto had a poker face.

Poner cara larga (📖 To make a long face)
— To look upset, sulky or down in the mouth

Expressions

- **La niña está poniendo cara larga porque no la dejan salir a jugar.**
  The little girl is sulking because she's not allowed to go out and play.

▷ Poner como camote a ☺; poner como Dios puso al perico a ☺
— To scold ☺
- **Si vuelvo a llegar tarde, mi jefe me va a poner como camote (como Dios puso al perico).**
  If I arrive late again, my boss is going to let me have it.

⇩ Poner como lazo de cochino a ☺ (📖 To make ☺ look like a pig's ribbon); ⇩ poner como palo de gallinero a ☺ (📖 To make ☺ look like the roosting stick in a chicken coop)
— To give ☺ hell
- **Rompiste ese vidrio de la ventana, ¿verdad? Cuando lo sepa tu papá, te va a poner como lazo de cochino (como palo de gallinero).**
  You broke that window, didn't you? When your father finds out, he's going to give you hell!

⇩ Poner como palo de gallinero a ☺ (see Poner como lazo de cochino a ☺)

Poner el dedo en la llaga (📖 To put your finger on the sore)
— To touch a sore spot (to put salt on a wound)
- **Cuando le hablaste de su divorcio, pusiste el dedo en la llaga.**
  When you spoke of her divorce, you touched a sore spot.

Poner el grito en el cielo (📖 To put the scream in the sky); colgar(se) de la lámpara (📖 To hang from the lamp); parar(se) de pestañas (📖 To stand over your eyelashes)
— To hit the ceiling; to make a fuss; to make a stink about ❑
- **Puso el grito en el cielo cuando se dio cuenta de que le habían robado el bolso.**
  She made a terrific fuss when she realized her bag had been stolen.

Poner(se) en ridículo
— To make a fool of yourself
- **Joaquín se puso en ridículo con esa tonta afirmación.**
  Joaquin made a fool of himself with that silly statement.

Poner en ridículo a ☺
— To make ☺ look bad
- **Quiso poner a Lina en ridículo, pero no pudo.**
  He wanted to make Lina look bad, but it didn't work.

Poner en tela de juicio ❑
— To doubt or mistrust ❑
- **Creemos absolutamente en sus palabras. No las ponemos en tela de juicio.**
  We believe him absolutely. We're not doubting his word.

Poner peros
— To make objections

- **El director le puso muchos peros a mi reporte.**
  The director made a lot of objections to my report.

Predicar en el desierto (📖 To preach in the desert)
— To fall upon deaf ears

- **Nadie te hará caso. Estás predicando en el desierto.**
  No one will pay any attention to what you say. It will fall on deaf ears.

⏾ Prender(sele) el foco a ☺ (📖 To have your light bulb light up) (see **Caerle el veinte** in *Common Slang Expressions*)
— To get a bright idea

- **No tenía idea dónde conseguir el dinero para el nuevo negocio, pero de repente se me prendió el foco.**
  I had no idea where I was going to get the money for the new business, but I suddenly had a brainwave.

— To finally understand or remember ❑; to have everything fall into place

- **No recordaba dónde había visto al hombre del bigote, pero finalmente se me prendió el foco.**
  I couldn't recall where I had seen the man with the moustache, and then it all came back.

- **No entendía por qué el niño no me hacía caso, hasta que se me prendió el foco. Era sordomudo.**
  I didn't understand why the kid paid no attention to me. Then it dawned on me that he was a deaf-mute.

Quedar(se) a (para) vestir santos (📖 To be left to dress figures of saints)
— To be left unmarried; to miss the last marital train; to be an old maid; to remain single

- **Ya rechazaste a tres novios. Si no aceptas a Telésforo, te vas a quedar a vestir santos.**
  You've turned down three admirers. If you don't say yes to Telésforo, you'll never get married.

Quedar bien (o mal)
— To fit (clothing, etc.) properly (or badly)

- **No sé si esto me va a quedar bien.**
  I don't know if this is going to fit me.

- **Ese vestido de tu mamá te queda muy mal.**
  That dress of your mother's doesn't fit you at all. It's awful.

— To do a good (or bad) job

- **Mi mecánico está quedando muy mal con la entrega del coche.**
  My mechanic still hasn't finished my car (it should have been ready long before this).

— To turn out well (or badly)

- **La pintura del mueble quedó muy mal.**
  The paint job on that piece of furniture is awful (didn't turn out the way it was supposed to).

Expressions

Quedar(se) con la boca abierta (boquiabierto(a)) (📖 To be open-mouthed)
— To be astounded
- **¡Qué memoria la de Julián! Me dejó con la boca abierta (boquiabierto).**
  What a memory Julian has! I was left open-mouthed.

Quedar(se) con las ganas
— To feel like doing ❑ and be unable to
- **Me quedé con las ganas de ver esa película.**
  I wanted very much to see that movie, but never was able to.

Quedar(se) con un palmo de narices
— To have ☺'s nose thumbed at you
- **Después de tanto cortejar a Luisa, Jaime se quedó con un palmo de narices.**
  After pursuing Luisa for so long, Jaime got the brush-off.

Quedar(se) corto(a)
— To make an understatement
- **Me habías dicho que la catedral de Puebla era bonita. Te quedaste corto. Es preciosa.**
  You told me the Puebla Cathedral was pretty, but it's out of this world.

Quedar(se) en ayunas (📖 To go without breakfast)
— To be out of it; not to know what's going on
- **Todos se rieron de lo que dijo Julio, pero Laura se quedó en ayunas.**
  Everyone laughed at what Julio said, but Laura didn't get it.

Quemar(se) las pestañas (📖 To burn your eyelashes with the candle flame, presumably studying late at night)
— To burn the midnight oil
- **Voy a tener que quemarme las pestañas estudiando este proyecto.**
  I'll have to burn the midnight oil studying this project.

Rascar(se) con sus propias uñas (📖 To scratch yourself with your own nails)
— To solve your own problems
- **No podré seguir ayudándote. De ahora en adelante tendrás que rascarte con tus propias uñas.**
  I won't be able to keep on helping you. You'll have to solve your own problems from now on.

Rascar(se) la panza (📖 To scratch your belly)
— To do nothing; to lie around doing nothing
- **Hoy es domingo. Voy a estar en la alberca, rascándome la panza.**
  Today is Sunday. I'll be out by the pool, just lying around.

Saber a gloria (📖 To taste of glory)
— To taste delicious, out of this world
- **Con el hambre que tenía, la torta me supo a gloria.**
  I was so hungry that the sandwich tasted out of this world.

Expressions

Saber al dedillo ❑
— To know ❑ perfectly; to have at your fingertips
- **Me sé mi papel al dedillo.**
  I know my lines perfectly.

▶ Sacar boleto
— To ask for ❑ (usually trouble)
- **Sígueme molestando; estás sacando boleto.**
  If you keep that up, you're asking for it.

Sacar(le) canas verdes a ☺ (📖 To give ☺ green-gray hair)
— To drive ☺ to distraction; to give ☺ a hard time
- **Este escuincle me está sacando canas verdes.**
  That kid is driving me around the bend (up the wall).

Sacar las uñas (📖 To unsheathe your claws)
— To steal ❑ stealthily
- **Si te descuidas, tu sirvienta va a sacar las uñas.**
  If you're not careful, your maid will steal you blind.
— To seem mild, then become aggressive
- **No le demuestres mucha confianza, porque va a sacar las uñas.**
  Don't get too chummy because he's sure to try to take advantage of you.

Salir bien (mal)
— To turn out well (or badly)
- **Todo salió bien, gracias a ti.**
  Everything turned out fine, thanks to you.
- **Voy a repetir esta hoja. Me salió mal.**
  I'm going to do this page over. It doesn't look right.

Salir(se) con la suya (📖 To end up having your way)
— To get away with ❑; to get your way
- **Esta vez no te vas a salir con la tuya.**
  This time you're not going to get away with it.

▶ Salir del paso
— To do ❑ just to get by, or to get ❑ over with
- **¿Qué puedo cocinar para la fiesta de Raúl, nada más para salir del paso?**
  What can I cook for Raul's party, just to get it over with?

Salir el tiro por la culata (📖 To have the bullet come out the butt end)
— To backfire; to be hoist on your own petard
- **No te pongas intransigente; corres el riesgo de que te salga el tiro por la culata.**
  Don't be so stubborn; you risk having this thing backfire.

Expressions

Seguir(se) de frente

— To continue on with □; not to stop; to be unable to stop

- **El libro estaba tan interesante que me seguí de frente leyendo toda la noche.**
  I couldn't put the book down; I read straight through the night.

- **No se dio vuelta donde le dije; se siguió de frente.**
  He didn't turn where I told him to; he just kept right on going.

Seguir(le) la corriente a ☺ (see **Dar(le) por su lado a** ☺)

— To humor ☺

- **Es muy necio. Más vale seguirle la corriente.**
  He's very stubborn. It's better to humor him.

— To go along with ☺

- **Si no quieres problemas con el jefe, simplemente síguele la corriente.**
  If you want to avoid problems with the boss, just go along with everything he says and does.

Sentir(se) la mamá de los pollitos (📖 To feel that you're the mother of the little chicks)

— To feel self important, self satisfied

- **Mi vecina es insoportable. Se siente la mamá de los pollitos.**
  My neighbor is unbearable. She thinks she's the cat's pajamas.

Ser aplicado(a)

— To be very studious

- **Lucrecia es una niña muy aplicada.**
  Lucrecia is a very studious girl.

Ser buen partido

— To be eligible; to be a good match

- **¿Por qué Conchita no le hace caso a Pepe? Creo que es un buen partido.**
  Why is Conchita giving Pepe the cold shoulder? I think he's a good match.

Ser de buen ver (see **No ser de mal ver**)

— To be good looking

- **Susana es de buen ver.**
  Susana is very good looking.

Ser de buena pasta

— To be made of good stuff

- Speaker A: **A sus años, tu padre está estupendamente.**
  Your father is in great shape for his age.

- Speaker B: **¡Es de muy buena pasta!**
  He's made of good stuff! (He comes from good stock!)

Ser de mírame y no me toques (📖 To be a look-at-me-but-touch-me-not)
— To be very fragile
- ▪ **Esa vajilla es de mírame y no me toques.**
  That china set is very fragile.
— To be very touchy
- ▪ **No se te puede decir nada. Eres de mírame y no me toques.**
  I can't say anything to you. You're really touchy.

Ser del día
— To be very fresh or of that same day (Before refrigeration, it was important to know whether produce (food) had been put on sale that very day or was left over from the day before.)
- ▪ **Este pan está duro. No es del día.**
  This bread is stale. It's not from today's batch.

Ser del montón (📖 To be of the heap)
— To be ordinary, common, mediocre
- ▪ **Hijo, tienes que prepararte muy bien, para no ser del montón.**
  Son, you have to study like hell so that you're not just one more in the heap.

♭ Ser fodongo(a)
— To be lazy (and sometimes dirty or messy as well)
- ▪ **Hija, levanta tu ropa, ¡no seas fodonga!**
  Pick your clothes up! Don't be lazy (messy).

Ser flojo(a) (📖 To be limp) (see **Ser fodongo**)
— To be lazy
- ▪ **¿Por qué eres tan flojo? Búscate un trabajo.**
  Why are you so lazy? Find yourself a job!

Ser harina de otro costal (📖 To be flour from another sack)
— To be another matter; to be another kettle of fish.
- ▪ **Ese asunto ya es harina de otro costal.**
  That's another matter.

Ser la piel de Judas (📖 To be the skin of Judas)
— To be a holy terror
- ▪ **Este muchachito es la piel de Judas.**
  This kid is a holy terror.

Ser letra muerta
— To be no longer in effect or effective
- ▪ **Actualmente esa ley es letra muerta.**
  That law is no longer in effect.

♭ Ser malinchista (see **Malinchismo**)
— To practice **malinchismo** or admire foreigners and foreign cultures overmuch
- ▪ **No seas tan malinchista.**
  You're too much fond of everything foreign.

Expressions

Ser mosca muerta (📖 To be a dead fly)
— To be a dull and inconspicuous person on the surface
- **Cuidado con esa mosca muerta de Connie. Es una amenaza.**
  Careful with that insignificant looking Connie. She's a mean one.

Ser mucha hembra
— To be an A#1 woman (good-looking, bright, assertive, self-reliant, etc.)
- **Jacinta es mucha hembra para Héctor, ¿no crees?**
  Jacinta is too much of a woman for Héctor, don't you think?

Ser muy mujer
— To be an excellent housekeeper
- **Juana lleva su casa admirablemente. Es muy mujer.**
  Juana runs her house beautifully. She's a great housekeeper.

Ser pasto de ❏
— To be fuel for ❏
- **La casa de madera fue fácil pasto de las llamas.**
  The wooden house was fuel for the flames.

Ser traga años
— To look a lot younger than you really are
- **Gonzalo parece más joven que su esposa, pero en realidad es traga años.**
  Gonzalo appears to be younger than his wife, but he just looks young for his years.

⏍ Ser un estuche de monerías (📖 To be a chest full of cute abilities)
— To be accomplished in many different skills
- **Diana, aparte de ser pediatra, mamá y ama de casa, también sabe afinar su coche y juega tenis muy bien. De veras que es un estuche de monerías.**
  Aside from being a pediatrician, a mother and a housewife, Diane knows how to tune up her car, and plays tennis very well. She's really very accomplished.

Ser un pan de Dios (📖 To be a piece of God's bread)
— To be a truly good person
- Speaker A: **¿Sabías que Marcos adoptó dos perritos que se encontró en la calle?**
  Did you know that Marcos adopted two stray dogs he found in the street?
- Speaker B: **¡Ay!, ese hombre es un pan de Dios.**
  Gosh! He's an angel!

⏍ Ser un plomo (📖 To be a piece of lead)
— To be dull, uninteresting and unpleasant (people only); to be a jerk
- **César no es mal muchacho pero es un plomo.**
  Cesar is not a bad guy, but he's really dull as dishwater.

Ser una lata
— To be a pain or bother
- **Es una lata tener que llenar todas estas formas.**
  What a pain to have to fill out all these forms!

Ser una nata (📖 To be like the skin that forms on boiled milk)
— To be totally inept, useless
- **Odilón no sirve para nada. Es una nata.**
  Odilon is totally inept. He's hopeless.

Sonar(se) a ☺
— ♌ To beat ☺ up
- **Joaquín amenazó con sonarse a Jaime.**
  Joaquin threatened to beat Jaime up.
— To blow your nose
- **No te suenes tan fuerte.**
  Don't blow your nose so hard.
— ♌ To spank ☺
- **Voy a sonarle unas buenas nalgadas a mi nieto.**
  I'm going to spank my grandson.

♌ Tener buena cara (📖 To have a good face)
— To look good or appealing
- Speaker A: **Aquí está el bufet. ¿Qué vas a comer?**
  Here's the buffet. What'll you have?
  Speaker B: **Pues este rosbif tiene muy buena cara.**
  Well, this roast beef looks very good.
- Speaker A: **¿Qué película se te antoja?**
  What movie do you want to see?
  Speaker B: **Ésta de suspenso tiene buena cara.**
  This suspense film looks good.

Tener en cuenta ❑ (see Tomar en cuenta ❑)
— To keep ❑ in mind
- **Si vas a llevar a tu abuelito al gimnasio, ten en cuenta que no puede seguirte el paso, así que vete con calma.**
  If you are going to the gym with your grandpa, keep in mind he can't keep up with you.

Tener ganas de ❑
— To feel a desire; to feel like ❑
- **Tengo ganas de un chocolate.**
  I feel like (eating) a chocolate.

Tener ganas de hacer ❑
— To feel like doing ❑

Expressions

- **No tuve ganas de estudiar.**
  I didn't feel like studying.

Tener harto(a) (see Estar harto(a))
— To irk ☺

- **¡Este calor me tiene harto!**
  I'm fed up with this heat!

- **Me fui de casa porque me tenían harto con sus regaños.**
  I left home because I was fed up with the scolding.

Tener presente ☺□
— To have ☺□ on your mind

- **Tengo muy presente la fecha de su muerte.**
  The date of his death is constantly on my mind.

▷ Tener sangre de atole (📖 To have blood made of **atole** (corn gruel))
— To have no gumption

- **¡Cómo permites que tu suegra te trate así! Tienes sangre de atole.**
  How can you let your mother-in-law treat you like this? You're such a wimp.

Tener sentido
— To make sense (Do not translate "make sense" as "**hacer sentido**")

- **Este recado no tiene sentido.**
  This message doesn't make sense.

Tener sus bemoles (📖 To have flat notes (in music))
— To have its cons (problems)

- **El trabajo parece fácil, pero tiene sus bemoles.**
  The work looks easy, but it's got its cons (problems).

Tener (hacer(sele)) un nudo en la garganta
— To have a lump in your throat

- **Con la emoción, tengo un nudo en la garganta.**
  I am so overcome that I have a lump in my throat.

Tener un trabajo de locos
— To be loaded with work

- **Con la preparación del campeonato, hemos tenido un trabajo de locos.**
  We're been loaded with work getting ready for the championship.

Tomar a pecho □ (📖 To take □ to your breast)
— To take □ seriously; to be hurt or offended by □; to take □ to heart

- **¡Ay Efrén! ¡No tomes tan a pecho lo que dijo ese tonto de Jorge!**
  Oh Efren! Don't take what George says so seriously! He's a jerk!

Tomar en cuenta □
— To keep ☺□ in mind while making a decision; to consider ☺'s opinion or presence

- **Ahora que van a preparar el presupuesto, tomen en cuenta que Joe ya no está aquí.**
  Now you're preparing the budget, don't forget Joe is no longer here.
- **A pesar de que él va a pagar la fiesta, no lo tomaron en cuenta para nada.**
  Even though he is going to pay for the party, nobody asked for his opinion regarding the details.

Tomar(se) el trabajo (see Tomar(se) la molestia)

— To take the trouble; to go to the trouble; to bother
  - **Le agradezco que se haya tomado el trabajo de leerlo.**
    I appreciate your taking the trouble to read it.

Tomar(se) la molestia (see Tomar(se) el trabajo)

— To take the trouble; to go to the trouble; to bother
  - **Se tomó la molestia de llevarme hasta mi casa.**
    He went to the trouble of driving me all the way home.

Tomar la sartén por el mango (📖 To take the frying pan by the handle)

— To take the bull by the horns
  - **Esto no puede seguir así. Alguien va a tener que tomar la sartén por el mango.**
    This can't go on. Someone is going to have to take the bull by the horns.

Traer entre ceja y ceja a ☺❑ (📖 To have ☺❑ between your two eyebrows)

— To have a grudge against ☺; to have it in for ☺
  - **Este gruñón de Enrique trae entre ceja y ceja a mi hermana.**
    That grouch Henry has it in for my sister.

Tragar(se) la tierra a ☺❑ (📖 To be swallowed up by the earth)

— To disappear
  - **Hace años que no vemos a Sergio. Se lo tragó la tierra.**
    We haven't seen Sergio for ages. He just disappeared.

Valer la pena + verb (📖 To be worth the pain)

— To be worthwhile
  - **Valió la pena venir hasta acá para ver esta preciosa iglesia.**
    It was worthwhile coming all the way up here to see this beautiful church.
  - **Lourdes anda con un muchacho que no vale la pena.**
    Lourdes is going out with a guy who is pretty much of a washout.

Venir al caso; no venir al caso

— To be the point; to have ❑ to do with ❑; to be relevant
  - **Creo que viene al caso citar este ejemplo.**
    I think this example is relevant.
  - **Lo que estás diciendo no viene al caso.**
    That has nothing to do with it.

Venir(le) bien a ☺

— To be welcome

Expressions

- **Me vino muy bien su ayuda.**
  His help was most welcome.
— To suit ☺; to be convenient or helpful
  - **A Leticia le vinieron muy bien esas vacaciones.**
    That vacation was just what Leticia needed.
— To fit (see **Quedar bien**)
  - **Ese pantalón ya no te viene.**
    Those pants don't fit you anymore.

Ver los toros desde la barrera (📖 To watch the bullfight from the safety of the spectator's stalls)

— To avoid getting involved; to be an onlooker when there is trouble
  - **¡Tú cállate! Si vas a ver los toros desde la barrera, no tienes derecho a opinar.**
    You keep quiet! If you're not going to shoulder part of the risk, you have no right to butt in.

Ver moros con tranchetes (📖 To see Moors with battle axes, from the time the Moors occupied Spain)

— To imagine danger or trouble where there is none
  - **Las cosas no son tan graves; Alma está viendo moros con tranchetes.**
    Things aren't all that serious; Alma is imagining things.

Vivir al día

— To live from day to day; to have just enough money for the day's needs.
  - **Necesito ganar más. Ya estoy cansado de vivir al día.**
    I need to earn more. I'm sick of being broke all the time (of not knowing where my next meal is coming from).

2. Expressions Used as Part of a Sentence (Non-Verbs)

The expressions in this section cannot stand alone, but must be used as part of a sentence.

A disgusto (adj.) (adv.)
—— Unhappy; uncomfortable
- **Estuve muy a disgusto en la fiesta.**
  I was very uncomfortable at the party.
—— Reluctantly
- **Los muchachos hicieron su tarea a disgusto.**
  The boys did their homework reluctantly.

A duras penas (adv.)
—— Barely
- **A duras penas salió un vaso de jugo.**
  We barely got one glass of juice (from the oranges).

A eso de . . . (adv.)
—— At about (x time)
- **Estaré contigo a eso de las seis.**
  I'll be with you around six.

A fin de . . .
—— In order to . . .
- **Repetí la frase, a fin de ser más claro.**
  I repeated the phrase, in order to make myself clear.

A fin de □; a fines de □; a finales de □ (adv.)
—— At the end of □; late in the month (week, etc.); in late □
- **Sucedió a fin de año.**
  It happened late in the year.

A fin de cuentas (📖 Once the calculations are done) (adv.)
—— In the end; when you come right down to it
- **A fin de cuentas, no valía la pena.**
  In the end, it wasn't worth it.
- **A fin de cuentas, ¿qué importa?**
  When you come right down to it, who cares?

A fondo (adv.)
—— In depth

Expressions

- **Hay que hacer un estudio a fondo.**
  We must make an in-depth study.
— Thoroughly
  - **Hay que investigar esto a fondo.**
  This has to be investigated thoroughly.

A la hora de la hora (adv.)
— When the going gets tough; when the time comes
  - **No vayas a echarte para atrás a la hora de la hora.**
  Don't back down when the going gets tough.

A la hora de la verdad (adv.)
— When the time comes
  - **A la hora de la verdad, van a negar que lo dijeron.**
  When the time comes, they are going to deny what they said.

A la larga (adv.)
— Eventually; in the long run
  - **Si ahorras un poquito cada mes, a la larga tendrás una buena cantidad.**
  If you save a bit every month, you will eventually have a good sum.
  - **Parece chica, pero a la larga nos acomodaremos en esta casa.**
  It seems small, but eventually we'll make ourselves at home in this house.

A las mil maravillas (adv.)
— Wonderfully well
  - **Esa blusa te queda a las mil maravillas.**
  That blouse fits beautifully.

A las primeras de cambio (adv.)
— At the first chance; straight off; right away
  - **Les metieron el gol a las primeras de cambio.**
  The team made a goal right away.
  - **Estoy seguro de que Arcadio va a meter la pata a las primeras de cambio.**
  I'm sure Arcadio is going to do something dumb the very first chance he has.

A más no poder (adv.)
— With all your might and main
  - **Para entrar a la competencia, se esforzó a más no poder, pero no logró calificar.**
  He worked with all his might and main to enter the competition, but he wasn't able to qualify.

A más tardar (adv.)
— At the latest; no later than
  - **Este impuesto se tiene que pagar a más tardar el jueves.**
  This tax must be paid by Thursday at the latest.

A mediados de ☐
— In the middle of ☐; in mid-☐ (adv.)
- **Llegará a mediados de semana.**
  He's arriving in the middle of the week.

A menos que
— Unless
- **El pago se debe hacer en efectivo, a menos que se especifique lo contrario.**
  The payment must be made in cash, unless otherwise stipulated.

A morir (adv.)
— Until ☐ dies, runs out, peters out, comes to an end, etc.
- **La fiesta va a ser a morir.**
  The party will go on until there's no one left standing.

A no ser que
— Unless
- **Estamos a punto de terminar, a no ser que se presente alguna complicación.**
  We are about to finish, unless some complication arises.

A pedir de boca (adv.) (see Ni mandado(a) a hacer (adv.))

A principios de ☐ (adv.)
— At the beginning of ☐; in early ☐
- **El curso empieza a principios de abril.**
  The course starts in early April.

A propósito (adv.) (see Entre paréntesis and Por cierto)
— Incidentally; by the way
- **Estuve hablando con Leticia ayer. A propósito, te manda saludar.**
  I was talking to Leticia yesterday. By the way, she says hello.
— On purpose
- **No fue un accidente. Lo hizo a propósito.**
  It wasn't an accident. She did it on purpose.

A regañadientes (adv.) (see De mala gana)
— Reluctantly; grudgingly
- **Mi hija siempre va a visitar a su abuela a regañadientes.**
  My daughter always has to be pushed into going to visit her grandma.

A ☺ se le cocina (guisa) aparte (📖 Special food is prepared separately for ☺, because ☺ is superior or more important)
— ☺ is super special (in ☺'s trade or specialty); to be in a class by yourself
- **Todos los atletas del equipo son buenos, pero a Mario García se le cocina aparte.**
  All the athletes on the team are good, but Mario Garcia is in a class by himself.

Expressions

A tiro limpio (adv.)
— In a hail of bullets
- **Villa entró en el pueblo a tiro limpio.**
  Villa and his men shot their way into the town.

A título de . . .
— In the capacity of . . .
- **Está actuando a título de representante.**
  He is acting as a (in the capacity of) representative.

¿A título de qué?
— For what reason . . . ?; in what capacity?
- **¿A título de qué te metes en nuestros asuntos?**
  For what reason (in what capacity) are you butting into our affairs?

A toda costa (adv.) (see **Cueste lo que cueste**)
— At whatever cost; no matter what, how, when, etc.
- **Hay que mejorar la producción a toda costa.**
  The production has to be improved, no matter how.

A ver si pega (📖 To see if it sticks)
— To see if ❑ takes root; to see if some strategy scheme or plan works
- **Voy a decir que el viaje de Acapulco fue de negocios, a ver si pega, porque en ese caso los gastos son deducibles.**
  I'm going to claim the trip to Acapulco was for business purposes and see if they fall for it, in which case, the expenses are deductible.

Ahora bien
— Nevertheless; however (a synonym of **sin embargo**)
- **No me entusiasma emplear a Joe; ahora bien, si me demuestra capacidad, puedo cambiar de idea.**
  I'm not inclined to hire Joe; nevertheless, if he proves he's capable, I may change my mind.

Ahora mismo; ahorita; ahorita mismo; ahoritita
— Right now; right away
- **Si no nos vamos ahorita mismo, vamos a perder el avión**
  If we don't leave right now, we'll miss the plane.
- **Lo haré ahora mismo (ahorita mismo, ahoritita).**
  I'll do it right away.

Al abrigo de ❑ (adv.)
— In the shadow of ❑
- **Hizo su fortuna al abrigo de su padre, que le ayudó siempre.**
  He made his fortune in the shadow of his father, who always helped him.

Al fin y al cabo; después de todo
— After all
- **Esther se merece el premio. Al fin y al cabo (después de todo), nos lleva muchos años de experiencia.**
  Esther deserves the prize. After all, she's had years more experience than we have.

Al hilo (adj.) (adv.)
— One after another; in a row
- **En este invierno me han dado tres resfriados al hilo.**
  This winter I've had three colds in a row.

Al otro día (adv.) (not to be confused with **el otro día,** which means "the other day")
— The next day
- **Dijo que estaría listo al otro día, pero no fue así.**
  He said it would be ready the next day, but it wasn't.

Al parecer (adv.)
— Apparently; supposedly
- **Se metieron a su casa y le robaron todo. Al parecer, la sirvienta es cómplice.**
  They broke into his house and got away with everything. Supposedly, the maid is an accessory.

Al tanteo (adv.)
— Haphazardly; by guesswork; said of ❏ that is done without really knowing what you're doing
- **Al tanteo, yo diría que son tres metros.**
  Roughly, I'd say it's three meters.
- **¿Me sabes algo o me lo dices al tanteo?**
  Do you know some secret about me, or are you just saying that?

Alma de Dios (📖 A soul of God) (see **Ser un pan de Dios**)
— A lovely person; a dear (kind, generous, sympathetic, etc.) person.
- **Tu abuelo es un alma de Dios.**
  Your grandfather is a dear.

Cara de pocos amigos (📖 A face of few friends)
— A nasty look
- **No te acerques a ese perro. Tiene cara de pocos amigos.**
  Stay away from the dog. He looks nasty.

Como alma en pena (adj.)
— Like a troubled soul
- **Aquí estoy solo y a oscuras, como alma en pena.**
  Here I am, alone and in the dark like some restless ghost.

Como Dios manda (adj.) (📖 As God dictates)

— Properly; correctly
  ▪ **Finalmente encontré a una muchacha que sabe limpiar la plata como Dios manda.**
    I finally found a girl who can clean the silver properly.

Con ganas
— With great effort; with great enthusiasm
  ▪ **Le pegó a la pelota con todas sus ganas.**
    He hit the ball as hard as he possibly could.

Con la mano en la cintura (adj.) (📖 With your hand on your hip)
— With the greatest of ease
  ▪ **Yo le gano a Gina en tenis con la mano en la cintura.**
    I can beat Gina at tennis with one hand tied behind my back.

Con toda su humanidad (adv.)
— With all ☺'s bulk
  ▪ **Arturo rodó por la escalera con toda su humanidad.**
    Arturo fell down the stairs . . . all 250 pounds of him.

Con trabajo(s) (adv.) (see **Costar (mucho) trabajo** and **Dar trabajo**)
— With great difficulty
  ▪ **Leo el francés con trabajos.**
    I read French with a great deal of difficulty.

Cortados(as) por la misma tijera (📖 Cut with the same scissors)
— Made from the same pattern; cut from the same cloth
  ▪ **Sandro y Saúl parecen cortados por la misma tijera.**
    Sandro and Saul seem to have been made from the same pattern.

Cueste lo que cueste (v.)
— At whatever cost; no matter what, how, when, etc.
  ▪ **Voy a hacer mi maestría, cueste lo que cueste.**
    I'm going to get my master's degree, no matter what.

Chistes (cuentos) colorados (n.)
— Dirty jokes
  ▪ **¿Cómo les voy a contar a mis hijos esos chistes colorados?**
    How can I tell my kids those dirty jokes?

De ahí que . . .
— Therefore; so that is why . . .
  ▪ **La deducción se basa en la ley. De ahí que el fisco deberá aceptarla.**
    The deduction is based on the law. Therefore, the tax authorities will have to accept it.

De buena gana (adv.)
— Willingly; gladly

- **Me ayudó a pintar la casa de muy buena gana.**
  He helped me to paint the house quite gladly.

De buenas a primeras (adv.) (see De repente)
— Without warning; suddenly; out of the blue
- **De buenas a primeras la empresa me mandó a trabajar a Paraguay.**
  The company sent me off to work in Paraguay without any warning.

De cualquier modo; de cualquier manera; de cualquier forma (adv.) (see De todos modos)
— Anyway; just the same (**de cualquier modo** also means carelessly)
- **Ya desayuné, pero de cualquier modo, me comeré este taco.**
  *I've already had breakfast, but I'll have this *taco* anyway.*

— Carelessly
- **Lupe puso la mesa de cualquier modo.**
  Lupe set the table sloppily.

De (las seis, hoy, ahora, etc.) en adelante (adv.)
— From now on; from (x moment) on; in the future . . .
- **De ahora en adelante, hágame el favor de tocar.**
  In the future, be kind enough to knock.

De igual a igual (adv.)
— On the same footing
- **Carlos y Enrique no pueden competir de igual a igual.**
  Carlos and Enrique can't compete on the same footing.

De improviso (adv.)
— On the spur of the moment
- **El viaje se hizo de improviso.**
  We took the trip on the spur of the moment.

De lo lindo (adv.)
— Very pleasantly or pleasurably
- **Comimos, cantamos y bailamos de lo lindo.**
  We had a great time eating, singing and dancing.

De mala gana (adv.) (see A regañadientes)
— Reluctantly
- **Ernesto siempre viene a las juntas de mala gana.**
  Ernesto always comes to the meetings reluctantly.

De manera que . . .
— So; therefore

Expressions

- **Voy a tener que salir de la ciudad mañana, de manera que no podré verte el sábado.**
  I have to go out of town tomorrow, so I won't be able to see you on Saturday.
- **Vamos a constituir una nueva empresa, de manera que necesitamos un buen abogado.**
  We are going to set up a new company; therefore, we need a good lawyer.

De maravilla (adv.)
— Wonderfully well
- **Nos fue de maravilla.**
  Everything went wonderfully well.

De por sí
— As it is; as things are; anyway; already; without any further aggravation
- **No podemos invitar más gente a la boda; de por sí no van a alcanzar las mesas para los que ya tenemos en la lista.**
  We can't invite anyone else to the wedding; as it is there won't be enough tables for everyone on the list.
- **"Ya de por sí la vida se lleva con trabajo."** (*Pedro Páramo*, by **Juan Rulfo**)
  "Life is difficult as it is."

De refacción; de repuesto
— Spare; replacement
- **No quiero salir a carretera porque no tengo llanta de repuesto (de refacción).**
  I don't want to drive on the highway because I don't have a spare tire.

De repente (adv.) (see De buenas a primeras)
— Suddenly
- **Estábamos cenando cuando de repente cayó un rayo.**
  We were having supper when suddenly there was a flash of lightning.

Después de todo (see Al fin y al cabo)

De su (mi, tu) cosecha
— ☐ of ☺'s invention (creation, making)
- **Todas las muchachas usaron modelos de modistos parisinos o italianos, pero yo llevé un diseño de mi cosecha.**
  All the girls wore Parisian or Italian designs, but my dress was of my own design.
- **Ella me dijo lo que pasó, pero evidentemente le puso de su cosecha.**
  She told me what happened, but she obviously made up some of the details.

De su (mi, tu) puño y letra
— In ☺'s own handwriting
- **El gobernador me mandó una nota de su puño y letra**
  The Governor sent me a note in his own handwriting.

De suyo
— It is in the nature of ☐ to be (adj.)

- **Esto de suyo es difícil.**
  This is naturally difficult. (It is the nature of this (thing) to be difficult.)
- **Rigoberto es flojo de suyo.**
  It is in the Rigoberto's nature to be lazy.

De todos modos; de todas maneras (see De cualquier modo; de cualquier manera; de cualquier forma)
— Anyway; just the same
- **Ya desayuné, pero me comeré este taco de todos modos.**
  *I've already had breakfast, but I'll have this **taco** anyway.*

De una vez (adv.) (See Ahora mismo; ahorita mismo; ahoritita and Luego luego)
— Right away; once and for all
- **Si lo vamos a tener que hacer tarde o temprano, vamos a hacerlo de una vez.**
  If we're going to do it sooner or later, let's do it right away (once and for all).

De una vez por todas (adv.)
— Once and for all
- **Quiero terminar de hacer estos estantes de una vez por todas.**
  I want to finish making these shelves once and for all.

Después de todo (see Al fin y al cabo)

El último grito de la moda (📖 The last scream of fashion)
— The latest rage
- **El vestido que trae Gloria es el último grito de la moda.**
  Gloria's dress is the latest rage.

En cuanto . . .
— As soon as
- **Te llamaré por teléfono en cuanto tenga la información.**
  I'll call you as soon as I have the information.

En el entendido de que . . . (see En la inteligencia de que . . .)

En el fondo
— At heart; deep down; when you come right down to it
- **Habla como mexicano, pero en el fondo sigue siendo español.**
  He talks like a Mexican, but he's a Spaniard at heart.
- **En el fondo, Jaime es romántico.**
  Deep down, Jaime is romantic.
- **En el fondo, este informe no dice nada.**
  When you come right down to it, this report doesn't say a thing.

En la inteligencia de que . . . (adv.)
— On the understanding that

Expressions

- **Asistiré a la reunión en la inteligencia de que (en el entendido de que) no estoy de acuerdo con el temario.**
  I'll attend the meeting, on the understanding that I am not in agreement with the agenda.

En limpio (adv.)
— Said of the final, corrected, clean version of ❑ written
- **Señorita, es urgente que pase esta carta en limpio.**
  Miss, it's urgent that you type this letter (in the final, clean version).

En lo sucesivo (adv.) (Slightly formal. See De (x momento) en adelante)

En pleno día (adv.)
— In broad daylight
- **Se fue caminando hasta el puesto de periódico en pijama, en pleno día.**
  He walked to the newspaper stand in his pajamas, in broad daylight.

En sucio (adv.)
— Said of the first draft of ❑ written (not the clean final version) (either handwritten or typed)
- **No importa que me traigas la propuesta en sucio.**
  I don't mind if you just bring the first draft of the proposal.

En toda la línea (adv.)
— Hands down; beyond a shadow of a doubt
- **Los Rojos vencieron en toda la línea.**
  The Reds won hands down.
- **Esta tela es mejor que la otra en toda la línea.**
  This cloth is better than the other, beyond a shadow of a doubt.

En virtud de
— Due to; because of
- **Pudo lograrlo en virtud de su talento.**
  He was able to achieve success because he is talented.

Entre comillas (📖 In quotation marks)
— Said when something is being taken with a grain of salt
- **Juana limpió la oficina, entre comillas.**
  Juana cleaned the office up, so she claims.

Entre paréntesis (adv.) (see A propósito and Por cierto)
— Incidentally; by the way
- **Hice la cita con la secretaria del Sr. Gómez. Entre paréntesis, ¡qué guapa está!**
  I made the appointment with Mr. Gomez's secretary. Incidentally, she's awfully good-looking!

Entre que (Mientras) son peras o son manzanas
— Until this can be cleared up or figured out . . .

Expressions

- **Usted dice que no conoce a los asaltantes y este testigo dice que sí. Entre que (Mientras) son peras o son manzanas, usted no se mueve de aquí.**
  You say you don't know the robbers, and this witness says you do. Until we can settle the matter, you're not going anywhere.

Gritos y sombrerazos (📖 Shouting and hitting with the hat)
— A ruckus; a to-do; shouts and yells (of upset people); with a great hullabaloo; in an uproar
- **Cuando sepan que la mercancía está dañada, van a haber gritos y sombrerazos.**
  When they realize the goods are damaged, there's going to be a ruckus (a to-do).
- **Cuando a la Sra. Gómez le dijeron que su sirvienta había metido a su novio a la casa, la corrió a gritos y sombrerazos.**
  When Mrs. Gomez found out her maid had let her boyfriend into the house, she made a huge stink and ran her out.

Hoy por hoy
— Nowadays; at the present time
- **Hoy por hoy, es el mejor tenista del país.**
  Nowadays he is the country's best tennis player.

📖 Luego luego (see De una vez and Ahora mismo)
— Right now; right away
- **Esto hay que enviarlo luego luego.**
  This has to be sent right away.

📖 Mala pasada
— A dirty trick
- **Al pobre Julián le jugaron una mala pasada.**
  They played a very dirty trick on poor Julian.

📖 Malinchismo (n.)
— Exaggerated love for foreigners (From **Malinche**, the Indian mistress of Hernan Cortes).
- **El malinchismo sigue muy arraigado en México.**
  In Mexico, people are still awed by everything foreign.

Mientras son peras o son manzanas (see Entre que son peras o son manzanas)

Ni mandado(a) a hacer (adv.); a pedir de boca (adv.)
— Just perfect
- **Tu regalo queda en este cuarto, que ni mandado a hacer (a pedir de boca).**
  Your present fits in this room to perfection.
- **Tenía mil cosas que hacer esta semana, pero todo salió que ni mandado a hacer (a pedir de boca).**
  I had lots of work to do this week, but everything came out just fine.

No haber (tener) para cuando
— To show no signs of happening or being ready yet; to take ages
- Speaker A: **¿Ya te propuso matrimonio Alfonso? Ya llevan tres años de novios.**
  Has Alfonso proposed yet? You've been going steady for three years.
- Speaker B (shaking her head):   **No hay (tiene) para cuando.**
  No sign of him proposing yet.

No hay pero que valga
— No buts
- **¡Vendrán a comer mañana! No hay pero que valga.**
  You're coming to dinner at my place tomorrow. No buts.

No tener para cuándo (see **No haber para cuándo**)

Para colmo (see **¡Es el colmo!**)
— To make things worse; to top things off
- **Acá está lloviendo, y para colmo, se fue la luz.**
  It's raining here, and to make things worse, there's no electricity.

Para quitar el hipo (adj.) (📖 Enough to cure the hiccups)
— Very impressive, astonishing
- **Es un proyecto verdaderamente inmenso . . . para quitar el hipo.**
  It's a huge project . . . really tremendous.

Pez gordo (n.) (📖 Fat fish)
— Fat cat
- **Con la investigación caerán varios peces gordos.**
  Several fat cats will be caught as a result of this investigation.

Por cierto (adv.) (see **A propósito** and **Entre paréntesis**)
— Incidentally; by the way
- **Entregué los documentos en el tercer piso. Por cierto, no había elevador.**
  I delivered the documents on the third floor. By the way, there was no elevator.

Por debajo del agua (adv.) (📖 Under the water)
— Under the table
- **Mario recibió por debajo del agua una cantidad por poner al contratista en contacto con el cliente.**
  Mario got some money under the table from the contractor for putting him in touch with the client.

Por la buena (adv.)
— Nicely; without having to be forced
- **Por la buena, pueden sacarme lo que quieran.**
  If you're nice about it, you can get anything you want out of me.

Por las dudas (see **Por si acaso**)

Por la mala (adv.)

— Only when forced

- **A este muchacho le gusta ser llevado por la mala.**
  That boy has to be forced to do things.

Por lo pronto

— In the meantime; until we see what happens next

- **No han resuelto nuestro préstamo; por lo pronto, tenemos que esperar.**
  No decision has been reached concerning our loan. In the meantime, all we can do is wait.

Por los suelos (adv.) (📖 On the floors)

— Down in the dumps; completely depressed

- **Desde la crisis, la divisa del país ha estado por los suelos.**
  Ever since the crisis, that country's currency has been down in the dumps.

Por otra parte (see **Por otro lado**)

Por otro lado; por otra parte

— On the other hand

- **El verano es mala época para ir a Acapulco, porque hace mucho calor; por otro lado (por otra parte), los precios son mucho mejores que en temporada alta.**
  It's really hot in Acapulco in the summertime; on the other hand, the prices are much better than in the high season.

Por poco; por poquito

— Almost

- **¡Qué horror! ¡Por poco (por poquito) atropellas a esa señora!**
  Good Lord! You almost ran that woman down!

Por poquito (see **Por poco**)

Por si acaso; por las dudas

— Just in case

- **Mejor cierra la puerta con llave, por si acaso (por las dudas).**
  Better lock the door, just in case.

ꀸ **Se me hace** ☐; **se me hace que** + verb

— It seems ☐; It seems to me that ☺☐ + verb; it strikes me as being ☐; I have a feeling that

- **No me gusta esta casa. Se me hace tenebrosa.**
  I don't like this house. It seems spooky to me.
- **Se me hace que va a llover.**
  I have a feeling it's going to rain.

Expressions

♫ **Siempre no**
— ☐ is not going to be done after all
- Speaker A: **¿Vas a Europa este verano, ¿verdad?**
  You're going to Europe this summer, aren't you?
- Speaker B: **Siempre no. No nos alcanzó (el dinero) para ir.**
  No, we're not going after all. We didn't have enough money.

♫ **Siempre sí**
— ☐ is going to be done after all
- **Dice Amalia que siempre sí va a querer que le cuides a la niña.**
  Amalia says she's going to want you to take care of her little girl after all.

♫ **Sin decir agua va** (adv.)
— Without warning
- **Me quitaron mi oficina sin decir agua va.**
  My office was taken from me without a word of warning.

Sin tasa ni medida (adv.)
— In an unbridled way
- **Se la pasa comprando sin tasa ni medida.**
  She spends her time going on shopping sprees.

Sin ton ni son (adv.)
— Making no sense
- **Se puso a discutir sin ton ni son.**
  He began to argue senselessly.

Tan pronto (adv.) (see **En cuanto**)
— As soon as
- **Tan pronto termine, me voy para allá.**
  I'll be over as soon as I finish.

Tarde o temprano (adv.)
— Sooner or later
- **Tarde o temprano vas a tener que ir a ver al médico.**
  You're going to have to see the doctor sooner or later.

Todo el santo día (adv.)
— All the live-long day; the whole day long
- **Ese maldito perro ladra todo el santo día.**
  The damned dog barks the whole day long.

Un ojo al gato y otro al garabato (see **Echar un ojo al gato y otro al garabato**)

Vamos bien
— So far, so good

- **Sólo llevamos tres días con el programa, pero vamos bien.**
  This is only the third day of the program, but so far, so good.

❑ **y pico**
— ❑ and a bit

- Speaker A: **¿Cuánto entregaron de arena?**
  How much sand was delivered?

  Speaker B: **Tres toneladas y pico.**
  Three tons and a bit.

- Speaker A: **¿Cuánto te costó tu reloj?**
  How much did your watch cost?

  Speaker B: **Dos mil y pico.**
  Two thousand and something.

- Speaker A: **¿A qué hora llegaste?**
  What time did you get here?

  Speaker B: **A las ocho y pico.**
  A bit after eight.

3. Stand-alone Expressions

A lo mejor
— Maybe; could be

- Speaker A: **No ha llegado Leonor. ¿Estará enferma?**
  Leonor hasn't arrived. I wonder if she's sick.

  Speaker B: **A lo mejor.**
  Could be.

¡A poco!
— Really?; no kidding!; seriously?

- Speaker A: **Me saqué la lotería.**
  I won the lottery.

  Speaker B: **¡A poco!**
  No kidding!

¿A poco no?
— Don't you agree?; am I right?

- **Linda es mucho más bonita que su hermana. ¿A poco no?**
  Linda is a lot prettier than her sister. Don't you agree?

¡A que sí!
— Want to bet? (aff.)

- Speaker A: **Panamá es una de las repúblicas de Centroamérica.**
  Panama is one of the Central American republics.

  Speaker B: **No es cierto.**
  No, it's not.

  Speaker A: **¡A que sí!**
  Want to bet?

¡A que no!
— Want to bet? (neg.)

- Speaker A: **¡A que no!**
  Want to bet it isn't?

  Speaker B: **¡A que sí!**
  Want to bet it is?

¡Águila o sol! (📖 Eagle or sun, on Mexican coins)
— Head or tails

Algo es algo (📖 Something is something) (see **Peor es nada**)
— It's better than nothing

- Speaker A: **Esto es todo lo que podemos darte de aumento. No nos va bien.**
  This is all the raise we can give you. We're not doing well.

Speaker B: **Algo es algo.**
                    It's better than nothing.

¡Ándale!; ¡Ándale pues!
— Go on!; get moving!; get going!; go ahead!
- ▪ **¿No ibas a ir al centro? ¿Qué esperas? ¡Ándale pues!**
  Weren't you going downtown? What are you waiting for? Get going!
— Yes, that's it; you're right!
- ▪ Speaker A: **No recuerdo la clave LADA de Orlando.**
                       I can't remember the area code of Orlando.
  Speaker B: **Es 406.**
                       It's 406.
  Speaker A: **¡Ándale!**
                       That's it!
— OK (you have my permission or approval); it's all right with me; that's fine
- ▪ Speaker A: **Mamá, ¿puedo ir al cine con Paco?**
                       Mom, can I go to the movies with Paco?
  Speaker B: **¡Ándale!**
                       Yes, OK.

Note: **¡Ándale!** has become an all-purpose word, sometimes without much meaning, or at least nothing really definite. It is often used to express surprise, admiration or agreement. A lot depends on the tone of voice, facial expression or gestures.

Aquí hay gato encerrado
— There's something fishy here
- ▪ **No veo claro el asunto. Aquí hay gato encerrado.**
  I can't figure out the situation. There's something fishy about it.

¡Basta!
— That's enough! (used when a person is really fed up; otherwise, a plain **es suficiente** or **ya no más, gracias** is used)

¡Claro!; ¡Claro que sí! (see ¡Cómo no!)
— Of course!; Naturally!
- ▪ Speaker A: **¿Me das una mano con mi tarea?**
                       Will you give me a hand with my homework?
  Speaker B: **¡Claro que sí!** or **¡Cómo no!**
                       Of course!

¡Cómo!
— This means *how* but is often used to mean What . . . ! (I can hardly believe my ears!)
- ▪ Speaker A: **Me temo que esta semana no te puedo dar nada de dinero.**
                       I'm afraid I can't give you any money this week.
  Speaker B: **¡Cómo! ¿Y qué quieres que comamos?**
                       What! And what do you expect us to eat?

Expressions

¡Cómo no!

— Of course!

- Speaker A: **¿Me ayuda?**
  Will you help me?

  Speaker B: **¡Cómo no!**
  Of course!

— Also used sarcastically as in:

- Speaker A: **Papá, he decidido que voy a ser estrella de cine.**
  Dad, I've decided I'm going to be a movie star.

  Speaker B: **¡Cómo no!**
  Suuure . . . !

¡Con razón!

— No wonder!

- Speaker A: **¿Sabes por qué no encontrabas las llaves? Pedro se las llevó por error.**
  You know why you couldn't find your keys? Pedro took them by mistake.

  Speaker B: **¡Con razón!**
  No wonder!

Da lo mismo

— It's all the same; it makes no difference

- Speaker A: **¿Quieres que lo haga hoy o mañana?**
  Do you want me to do that today or tomorrow?

  Speaker B: **Da lo mismo**
  It makes no difference.

¡De ninguna manera! (see ¡Ni pensarlo!)

— No way!; It's unthinkable!; It's out of the question!

- Speaker A: **Linda se quiere ir temprano hoy. ¿Usted lo autoriza?**
  Linda wants to leave early today. Will you OK that?

  Speaker B: **¡De ninguna manera! Hay mucho trabajo que hacer.**
  No way! There's a lot of work to do.

De vez en cuando

— Once in a while; every now and then; from time to time

- Speaker A: **¿Con qué frecuencia vas al centro?**
  How often do you go downtown?

  Speaker B: **De vez en cuando.**
  Once in a while.

¡Es el colmo!

— It's the last straw!; This is the limit!

- **Ahora me está echando la culpa de su última estupidez. ¡Es el colmo!**
  Now he's blaming me for his latest stupidity. It's the last straw!

Es igual (see Da lo mismo)

Es pan comido
— That's easy as a pie; That's duck soup
- Speaker A: **¡Mira! Estos son los requisitos para entrar al club.**
  Look! These are the requirements to get into the club.
- Speaker B: **A ver . . . ¡Están muy fáciles! Es pan comido.**
  Let's see . . . They're easy as pie!

¡Hágame el favor!; ¡Hazme el favor!
— Can you believe it?
- **Después de diez años de casada, mi hija mandó a su marido al diablo y se trajo a sus tres hijos a vivir con nosotros. ¡Hágame el favor!**
  After ten years of marriage, my daughter sent her husband to hell and brought her three kids to live with us. Can you believe it?

¡Hombre!
— Friend!; buddy!
- **¡Pero hombre! No se contesta de ese modo.**
  Hey, friend! That's no way to answer.
— Certainly!
- Speaker A: **¿A poco eres muy madrugador..?**
  Do you really get up early?

  Speaker B: **¡Hombre!**
  Certainly!

¡Menos mal!
— Thank goodness!
- Speaker A: **Tranquilízate. Los niños ya llegaron.**
  You can relax. The kids have arrived.

  Speaker B: **¡Menos mal!**
  Thank goodness!

¡Ni modo(s)!
— It can't be helped!; There's nothing we can do about that!; That's the way the ball bounces!; That's too bad!; That's bad luck!
- Speaker A: **¡Mira nomás! Linda se ganó el viaje al Canadá, y yo no me gané nada.**
  Just look at that! Linda won the trip to Canada, and I didn't win a damned thing!

  Speaker B: **¡Ni modo!**
  That's the way things go!

Expressions

Ni pensarlo (see De ninguna manera)

— No way!; It's unthinkable!; It's out of the question

- Speaker A: **Veo que estás necesitado. Permíteme prestarte algo de dinero.**
  I can see you're in a bad way. Let me lend you some money.

  Speaker B: **¡Ni pensarlo! Pero gracias de todas maneras.**
  Out of the question! But thanks anyway.

♪ Ni yendo a bailar a Chalma (📖 Not even if you go to do a ritual dance in Chalma.)

— No matter what. No matter how hard you try.

- **No vas a poder ganar ese torneo, ni yendo a bailar a Chalma.**
  You'll never be able to win that tournament, no matter what.

Note: This comes from the custom of doing a religious dance in front of the church in Chalma when requesting a great favor of God.

♪ ¡No son enchiladas! (📖 It's not like making enchiladas!)

— It's not that easy!

- Speaker A: **¿Por qué no puedes armar el motor hoy mismo?**
  Why can't you put the engine back together today?

- Speaker B: **¡Oye! ¡No son enchiladas!**
  Hey! It's not that easy!

¡Oiga!

— Listen!; Hey!; What do you think you are doing?; Who do you think you are?, etc.

A person shoves into line ahead of you at the bank. You say:

- **¡Oiga! ¡Hay que hacer cola!**
  What do you think you are doing? Go to the end of the line!

♪ Para eso me pinto solo (📖 I paint myself without any help)

— That's what I'm really good at

- Speaker A: **¿Conoces a alguien que sepa arreglar esta silla?**
  Do you know someone who can fix this chair?

  Speaker B: **¡Para eso me pinto solo!**
  I'm particularly good at that.

Para variar

— For a change

- **Hoy tú vas al super, para variar.**
  Today, you go to the supermarket, for a change.

Peor es nada

— It's better than nothing.

- Speaker A: **El abuelo sólo me dejó este anillo.**
  Grandfather left me only this ring.

Speaker B: **Peor es nada.**
                    It's better than nothing.

¡Por amor de Dios!

— For God's sake!; For the love of God!

- **¡Por amor de Dios, bájale al radio!**
  For God's sake, turn the radio down!

- **¡No me hagas eso, por amor de Dios!**
  For the love of God, don't do that to me!

¡Qué barbaridad! (📖 What a barbarity!)

— Oh, no!; How awful!; How incredible!; What a disaster!; Imagine that!; Good God!

- Speaker A: **Teddy se fugó con su secretaria.**
                      Teddy ran off with his secretary.

  Speaker B: **¡Qué barbaridad!**
                      How incredible!

- Speaker A: **Hubo 25% de inflación el mes pasado.**
                      There was 25% inflation last month.

  Speaker B: **¡Qué barbaridad!**
                      What a disaster!

- Speaker A: **El pobre de Javier tiene hepatitis.**
                      Poor Javier has hepatitis.

  Speaker B: **¡Qué barbaridad!**
                      Good God!

- Speaker A: **Mira, tienes caspa.**
                      Look, you have dandruff.

  Speaker B: **¡Qué barbaridad!**
                      Oh, no!

¡Qué bárbaro(a)! (📖 What a barbarian!)

— Said of ☺ when he or she has done ❑ outstandingly good or bad, as in the following situations:

— Someone has won the lottery.
     What terrific luck!

— Someone stays up all night working.
     Boy! What a workaholic!

— Someone cracks up a car and breaks 25 bones.
     Gosh! What a mess! Poor bastard!

— Someone is thinking of climbing Mt. Everest singlehanded.
     The guy is out of his mind! But what guts!

— Someone prepares a six-course dinner for ten in under an hour.
     What an incredible cook!

— Someone wins the Nobel prize for something.
     Wow!

Expressions

— Someone is disrespectful of his or her mother.

How dare he (she)?

¡Qué le vamos a hacer!

— Same as ¡Ni modo!

¡Qué milagro! (📖 What a miracle!)

— What a surprise! How unexpected! Usually referring to someone who has not been seen or heard from for quite a long time, or who has done something out of character, as in the following situations:

— You call someone on the phone.

Well, it is been ages since you called!

— Someone gets up and dances.

That guy never dances. How unbelievable!

— Someone's check bounces.

Incredible! This has never happened with one of his checks in all these years!

— You arrive at school early.

How come you're not late as usual?

— Someone has an alcoholic drink.

I didn't know you drank!

— A boss gives his secretary some expensive perfume on her birthday.

That's more like it! This fellow is usually such a tightward!

¡Qué pena!

— What a shame!; Too bad! (also see ¡Qué lástima!)

- **¡Qué pena! Armando no nos puede acompañar.**
  What a shame! Armando can't come with us.

— How embarrassing!; How mortifying!

- **¡Qué pena! Se me cayó la sopa.**
  How embarrasing! I spilled the soup.

📖 ¿Qué tienes?

— What's wrong?

- Speaker A: **¿Qué tienes, Pepe?**
                What's wrong, Pepe?

  Speaker B: **Me duele la panza.**
                I've got a stomach ache.

¡Qué va!

— Certainly not!; That's not true!

- Speaker A: **¿Será cierto que Liliana estudió en Italia?**
                Do you think it's true that Liliana studied in Italy?

Expressions

Speaker B: **¡Qué va! Ni siquiera conoce Europa.**
                    Certainly not! She's never even been in Europe.

Tal cual

— Just as it is; exactly the same.

▪ Speaker A: **¿Quieres que tu coche se pinte otra vez del mismo color?**
                    Do you want your car painted the same color again?

  Speaker B: **Tal cual.**
                    Exactly the same.

▪ Speaker A: **¿Se lleva usted el escritorio así como está?**
                    Will you take the desk as it is?

  Speaker B: **Tal cual.**
                    Just as it is.

¡Trágame tierra! (📖 Swallow me, Earth!)

— I'm so embarassed, I could die!

▪ **Cuando le vacié la tinta en el vestido, pensé: "¡trágame tierra!"**
  When I spilled ink over her dress, I could have died of embarassment.

¡Válgame Dios!

— Dear me!; Dear God!; God help us!; Oh my God!; Well, I'll be!

▪ **¡Válgame Dios! Mira lo que me están cobrando por el ajuste del coche.**
  Dear God! Look what they're charging me to overhaul my car!

¡Vaya!

— Well!; Well, well!; So!; It's about time!

▪ Speaker A: **Mira, aquí está el dinero que se había perdido.**
                    Look, here's the money that was lost.

  Speaker B: **¡Vaya!**
                    Well, well, well!

▪ **¡Vaya! Hasta que llegaste.**
  Well! You finally arrived.

¡Ya lo creo!

— I should say so!; Of course!; Certainly!; Absolutely!; Naturally!

▪ Speaker A: **¿Piensas que Alberto debe pagarle algo a Nora por haberle abollado su coche?**
                    Do you think Alberto should pay Nora something for denting her car?

  Speaker B: **¡Ya lo creo!**
                    I should say so!

Expressions

B. Common Expressions in English

This section contains a list of expressions in English, followed by the Spanish equivalents, which are sometimes not as apt or colorful as the English version, simply because it's a little too much to expect every single expression in English to have an exact counterpart in another language. When the Spanish version is not an actual expression but merely the best way to get that particular idea across, it is enclosed in brackets. If two or more words or expressions are given, it means that they are interchangeable.

As in *Section A*, this section has been divided into:

1. *Verbs (must be conjugated)*
2. *Expressions used as a part of a sentence (Non-Verbs)*
3. *Stand-alone expressions*

You will note that some of the Spanish equivalents of English expressions have the symbol for slang ♨. Expressions used only in Mexico have the ᕮ symbol.

1. VERBS

To add fuel to the fire; to pour oil on the flames
— **Echar leña al fuego**
- *My husband was mad at me, and what my mother-in-law said just added fuel to the fire.*
  Mi esposo estaba enojado conmigo, y lo que dijo mi suegra fue echarle leña al fuego.

To add insult to injury
— **Como (Por) si fuera poco**
- *I have a really small salary, and to add insult to injury, I haven't been paid for the last two months.*
  El sueldo que me pagan es bajo, y por si fuera poco, tengo dos meses sin cobrar.

To ask for it (see To burn the candle at both ends; to look for trouble)

To badmouth ☺
— **[Criticar a ☺]; echar(le) tierra a ☺**
- *Don't be badmouthing Sam. He's supposed to be your friend.*
  No estés criticando a Sam. Se supone que es tu amigo.

To be a big frog in a little puddle
— **Ser cabeza de ratón**
- *The president of that second-rate company is just a big frog in a little puddle.*
  El presidente de esa compañía de segunda no es más que cabeza de ratón.

To be a bone of contention
— **Ser la manzana de la discordia**
- *The inheritance was the bone of contention in the family.*
  La herencia fue la manzana de la discordia para la familia.

To be a busybody
— **Ser metiche**
- *Let your daughter-in-law decide what she wants to wear. Don't be such a busybody!*
  Deja que tu nuera decida cómo vestirse. ¡No seas tan metiche!

To be a far cry from ☐
— **Estar lejos de** ☐
- *The service in this hotel is a far cry from what it used to be when Mr. Young was manager.*
  El servicio de este hotel está lejos de ser lo que era cuando el Sr. Young era el gerente.

To be a feather in ☺**'s cap**
— **Anotar(se) un tanto (un triunfo) para** ☺
- *He won the prize again; this is another feather in his cap.*
  Otra vez ganó el premio; volvió a anotarse un tanto (triunfo).

To be a great guy (gal)
— **Ser buena gente**

Expressions

- *Did you know that Marcia works as a volunteer at a handicapped kids camp every summer? She's really a great gal.*
  ¿Sabías que cada verano Marcia trabaja de voluntaria en un campamento para niños minusválidos? De veras que es buena gente.

To be a jalopy
— **Ser una carcacha**
- *Help us push John's jalopy.*
  Ayúdanos a empujar la carcacha de Juan.

To be a nerd; to be a horse's backside
— **[Ser un menso(a) (pesado(a))]**
- *Don't put me at the same table with Victor. He's a nerd.*
  No me pongas en la misma mesa con Víctor. Es un menso pesado.

To be a tempest in a teapot; to make a mountain out of a molehill
— **Hacer una tempestad en un vaso de agua** (📖 To make a tempest in a glass of water)
- *It doesn't really matter if there's a towel missing. It's a tempest in a teapot. (You're making a mountain out of a molehill.)*
  Realmente no importa que falte una toalla. Estás haciendo una tempestad en un vaso de agua.

To be able to cope with ☺□
— 👃 **Poder con el paquete; poder con ☺□; [poder manejar ☺□]**
- *Just look at all these kids! I really don't know if you'll be able to cope with them.*
  Mira nada más todos esos niños. No sé si vas a poder con ellos (poder manejarlos, poder con el paquete).

To be able to do □ blindfolded
— **Poder hacer □ con los ojos cerrados**
- *Juan can take an engine to pieces and put it back together again blindfolded.*
  Juan es capaz de desarmar y armar un motor con los ojos cerrados.

To be able to tell that . . .
— **Se nota que . . .**
- *You can tell she's had cosmetic surgery.*
  Se nota que se hizo la cirugía plástica.

To be alive and kicking
— **Estar vivito(a) y coleando** (📖 To be alive and wagging your tail)
- *You can stop worrying now; the baby is alive and kicking.*
  Ya pueden dejar de preocuparse; el bebé está vivito y coleando.

To be all beat-up (cars)
— 👃 **Estar como (parecer) muégano** (📖 To be like a Mexican confection that is full of lumps)
- *Jane's car is only two years old, but it's already all beaten-up.*
  El coche de Jane tiene sólo dos años, pero ya está como muégano (pero ya parece muégano).

Expressions

To be all thumbs
— **[Ser de manos torpes; ser torpe de manos]**
- *Would you be kind enough to help me assemble these shelves? I am all thumbs.*
  ¿Podrías ser tan amable de ayudarme a ensamblar esta estantería? Yo soy muy torpe de manos.

To be as bald as a coot
— **Ser calvo como bola de billar** (📖 To be as bald as a billiard ball)
- *The school principal is as bald as a coot.*
  El director de la escuela es calvo como bola de billar.

To be as black as night
— **Ser (estar) como boca de lobo; ser (estar) negro; ser (estar) como la noche***
- *I can't see a thing in the basement; it's as black as night.*
  No veo nada en el sótano; está como boca de lobo.

Note: Used only for rooms or other spaces. For people, animals and things, see To be black as the ace of spades.

To be as good as done
— **Poder dar(lo) por hecho**
- *I'll quit my job today; it is as good as done.*
  Hoy presentaré mi renuncia; puedes darlo por hecho.

To be at someone's beck and call
— **[Estar a la disposición de ☺]**
- *The manager seems to think I'm at his beck and call round the clock.*
  El gerente piensa que estoy a su disposición día y noche.

To be at wit's end
— **Estar al borde de la locura; [estar desesperado(a)]**
- *I can't find that child anywhere and I'm at wit's end.*
  No encuentro al niño por ninguna parte y estoy desesperado (al borde de la locura).

To be bats (see To be out of your mind)

To be behind the eight ball (see To be on your toes)

To be bent on □
— **Estar empeñado(a) en □**
- *My father is bent on checking the homework of his 50 students all by himself.*
  Mi papá está empeñado en revisar sin ayuda las tareas de sus 50 alumnos.

To be better than nothing
— **Ser mejor que nada**
- *This apartment isn't much, but it's better than nothing.*
  Este departamento no es gran cosa, pero es mejor que nada.
— **Peor es nada**

Expressions

- *Speaker A:* *Look, this is the only kind of painkiller I was able to find.*
  Mira, es el único tipo de analgésico que pude encontrar.
- *Speaker B:* *It's better than nothing.*
  Peor es nada. (Es mejor que nada.)

To be between the devil and the deep blue sea; to be between a rock and a hard place
— **Estar entre la espada y la pared** (📖 To be between the sword and the wall)
  - *My husband won't let me work, but he has no money to give me. I'm between the devil and the deep blue sea.*
    Mi marido no me deja trabajar, pero no tiene para darme dinero. Estoy entre la espada y la pared.

To be black and blue
— **[Estar todo amoratado(a)]** (bruised); **[estar lleno(a) de moretones]** (full of bruises)
  - *He fell down the stairs and he's black and blue.*
    Se rodó por las escaleras y está lleno de moretones.

To be black as the ace of spades; to be jet black
— **Ser negro azabache**
  - *That's Ruben's horse, the one that's black as the ace of spades (the one that's jet black).*
    Ese es el caballo de Rubén, el negro azabache.

To be blind as a bat
— **Estar más ciego(a) que un topo** (📖 To be blind as a mole)
  - *Greg doesn't recognize me. He's blind as a bat.*
    Greg no me reconoce. Está más ciego que un topo.

To be blue
— 🔲 🔺 **Sentirse (estar) apachurrado(a)** (📖 To be squashed); **[estar deprimido(a)]**
  - *I don't know why I'm down in the dumps today.*
    No sé por qué me siento apachurrado hoy.

To be bonkers (see To be out of your mind)

To be cold comfort
— **Ser pobre consuelo; ¡Valiente consuelo!**
  - *The kid was not permitted to go camping, but they took him to the movies, which was cold comfort.*
    Al niño no lo dejaron ir a acampar, pero lo llevaron al cine. ¡Valiente consuelo!

To be completely at sea; to be all mixed up
— 🔺 🔲 **Estar hecho(a) bolas (pelotas)**
  - *I can't figure out my checkbook balance; I'm completely at sea.*
    No logro sacar el saldo de mi chequera; estoy hecho bolas (estoy hecho pelotas).
— **[Estar completamente perdido(a)]**
  - *I don't know the city, and I'm going around in circles.*
    No conozco la ciudad y estoy completamente perdido.

Expressions

To be dead to the world (asleep)
— **[Estar profundamente dormido(a)]**
  - *I can't wake him up. He's dead to the world.*
    No lo puedo despertar. Está profundamente dormido.

To be down in the dumps (see To be blue)

To be dressed to kill
— **Ir con sus mejores galas**
  - *Everyone there was in their best bib and tucker.*
    Todo el mundo iba con sus mejores galas.
— **Ir emperifollado(a); emperifollar(se)**
  - *We really have to dress to kill for Robert's party.*
    Realmente tenemos que emperifollarnos (ir emperifollados) para la fiesta de Roberto.

To be dressed to the nines (see To be dressed to kill)

To be dressed to the teeth (see To be dressed to kill)

To be dumbfounded
— **Quedar(se) atónito(a); perder el habla; quedar(se) con la boca abierta**
  - *I'm dumbfounded. I didn't know Javier had got married.*
    Me dejaste atónita (me hiciste perder el habla, me dejaste con a boca abierta). No sabía que Javier se había casado.

To be falling on your face (see To drop (into bed))
— **Estar(se) cayendo de cansancio** (fatigue)
  - *I've been working nonstop for 18 hours and I'm falling on my face.*
    Llevo 18 horas trabajando y me estoy cayendo de cansancio.
— **Estar(se) cayendo de borracho(a)** (drunk)
  - *Peter has been drinking for hours and now he is falling on his face.*
    Pedro ha estado tomando durante horas y se está cayendo de borracho.

To be famished (see To be starved)
— **Estar muerto(a) de hambre**
  - *The poor dog was famished (starved) when we found him.*
    El pobre perro estaba muerto de hambre cuando lo encontramos.

To be far from ☐
— **Estar lejos de ☐**
  - *These clothes are far from new.*
    Esta ropa está lejos de ser nueva.

To be fed up; to be up to here
— **Estar harto(a); estar hasta la coronilla**
  - *I'm completely fed up with having to answer that confounded phone.*
    Estoy harto (estoy hasta la coronilla) de tener que contestar ese maldito teléfono.

Expressions

To be hand in glove
— **Ser uña y carne** (📖 To be nail and finger); 🔱 ⬇ **Ser uña y mugre** (📖 To be nail and dirt)
- *I knew all along that those two were hand in glove.*
  Yo siempre supe que esas dos eran uña y carne (eran uña y mugre).

To be head over heels in love; to be madly in love
— **Estar locamente (perdidamente) enamorado(a)**
- *He used to be madly in love with Laura, didn't he?*
  Estaba locamente enamorado de Laura, ¿no?

To be hooked on ☺□ *
— **Estar enamorado(a) de ☺□; estar fascinado(a) con ☺□**
- *I've been hooked on skiing since I lived in Colorado.*
  He estado enamorado del (fascinado con el) esquí desde que viví en Colorado.

Note: When referring to alcohol, cigarettes, drugs, etc., use **Ser adicto(a) a □**.

To be in ☺'s way; to hinder
— **[Estorbar]**
- *Am I in your way?*
  ¿Le estorbo? (¿No Le estorbo?)
- *There's a big truck in my way.*
  Me está estorbando un camionsote.

To be in a tight spot; to be in deep water
— **[Estar en aprietos]; [estar en dificultades]**
- *Poor Hank! He lost all he had gambling and he's in a tight spot.*
  ¡Pobre Hank! Perdió todo apostando y está en aprietos.

To be in apple pie order
— **Estar como Dios manda; [estar perfectamente ordenado(a)]**
- *It took me a long time, but everything is now in apple pie order.*
  Me tardé bastante, pero ya está todo como Dios manda (perfectamente ordenado).

To be in deep water (see To be in a tight spot)

To be in disgrace (see To be in the doghouse)

To be in deep water (see To be in a tight spot)

To be in the doghouse; to be in disgrace
— **[No dirigir(le) la palabra a ☺]; aplicar(le) la ley del hielo a ☺**
- *Jack's in the doghouse for forgetting his wife's birthday.*
  Jack olvidó el cumpleaños de su esposa, y ella sigue sin dirigirle la palabra (sigue aplicándole la ley del hielo).

To be in the limelight
— **[Ser el centro de atracción]; [ser el centro de atención]**
- *Adriana loves to be in the limelight.*
  A Adriana le encanta ser el centro de atracción (de atención).

To be in your birthday suit
— **Estar como Dios lo trajo al mundo** (📖 To be as God brought you into this world); ♫☝⇓**Estar encuerado(a) (en cueros)** (📖 To be in your hide)
- *I can't open the door. I'm in my birthday suit.*
  No puedo ir a abrir la puerta; estoy como Dios me trajo al mundo (estoy encuerado).

To be left holding the baby
— **Tener que cargar con el muerto** (📖 To have to dispose of the corpse)
- *Everyone disappeared and left me holding the baby.*
  Todos desaparecieron y yo tuve que cargar con el muerto.

To be made the scapegoat
— **Ser el chivo expiatorio; pagar los platos rotos**
- *Juana really is a good friend. She did not let my boss make me the scapegoat for her mistake.*
  Juana demostró ser mi amiga al no permitir que mi jefe me convirtiera en el chivo expiatorio (me hiciera pagar los platos rotos) por el error que ella cometió.

To be madly in love (see To be head over heels in love)

To be nuts (see To be out of your mind)

To be on duty
— **Estar de guardia; estar de turno**
- *Don't offer me anything to drink now. I'm still on duty.*
  No me ofrezcas nada de tomar ahorita. Todavía estoy de guardia.

To be on the go
— **Andar a la carrera** (📖 To be racing around)
- *I've never seen such stamina! He's always on the go.*
  Jamás he visto tanto aguante. Siempre anda a la carrera.

To be on the level
— **[Hablar en serio]**
- *Joe says his salary is going to be doubled. Do you think he's on the level?*
  Joe dice que le van a duplicar el sueldo. ¿Hablará en serio?

To be on the spot
— **Estar en aprietos (en un aprieto)**
- *I accepted two invitations for the same evening. Now I'm really on the spot.*
  Acepté dos invitaciones para la misma noche. Ahora sí que estoy en aprietos.

To be on your toes
— **Estar abuzado(a); ponerse vivo(a)**
- *You'll have to be on your toes if you want to catch that mouse.*
  Vas a tener que estar abuzado (ponerte vivo) si quieres agarrar ese ratón.

To be onto ☺
— ♫ **Tener fichado(a) a** ☺

Expressions

- *I'm onto that guy. Now I know how he gets in and out of the building without being seen.*
  Ya tengo fichado a ese tipo. Ahora sé cómo le hace para entrar y salir del edificio sin ser visto.

To be on a first-name basis
— **Tutearse; romper el turrón**
- *We got along so well that from the beginning we were on a first-name basis.*
  Nos caímos tan bien que desde el primer momento nos tuteamos (rompimos el turrón).

To be on your last legs
— **Estar en las últimas**
- *Can we take your car? Mine's on its last legs.*
  ¿Podemos ir en tu coche? El mío está en las últimas.

To be on your way
— **Estar en camino**
- *The shipment is on it's way.*
  El embarque está en camino.
- *We are on our way to Toronto.*
  Estamos en camino a Toronto.

Note: Unless you must, it is advisable not to get involved in details like I'm on my way up, down, through, over, etc., as these can get complicated and are not really necessary in most cases. *On my way back* is **En camino de regreso.**

To be out of your mind
— **Estar demente; estar loco(a); 🖰🖐 estar mafufo(a); 🖰🖐 estar tocado(a); 🖰🖐 estar zafado(a)**
- *Speaker A:*   *Did you hear that old Mr. Lewis is having his house painted red?*
  ¿Supiste que el viejo Lewis mandó pintar su casa de rojo?
- *Speaker B:*   *Yeah. He must be out of his mind.*
  Sí, debe estar demente (loco, mafufo, tocado, zafado).

To be peculiar
— **Ser raro(a); 🖐⬇ ser (un) bicho raro (📖 To be a strange bug)**
- *That's my sister's violin teacher. He's a little peculiar.*
  Este es el maestro de violín de mi hermana. Es raro (un bicho raro).

To be plastered (see To be falling on your face) (see *Slang*)
— **Estar tomado(a); estar borracho(a); ⬇🖐 estar hasta atrás; ⬇🖐 andar(se) cayendo; ⬇🖐 estar beodo(a)**
- *Tomas has had about ten rum and cokes; he's plastered.*
  Tomás lleva como diez cubas; ya está borracho (está hasta atrás, se anda cayendo, está beodo).

To be saddled with ☺□
— **Tener que cargar con ☺□**

- *If I marry Nelly, I'm going to be saddled with her mother for life.*
  Si me caso con Nelly, voy a tener que cargar con su mamá de por vida.

To be second to none
— **No tener rival**
- *As a teacher, he's second to none.*
  Como maestro, no tiene rival.

To be snotty (see To play the big shot)
— **Ser un(a) creído(a)**
- *I'm afraid my mother is a little snotty. My friends don't like her.*
  Me temo que mi mamá es un poco creída; por eso le cae mal a mis amigos.

To be starved; to be famished; to be starving
— **Estar muerto(a) de hambre**
- *The poor dog was starved when we found him.*
  El pobre perro estaba muerto de hambre cuando lo encontramos.
— **Estar muriéndose de hambre**
- *I didn't have breakfast, and I'm starving.*
  No desayuné y me estoy muriendo de hambre.

To be starving (see To be starved)

To be stingy
— **Ser tacaño(a); [ser avaro(a)]; ☟☺ ser codo(a)**
- *Your girl friend is extremely stingy.*
  Tu amiga es muy tacaña (es muy avara; es codísima).

To be supposed to + verb
— **Se supone que debe + verb (Suponer and deber are both conjugated)**
- *I'm supposed to be there at 5:00.*
  Se supone que debo estar ahí a las 5:00.
- *Raul was supposed to fix this chair.*
  Se suponía que Raúl debía arreglar esta silla.

To be the apple of ☺'s eye
— **Ser la niña de los ojos de ☺**
- *Gertrude adores her little grandson. He's the apple of her eye.*
  Gertrudis adora a su nietecito. Es la niña de sus ojos.

To be the black sheep of the family
— **Ser la oveja negra de la familia**
- *You never met him before because he hardly comes. He is the black sheep of the family.*
  No lo conocías porque casi nunca viene. Es la oveja negra de la familia.

To be the last straw
— **Ser la gota que derramó el vaso (📖 To be the drop that overflowed the glass)**
- *This is the last straw! I'm quitting right now!*
  ¡Es la gota que derramó el vaso! ¡Renuncio!

Expressions

To be tickled pink (see To be tickled to death)

To be tickled to death; to be tickled pink
— **Estar encantado(a); estar fascinado(a); estar feliz de la vida**
- *My mother is tickled to death (tickled pink) with her birthday gift.*
Mi mamá está encantada (fascinada, feliz de la vida) con su regalo de cumpleaños.

To be tight
— **Estar mareado(a);** 📖😃 **andar (estar) a medios chiles;** 📖😃 **andar (estar) pasado(a) de tueste**
- *Linda hasn't even finished her first drink and she's already tight.*
Linda todavía ni se acaba su primera copa y ya está mareada (anda a medios chiles, está pasada de tueste).

To be tipsy (see To be tight)

To be (to get) too big for your britches
— **Dejar que se le suban los humos a la cabeza a** ☺
- *You have been very successful lately, but don't get too big for your britches.*
Has tenido mucho éxito últimamente, pero no dejes que se te suban los humos a la cabeza.

To be unable to put up with ☺□ (see To (be unable to) put up with ☺□)

To be unable to stand ☺□ (see To (be unable to) put up with ☺□)

To be up and about
— **[Estar levantado(a)]** (in the morning)
- *Mr. Black is always up and about by six.*
El Sr. Black ya está levantado a las seis todos los días.
— **[Ya no estar en cama]** (after an illness/operation)
- *Lolita is up and about, but not yet out of the hospital.*
Lolita ya no está en cama, pero todavía no la dejan salir del hospital.

To be up to here (see To be fed up)

To be very bright (see To have a lot on the ball)

To be (way) overdressed
— **Estar muy emperifollado(a);** 📖 **colgarse hasta el molcajete;** 📖 **colgarse hasta la mano del metate** (📖 To hang around your neck the Mexican stone mortar and pestle for making sauces, or the stone rolling pin used to grind corn, chilies, etc. on the **metate**, which is a flat, open version of the **molcajete**)
- *Did you see Pilar's mother at the graduation? She was grossly overdressed.*
¿Viste a la mamá de Pilar en la graduación? Se colgó hasta el molcajete (hasta la mano del metate).

To be worn out (very tired)
— **[Estar exhausto(a); Estar muerto(a); Estar agotado(a); Estar rendido(a)]**

- *I didn't get any sleep at all last night; I'm worn out.*
  Anoche no dormí nada; estoy exhausta (muerta, agotada, rendida).
— 📖 **Poner(se) una soba**
- *We need a couple of days to rest. We are worn out after the move.*
  Necesitamos un par de días de descanso. Nos pusimos una soba con la mudanza.

To beat around the bush
— **Andar con rodeos**
- *Don't beat around the bush. Just say what you mean.*
  No andes con rodeos. Simplemente dime lo que quieres decir.

To bend over backwards for ☺
— **[Hacer un esfuerzo sobrehumano para ayudar a ☺]**
- *Your sister really bent over backwards to get the blood we needed for our son.*
  Tu hermana hizo un esfuerzo sobrehumano para conseguir la sangre que necesitábamos para nuestro hijo.
- *Terry was very nice while I was in Mexico. He bent over backwards to make sure I had everything I needed for my research.*
  Terry se portó estupendamente mientras estuve en México. Hizo un esfuerzo sobrehumano para conseguir lo necesario para mi investigación.

To bite ☺'s head off
— **[Regañar a ☺]** (📖 To scold); **[gritar(le) a ☺]** (📖 To yell)
- *OK, OK, I apologize. Don't bite my head off.*
  Está bien, perdóname. No me regañes (no me grites).

To bite off more than you can chew
— **Meter(se) en camisa de once varas (v.)** (📖 To wear a shirt eleven "**varas**" long; one **vara**, a measure no longer used, is equivalent to 0.835 meters)
- *He bit off more than he could chew when he took on that job in Spain.*
  Se metió en camisa de once varas cuando aceptó ese empleo en España.

To blow it (see To put your foot in it)

To blow off steam
— **[Desahogarse]**
- *It's not good to bottle up your anger. You have to blow off some steam every now and then.*
  Hace daño guardarse el enojo. Hay que desahogarse de vez en cuando.

To blow your own horn
— **Alabar(se) a ☺ mismo(a)**
- *Please don't invite me again if your brother is going to be around. He does nothing but blow his own horn.*
  Por favor, no vuelvas a invitarme si también va tu hermano. No hace sino alabarse a sí mismo todo el tiempo.

To boot ☺ out (see To throw ☺ out)

Expressions

To break the ice
— **Romper el hielo**
- *The two drinks broke the ice.*

   Después de un par de tragos, rompimos el hielo.

To bring home the bacon
— **Sacar para el gasto**
- *Robert can't bring home the bacon anymore since he lost his leg in the accident.*

   Roberto ya no saca para el gasto desde que perdió la pierna en el accidente.

To burn the candle at both ends; to look for trouble; to ask for it
— **[Buscar(se) un problema]; ♉♫ ganar(sela) a pulso**
- *Nick knew he was burning the candle at both ends (he was looking for trouble, he was asking for it).*

   Nicolás sabía que se estaba buscando un problema (se la estaba ganando a pulso).

To burn your bridges behind you
— **Quemar sus naves** (📖 To burn your ships)
- *Before he started his new business, Ernesto had to burn his bridges behind him and put an end to all relationships with the companies he had worked for.*

   Para empezar su nuevo negocio, Ernesto tuvo que quemar sus naves con las compañías en las que había trabajado antes.

To bury your head in the sand
— **Cerrar los ojos a (negar) la realidad; [esconder la cabeza (como el avestruz)]; hacer lo que el avestruz**
- *You can't bury your head in the sand that way.*

   No puedes cerrar los ojos a la realidad (esconder la cabeza como el avestruz).

To bury the hatchet
— **Hacer las paces**
- *She waited for me over two hours to apologize, so we finally buried the hatchet.*

   Me esperó más de dos horas para disculparse, así que finalmente hicimos las paces.

To buy a pig in a poke
— **Comprar a ciegas; ♉ [comprar 🔲 a lo tarugo]; [comprar 🔲 a lo tonto]; [comprar 🔲 sin saber lo que se hace]** (both **comprar** and **hacer** are conjugated)
- *This is what you get for buying a pig in a poke.*

   Eso te pasa por comprar las cosas a ciegas (a lo tarugo, a lo tonto, sin saber lo que haces).

To call ☺🔲 all the names in the book
— **Echar pestes de ☺🔲; [hablar mal de ☺🔲]; [hablar horrores de ☺🔲]**
- *Mr. Stuart is furious. He's calling you all the names in the book.*

   El Sr. Stuart está furioso. Está echando pestes de ti (habla mal de ti, habla horrores de ti).

To call a spade a spade
— **Llamarle al pan pan, y al vino vino**
- *Tell me what bothers you. Don't be afraid to call a spade a spade.*

   Dime lo que te molesta. No tengas miedo de llamarle al pan pan y al vino vino.

To cook ☺'s goose
— **Hacer que ☺ pague el precio**
  - *Allen thinks he can get away with stealing my girlfriend. I'll cook his goose!*
    Allen cree que puede salirse con la suya y robarme la novia. Voy a hacer que pague el precio!

To dawn on ☺
— **Venir(le) ☐ de pronto (o de repente) a ☺; ♫⇩ prender(sele) el foco** (📖 The light bulb lights up). **♫ Caer(le) el veinte** (📖 The coin drops in the machine and it starts working).
  - *I had been mulling over the problem for days when the answer suddenly dawned on me.*
    Tenía días dándole vueltas al problema cuando de pronto me vino la solución (se me prendió el foco, me cayó el veinte).

To dig your own grave (see To put the noose around your neck)
— **Cavar su propia tumba**
  - *I'm sure she thought I believed everything she said as usual, but she dug her own grave lying to me again.*
    Pensó que me estaba engañando como siempre, pero cavó su propia tumba mintiéndome otra vez.

To die with ☺'s boots on
— **Morir(se) con las botas puestas**
  - *My grandfather never retired. He died with his boots on.*
    Mi abuelo nunca se jubiló. Murió con las botas puestas.

To dress to kill (see To be dressed to kill)

To drop (into bed) (from exhaustion) (see To be falling on your face)
— **♫ Clavar el pico** (📖 To fall forward so hard that your "beak" is pushed into the ground); **♫ Caer como tabla** (📖 To fall like a board)
  - *He could hardly keep his eyes open, and a few minutes later he fell into a deep sleep.*
    Ya no podía tener los ojos abiertos, y unos momentos después clavó el pico (cayó como tabla).

To drop in on ☺; to pop in on ☺
— **♫ Dar(se) una vuelta; ♫⇩ caer(le) a ☺**
  - *I think I'll drop in on my parents this Sunday for a while.*
    Creo que me daré una vuelta por casa de mis padres (creo que voy a caerles a mis padres) este domingo.

To end (wind) up + verb + ing
— **Terminar en**
  - *Harry ended up in the hospital with yellow fever.*
    Harry terminó en el hospital con fiebre amarilla.
— **Terminar verb + ndo**
  - *Poor Martha ended up washing the dishes.*
    La pobre de Marta terminó lavando los platos.

Expressions

To fall in love with ☺
— **Enamorar(se) de** ☺
- *You can tell Pepe is falling in love with Concha.*
  Se nota que Pepe se está enamorando de Concha.

To fall short of
— **[No lograr el objetivo]; quedar(se) corto(a)**
- *Well, I didn't make it, but it wasn't because I didn't try.*
  No logré el objetivo (me quedé corto), pero no fue por no hacer el intento.
— ⌂ **No hacer(la)**
- *Darn! I thought I was going to pass the test, but I didn't make it.*
  ¡Diablos! Pensé que iba a aprobar el examen, pero no la hice.

To feel ☐ in your bones
— ℗ ⌂ **Latir(le) ☐ a ☺; [tener el presentimiento]**
- *This won't work. I can feel it in my bones.*
  Me late (tengo el presentimiento de) que esto no va a funcionar.

To feel like ☐; to feel like + verb + ing
— **Tener ganas de ☐; [antojar(sele) ☐]**
- *I feel like a big steak and fries.*
  Tengo ganas de (se me antoja) una carne grandota con papas fritas.
— **Tener ganas de + verb in infinitive**
- *I feel like going to the beach today.*
  Hoy tengo ganas de ir a la playa.

To feel like a million dollars
— **Sentir(se) de maravilla** (physically)
- *Liza feels like a million dollars since she got her pacemaker.*
  Liza se siente de maravilla desde que le pusieron su marcapaso.
— **Sentir(se) realizado** (morally/emotionally)
- *I was just promoted to Vice President, and I feel like a million bucks.*
  Me acaban de ascender a vicepresidente, y me siento realizado.

To fight a losing battle
— **[Estar perdido(a) de antemano]**
- *The deadline is in a week and I haven't even finished the second chapter yet. I really feel I'm fighting a losing battle.*
  La fecha de entrega es en una semana, y aún no termino el capítulo dos. Realmente siento que esto está perdido de antemano.

To fight tooth and nail
— **Defender(se) hasta con los dientes; defender(se) como gato boca arriba**
- *Her relatives tried to take her house from her, but she fought tooth and nail for it.*
  Sus parientes trataron de quitarle la casa, pero ella la defendió hasta con los dientes (como gato boca arriba).

To figure ☺◻ out

— **Encontrar(le) sentido a ☺◻; [entender ◻]; [entender a ☺]**

- *I can't figure out the hospital bill.*
  No le encuentro sentido (no le entiendo) a la cuenta del hospital.

To figure out how to . . .

— **Encontrar la manera de . . . ; ingeniar(selas) para . . .**

- *I've got to figure out how to make enough money to pay for the house.*
  Tengo que encontrar la manera de (ingeniármelas para) ganar lo suficiente para pagar la casa.

To fill the bill

— **[Servir]**

- *I only have this old projector, but it fills the bill quite nicely.*
  Sólo tengo este proyector viejo, pero sirve muy bien.

— **Dar el ancho; [ser lo que se necesita]; [cumplir con los requisitos]**

- *I've seen her application, and she does not fill the bill.*
  He visto su solicitud, y no da el ancho (no es lo que se necesita; no cumple con los requisitos).

To fly off the handle

— **Perder los estribos** (📖 To lose your stirrups)

- *The accountant is the kind of person who flies off the handle all the time.*
  El contador es el tipo de persona que pierde los estribos a cada rato.

To fool ☺ (see To pull a fast one)

To fool around (see To horse around)

To fork out the dough (see To fork out the money)

To fork out the money; to fork out the dough

— **Pagar; ⌂⇓ caer(se) con la lana; ⌂ poner(se) a mano**

- *I've been waiting for two weeks for you to fork out the dough.*
  Llevo dos semanas esperando que me pagues (que te caigas con la lana, que te pongas a mano).

To get along in years

— **[Envejecer]**

- *I saw David today. He's really getting along in years.*
  Hoy vi a David. Está envejeciendo.

To get along on a shoe string

— **[Vivir con muy poco dinero]**

- *While I was a student, I had to get along on a shoe string.*
  Mientras fui estudiante, tuve que arreglármelas para vivir con muy poco dinero.

To get away with ◻

— **Salir(se) con la suya**

Expressions

- *Allen thinks he can get away with stealing my girlfriend.*
  Allen cree que puede salirse con la suya y robarme la novia.

To get back at ☺; to get your own back (see To cook ☺'s goose)
— **[Desquitar(se)]; [vengar(se)] ***
- *I've waited a long time, but now I'm going to get my own back.*
  Llevo mucho tiempo esperando, pero ahora me voy a desquitar.

Note: **Vengarse** is a very strong word . . . for serious vengeance only

To get □ by hook or by crook
— **Conseguir □ por las buenas o por las malas**
- *You know her. She's going to get her way by hook or by crook.*
  Ya la conoces. Va a conseguir lo que quiere por las buenas o por las malas.

To get carried away
— ☺ **Alocar(se)**
- *I got carried away and bought all the canaries in the pet shop.*
  Me aloqué y compré todos los canarios que había en la tienda.
— ☺ **Acelerar(se)**
- *Steve is the type that gets carried away at a baseball game.*
  Steve es de los que se acelera mucho en un juego de beisbol.
— ☺ **Pasar(sele) la mano**
- *I apologize. I got carried away because I was angry and said a lot of things I didn't mean.*
  Discúlpame. Se me pasó la mano porque estaba enojada y dije cosas que no sentía.

To get hooked on □ (see To be hooked on □)

To get on your nerves
— **[Irritar]; [poner de mal humor]; ☺👃 caer gordo(a); ☺ poner de malas**
- *That barking dog is really getting on my nerves.*
  El ladrido de ese perro de veras me está irritando (me está cayendo gordo, me está poniendo de malas).

To get the hang of □
— **Encontrar(le) el modo a □**
- *It was hours before I finally got the hang of how the lawnmower works.*
  Me tomó horas encontrarle el modo a la podadora.

To get the show on the road
— **Echar a andar + (event); [arrancar con + (event)]**
- *It's late. Let's get the show on the road.* (e.g. referring to a meeting)
  Ya es tarde. Hay que echar a andar (arrancar con) la junta.

To get too big for your britches (see To be too big for your britches)

To get up on the wrong side of the bed
— **[Estar de malas]; [estar de mal humor]**
- *Boy, what a grump! You must've gotten up on the wrong side of the bed.*
  ¡Caray! ¡Qué gruñón! (¿Estás de mal humor?, ¿Estás de malas?).

To get your own back (see To get back at)

To give ☺ a hand

— **Dar(le) una mano a ☺; echar(le) una mano a ☺**

  ▪ *I can't do this alone. Can you give me a hand?*
    No puedo hacer esto solo. ¿Me das una mano? (¿Me echas una mano?)

To give ☺ a hard time

— **Cargar(le) la mano a ☺**

  ▪ *The boss is giving Efren a hard time about the lost keys.*
    El jefe le está cargando la mano a Efrén por lo de las llaves perdidas.

To give ☺ a piece of your mind

— **Cantar(le) sus verdades a ☺**

  ▪ *As soon as I see Paul I'm going to give him a piece of my mind.*
    En cuanto vea a Paul le voy a cantar sus verdades.

To give ☺ a ride

— **Llevar a☺; 🖐🔊 dar(le) un aventón a ☺**

  ▪ *I got home early because Wolf gave me a ride.*
    Llegué temprano a casa porque Wolf me llevó (me dio un aventón).

To give ☺ a taste of his own medicine (see To give ☺ what he's got coming to him)

To give ☺ what he's got coming to him

— **Dar(le) una sopa de su propio chocolate a ☺ (📖 To give ☺ a soup of his own chocolate)**

  ▪ *I often dream of giving that bully a taste of his own medicine (what he's got coming to him).*
    Muchas veces sueño con darle a ese abusivo una sopa de su propio chocolate.

To give ☺◻ a wide berth

— **Sacar(le) la vuelta a ☺◻**

  ▪ *I suggest you give that manager a wide berth. He's unbearable.*
    Sugiero que le saques la vuelta a ese gerente. Es insoportable.

To give ☺ free rein

— **Soltar(le) la rienda a ☺**

  ▪ *As soon as her daughter graduated, Tom gave her free rein. Now she is living in Germany.*
    Tan pronto como su hija se recibió, Tomás le soltó la rienda. Ahora vive en Alemania.

— **Dar rienda suelta a ◻**

  ▪ *When his wife died, he gave free rein to his grief; he got drunk for a whole week.*
    Cuando murió su esposa, le dio rienda suelta a su tristeza; se puso una borrachera de una semana.

To give ☺ the cold shoulder

— **Volver(le) la espalda a alguien; 🖐⬇no pelar a ☺; [tratar fríamente a ☺]; 🔊 hacer(se) el (la) que no conoce a ☺**

  ▪ *I can't understand why Meg is giving me the cold shoulder.*

Expressions

No comprendo por qué Meg me volvió la espalda (me trata tan fríamente, no me pela, se hace la que no me conoce).

To give ☺ the once over
— **Comer(se) con los ojos a ☺**; **[mirar de arriba a abajo a ☺]** (this expression also means to look at ☺ in a very snotty way)
- *The guy at the next table is giving Rita the once over.*
  El tipo de la mesa de junto se está comiendo a Rita con los ojos (está mirando a Rita de arriba a abajo).

To give ☺ the slip
— ☺ **Pelar(sele) a ☺**
— **[Escapar(sele) a ☺]**
- *The guards didn't let the convict give them the slip.*
  Los guardias no dejaron que el reo se les pelara.
- *That brat has given me the slip again.*
  Ese niño se me volvió a escapar.

To give up + verb (stop a habit)
— **Dejar de** + (verb)
- *I have to give up smoking.*
  Tengo que dejar de fumar.

To give up □
— **Dejar □**
- *The doctor told me I have to give up coffee.*
  El médico me dijo que tengo que dejar el café.

To give up (stop trying)
— **[Rendir(se)]** ; **[Dar(se)]** (to surrender)
- *OK, I give up. What's the answer?*
  Bueno, me doy (me rindo). ¿Cuál es la respuesta?
— ☺ **Dar(se) (por vencido(a))** (used without **por vencido** just as often as it is used with it)
- *Martin gave up before he had really started.*
  Martín se dio por vencido antes de haber empezado.
- *OK, I give up..*
  Está bien. Me doy.

To go against the grain
— **Ir contra la corriente** (📖 To go against the current)
- *I know I'm going against the grain, but I can't give my approval for this plan.*
  Sé que es ir contra la corriente, pero no puedo dar mi aprobación para este plan.

To go all out
— **Echar (tirar) la casa por la ventana**
- *My husband went all out when we celebrated our first anniversary.*
  Mi esposo echó (tiró) la casa por la ventana para celebrar nuestro primer aniversario.

To go it alone (see To shift for yourself)

To go at ❑ hammer and tongs
— **Meter(le) (echarle) muchísimas ganas; echar(le) los kilos**
  ▪ *Sam is already on chapter 15 of his book. He's going at it hammer and tongs.*
    Sam ya va en el capítulo 15 de su libro. Le está metiendo (echando) muchísimas ganas (echando los kilos).

To go crazy
— **Volver(se) loco(a)**
  ▪ *The boss went crazy and fired all the truck drivers.*
    El jefe se volvió loco y despidió a todos los choferes de camión.

To go from bad to worse
— **Ir de mal en peor**
  ▪ *Leon's grades have gone from bad to worse in the last few months.*
    Las calificaciones de León han ido de mal en peor en los últimos meses.

To go it alone (see To shift for yourself)

To go jump in the lake
— **Ir(se) al diablo; ir(se) al demonio; ⇩ ir(se) a la porra**
  ▪ *I told the idiot to go jump in the lake.*
    Le dije al estúpido que se fuera al diablo (al demonio, a la porra).

To go nuts (see To go crazy)

To go on a binge
— **Ir(se) de parranda; ir(se) de juerga**
  ▪ *It has been a long time since Humberto and Leon went on a binge.*
    Hace mucho tiempo que Humberto y León no se van de parranda.

To go under
— **[Hundir(se)]** (📖 To sink)
  ▪ *I'm afraid that savings and loan company is going under.*
    Me temo que esa institución de crédito se está hundiendo.

To grease ☺'s palm
— **[Sobornar a ☺];** ⌧ ⌂ **dar mordida a ☺;** ⌂ **pasar(le) una feria a ☺; untar(le) la mano a ☺**
  ▪ *I don't like to do it, but the only way to get this done is to grease that guy's palm.*
    No me gusta hacerlo, pero la única manera de que esto se resuelva es sobornando (dando una mordida, pasándole una feria, untándole la mano) al individuo ése.

To have a bone to pick with ☺; to have an ax to grind
— **[Tener cuentas pendientes]; [tener un pleito pendiente con ☺];** ⌂ **traer(le) ganas a ☺**
  ▪ *I have a bone to pick with John, when I can get my hands on him.*
    Le traigo ganas a Juan (tengo un pleito pendiente con Juan). Deja que me lo encuentre.
  ▪ *Peter never came back. He knows very well I have an ax to grind.*

Expressions

Pedro ya no regresó. Sabe que tiene cuentas pendientes conmigo (le traigo ganas).

Note: **Pleito** (fight) is used figuratively here. It is normally used for nastier unpleasantness.

To have a chip on your shoulder

— **[Ser una persona desagradable];** ☝ **ser pesado(a);** ☝ **ser sangrón(a);** ☝ **ser sangres**

- *It's a pain to have to work with Peter. He has a chip on his shoulder.*

  No me gusta trabajar con Pedro. Es una persona desagradable (es un pesado, es un sangrón, es sangres).

To have a fit

— ☝ **Hacer un tango** (📖 To sing or dance a tango, which is considered extremely melodramatic by non-Argentine Latins); ☝ **hacer un drama o dramón** (📖 To be very dramatic about ☐); ☝ **dar(le) el infarto** (📖 To have a heart attack); 👥☝ **dar(le) el (un) patatús**; 👥☝ **dar(le) un soponcio**

- *Alvin had a fit when he saw what had happened to his car.*

  Alvin hizo un drama (hizo un tango, un dramón) (A Alvin le dio el infarto (el patatús, el soponcio)) cuando vio lo que le había sucedido a su coche.

- *When Ann found out her daughter was pregnant, she had a fit.*

  Cuando Ana supo que su hija estaba embarazada, le dio un patatús (un soponcio, el infarto).

(Not) to have a ghost of a chance

— **[No va a lograr(se)]; ni de chiste;** 👥 **ni yendo a bailar a Chalma**

- *Peter thinks he's going to finish on time, but he hasn't got a ghost of a chance.*

  Pedro piensa que terminará a tiempo, pero no va a lograrlo (no va a terminar ni de chiste; no va a terminar ni yendo a bailar a Chalma).

To have a green thumb

— **Tener el don para la jardinería; [Tener buena mano para las plantas]**

- *When my mother-in-law was alive, this garden was beautiful. She had a green thumb.*

  Cuando vivía mi suegra, este jardín estaba precioso. Tenía muy buena mano (tenía el don para la jardinería).

To have a hunch

— **Tener una corazonada;** ☝ **Latir(le) a** ☺

- *I have a hunch that the old mine is around here somewhere.*

  Tengo la corazonada de que la vieja mina queda por aquí.

- *Something tells me Celia isn't coming back.*

  Me late que Celia ya no va a regresar.

To have a lot on the ball; to be very bright

— **[Ser muy listo(a)]; [Ser muy vivo(a)]**

— ☝ **Ser aguzado** (📖 To be sharp)*

- *Get George to explain it to you. He's got a lot on the ball.*

  Que te lo explique Jorge. Él es muy listo (es muy vivo, es muy aguzado).

Note: Very often also spelled (and said) **abuzado** . . . nothing to do with the verb **abusar**, to abuse.

To have a lump in your throat
— **Tener un nudo en la garganta**
  - *Cristina could barely talk. She had a lump in her throat.*
  Cristina apenas podía hablar. Tenía un nudo en la garganta.

To have a soft spot for ☐☺
— **Tener predilección por ☐☺**
  - *It's so obvious that the teacher has a soft spot for Ivonne.*
  Es tan obvio que el profesor tiene predilección por Ivonne.
— **Estar encariñado(a) con ☐☺**
  - *I can't understand why George has a soft spot for that ugly dog.*
  No entiendo por qué Jorge está encariñado con ese perro tan feo.

To have a screw loose (see To be out of your mind)

To have an ax to grind (see To have a bone to pick with ☺)

To have bats in the belfry (see To be out of your mind)

To have ☺ figured out (see To have ☺'s number)
— 🔔 **Tener fichado(a) a ☺**
  - *After working for my boss for ten years, I have him all figured out (I have his number).*
  Después de trabajar diez años con mi jefe, ya me lo tengo fichado (ya le tengo tomada la medida, ya me lo conozco de memoria).

To have ☐ figured out
— **Tener todo resuelto; tener todo calculado**
  - *I'm not calling a plumber to install the dishwasher; I've got the whole thing figured out.*
  No voy a traer al plomero a instalar el lavaplatos; ya lo tengo todo resuelto (calculado).

To have irons in the fire (see To have ☐ on the back burner)
— **Estar dándole vueltas a ☐**
  - *Luis is very tight lipped, but I think he has some irons in the fire.*
  Luis no dice nada, pero creo que le está dando vueltas a algo.

To have no choice
— **No tener alternativa; 🔔 no quedar(le) de otra**
  - *Why fight it? I have no choice.*
  ¿Para qué oponerme? No tengo alternativa (no me queda de otra).

To have ☺'s number (see To have ☺ figured out)
— 🔔 **Tener fichado(a) a ☺**
  - *Kevin and I had a long talk about Aldo's past. Don't worry. I have Aldo's number now.*
  Kevin y yo platicamos largamente sobre el pasado de Aldo. No te preocupes, ya lo tengo fichado.

To have one too many
— 🔔 **Pasar(sele) las cucharadas** (📖 To have had too many spoonfuls)

Expressions

- *I hope you don't have one too many tonight, like you did last time.*
  Espero que esta noche no se te pasen las cucharadas como la última vez.

To have □ on your mind
— **[Estar preocupado(a)]** (📖 To be worried)
- *Leonard isn't himself. I think he has something on his mind.*
  Leonardo está muy raro. Creo que está preocupado por algo.

To have □ on the back burner (see To have irons in the fire)
— **Estar en veremos** (📖 To be in "we'll-see" status)
- *We had to shelve the project for now, but we have it on the back burner.*
  Tuvimos que cancelar el proyecto por el momento, pero todavía está en veremos.

To have the gift of the gab
— **Tener labia**
- *I didn't want to buy the books, but she has the gift of the gab and I ended up buying them all.*
  Yo no quería comprar los libros, pero ella tiene mucha labia y terminé comprándoselos todos.

To have your hands full with □
— **Tener un paquete con □**
- *You certainly have your hands full with the wedding plans.*
  Sí que tienes un paquete con los planes para la boda.

To help yourself
— **Servir(se) lo que se apetece; [Hacer lo que se desea]**
- *Help yourself to anything you want, please.*
  Sírvase todo lo que quiera, por favor.
- *Speaker A:*   *May I have one of these magazines?*
  ¿Puedo tomar una de estas revistas?
  Speaker B: *Help yourself.*
  ¡Adelante!

To hit the ceiling
— **Colgar(se) de la lámpara** (📖 To leap onto the lamp); **poner el grito en el cielo** (📖 To scream up into the sky); **parar(se) de pestañas** (📖 To stand on your eyelashes)
- *I bet he hit the ceiling when you told him you were quitting.*
  Apuesto a que se colgó de la lámpara (puso el grito en el cielo, se paró de pestañas) cuando le dijiste que renunciabas.

To hit the hay (see To Turn in)

To hit the nail on the head
— **Dar en el clavo**
- *You were right. You hit the nail on the head.*
  Tenías razón. Diste en el clavo.

To hit the sack (see To Turn in)

(Not) to hold a candle to ☺

— **No le llega ni al tobillo; no se compara; no hay punto de comparación**

- *Your present secretary cannot hold a candle to the previous one.*
  Tu actual secretaria no le llega ni al tobillo a la anterior (no se compara con la anterior). No hay punto de comparación entre esta secretaria y la anterior.

To hold the fort

— **Encargar(se) de** ☐

- *I have to be away for a few days. You hold the fort, will you?*
  Tengo que ausentarme unos cuantos días. Encárgate por favor de la oficina.

To hold ☺ **up; to mug** ☺**; to rob** ☐

— **[Asaltar]** (from an amateur stick-up to a full scale bank robbery)

- *My neighbor was mugged last night as she was leaving the building.*
  Anoche asaltaron a mi vecina al salir del edificio.
- *Ten well-trained crooks robbed the main office of the bank on payday.*
  Diez tipos bien entrenados asaltaron la central del banco el día de quincena.

To horse around

— ☖ **Echar relajo**

- *When the teacher stepped into the room, everyone was horsing around.*
  Cuando el maestro entró al salón, todo el mundo estaba echando relajo.

To hush ☐ **up**

— **Dar carpetazo; echar tierra al asunto**

- *Carlos had to fork out a lot of money, but he finally succeeded in hushing up the affair with that woman.*
  Carlos le metió mucho dinero, pero finalmente logró que se le diera carpetazo (se le echara tierra) a su relación con esa mujer.

To jump down ☺**'s throat**

— **Regañar severamente a** ☺**; regañar feo a** ☺**; [gritar(le) a** ☺**];** ☖⇩ **poner como lazo de cochino a** ☺ **(**📖 To dirty ☺ like a pig's bow)**;** ☖⇩ **poner como palo de gallinero a** ☺ **(**📖 To dirty ☺ like a perch in a chicken coop)

- *All I did was look out the window, and he jumped down my throat.*
  Todo lo que hice fue asomarme por la ventana, y me regañó severamente (me regañó feo, me gritó, me puso como lazo de cochino, me puse como palo de gallinero).

To jump out of the frying pan into the fire

— **Huir del fuego para caer en las brasas; salir de Guatemala para entrar a Guatepeor (**📖 To leave Guate-bad to enter Guate-worse)**; salir de ansias para entrar en congojas**

- *Speaker A:*   *After his divorce, Ramon married an unbearable woman.*
  Después de su divorcio, Ramón se casó con una mujer insoportable.
- *Speaker B:*   *Out of the frying pan into the fire, poor man.*
  Pobre, huyó del fuego para caer en las brasas (salió de ansias para entrar en congojas, salió de Guatemala para entrar a Guatepeor).

Expressions

To jump to conclusions
— **Juzgar a la ligera; sacar conclusiones gratuitas (falsas)**
  ▪ *My mother saw us together and jumped to conclusions.*
    Mi mamá nos vio juntos y sacó conclusiones falsas.

To keep a stiff upper lip
— **[Conservar la compostura]**
  ▪ *Marcela is keeping a stiff upper lip in this business of her divorce.*
    Marcela está conservando la compostura con esto de su divorcio.

To keep ☺ at arm's length
— **[Mantener a prudente distancia a ☺]**
  ▪ *I have a feeling I should keep Gustavo at arm's length.*
    Me late que debo mantener a Gustavo a prudente distancia.

To keep the ball rolling
— **[Mantener el ritmo]; [hacer algo para que no se muera (el interés por) ❑]**
  ▪ *We've got to do something to keep the ball rolling.* (e.g. in a class)
    Tenemos que hacer algo para mantener el ritmo de la clase (para que no se muera la clase, para que no se muera el interés por la clase).

To kick ☺ out (or off) ❑ (see To throw ☺ out)
— 🔊 **Sacar a ☺**; 🔊 **correr a ☺**; 🔊**sacar a patadas a ☺** (this expression is quite a bit nastier in Spanish than in English)
  ▪ *Walter was kicked off the team because he never wore the uniform.*
    A Walter lo sacaron (corrieron) del equipo porque nunca usaba el uniforme.
  ▪ *I kicked that bastard out of my house; I should have broken his neck after what he did to my daughter.*
    Saqué al infeliz ese a patadas de mi casa; debí haberlo estrangulado después de lo que le hizo a mi hija.

To kick the bucket
— **Morir(se);** 🔊 **colgar los tenis** (📖 To hang up (or hand in) your tennis shoes); 🔊 **estirar la pata** (📖 To stretch out your leg); 📖**petatear(se)** (📖 To lie or fall on the **petate** (straw sleeping mat))
  ▪ *The old geezer finally kicked the bucket.*
    El vejete por fin colgó los tenis (estiró la pata, se petateó).

To kill the goose that lays the golden eggs
— **Matar la gallina de los huevos de oro**
  ▪ *He insulted his best client; in other words, he killed the goose that lays the golden eggs.*
    Insultó a su mejor cliente; para mí que mató la gallina de los huevos de oro.

To kill two birds with one stone
— **Matar dos pájaros de un tiro (de una pedrada)**
  ▪ *Joe is at the same hospital where Joan is recovering, so you can kill two birds with one stone.*
    José está en el mismo hospital en el que está internada Joan. Así que puedes matar dos pájaros de un tiro (de una pedrada).

To knock yourself out
— **Poner(se) una soba; dar(se) una matada; matar(se)**
  - *I worked all night; I knocked myself out.*
    Me puse una soba (me di una matada, me maté) toda la noche trabajando.

To know the ropes
— **Conocer el tejemaneje**
  - *I'm taking John with me to request the import license because he knows the ropes.*
    Me voy a llevar a Juan para hacer la solicitud del permiso de importación, porque él conoce el tejemaneje.

To know what side his/her bread is buttered on
— **Saber lo que le conviene**
  - *She won't come ever again. She knows what side her bread is buttered on.*
    Nunca volverá a venir. Sabe lo que le conviene.

To lay down the law
— **Leer(le) la cartilla a** ☺
  - *We met the new boss today, and he immediately laid down the law.*
    Hoy conocimos al nuevo jefe, y luego luego nos leyó la cartilla.

To lead ☺ by the nose
— **Tener idiotizado(a) a** ☺; **traer marcando el paso a** ☺; **traer cortito(a) a** ☺
  - *Gonzalo lets Marcela lead him around by the nose, poor guy, in front of everybody.*
    Marcela tiene idiotizado a Gonzalo (lo trae marcando el paso, lo trae cortito) delante de todos, y el pobre se lo permite.

To leave a lot to be desired
— **Dejar mucho que desear**
  - *John's work leaves a lot to be desired.*
    El trabajo de John deja mucho que desear.

To leave ☺ breathless
— **Dejar sin aliento a** ☺
  - *The trapeze artist left us all breathless.*
    El trapecista dejó al público sin aliento

To let the cat out of the bag
— **[Revelar un secreto]; ☝ salir(sele) ☐ a** ☺; ☝ **regar el tepache** (drink made from fermented pinneapple)
  - *I'm sorry I let the cat out of the bag. I didn't mean to.*
    Se me salió; lo siento. Fue sin querer.
    Siento mucho haber revelado el secreto (regado el tepache). No fue mi intención.

To let your arm be twisted
— **Dar el brazo a torcer** (this is used in the negative more often than not)
  - *Pepe knows I don't want to go to the dance, and I'm not going to let him twist my arm.*
    Pepe sabe que no quiero ir al baile, y no voy a dar mi brazo a torcer.
  - *Pamela always lets her arm be twisted if it's a question of going to the movies.*
    Pamela siempre da el brazo a torcer si se trata de ir al cine.

Expressions

To let your hair down
— **[Sentir(se) en confianza]**
- *After the Merinos left, we all let our hair down.*
  Cuando se fueron los Merino, nos sentimos en confianza.

To lick your chops
— **Estar saboreándose** ❑
- *Michael sat there licking his chops while I made the sausages.*
  Miguel estaba sentado, saboreándose las salchichas que yo preparaba.
- *Aldo is licking his chops at the thought of the coming weekend of deep sea fishing.*
  Aldo se está saboreando el próximo fin de semana de pesca en alta mar.

(Not) to lift a finger
— **No mover ni un dedo**
- *We all work like crazy, but my daughter-in-law never lifts a finger.*
  Todos trabajamos como locos, pero mi nuera no mueve ni un dedo.

To live from hand to mouth
— **Vivir al día**
- *I cannot make any vacation plans. I'm living from hand to mouth.*
  No puedo hacer planes para las vacaciones. Vivo al día.

To look for trouble (see To burn the candle at both ends)

To look forward to ❑
— **Esperar** ❑ **con ansias; dar gusto** (used mostly in the affirmative)**; tener ganas** (also means to feel like doing ❑)**; entusiasmar** (used mostly in the negative)
- *I'm looking forward to seeing you on your next visit to Mexico.*
  Espero con ansias (Me va a dar mucho gusto, Tengo muchas ganas de) verte en tu próxima visita a México.
- *I'm not really looking forward to going to the dentist today.*
  Realmente no tengo ganas de (no me entusiasma) ir hoy al dentista. (This could mean either that he doesn't like the idea but is going anyway, or that he doesn't like the idea and he has decided not to go.)

Note: In English this expression is used to refer only to something that one is sure is going to happen. There is no exact equivalent in Spanish.

To make a booboo (see To put your foot in it)

To make a mountain out of a molehill (see To be a tempest in a teapot)

To make a beeline for ❑
— **Salir disparado(a) hacia** ❑**;** ⚥⬇ **salir hecho(a) la mocha;** ⚥⬇**salir hecho(a) la raya**
- *As soon as Nacho was told his wife was about to give birth, he made a beeline for the hospital.*
  Cuando le dijeron que su esposa estaba a punto de dar a luz, Nacho salió disparado (salió hecho la mocha, salió hecho la raya) para el hospital.

Expressions

To make ends meet
— 🔊 **Ir(la) librando** (affirmative); **ir(la) pasando** (affirmative); **[no ganar lo suficiente]** (negative); **[no alcanzar]** (negative); **[no dar para todo]** (negative)

- *Speaker A:*   *I haven't seen you for ages. How are you doing?*
  Hace años que no te veo. ¿Cómo te va?

  Speaker B: *Not great, but I'm more or less making ends meet.*
  No muy bien, pero ahí la voy librando (la voy pasando).

or

        Awful, I can't seem to make ends meet.
        Muy mal. Nomás no me alcanza para los gastos (lo que gano no da para los gastos, or **no gano lo suficiente para cubrir mis gastos).**

To make no sense
— **No tener pies ni cabeza; no tener sentido**

- *I guess this is written in code. It makes no sense.*
  Esto debe estar escrito en clave. No tiene pies ni cabeza (no tiene sentido).

To make sense
— **Tener sentido**

- *These instructions for the VCR make sense after your explanation.*
  Con tu explicación, estas instrucciones para la videocasetera tienen sentido.

To make the best of a bad bargain
— **Al mal tiempo, buena cara** *(Saying)*

- *We didn't exactly get the best room. Well, I guess we'll just have to make the best of a bad bargain.*
  Nos dieron un cuarto bastante feo. Pero al mal tiempo, buena cara.

To make the most of ☐
— **Aprovechar al máximo ☐**

- *These big closets really allow me to make the most of the space in this room.*
  Estos grandes closets realmente me permiten aprovechar al máximo el espacio de este cuarto.

To make yourself scarce
— **Esfumar(se); [desaparecer]**

- *Here comes Julian. You had better make yourself scarce.*
  Ahí viene Julián. Mejor te esfumas (mejor desapareces).

To meet your match
— **Encontrar (hallar) la horma de su zapato**

- *I notice you don't fool around with him. You've finally met your match.*
  Con él no te andas con juegos. Hasta que encontraste la horma de tu zapato.

To mess with ☺☐
— **Meter(se) con ☺☐**

- *Don't mess with Butch or you'll be sorry.*

Expressions

No te metas con Butch o te arrepentirás.
- *I warned you not to mess with the union.*
Te advertí que no te metieras con el sindicato.

To mind the store
— **Encargar(se) del negocio;** ↔⇓ **encargar(se) del changarro** (📖 To look after the store)
- *Who's minding the store while you are on holiday?*
¿Quién se está encargando del negocio (changarro) mientras tú estás de vacaciones?

To monkey with □
— **Meter(le) mano a □**
- *Someone monkeyed with the copy machine and now it just won't work.*
Alguien le metió mano a la copiadora y ya no funciona.
Note: Also a very rude way of saying that a guy is going too far with a girl.

To mug (see To hold ☺ up)

To nip □ in the bud
— **Cortar de raíz** (📖 To cut □ at root level)
- *If you don't nip that relationship in the bud, you are going to have a real problem.*
Si no cortas de raíz ese noviazgo, vas a tener un verdadero problema.

To pass ☺ or □ off as a □
— **Hacer pasar ☺ o □ por □**
- *Joan is trying to pass off her Italian boyfriend off as a count.*
Joan está tratando de hacer pasar a su amigo italiano por conde.

To pay lip service to ☺
— **[Fingir estar de acuerdo con ☺]; decir □ de dientes para fuera**
- *I'm telling you right now. I refuse to pay lip service to Mr. Brant just because he's the boss.*
Te digo de una vez que no voy a fingir que estoy de acuerdo con el Sr. Brant simplemente porque es el jefe.
- *Don't believe everything Beto said about your painting. I know him. He was just paying lip service.*
No creas todo lo que Beto dijo de tu cuadro. Lo conozco: lo dijo de dientes para fuera.

To pay through the nose
— **[Pagar un precio exorbitante]; [pagar una fortuna]**
- *I had to pay through the nose to get these tickets.*
Tuve que pagar una fortuna por estos boletos.

To pick a quarrel
— **Buscar pleito;** ↔⇓ **buscar camorra;** ⇓**buscar bronca;** ↔⇓ **sacar boleto**
- *Ronny has had too much to drink and he's picking a quarrel with Sam.*
Ronny ha bebido demasiado y está buscando pleito (está buscando bronca, sacando boleto) con Sam.

To play around (see To horse around)

To play ball
— **[Cooperar];** ♭⇩ **jalar parejo**
- *All the guard has to do is look the other way, but he won't play ball.*
  Todo lo que tiene que hacer el guardia es hacerse el disimulado, pero no quiere cooperar (jalar parejo).

To play dead; to play dumb
— **Hacer(se) el (la) tonto(a);** ⌂ **hacer(se) el (la)loco(a)**
- *Don't play dumb. I know you know all about it.*
  No te hagas el tonto (el loco). Ya sé que estás enterado.

To play ☐ down
— **[Minimizar ☐]**
- *The governor's press agent tried to play down his boss's affair with the starlet.*
  El jefe de prensa del gobernador trató de minimizar el enredo de su jefe con la actriz.

To play dumb (see To play dead)

To play hard to get
— **Hacer(se) el (la) interesante; hacer(se) el (la) difícil**
- *She refuses to get on the phone; she's still playing hard to get.*
  Se niega a ponerse al teléfono; se está haciendo la interesante (la difícil).

To play hookey
— **Ir(se) de pinta**
- *The reason Paul has bad grades is because he plays hookey all the time.*
  Paul tiene malas calificaciones porque a cada rato se va de pinta.

To play it cool
— ⌂ **Actuar como si nada**
- *If anyone asks where we got this, just play it cool.*
  Si alguien pregunta dónde conseguimos esto, actúa como si nada.

To play it safe (see Just in case)
— **[No arriesgar(se)]**
- *I think we had better play it safe and not drink the water.*
  Yo creo que mejor no bebemos el agua, para no arriesgarnos.

To play the big shot; to play the (anything); to be snotty
— ⌂ **Dar(selas) de importante;** ⌂ **sentir(se) el (la) muy muy;** ⌂ **dar(selas) de ☐**
- *Arturo likes to play the big shot, doesn't he?*
  Arturo se las quiere dar de importante, ¿verdad? or **A Arturo le gusta dárselas de importante, ¿verdad?**
- *I don't like Sonia. She's always playing the executive.*
  Sonia me cae muy mal. Se siente la muy muy.
- *Anastasio likes to play the architect, but he hasn't even started college yet.*
  Anastasio se las da de arquitecto, pero todavía ni empieza la carrera.

Expressions

To play the horses
— **[Apostar a las carreras de caballos]**
- *I can't get Luis to stop playing the horses.*
  No logro que Luis deje de apostar a las carreras de caballos.

To pop in on ☺ (see To drop in)

To pour oil on the flames (see To add fuel to the fire)

To promise the Earth
— **Prometer el oro y el moro; prometer la luna y las estrellas**
- *Cindy married Kevin because he promised her the world.*
  Cindy se casó con Kevin porque le prometió el oro y el moro (la luna y las estrellas).

To pull a fast one; to fool ☺
— **[Engañar]; [defraudar];** ☺ **ver(le) la cara a** ☺; ☺⇩ **ver(le) la cara de tonto(a) a** ☺
- *The gas station attendant pulled a fast one. He gave me 20 liters and charged me for 30.*
  El fulano de la gasolinera me engañó (me defraudó, me vio la cara, me vio la cara de tonto). Me puso 20 litros y me cobró 30.

To pull ☺'s leg
— ☺ **Tomar(le) el pelo a** ☺ (📖 To take ☺'s hair)
- *Don't take it so seriously! He's pulling your leg.*
  ¡No lo tomes tan en serio! Te está tomando el pelo.

To pull strings
— **[Mover influencias];** ☺ **mover (usar) palancas** (📖 To move (to use) levers)
- *If there are no tickets left, I'll have to pull some strings.*
  Si ya no quedan boletos, tendré que mover mis influencias (usar mis palancas).

To pull through
— **[Salir de un aprieto];** ☺ **salir de ésta; [aliviar(se)]** (from an illness)
- *I don't know how I'm going to pull through this crisis.*
  No sé cómo voy a salir de este aprieto (a salir de ésta).
- *Of course tuberculosis is serious, but I know you are going to pull through.*
  Por supuesto que la tuberculosis es grave, pero sé que te vas a aliviar.

To pull □ to pieces
— **Despedazar □; hacer pedazos □; hacer trizas □**
- *The dog pulled the sofa to pieces.*
  El perro despedazó (hizo pedazos, hizo trizas) el sofá.

To pull yourself together
— **[Controlar(se)]; [calmar(se)]**
- *I understand how you feel, but you must pull yourself together.*
  Comprendo tus sentimientos, pero tienes que controlarte (calmarte).

To put in your two cents' worth
— **Meter su cuchara**
- *Your brother knows nothing about medicine, but he had to put in his two cents' worth.*
  Tu hermano no sabe nada de medicina, pero tenía que meter su cuchara.

To put the cart before the horse
— **Adelantar(se) a los hechos**
- *Why don't you wait until John proposes before you choose a wedding dress? You're putting the cart before the horse.*
  ¿Por qué no esperas a que Juan te proponga matrimonio antes de escoger tu vestido? Estás adelantándote a los hechos.

To put the noose around your neck (see To dig your own grave)
— **Poner(se) la soga al cuello; echar(se) la soga al cuello**
- *She didn't realize that by calling that lawyer, she was putting the noose around her own neck.*
  No se daba cuenta de que al llamar a ese abogado se estaba echando la soga al cuello.

To (be unable to) put up with ☺□; to (be unable to) stand ☺□
— **[(No poder) tolerar a ☺□]; [(no poder) soportar a ☺□]; [(no poder) aguantar □ or a ☺]**
- *I simply cannot put up with (stand) this heat!*
  ¡Sencillamente no tolero (no soporto, no aguanto) este calor!
- *Let's get out of here. I can't stand the guy at the next table another minute!*
  ¡Vámonos! Ya no soporto (no aguanto, no tolero) al tipo de la mesa de junto.

To put your foot in it; to put your foot in your mouth; to make a booboo; to blow it; to screw (things) up
— ♒ **Meter la pata*** (📖 To stick your foot in it)
- *Can't you keep your mouth shut? You put your foot in it again.*
  ¿No puedes mantener la boca cerrada? Ya volviste a meter la pata.
— ♒ **Regar(la)** (📖 To spill it)
- *You blew it, dumbbell! That isn't Lulu, it's Marta!*
  ¡La regaste, baboso! ¡Esa no es Lulú, es Marta!
— ♒ **Regar el tepache** (📖 To spill the beer)
- *I just knew you were going to put your foot in it!*
  ¡Sabía que ibas a meter la pata!
- *If Janet makes a booboo, I'm going to pretend I don't know her.*
  Si Janet riega el tepache, voy a hacer que no la conozco.

Note: This also means to get pregnant out of wedlock.

To put your foot in your mouth (see To put your foot in it)

To put your nose to the grindstone
— **Poner(se) a trabajar (a estudiar**, or whatever verb applies)
- *Jim really has to put his nose to the grindstone if he wants to pass the final exams.*
  Jim se tiene que poner a estudiar duro si quiere aprobar los exámenes finales.

Expressions

To rave about ☺□
— **Hablar maravillas de** ☺□
  - *Everybody is raving about the new French film.*
  Todo el mundo habla maravillas de la nueva película francesa.

To reach a point of no return
— **Llegar al punto en que ya no tiene remedio** □; **[llegar a un punto en que ya no puede arrepentir(se) (regresar(se), hacer(se) para atrás)]; llegar al punto sin regreso (retorno)**
  - *You should have thought of that sooner, before you reached a point of no return.*
  Eso se te hubiera ocurrido antes de llegar al punto en que ya no tiene remedio (al punto sin regreso, sin retorno) (en que ya no te puedes (o podías) hacerte para atrás (arrepentirte)).

To rest on your laurels
— **Dormir(se) en sus laureles**
  - *Your competitor is getting a bigger share of the market while you're resting on your laurels.*
  Tu competidor está logrando aumentar su participación en el mercado, mientras tú te duermes en tus laureles.

To rise to the occasion
— **Estar (poner(se)) a la altura de las circunstancias**
  - *Although your wife is not used to rubbing shoulders with these people, she rose to the occasion and did very well.*
  A pesar de que no está acostumbrada a codearse con estas personas, tu esposa se puso a la altura de las circunstancias y lo hizo muy bien.

To rub shoulders with ☺
— **Codear(se) con** ☺
  - *Because of his job, Peter rubs shoulders with a lot of government bigwigs.*
  Por su trabajo, Peter se codea con muchos altos funcionarios del gobierno.

To run across ☺□; to run into ☺□
— **Encontrar(se) (de casualidad)** □
  - *I ran across these old letters in the closet.*
  Me encontré (de casualidad) estas viejas cartas en el closet.
— **Encontrar(se) a** ☺; **topar(se) con** ☺
  - *Abigail says she ran into Gordon at the library yesterday.*
  Dice Abigail que se encontró a (se topó con) Gordon ayer en la biblioteca.

To run ☺ out (see To throw ☺ out)
— **[Despedir a** ☺**]** (from a job); **correr a** ☺
  - *Alan was run out of the company.*
  Despidieron (corrieron) a Alan de la empresa.

To run out of □
— **Acabar(sele)** □ a ☺
  - *I've run out of paper*
  Se me acabó el papel.

To save face
— **[Guardar las apariencias]; [no quedar mal]**
  ▪ *I made an appointment with the wrong person. Please help me to save face.*
  Hice una cita con la persona equivocada. Por favor, ayúdame a guardar las apariencias (a no quedar mal).

To screw □ up
— **Echar a perder □; descomponer □**
  ▪ *Tony screwed up the stapler.*
  Tony echó a perder (descompuso) la engrapadora.

To screw up the courage to do □
— **Tener (Encontrar) el valor para** + verb
  ▪ *I couldn't screw up the courage to ask her out.*
  No (tuve) encontré el valor para invitarla a salir.

To see eye to eye about □
— **[Estar (perfectamente) de acuerdo en (o sobre) □]**
  ▪ *It's a good thing you and I see eye to eye about this matter.*
  ¡Qué bueno que tú y yo estamos perfectamente de acuerdo en este asunto!
  ▪ *I don't think Ron and Linda see eye to eye about the decor she wants for the house.*
  No creo que Ron y Linda estén muy de acuerdo sobre la decoración que ella quiere para la casa.

To see ☺ off; to see ☺ out
— **[Ir a despedir a ☺]**
  ▪ *Reggie is going to be too busy to see me off at the airport.*
  Reggie va a estar demasiado ocupado como para ir a despedirme al aeropuerto.
— **[Acompañar a la puerta a ☺]**
  ▪ *Please forgive me if I don't see you out.*
  Perdóneme por no acompañarlo a la puerta.

To see red
— **[Enfurecer(se)]; ☺ trabar(se) de coraje**
  ▪ *When Joan turned up with Paul, I saw red.*
  Cuando Joan se apareció con Paul, me enfurecí (me trabé de coraje).

To see the handwriting on the wall
— **Dar(se) cuenta de lo inevitable**
  ▪ *Joe finally stopped smoking. He has seen the handwriting on the wall.*
  Joe finalmente dejó de fumar. Ya se dio cuenta de lo inevitable.

To sell ☺ down the river
— **[Traicionar a ☺]**
  ▪ *I'm afraid Johnson sold me down the river with the car deal.*
  Me temo que Johnson me traicionó con el trato de los autos.

Expressions

To sell like hotcakes
— **Vender(se) como pan caliente**
- *The new recording is selling like hotcakes.*
  El nuevo disco se está vendiendo como pan caliente.

To send ☺ to hell
— ☺ **Mandar al diablo a** ☺; ☺ **mandar al demonio a** ☺
- *I don't dare ask for a raise because I know the boss will just send me to hell.*
  No me atrevo a pedir un aumento porque sé que el jefe me va a mandar al diablo.

To set ☺ up
— **Tender(le) una trampa a** ☺; ☺ **Poner(le) un cuatro a** ☺
- *The boss set the accountant up to prove she had been stealing the company's money.*
  El jefe le tendió una trampa (le puso un cuatro) a la contadora, para probar que había estado robando dinero de la empresa.

To set ☐ up
— **[Establecer; organizar; arreglar]**
- *Mrs. Smith is going to set up three of the stalls at the fair.*
  La Sra. Smith va a organizar (a poner) tres de los puestos de la feria.
— **[Constituir ☐]** (for corporations)
- *My father set up the company when he was 25.*
  Mi padre constituyó (puso, estableció) la empresa a los 25 años.

To shift for yourself; to go it alone
— ☺ **Arreglar(selas) solo**; ☺ **rascar(se) con sus propias uñas**
- *Now that Peter is gone, I'm going to have to shift for myself (go it alone).*
  Ahora que ya no está Pedro, voy a tener que arreglármelas solo (que rascarme con mis propias uñas).

To show up
— **[Llegar]; aparecer(se)**
- *My sisters didn't show up until after the ceremony had started.*
  Mis hermanas no llegaron (no se aparecieron) hasta después de empezada la ceremonia.

To shut ☐ down
— **[Cerrar ☐]**
- *The factory was shut down because it was polluting.*
  Cerraron la fábrica porque estaba contaminando.

To shut up
— **[Callar a** ☺**]; [callar(se)]** (also means to keep quiet)
- *If you don't shut up, I'll have to shut you up.*
  Si no te callas, voy a tener que callarte.

To skate on thin ice
— **[Arriesgar(se)]; jugar con fuego** (📖 To play with fire)

- *Those people are really skating on thin ice; their visa ran out two days ago and they haven't left the country.*
  Esa gente se está arriesgando mucho (está jugando con fuego); su visa se venció hace dos días y aún no ha salido del país.

To sleep like a log
— **Dormir como tronco** (📖 To sleep like a log)**; dormir como un lirón** (📖 To sleep as if hibernating)**; dormir a pierna suelta**
- *I always sleep like a log when I'm up in the mountains.*
  Cuando estoy en las montañas, siempre duermo como tronco (como un lirón, a pierna suelta).

To sleep on ☐
— **Consultar ☐ con la almohada**
- *I think I'm going to have to sleep on your proposal.*
  Me parece que voy a tener que consultar tu propuesta con la almohada.

To sow your wild oats
— **Andar de picos pardos**
- *I can tell from the expression on your face that you were out sowing your wild oats all night.*
  ¡Mira qué cara tienes! Seguramente anduviste de picos pardos toda la noche.

To split hairs
— **[Discutir pequeñeces]**
- *I hate arguing with Ethel; she always loses sight of the main point and starts splitting hairs.*
  Odio hablar con Ethel; siempre se le olvida el tema principal y empieza a discutir pequeñeces.

To stand out
— **[Sobresalir]**
- *Isn't it wonderful? Pricilla stands out in everything she does.*
  ¿No es maravilloso? Priscila sobresale en todo lo que hace.

To (be unable to) stand ☺☐ (see To (be unable to) put up with ☺☐)

To stand up for ☺☐ (see To stick up for ☺☐)
— **[Salir en defensa de ☺☐]**
- *You don't have to stand up for me anymore. Thank you.*
  Ya no tienes que salir en mi defensa. Gracias.

To start at the bottom of the ladder
— **(Empezar) sin nada; desde abajo; desde el fondo**
- *He is director now, but he started at the bottom of the ladder.*
  Ahora es el director, pero empezó desde abajo.

To stay in; to stay home
— **[Quedar(se) en casa]**
- *I think I'll stay home tonight.*
  Me parece que esta noche me quedaré en casa.

Expressions

To stick out like a sore thumb
— **Disparar(se)**
  - *That modern building sticks out like a sore thumb in this area of old houses.*
    Ese edificio moderno se dispara en esta zona de antiguas residencias.
— **[Ser muy notorio, resaltar]**
  - *The visiting basketball player stuck out like a sore thumb in the group of school children.*
    El basquetbolista era muy notorio (resaltaba) entre los niños de primaria.
— **Ver(se) a la legua** (📖 To be visible from a league away)
  - *You can easily tell that the suit Ernesto is wearing is not his.*
    Se ve a la legua que Ernesto trae un traje prestado.
— **Ver(se) mal (feo(a), horrible, espantoso(a))**
  - *Your pick-up sticks out like a sore thumb among all these European imports in the parking lot.*
    Tu camioneta se ve horrible entre todos estos coches europeos en el estacionamiento.
— 🔔 **Ver(se) de la cachetada** (📖 To look like a slap in the face)
  - *If I were you, I'd wear something with a longer skirt to the funeral. That dress is going to stick out like a sore thumb.*
    Si fuera tú, me pondría algo con la falda más larga para el funeral. Con ese vestido te ves de la cachetada.

To stick up for ☺□ (see To stand up for ☺□)
— **[Defender a ☺□]**
  - *I stick up for Ernie because no one else ever does.*
    Yo defiendo a Ernie, porque nadie más lo hace.

To stop at nothing
— **[Scr capaz de todo]; [ser capaz de cualquier cosa]; 🔔 no medir(se)**
  - *Dave will stop at nothing to get to the top.*
    Dave no se mide (es capaz de todo, es capaz de cualquier cosa) por llegar hasta arriba.

To stop □ cold turkey
— **Parar □ de golpe; dejar □ de golpe; dejar de hacer □ de golpe; dejar de hacer □ sin más ni más; dejar de hacer □ así nada más; dejar de hacer □ de buenas a primeras**
  - *John stopped smoking cold turkey.*
    Juan dejó de fumar (el cigarro) de golpe (sin más ni más, así nada más, de buenas a primeras).

To suit ☺ to a tee
— **Caer(le) como anillo al dedo a ☺** (📖 To fit like a ring on a finger); 🏮 **caer(le) al (puro) pelo a ☺**
  - *You may not like this little office, but it suits me to a tee.*
    A ti tal vez no te guste esta oficinita, pero a mí me cae como anillo al dedo (me cae al puro pelo).

To swallow □ hook, line and sinker
— **Tragar(se) el anzuelo; tragar(se) la mentira; creer □ sin sospechar que es mentira**
  ▪ *Ellen made up a story about her mother's illness, which her boss swallowed hook, line and sinker.*
    Ellen inventó un cuento sobre la enfermedad de su mamá, y el jefe se tragó el anzuelo (la mentira).

To take (unfair) advantage of ☺□
— **Aprovechar(se) de ☺□**
  ▪ *I don't think Gordon is ever going to give me a raise. He's just taking advantage of me.*
    Creo que Gordon jamás me va a dar el aumento. Simplemente se está aprovechando de mí.

To take after ☺
— **[Parecer(se) a ☺]; ⌂ salir a ☺**
  ▪ *I'm the only one in the family who takes after my father.*
    Soy el único de mis hermanos que se parece a mi papá (que salió a mi papá).

To take □ apart (see To take to pieces)
— **[Desarmar □]**
  ▪ *I'll never hit on the problem unless I take the whole engine apart.*
    Jamás voy a dar con el problema a menos que desarme todo el motor.

To take ☺'s breath away (see To leave ☺ breathless)
— **Dejar atónito(a) a ☺; dejar anonadado(a) a ☺; dejar boquiabierto(a) a ☺; dejar con la boca abierta a ☺**
  ▪ *The sight of the school of porpoise in the moonlight took my breath away.*
    El espectáculo del cardumen de delfines a la luz de la luna me dejó atónito (anonadado, boquiabierto).

To take ☺□ for granted*
— **Dar por hecho □; dar por sentado □**
  ▪ *John never appreciates anything I do for him. He just takes me for granted.*
    John nunca agradece nada. Da por hecho (Da por sentado) que tengo la obligación de ayudarlo.
Note: In Spanish you cannot take a person for granted, only a thing.

To take it easy
— **Tomar las cosas con calma**
  ▪ *I really have to take it easy for a few days; I've been run ragged.*
    Tengo que tomar las cosas con calma por unos días; me he estado poniendo una soba.

To take it or leave it
— **Tomar(lo) o dejar(lo)**
  ▪ *This is what I have to offer. Take it or leave it.*
    Esto es lo que ofrezco. Tómelo o déjelo.

Expressions

To take the bull by the horns
— **Agarrar al toro por los cuernos**
- *The time has come to face up to the problem and take the bull by the horns.*
  Ya llegó el momento de encarar el problema y agarrar al toro por los cuernos.

To take the cake; to take the prize
— **Ser el colmo; llevar(se) la palma**
- *How could you bring your mechanic to the party as your date? That really takes the cake!*
  ¿Cómo pudiste llevar a tu mecánico a la fiesta? ¡Te llevaste la palma!

To take the law into your own hands
— **Hacer(se) justicia por su propia mano**
- *The police are turning a blind eye. We're going to have to take the law into our own hands.*
  La policía se está haciendo guaje. Vamos a tener que hacernos justicia por nuestra propia mano.

To take □ to pieces
— **Desarmar □**
- *I'll have to take the carburetor to pieces.*
  Tendré que desarmar el carburador.

To take ☺ under your wing
— **[Tomar bajo su protección a ☺]**
- *When Julie's mother died, I took the kid under my wing.*
  Al morir la madre de Julie, tomé a la niña bajo mi protección.

To take □ up with ☺
— **[Tratar □ con ☺]; [discutir □ con ☺]**
- *I suggest you take that up with Mr. Dillon.*
  Sugiero que trates (discutas) ese asunto con el Sr. Dillon.

To take □ with a grain of salt
— **Tomar □ con reservas**
- *She told me she is getting married in two months, but you know her. Take it with a grain of salt.*
  A mí me dijo que se casa en dos meses, pero ya la conoces. Tómalo con reservas.

To talk ☺'s ear off
— **Hablar hasta por los codos; ⏏poner(le) gorro a ☺ hablando hasta por los codos**
- *If your father-in-law is going too, I better not go. He will talk my ear off.*
  Si tu suegro también va a ir, mejor no voy. Habla hasta por los codos (me va a poner gorro hablando todo el tiempo).

To talk nonsense; to talk through your hat
— **Hablar tonterías; decir disparates**
- *Mario is talking through his hat. I think he's a bit drunk.*
  Mario está diciendo disparates (hablando tonterías). Creo que está un poco tomado.

To talk through your hat (see To talk nonsense)

To talk turkey

— **[Hablar sin rodeos]**

▪ *Let's talk turkey; we have a serious problem on our hands and we're not going to solve it by pussyfooting.*
Hablemos sin rodeos; tenemos un problema grave y no lo vamos a resolver con diplomacia.

To think better of ❐

— **[Cambiar de opinión]; [cambiar de parecer]**

▪ *I thought better of what we decided yesterday; we'll have to think up something else.*
Cambié de parecer (de opinión) con respecto a lo que decidimos ayer; vamos a tener que idear alguna otra cosa.

— **Pensar(lo) mejor**

▪ *I thought better of going to Taxco today.*
Ya pensé mejor lo de ir hoy a Taxco.

To think highly of ☺❐; to think the world of ☺❐

— **Tener en gran estima a ☺❐; [estimar a ☺; estimar ❐]; [apreciar a ☺; apreciar ❐]; [querer mucho a ☺]**

▪ *We all think the world of the director; aside from being a whiz at his job, he's a wonderful human being.*
Todos tenemos en gran estima (estimamos, apreciamos, queremos mucho) al director; aparte de ser eficiente en su trabajo, es buenísima gente.

To throw a party

— **Hacer una fiesta**

▪ *I'm throwing a party this weekend.*
Voy a hacer una fiesta este fin de semana.

To throw in the towel

— **Tirar la toalla; dar(se) por vencido**

▪ *Geoffrey has received seven rejection slips from publishers, but he is not throwing in the towel.*
A Geoffrey le han rechazado su libro siete editoras, pero no va a tirar la toalla (a darse por vencido).

To throw cold water on ❐

— **Echar por tierra ❐**

▪ *Doug threw cold water on my suggestion for the weekend.*
Doug echó por tierra mi sugerencia para el fin de semana.

To throw ☺ out (on their ear); to boot ☺ out (see To kick ☺ out)

— ⌂ **Poner de patitas en la calle a ☺; ⌂ sacar a ☺; correr a ☺**

▪ *They threw Alejandro out (on his ear).*
A Alejandro lo pusieron de patitas en la calle.

▪ *My brother was booted out of the rifle club.*
A mi hermano lo sacaron (lo corrieron) del club de tiro.

Expressions

To touch a sore spot
— **Poner el dedo en la llaga**
- *When you spoke of her divorce, you touched a sore spot.*
  Cuando le hablaste de su divorcio, pusiste el dedo en la llaga.

To turn a blind eye
— **Hacer(se) de la vista gorda**
- *Parents who turn a blind eye to their kid's drinking are asking for trouble.*
  Los padres que se hacen de la vista gorda cuando sus hijos beben, pronto tendrán problemas.

To turn ☺□ down
— **[Rechazar ☺□]** (to reject)
- *I have a feeling they're going to turn me down for the job.*
  Me late que me van a rechazar para el puesto.
— **[Negar]** (to deny a request)
- *My request to leave the country was turned down.*
  Me negaron el permiso para salir del país.

To turn in (go to bed), to hit the hay; to hit the sack
— **[Ir(se) a la cama]; [acostar(se)]**
- *I think I'll turn in (hit the hay, hit the sack) now.*
  Creo que es hora de ir a la cama (de acostarse).

To turn or shut □ off
— **[Apagar □]**
- *Remember to turn off the gas before we go away.*
  Recuerda (no olvides) apagar el gas antes de irnos de viaje.
— **[Cortar □]** (when the utility company does it)
- *Our electricity was cut off because we forgot to pay the bill.*
  Nos cortaron la luz porque se nos olvidó pagar el recibo.

To turn over a new leaf
— **[Reformar(se)]**
- *Jacinto has promised to turn over a new leaf.*
  Jacinto ha prometido reformarse.

To turn □ over to ☺
— **[Entregar □ a ☺]; [hacer entrega de □ a ☺]**
- *Tomorrow is the day I turn the documents over to the court.*
  Mañana entrego (hago entrega de) los documentos al tribunal.

To turn up your nose at □
— **[Despreciar □]; ⌕ hacer(le) el fuchi a □; ⌕ hacer(le) el feo a □**
- *Glenda turned up her nose at the job she was offered.*
  Glenda despreció el (le hizo el fuchi al, le hizo el feo al) puesto que le ofrecieron.

Expressions

To twist ☺'s arm
— 🤚 **Hacer(le) manita de puerco a ☺; [presionar a ☺]; ✋apretar(le) el pescuezo (hasta convencer) a ☺**
- *I'm going to have to twist Greg's arm a bit to get him to go with us.*
  Voy a tener que presionar (apretarle el pescuezo, hacerle manita de puerquito) a Greg para que nos acompañe.

To upset the applecart
— **Echar(lo) todo a perder; estropear los planes**
- *Janice upset the applecart because she told Jim everything.*
  Janice echó todo a perder (estropeó los planes) porque se lo dijo a Jim.

To wait on ☺
— **[Atender a ☺]**
- *It took the waitress ages to wait on me.*
  La mesera se tardó mucho para atenderme.

To wait on ☺ hand and foot
— **Atender a cuerpo de rey a ☺**
- *When we visit my sister, she waits on us hand and foot*
  Cuando visitamos a mi hermana, nos atiende a cuerpo de rey.

To wait up for ☺
— **Esperar despierto(a) a ☺**
- *I don't know what time I'll be home, so don't wait up.*
  No sé a qué hora volveré a casa, así que no me esperes despierta.

To wash your dirty linen in public
— **Sacar los trapos (trapitos) (sucios) al sol**
- *Did you read the newspaper. They are washing your friend's dirty linen in public.*
  ¿Ya leíste el periódico? A tu amigo le sacaron sus trapitos sucios al sol.

To wear your heart on your sleeve
— **No poder disimular los sentimientos (amorosos)**
- *Jim has bad luck with the girls because he wears his heart on his sleeve.*
  A Jim le va mal con las muchachas porque no sabe disimular sus sentimientos.

To wind ☺ around your little finger
— **Tener en el bolsillo a ☺ (📖 To have ☺ in your pocket); tener comiendo de la mano a ☺ (📖 To have ☺ eating out of your hand); [manejar a ☺ a su antojo]**
- *Don't worry about the teacher; I've got her wound around my little finger.*
  No te preocupes por la maestra; la tengo en el bolsillo (la tengo comiendo de mi mano, la manejo a mi antojo).

Expressions

To work □ out (to resolve a problem)
— **[Solucionar □]; [buscar una solución]**
- *We have to let them work this out between them.*
  Tenemos que dejar que ellos solos busquen una solución (lo solucionen).
— **[Resultar]; [salir]**
- *Everything worked out just great.*
  Todo resultó (salió) muy bien.

To work your way up
— **Abrir(se) paso; abrir(se) camino**
- *The chairman of the Board worked his way up from the bottom.*
  El presidente del Consejo se abrió paso (se abrió camino) desde abajo.

2. Expressions Used as Part of a Sentence

A cock-and-bull story
— **Un cuento chino** (📖 A Chinese story)
  - *She gave the police a cock-and-bull story about the disappearance of the diamond.*
    Le contó a la policía un cuento chino sobre la desaparición del brillante.

A fair-weather friend
— **[Amigo(a) sólo en las buenas]; [amigo(a) sólo en las buenas]; [amigo(a) interesado(a)]**
  - *Adriana would leave you if you lose everything. She is nothing but a fair-weather friend.*
    Adriana te dará la espalda si te quedas sin nada. Es amiga sólo en las buenas (mientras le conviene).

A flash in the pan
— **♫Llamarada de petate**
  - *He'll stop coming to the gym before the week is out. This is just a flash in the pan.*
    Antes de una semana habrá dejado de venir al gimnasio. Esto es sólo llamarada de petate.

A left-handed compliment
— **Un cumplido falso**
  - *I don't understand. He doesn't usually make left-handed compliments.*
    No entiendo. Por lo general, no hace cumplidos falsos.

A long face
— **Cara larga**
  - *OK. Don't make that long face. You can borrow the car.*
    Está bien. No pongas cara larga. Te presto el coche.

A show of hands
— **[Votar levantando la mano]**
  - *Don't bother with ballots. Let's just have a show of hands.*
    Simplifiquemos las cosas. Vamos a votar levantando la mano.

A stab in the back
— **(Una) puñalada trapera; puñalada por la espalda**
  - *He quit a day before the high season began; I call that a stab in the back.*
    Renunció un día antes de que empezara la temporada alta. A eso le llamo una puñalada trapera (por la espalda).

A two-edged sword
— **(Un) arma de dos filos**
  - *Freedom can be a two-edged sword.*
    La libertad puede ser un arma de dos filos.

Expressions

A wolf in sheep's clothing
— **Lobo con piel de oveja**
- *Leon has lovely manners. But don't trust him. He's a wolf in sheep's clothing.*
  León es muy amable, pero no confíes en él. Es un lobo con piel de oveja.

Act of God
— **Desastre natural; caso de fuerza mayor**
- *I bought some insurance to cover my house against earthquakes or any other act of God.*
  Compré un seguro que protege mi casa en caso de terremoto o cualquier otro desastre natural.

An all-time high
— **Sin precedentes**
- *This year car sales were at an all-time high.*
  Este año logramos una venta de autos sin precedentes.

As a matter of fact; in fact
— **De hecho; es más**
- *Grey is a good man for the job; as a matter of fact, he has two degrees in economy.*
  Grey es un buen candidato para el puesto; de hecho, tiene dos títulos en economía.
- *No, I haven't seen Bruce today. As a matter of fact, I haven't seen him for a week.*
  No, hoy no he visto a Bruce. Es más, hace una semana que no lo veo.

As the crow flies
— **[En línea recta]** (📖 In a straight line)
- *Taxco is not really far as the crow flies, but on that winding road, it's three hours by car.*
  Taxco no está realmente lejos en línea recta, pero por ese camino sinuoso, son tres horas en coche.

Better half
— **Media naranja**
- *I'm going to have to ask my better half about this first.*
  Primero voy a tener que consultar a mi media naranja acerca de esto.

(A) big shot
— **Mandamás**
- *I didn't realize you were a big shot in that company, Walter.*
  No sabía que eras el mandamás en esa empresa, Walter.

By leaps and bounds
— **A pasos agigantados**
- *George's company is growing by leaps and bounds.*
  La empresa de Jorge está creciendo a pasos agigantados.

By the skin of your teeth
— **Por un pelito** (📖 By a little hair); 👄 **por un pelo de rana** (📖 By a frog's hair)
- *Pam passed the test by the skin of her teeth.*
  Pam aprobó el examen por un pelito (por un pelo de rana).

Expressions

By the way
— **Por cierto; a propósito**
- *Walter drove me to work today. By the way, he sent you these papers.*
  Walter me trajo a la oficina. Por cierto (a propósito), te manda estos papeles.

Come hell or high water
— **Contra viento y marea; cueste lo que cueste; pase lo que pase**
- *I'm going to buy Joan the house I promised her, come hell or high water.*
  Le voy a comprar a Joan la casa que le prometí, contra viento y marea (cueste lo que cueste, pase lo que pase).

Day in and day out
— **Día tras día; de día y de noche**
- *That kid does nothing but sit at the computer day in and day out.*
  Ese muchacho no hace nada más que estar sentado frente a la computadora día tras día (de día y de noche).

Dressed to kill
— **Con sus mejores galas**
- *Carla is dressed to kill tonight.*
  Carla está vestida con sus mejores galas esta noche.

Few and far between
— **Escasos(as); contados(as)**
- *In this town, bachelors are few and far between.*
  En este pueblo los solteros son escasos (contados).

First of all . . .
— **Primero que nada . . . ; antes que nada . . . ; antes que otra cosa**
- *It's time to get to work. First of all, we have to clean up the office.*
  Es hora de ponernos a trabajar. Primero que nada (antes que nada), vamos a limpiar la oficina.

For a change; as usual (sarcastic)
— **Para variar**
- *Let's go to a new restaurant for a change.*
  Vamos a otro restaurante, para variar.
- *Pollution is high again today, as usual.*
  Otra vez está muy alta la contaminación hoy, para variar.

For the time being
— **Por el momento; por ahora; ⌂ por mientras**
- *I'm sorry, but for the time being I don't want to buy a telescope.*
  Lo siento, pero por el momento (por ahora) no quiero comprar un telescopio.
- *Linda can't afford an apartment, so she'll be staying with us for the time being.*
  A Linda no le alcanza para pagar un departamento; así que se hospedará con nosotros por mientras.

Expressions

Hot air
— **Tonterías; sandeces**
  ▪ *You're just talking a lot of hot air.*
    Estás diciendo tonterías (sandeces).

In a nutshell
— **En pocas palabras**
  ▪ *That's the idea, in a nutshell.*
    Esa es la idea, en pocas palabras.

In every nook and cranny
— **Por todos los rincones**
  ▪ *I've looked in every nook and cranny, but I can't find my keys.*
    Ya busqué por todos los rincones, pero no encuentro mis llaves.

In fact (see As a matter of fact)

In the meantime, meanwhile
— **Mientras; mientras tanto**
  ▪ *We're still waiting for our new furniture to be delivered. In the meantime (meanwhile), we're using these ratty old things.*
    Seguimos esperando que nos entreguen los nuevos muebles. Mientras (tanto), estamos usando estos muebles viejos.

In the nick of time
— **Apenas a tiempo**
  ▪ *He got here in the nick of time.*
    Llegó apenas a tiempo.

In the small hours of the morning
— **A las mil y quinientas; a altas horas de la madrugada**
  ▪ *I'm really tired because we've been getting home in the small hours of the morning for three nights in a row.*
    Estoy bastante cansada porque ya van tres noches que regresamos a altas horas de la madrugada (a las mil y quinientas).

In this neck of the woods
— **Por estos rumbos**
  ▪ *What are you doing in this neck of the woods?*
    ¿Qué andas haciendo por estos rumbos?

Just in case
— **Por si + verb; por si acaso; por (si) las dudas; ⌂ por las cochinas dudas; ⌂ por (si) las moscas**
  ▪ *Bring the umbrella, in case it rains.*
    Tráete el paraguas por si llueve.
  ▪ *We'll only be out a second, but lock the door just in case.*
    Sólo vamos a salir un segundo, pero cierra con llave por si acaso.

- *We had better take some extra money, just in case.*
  Mejor llevemos algo de dinero extra, por si las moscas.
- *Those roadside tacos look really good, but I won't have any, just in case.*
  Los tacos de ese puesto se ven sabrosos, pero mejor no los como, por las dudas.
- *I'm going to hide this money, just in case.*
  Voy a esconder este dinero, por las cochinas dudas.

Like a bat out of hell
— **Como alma que lleva el diablo**
- *You should talk to Joe about speeding. When he passed me he was going like a bat out of hell.*
  Debes hablar con Joe acerca de cómo maneja. Cuando me rebasó, iba como alma que lleva el diablo.

Like it or lump it
— **Quiera o no; le guste o no**
- *I'm going to get married, like it or lump it.*
  Me voy a casar, quieras o no (te guste o no).

Meanwhile (see In the meantime)

More □ than you can shake a stick at
— **Para aventar para arriba** (📖 Enough to fling up in the air)
- *That woman has more cats than you can shake a stick at.*
  Esa señora tiene gatos para aventar para arriba.

No sooner said than done
— **Dicho y hecho**
- *Juan said: "If Pedro gets on that ladder, he's going to fall". No sooner said than done. Down he went.*
  Juan dijo: si Pedro se sube a esa escalera, se va a caer. Dicho y hecho, se cayó.
— **Tal dijo y tal hizo**
- *We said we'll go out for dinner, and no sooner said than done, Paula went up to change her clothes.*
  Acordamos salir a cenar. Tal dijo y tal hizo. Paula subió inmediatamente a cambiarse.

Not for love or money
— **Ni a tiros; ni por todo el oro del mundo; ⇩ni a patadas**
- *Alfred is never coming back, not for love or money.*
  Alfredo no regresa ni a tiros (ni por todo el oro del mundo, ni a patadas).

Now that I come to think of it . . .
— **Ahora que lo pienso . . .**
- *Here . . . I brought you these candies. However, now that I come to think of it, you're on a diet, right?*
  Toma . . . te traje estos dulces. Pero ahora que lo pienso, estás a dieta, ¿verdad?

Null and void
— **Sin efecto**

Expressions

- *From this week on, these regulations are null and void.*
  A partir de esta semana, estas reglas quedan sin efecto.

Once in a blue moon
— **Cada mil años**

- *I'm very fond of Bruce, but I only see him once in a blue moon.*
  Estimo mucho a Bruce, aunque lo veo cada mil años.

Out of a clear blue sky
— **De buenas a primeras**

- *They were talking quite amicably, when out of a clear blue sky, Joe socked Pete in the jaw.*
  Estaban hablando amistosamente, y de buenas a primeras, Joe le dio un puñetazo a Pete.

Out of order
— **Descompuesto(a)**

- *This elevator is out of order.*
  Este elevador está descompuesto.

Out of print
— **[Agotado(a)]**

- *I can't get that book anymore. It's out of print.*
  Ya no puedo conseguir ese libro. Está agotado.

Out of stock
— **[Agotado(a)]**

- *Sorry. That pen is out of stock.*
  Lo siento. Esta pluma está agotada.

Out of thin air
— **De la nada**

- *After one year of absence, today Pedro just appeared out of thin air.*
  Después de un año de no saber nada de él, hoy Pedro apareció de la nada.

Out of this world
— **Del otro mundo**

- *I don't know what you see in Jean. She's nothing out of this world.*
  No sé qué le ves a Jean. No es nada del otro mundo.

Over my dead body
— **Sobre mi cadáver**

- *She will set foot in this house over my dead body.*
  Ella entrará en esta casa pasando sobre mi cadáver.

Rain or shine
— **Llueva, truene o relampaguee**

- *Fred always goes out for a walk on Sundays, rain or shine.*
  Fred siempre sale a caminar los domingos, llueva, truene o relampaguee.

Right away
— **Ya; de inmediato; inmediatamente; enseguida; 🔔 luego luego; ahora (ahorita) mismo**
- *I want you to do it right away.*
  Quiero que lo hagas inmediatamente (ya, de inmediato, enseguida, luego luego, ahora mismo).

Small fry
— **Niños(as); chiquillos(as); 🐦 escuincles** (children)
- *The small fry will have lunch out on the porch.*
  Los chiquillos van a comer en la terraza.
— **🔔 Chaparrito(a), bajito(a)** (physical height) (adults)
- *The people in this part of the country are all small fry.*
  Los habitantes de esta parte del país son todos chaparritos (bajitos).
— **Poca cosa** (insignificance) (things)
- *We can't merge with those companies; they're small fry.*
  No debemos fusionarnos con esas empresitas; son poca cosa.

Sooner or later
— **Tarde o temprano**
- *Sooner or later you're going to have to tell them.*
  Tarde o temprano les vas a tener que decir.

Spick and span
— **[Limpio(a) y ordenado(a)]; reluciente** (📖 Sparkling)
- *Why can't you keep the kitchen spick and span like mother does?*
  ¿Por qué no eres capaz de tener la cocina limpia y ordenada (reluciente), como la tiene mi mamá?

Square meal
— **[Comida completa]; [comida en toda forma]**
- *Rick works out in the field and he needs three square meals a day.*
  Rick trabaja en el campo y necesita hacer tres comidas completas (en toda forma) al día.

Straight from the shoulder
— **[Francamente]; sin rodeos**
- *Give it to me straight from the shoulder: how long have I got to live?*
  Dígamelo sin rodeos (francamente). ¿Cuánto me queda de vida?

Stuck up
— **Presumido(a)**
- *Don't you think Eleanor is a bit stuck up, or is it my imagination?*
  ¿No te parece que Leonor es un poco presumida, o me lo estoy imaginando?

That's another kettle of fish (see That's a horse of a different color)

Expressions

That's a horse of a different color; that's another kettle of fish
— **Esa es harina de otro costal**
  ▪ *These two are inexpensive, but that one is a Christofle. That is a horse of a different color (another kettle of fish).*
    Estos dos no son caros, pero ése es un Christofle, que ya es harina de otro costal.

The coast is clear
— **No hay moros en la costa**
  ▪ *Please go outside and tell me if the coast is clear now.*
    Por favor, sal y dime si ya no hay moros en la costa.
  ▪ *I'm going to raid the fridge. Let me know if the coast is clear.*
    Voy a asaltar el refrigerador. Avísame si no hay moros en la costa.

The latest rage
— **El último grito (de la moda)**
  ▪ *Look, these boots are the latest rage.*
    Mira, estas botas son el último grito (de la moda).

There's more than meets the eye
— **Hay mar de fondo; ha gato encerrado**
  ▪ *I don't believe that. There's more here than meets the eye.*
    Eso no lo creo. Aquí hay mar de fondo (hay gato encerrado).

There is no point . . . verb + ing
— **No tiene caso . . . + verb**
  ▪ *Calm down. There is no point losing your cool.*
    Cálmate. No tiene caso perder los estribos.

Through the grapevine
— **[Rumor]; [chisme]**
  ▪ *I heard it through the grapevine.*
    Es un rumor (chisme) que me llegó.

Under the table
— **Por debajo del agua**
  ▪ *I think the director's nephew gets something extra under the table every month.*
    Creo que el sobrino del director recibe dinero extra cada mes, por debajo del agua.

Wild goose chase
— **[Búsqueda inútil, infructuosa]**
  ▪ *As usual, you sent me out on another wild goose chase.*
    Como de costumbre, me enviaste a otra búsqueda inútil (infructuosa).

With flying colors
— **[Con gran éxito]**
  ▪ *Our company finished the year with flying colors.*
    Nuestra empresa terminó el año con gran éxito.

Expressions

Without batting an eye
— **Sin pestañear**
- *Reggie raised the gun and shot his wife's lover without batting an eye.*
  Reggie alzó la pistola y le disparó al amante de su esposa sin pestañear.

Without rhyme or reason
— **Sin ton ni son**
- *He was so drunk that he began to argue with everyone without rhyme or reason.*
  Estaba tan borracho que empezó a discutir con todos nosotros, sin ton ni son.

3. Stand-alone Expressions

A penny for your thoughts.
— **¿En qué piensas?**

Don't panic!
— **¡Que no cunda el pánico!**

Give him (her) an inch, and he'll (she'll) take a mile.
— **Le das la mano (a ☺) y ☺ se toma hasta el pie (brazo).**

He doesn't eat enough to feed a bird
— **Come como pajarito.**

He's every inch a man.
— **Es un hombre hecho y derecho.**

Hold your horses!
— **¡No te aceleres!**

It beats me!
— **¡Ni idea!**

I can dream, can't I?
— **Soñar no cuesta nada.**

It doesn't ring a bell.
— **No me suena.**

I mean it.
— **Lo digo en serio.**

I wouldn't dream of it!
— **¡Ni soñarlo!**

I wouldn't touch it with a barge pole (or a 10 ft. pole).
— **No lo tocaría ni con pinzas.**

Is that a threat or a promise?
— **¿Es promesa o amenaza?**

It rings a bell.
— **Me suena.**

It's a stone's throw from here.
— **Está a tiro de piedra de aquí. (Está tras lomita.)**

It was a slip of the tongue.
— **Lo dijo sin querer.**
— **Se le fue la lengua.**

It's about time!
— **¡Ya era hora!**

It's like looking for a needle in a haystack.
— **Es como buscar una aguja en un pajar.**

It's none of your business!
— Formal: **No es de tu (su) incumbencia.**
— Familiar: **No te importa. (¿Qué te importa?)**

It's not all fun and games.
— **No todo es miel sobre hojuelas.**

It's out of the question.
— **¡Imposible!**
— **¡Ni de chiste!**

It's raining cats and dogs.
— **Está diluviando.**
— **Está lloviendo a cántaros.**

No go
— **No se puede.**
— **No hay modo.**

Pipe down!
— **¡Cállate! (¡Cállense!)**
— ☺ **¡Bájale! (¡Bájenle!)**

Speaking of the devil...
— **Hablando del rey de Roma...**

Step on it!
— **¡Apúrate!**

Take a hike!; Take a flying leap!
— ♫ **¡Vete a la goma!**
— **¡Vete al diablo!**

Tell it to the marines!
— **¡A otro perro con ese hueso!**

That goes without saying.
— **No hace falta decirlo. Se sobreentiende.**

There is method in his madness.
— **Es más cuerdo de lo que parece.**

There is no love lost between them.
— **La antipatía es mutua.**

There's something fishy here.
— **Aquí hay gato encerrado**

What a nerve!
— **¡Qué poca vergüenza!**

You can't miss it.
— ♫ **No tiene pierde.**

Expressions

C. Proverbs and Sayings

There are heaps of sayings in any language, and Spanish is no exception. Whole tomes could be filled with sayings in Spanish, but due to obvious limitations, we are including here only the most common; i.e., the ones you hear all the time. We are providing two parts: the first with proverbs and sayings in Spanish, the second with proverbs and sayings in English.

1. In Spanish

The proverbs and sayings in Spanish are organized as follows:

A caballo dado no . . .   (Spanish proverb or saying)
— It's not nice to examine . . .   (A literal translation to give the reader the true feel of the saying)

▪ *Don't look a gift . . .*   (Equivalent saying in English, when there is one)

A caballo dado no se le ve el colmillo.
— It's not nice to examine a horse's eye tooth when the horse is a gift.
▪ *Don't look a gift horse in the mouth.*

A Dios rogando y con el mazo dando.
— Praying to God while hitting with the mallet.
▪ *God helps him who helps himself.*

A la tierra que fueres, haz lo que vieres.
— To the place you go, do what you see others do.
▪ *When in Rome, do as the Romans do.*

A la vejez, viruelas.
— Said when ❑ happens to an elderly person that normally happens in childhood or youth.

Expressions

Al mal paso, darle prisa.

— An unpleasant step should be taken quickly (if you've got to do something you don't like, do it quickly and get it over with).

- *Let's get this over with.*

Al nopal lo van a ver sólo cuando tiene tunas.

— A cactus is sought only when it bears fruit.

- *A friend in need is a friend in deed.*

A lo hecho, pecho.

— A deed done must be faced (own up to what you've done).

- *You have to face the music.*

Al que madruga, Dios le ayuda.

— Gods helps people who get up early.

- *The early bird catches the worm.*

Antes de que te cases, mira lo que haces.

— Before you get married, look what you do.

- *Look before you leap.*

Aquí, el que no corre, vuela.

— Here, those who don't run, fly.

- *Hang on to your back teeth* (when in danger of having ☐ stolen).
- ☺ *is/are razor sharp* (when in danger of being outwitted by ☺).

Aquí hay gato encerrado.

— There is a cat locked up here somewhere.

- *There's more to this than meets the eye.*
- *There's something fishy here.*

Árbol que crece torcido, nunca su rama endereza.

— You can't straighten out a tree that has grown twisted.

- *Once a crook (thief, bum, etc.) always a crook (etc.).*

Aunque la mona se vista de seda, mona se queda.

— A monkey dressed in silk is still a monkey.

- *You can't make a silk purse out of a sow's ear.*

Expressions

Barriga llena, corazón contento.
— Full belly, happy heart (the soul feels at rest after a good meal).

Caballo grande, ande o no ande.
— Big horse, even if it doesn't move (said when ☺ chooses a big person, car, etc., giving priority to size over character or performance).

Cada loco con su tema
— Every lunatic has an obsession (everyone has his/her own favorite subject; said when two or more persons are talking of different topics).

Cada oveja con su pareja.
— There's a ewe for every ram.
  - *Every Raggedy Ann has a Raggedy Andy.*

Candil de la calle y oscuridad de su casa.
— ☺ is a bright light in the street, and darkness at home (said of those who are helpful to strangers, friends and acquaintances, but not to members of his/her family).

Camarón que se duerme, se lo lleva la corriente.
— A sleeping shrimp is carried away by the current (you've got to keep on your toes).

Con dinero baila el perro.
— With money, you can even make a dog dance.
  - *Money makes the world go round.*

Cuando digo que la mula es parda, es porque tengo los pelos en la mano.
— When I say the mule is brown, it's because I have its hairs in my hand (I make an statement only when I can back it up with evidence).

Cuando el pobre tiene para carne, es vigilia.
— When there's money for meat, it's a meatless day (in the Catholic Church, no meat is eaten on certain days of the year).

Cuando no le llueve, le llovizna.
— When it isn't raining on ☺, it's drizzling on ☺.
  - *When it isn't one thing, it's another.*

Cuando veas las barbas de tu vecino cortar, pon las tuyas a remojar.
— If you see your neighbor shaving, get ready to be shaved (your neighbor's troubles may soon be yours too, so be prepared).

Del árbol caído todos hacen leña.
— Everyone makes firewood out of the fallen tree (everybody takes advantage of a person when he is down).

Del dicho al hecho hay mucho trecho.
— It's a long way from the word to the deed.
  - *Easier said than done.*

De tal palo, tal astilla.
— From such stick, such a chip.
  - *Like father, like son.*
  - ☺ *is a chip off the old block.*

Después de niño ahogado, tapen el pozo.
— They cover the well after the child has drowned.
  - *They close the barn door after the horse has bolted.*

Dime con quién andas y te diré quién eres.
— Tell me who you go around with and I'll tell you who you are (the kind of company you prefer shows the kind of person you are).

Dios aprieta, pero no ahorca.
— God squeezes your neck just tight enough not to asphyxiate you.
  - *God tempers the shorn lamb.*

Dios dice: ayúdate, que yo te ayudaré.
— God says: help yourself and I will help you.
  - *God helps those who help themselves.*

Dios los cría y ellos se juntan.
— God creates them, they get together.
  - *Birds of a feather flock together.*

Expressions

Echando a perder se aprende.
— You learn by making mistakes.
- *Experience is the best teacher.*

El corazón no se arruga; el cuero es el que envejece.
— The heart doesn't wrinkle. It's the hide that grows old (the heart remains young as the body grows old).

El león cree que todos son de su condición.
— The lion thinks everyone is like him (not everyone thinks and acts the way you do).

El que a buen árbol se arrima, buena sombra le cobija.
— He who takes cover under a good tree gets good shade (if you stick to a good person you will reap the benefits).

El que al cielo escupe, en la cara le cae.
— If you spit the sky, it will fall in your face.
- *To cut off your nose to spite your face.*

El que con lobos anda, a aullar se enseña.
— You learn how to howl when you keep company with wolves.

El que mucho abarca poco aprieta.
— If you try to grasp too much, you can apply very little pressure.
- *Don't bite off more than you can chew.*

El que persevera alcanza.
— He who perseveres, achieves his objective.
- *If at first you don't succeed, try, try again.*

El que porfía mata venado.
— He who persists kills the deer.
- *If at first you don't succeed, try, try again.*

El que quiera azul celeste, que le cueste.
— He who wants light blue will have to pay the cost (you must be prepared to pay for what you want).

♫ El que se va a la villa, pierde su silla.
— He who goes to town, looses his chair.

El que se va se divierte con lo verde del camino.
— He who goes somewhere enjoys the greenery along the way (said of a person who enjoys every tiny detail when he goes out).

♌ El que tiene más saliva, traga más pinole.
— He who has the most saliva, can swallow the most **pinole** (ground corn mixed with sugar and cinnamon).

En arca abierta, el más justo peca.
— When the till is open, even the most honest man becomes a sinner.

En la casa del herrero, azadón de palo.
— In the house of the blacksmith, they use a wooden hoe.

En tierra de ciegos, el tuerto es rey.
— In the land of the blind, the one eyed-man is king.
- *The halt leading the blind.*

En todas partes se cuecen habas.
— They cook beans everywhere (human nature is the same pretty well everywhere).

Hijo de tigre, pintito.
— The tiger's offspring has stripes.
- *Like father, like son.*

Las apariencias engañan.
— Appearances are deceiving.
- *You can't judge a book by its cover.*

Lo barato sale caro.
— Cheap things turn out to be expensive.

Lo que no fue en tu año, no fue en tu daño.
— What didn't happen in your year, doesn't hurt you (you have no reason to feel hurt by something that happened before you met your sweetheart, spouse, etc.).

Expressions

Lo paseado (cantado) y lo bailado no hay quien (te) lo quite.
— No one can take away the good times you've had.

Mala hierba nunca muere.
— Weeds never die (bad people seem to live forever).

⌘ **Mala p'al metate, buena p'al petate.**
— She's bad at the **metate** (housework), but good for the **petate** (bed).

Manos frías, corazón ardiente.
- *Cold hands, warm heart.*

Más tiene el rico cuando empobrece que el pobre cuando enriquece.
— The rich man who loses his wealth is richer than the poor man who attains wealth.

Más vale tarde que nunca.
- *Better late than never.*

Más vale malo conocido que bueno por conocer.
— It's better to stick with something you know is bad, than to opt for something that you think is better, but you still haven't tried.

Más vale pájaro en mano que ciento volando.
— It's better to have a bird in hand than a hundred flying.
- *A bird in hand is worth two in the bush.*

Más vale paso que dure y no trote que canse.
— A slow pace that lasts is better than a tiring trot

Más vale que digan aquí corrió y no aquí murió.
— I'd rather people said "here he ran" than "here he died".

Más vale solo que mal acompañado.
— Better to be alone than in unpleasant company.

Matrimonio y mortaja, del cielo baja.
— Marriage and the shroud come from heaven (marriage and death happen when God decides it's time; one has nothing to do with the decision).

Nadie sabe el bien que tiene hasta que lo ve perdido.

— No one appreciates a good thing until he finds himself without it.

Ni amor reanudado, ni chocolate recalentado.

— A rekindled romantic relationship is as bad as reheated chocolate (don't try to fan up an old romance, as it will have the bitter flavor of reheated chocolate).

Ni tanto que queme al santo, ni tan poco que no le alumbre.

— Don't place the candle so close to the saint that you burn it, or so far away that it can't be seen (don't go to extremes).

No dejes que se te suban los humos a la cabeza.

— Don't let the smoke go up to your head.
  - *Don't get too big for your boots.*

No hay camino más seguro que el acaban de robar.

— There is no safer road than a road where a robbery has just occurred.

No hay mal que por bien no venga.

— There's nothing bad that does not come for good.
  - *Every cloud has a silver lining.*

No hay peor lucha que la que no se hace.

— There is no worse battle than that which is not fought (you should give things a try before giving up on them).

No puedes andar y quieres correr.

— You can't walk and you want to run.
  - *You have to walk before you run.*

No se puede repicar y andar en la procesión.

— You can't ring the church bells and take part in the procession at the same time.
  - *You can't have your cake and eat it too.*

No sirvas a quien sirvió, ni mandes a quien mandó.

— Don't serve ☺ who has been a servant, or boss ☺ who has been a boss.

No todo el monte es orégano.

— The vegetation on the hill isn't all oregano.
  - *It's not all peaches and cream.*

Expressions

No todo es miel sobre hojuelas.
— It's not all honey over the flakes.
- *It's not all fun and games.*

Nunca falta un roto para un descosido.
— It doesn't matter how undesirable or ugly a person may be, there's always ☺ somewhere who's in the same boat and is willing to have a relationship with ☺.
- *There's always a Raggedy Ann for a Raggedy Andy.*

Obras son amores, no buenas razones.
— Love is actions, not words.
- *Actions speak louder than words.*

Ojos que no ven, corazón que no siente.
— When eyes don't see, the heart doesn't feel.
- *What you don't know can't hurt you.*

O todos coludos o todos rabones.
— Either they all have tails, or none of them do (a call for equality and fairness).

Palo dado, ni Dios lo quita.
— When the blow has fallen, not even God can take it away.
- *Don't cry over spilt milk.*

Para que la cuña apriete, ha de ser del mismo palo.
— A wedge won't fit tightly unless it's made of the same wood.
- *It takes a thief to catch a thief.*

Para todo mal, mezcal; para todo bien, también.
— Take **mezcal** for all ills, and for all good things too.

Perro que ladra no muerde.
— A barking dog doesn't bite.
- *His bark is worse than his bite.*

Quien de su casa se aleja, no la halla como la deja.
— He who ventures away from his home does not find it the same on his return (a warning not to abandon home, business or valuable possessions).

Quien parte y comparte, se queda con la mejor parte.
— He who divides something up and hands it out keeps the best piece for himself.

Quien pega primero, pega dos veces.
▪ *He who strikes first strikes twice.*

Quien ríe al último ríe mejor.
▪ *He who laughs last laughs best.*

Sabe más el diablo por viejo que por diablo.
— The devil knows so much, not because he is the devil, but because he's old (age brings wisdom).

Salir más caro el caldo que las albóndigas.
— The broth is more expensive than the meatballs (something is more trouble than it's worth).

Santo que no es visto, no es venerado.
— A saint not seen is not revered (personal contact is important).

Siempre se rompe el hilo por lo más delgado.
— The thread always breaks where it is thinnest.
▪ *A chain is only as strong as its weakest link.*

Si una vela se te apaga, que otra te quede encendida.
— If one candle goes out, you had better have another one lit.
▪ *Don't put all your eggs in one basket.*

Soñar no cuesta nada.
— To dream costs you nothing.

Tanto peca el que mata la vaca como el que le tiene la pata.
— The man who ties up the cow is just as guilty as the fellow who slits its throat.

Todas las cosas se parecen a su dueño.
— All things resemble their owner.

Expressions

Todo por servir se acaba.
— All things wear out if you use them.

Todo cabe en un jarrito, sabiéndolo acomodar.
— Everything fits in a little pot if you know how to put things in (a bag or container will hold everything if it is properly arranged).

Una golondrina no hace verano.
- *One swallow does not a summer make.*

Una imagen dice más que mil palabras.
— A picture says more than a thousand words.
- *A picture is worth a thousand words.*

Un ojo al gato y otro al garabato.
— One eye on the cat, and the other one on the scribble.
- *Keep you eye on the eight ball.*

2. In English

Proverbs and sayings in English are organized as follows:

A bird in hand is . . . **(English proverb or saying)**
- **Más vale pájaro . . .** (Equivalent saying in Spanish)

A bird in hand is worth two in the bush.
- **Más vale pájaro en mano que cien (ciento) volando.**

A picture is worth a thousand words.
- **Una imagen dice más que mil palabras.**

A watched pot never boils.
- **El que espera, desespera.**

Actions speak louder than words.
- **Obras son amores, no buenas razones.**

All that glitters is not gold.
- **No todo lo que relumbra es oro.**

An ounce of prevention is worth a pound of cure.
- **Más vale prevenir que remediar (lamentar).**

Appearances are deceiving.
- **Las apariencias engañan.**

Better late than never.
- **Más vale tarde que nunca.**

Birds of a feather flock together.
- **Dios los cría y ellos se juntan.**

Blood is thicker than water.
- **Duele más el cuero que la camisa.**

Cold hands, warm heart.
- **Manos frías, corazón ardiente.**

Charity begins at home.
- **La caridad por casa empieza.**

Expressions

Don't cast pearls before swine.
- **No les tires margaritas a los puercos.**

Don't cry over spilled milk.
- **Palo dado, ni Dios lo quita.**
- **[Ya ni llorar es bueno]**

Don't bite off more than you can chew.
- **El que mucho abarca poco aprieta.**

Every cloud has a silver lining.
- **No hay mal que por bien no venga.**

Familiarity breeds contempt.
- **No hay rey para el ayuda de cámara.**

God helps him who helps himself.
- **A Dios rogando y con el mazo dando.**
- **Dios dice: ayúdate que yo te ayudaré.**

God tempers the shorn lamb.
- **Dios aprieta, pero no ahorca.**

He laughs best who laughs last.
- **El que ríe al último, ríe mejor.**

He's a chip of the old block.
- **De tal palo, tal astilla.**

He who pays the piper calls the tune.
- **El que paga, manda.**

His bark is worse than his bite.
- **Perro que ladra no muerde.**

If at first you don't succeed, try, try again.
- **El que porfía mata venado.**
- **El que persevera alcanza.**

If you can't beat 'em, join 'em.
- **Si no puedes con ellos, únete a ellos.**
- **Si no se puede vencer, hay que aliarse.**

In the land of the blind, the one-eyed man is king.
- **En tierra de ciegos, el tuerto es rey.**

It's a long lane that has no turning.
- **No hay mal que dure 100 años.**

It's always darkest before the dawn.
- **Nunca está más oscuro que cuando va a amanecer.**

Jack of all trades, master of none.
- **Aprendiz de todo, oficial de nada.**

Like father, like son.
- **Hijo de tigre, pintito.**
- **De tal palo, tal astilla.**

Look before you leap.
- **Antes de que te cases, mira lo que haces.**

Marriages are made in heaven.
- **Matrimonio y mortaja, del cielo baja.**

Money makes the world go round.
- **Poderoso caballero es don dinero.**
- **Con dinero baila el perro.**

One good turn deserves another.
- **El amor con amor se paga.**

One man's meat is another man's poison.
- **En gustos se rompen géneros.**

One swallow does not a summer make.
- **Una golondrina no hace verano.**

Out of sight, out of mind.
- **Ojos que no ven, corazón que no siente.**

Silence is consent.
- **El que calla, otorga.**

Still waters run deep.
- **Líbreme Dios del agua mansa, que de la brava me cuido (libro) yo.**

Expressions

The early bird gets the worm.
- **Al que madruga, Dios lo ayuda.**

The fat is in the fire.
- **La cosa ya no tiene remedio.**

The pot calling the kettle black.
- 🕮 **El comal le dijo a la olla.**
- **El burro hablando de orejas.**

The proof is in the pudding.
- **A las pruebas me remito.**

The road to hell is paved with good intentions.
- **El camino al infierno está empedrado de buenas intenciones.**

There are more ways than one to skin a cat.
- **Hay muchos modos de matar las pulgas.**

There's many a slip twixt the cup and the lip.
- **Del plato a la boca, se cae la sopa.**

There's more to it than meets the eye.
- **Aquí hay mar de fondo.**

Two's company, three's a crowd.
- **Dos es compañía, tres es multitud.**

What can't be cured must be endured.
- **A lo hecho, pecho.**

What's sauce for the goose is sauce for the gander.
- **Todos coludos o todos rabones.**
- **Todos hijos o todos entenados.**

When in Rome, do as the Romans do.
- **A la tierra que fueres, haz lo que vieres.**

When it rains, it pours.
- **Siempre llueve sobre mojado.**
- **Las desgracias nunca vienen solas.**

Where there's smoke, there's fire.
- **Cuando el río suena, agua lleva.**

Expressions

You can't get a leopard to change his spots.
- **Genio y figura, hasta la sepultura.**

You can't have your cake and eat it too.
- ⌕ **No se puede chiflar y comer pinole.**
- **No se puede repicar y andar en la procesión.**

You can't judge a book by its cover.
- **Las apariencias engañan.**

You can't make a silk purse out of a sow's ear.
- **Aunque la mona se vista de seda, mona se queda.**

You have to learn to walk before you can run.
- **No puedes andar y quieres correr.**

Expressions

II

SLANG IN MEXICO

A. Common Slang Expressions

Slang is not the easiest part of a language to get down in black and white in such a way as to convey to the non-native speaker the exact meaning and feeling of each of the thousands of juicy tidbits that are the hot sauce on the meat of any language. But that won't keep us from trying. However, what we can't offer to do is cover all regional slang in Latin America. That would take a lifetime of complicated research. A lot of these expressions are used in Mexico, but many are used throughout Latin America. Expressions used only in Mexico have the 🏵 symbol.

Generally speaking, we would advise students of Spanish to go easy on the use of slang. It's very easy to get things screwed up and look silly. Perhaps a good idea would be to take them gradually, one by one, and make sure you understand all the subtle nuances before you start using them. We are providing them here so that you'll have an idea of what native speakers are talking about when they use slang, which they do in practically every sentence in normal conversation.

Remember that slang in any language is usually coarse, often vulgar, and sometimes embarrassing in polite company, so be careful when and where you try it out. Latin Americans tend to be much more polite and refined with people they don't know well than Americans, who use slang in any and all situations. This Section is divided into:

1. *Verbs*
2. *Slang expressions used as part of a sentence (Non-Verbs)*
3. *Stand-alone slang expressions*

Unless otherwise indicated, you should assume that all the slang in this section is about a ⇩ level for vulgarity. In other words, it's plain ordinary slang that, although vulgar, would offend no one. Naturally, there is plenty of very vulgar (even filthy) slang, but you'll have to look under *Not for Polite Society* for that. Persons who are not criminals often use words or expressions marked as *underworld jargon*. Many of the words marked ✝✝ which are coined and used by teenagers, often seep into the speech of older people.

---

1. VERBS

Acabar(sele) el veinte a ☺ (📖 To have your coin run out)
— To be too late; to run out of time
- **Perdiste tu oportunidad. Ya se te acabó el veinte.**
  It's too late. That was your last chance.

†† Acelerar(se)
— To get uptight, annoyed, carried away, angry, etc.
- **Mira, chavo, no te aceleres, porque te puede ir mal.**
  Hey! Don't get all worked up, because you could get the short end of the stick.

⌐ Achicopalar(se)
— To become very sad, frightened and discouraged
- **Tu enfermedad no es nada grave. No te achicopales.**
  Your illness is nothing serious. Don't look so glum.

Agarrar con las manos en la masa a ☺
— To catch ☺ red-handed.
- **Agarramos a Juan con las manos en la masa.**
  We caught Juan red-handed.

⌐ Agarrar de botana a ☺
— To make fun of someone
- **¡Creo que ya te agarraron de botana!**
  I think they're making fun of you.

⌐ Agarrar(se) del chongo (📖 To grab each other by the bun of hair at the back of the head, figuratively speaking)
— To brawl; to fight (applied only to women)
- **Las sirvientas de mi vecina se agarraron del chongo.**
  My neighbor's maids got into a fight.

Agarrar en caliente a ☺◻
— To strike while the iron is hot
- **Hay que agarrarlos en caliente, antes de que se arrepientan.**
  We must strike while the iron is hot, before they change their minds.

⌐ Agarrar en curva a ☺
— To catch ☺ off-guard
- **Carlos me agarró en curva cuando me propuso matrimonio.**
  Carlos caught me off-guard when he proposed to me.

- **Algunas preguntas de la prueba me agarraron en curva.**
  I wasn't prepared for some of the questions on the test.

🔲➕ Agarrar la onda

— To get in the groove; to get the picture; to get with it

- **Ay, cuate, estás en la luna. ¡Agarra la onda!**
  Hey! You really don't have the foggiest idea what is going on. Get with it!

Agarrar su patín (📖 To grab your skate)

— To start and/or keep doing 🔲 and be unable to stop

- **Cuando tocamos el tema de la música, Jorge agarró su patín y no paró de hablar.**
  When we got on the subject of music, Jorge started to talk and nobody could stop him.

🔲 Agüitar(se)

— To become disheartened

- **¿Te sientes mal? Se te ve muy agüitado.**
  Are you all right? You look very down in the mouth.

Ahuecar el ala (📖 To curve your wings and take off)

— To leave; to go away; to take off

- **En un ratito voy a tener que ahuecar el ala.**
  In a little while, I'm going to have to take off.

🔲 Alebrestar(se)

— To get all riled up

- **No te metas con Chava. Se alebresta con mucha facilidad.**
  Don't pick on Chava. He gets upset very easily.

🔲➕ Alivianar(se)

— To cheer up; to get high

- **Ya no estés triste. ¡Aliviánate!**
  Don't be sad. Cheer up!

🔲 Amolar(la)

— To do 🔲 crumby; to spoil things

- **¡Cómo eres! ¡La amolaste!**
  That was a crumby thing to do!

🔲 Andar chueco(a) (📖 To be crooked)

— To be in trouble with the law, usually as concerns the authorities, especially the tax authorities

- **Tu empresa anda muy chueca fiscalmente.**
  Your company's tax situation is really not at all straight.

Andar en fachas (📖 To go around in sloppy clothes)

— To be dressed in dreadful old rags; to look awful (as concerns clothes)

- **¡Sí, vamos al cine! Ando en fachas, pero puedo estar lista en media hora.**
  Yes, let's go to the movies! I look awful, but I can be ready in half an hour.

♘†† **Andar erizo(a)**
— To be in need of a drug; to need a fix.
- **Mira al Beto: hace tres días que no se inyecta y anda bien erizo.**
  Look at Beto. He hasn't had a thing for three days and he really needs a fix.

♘†† **Andar hasta la madre**
— To be blind drunk
- **Cuando Pancho salió de la fiesta, andaba hasta la madre (hasta las manitas).**
  When Pancho left the party, he was totally plastered.

♘ **Andar hasta las manitas** (see **Andar hasta a madre**)

♘×†† **Andar jólidei** (euphemism for a very rude word. See *Not for Polite Society*)
— To be broke
- **Oye Jorge, pásame una feria, que ando jólidei.**
  Hey, George, lend me some dough. I'm flat broke.

♘ **Andar volado(a)**
— To be very keen on ☺; to be infatuated with ☺ who is not likely to pay much attention to you
- **Luis anda bien volado con la maestra.**
  Luis is gaga over the teacher.

♘ **Apantallar**
— To impress
- **Los voy a apantallar a todos con mi título.**
  I'm going to impress them all with my university degree.
- **No vas a apantallar a nadie con esos musculitos.**
  You're not going to impress anyone with those puny little muscles.

♘ **Apantallar(se)**
— To allow yourself to be impressed or to allow ☺ to put one over on you.
- **De veras me apantallé con todo lo que hablaba ella de su dinero, sus casas y sus viajes. Se lo creí todo.**
  She really took me in with all her talk about her money and houses and trips. I believed every word of it.

♘ **Apapachar a** ☺
— To cuddle; to neck (sweetly and tenderly)
- **Anoche te vi en el cine apapachando a tu novia.**
  I saw you cuddling with your girlfriend at the movies last night.

♘ **Apergollar a** ☺
— To take advantage of ☺; to use ☺
- **Ya me cansé de que mis parientes me estén apergollando.**
  I'm sick of my relatives using me.

Slang in Mexico

ᒍ **Apoquinar; caer(se); caer(se) con la lana**
— To pay up; to hand over the dough; to fork it over
- **Tarde o temprano vas a tener que apoquinar (caerte, caerte con la lana).**
  Sooner or later you're going to have to pay up.

ᒍ†† **Aterrizar**
— To come back down to Earth after the effects of marijuana
- **Con lo que te las tronaste, vas a aterrizar hasta mañana.**
  After all that grass, you're not going to come to your senses until tomorrow.

ᒍ†† **Atizar** (see **Tostar(se)**)

Averiguar(selas)
— To look out for yourself
- **¡No necesito tu ayuda! ¡Puedo averiguármelas solo!**
  I don't need your help. I can look out for myself.

Babosear a ☺
— To push ☺ around
- **Te equivocas si crees que me puedes babosear.**
  You're mistaken if you think you can push me around.

ᒍ **Barbear (**see **Hacer(le) la barba a** ☺ and **Ser barbero)**
— To suck up to ☺; to flatter ☺
- **No ganarás nada con barbear a tu profesor.**
  You won't get anywhere by sucking up to the teacher.

Bocabajear a ☺
— To humiliate ☺
- **Ni creas que me van a poder bocabajear.**
  You're not going to make me look bad, you know.

Cabecear
— To doze off in a sitting position.
- **Yo no era la única que estaba cabeceando durante el concierto.**
  I wasn't the only one who was dozing off during the concert.

Cachar granizo (📖 To catch hail as it falls)
— To be or act gay (men)
- **El sobrino de Raquel anda cachando granizo.**
  Rachel's nephew is acting effeminate.

ᒍ↓ **Cachondear(se)**
— To neck (with a lot of hand action)
- **No se estén cachondeando aquí.**
  Go neck somewhere else.

🔓 **Caer(se)** (see **Apoquinar**)

🔓 **Caer(se) con la lana** (see **Apoquinar, ¡Caifás con la lana!, ¡Cayitos!** and **Pasar una corta**)

🔓 **Caer(se) de la reata (del mecate)**
— To be caught or found out lying
- **No olvides que dijimos que estábamos de viaje. No nos vayamos a caer de la reata.**
  Don't forget we said that we were away on a trip. We don't want to be caught in a lie.

Caer(le) de variedad a ☺
— To be amusing to ☺
- **El baboso de tu primo me cayó de variedad.**
  That silly cousin of yours is really amusing.

🔓 **Caer(le) el chahuistle a** ☺ (📖 To have your corn suddenly blighted by a deadly plant disease **(chahuistle)**)
— To have really bad luck; to have ❒ awful happen (like an unpleasant visit)
- **Llegaron tus cuñados. ¡Ahora sí nos cayó el chahuistle!**
  Your brothers in law have arrived! Now we're really in for it!
- **A Toño le cayó el chahuistle. Le hicieron una auditoría fiscal y le estimaron 250 mil pesos de impuestos omitidos.**
  Toño is having a hard time. He had an official tax review and they assessed 250 thousand pesos in unpaid taxes.

Caer(le) (a ☺**) el veinte** (this refers to ❒ not working until the coin drops and makes things go, like a public telephone)
— To finally realize or understand ❒
- **No me cayó el veinte de lo que estaba sucediendo hasta que ya era demasiado tarde.**
  I didn't realize what was going on until it was too late.
— To catch on
- **¿Cuándo te cayó el veinte de que Marta no te quería, sino que te estaba utilizando?**
  When did you finally catch on that Marta didn't love you and was only using you?

🔓 **Caer(le) gordo(a) a** ☺ (📖 To fall heavily on ☺)
— To be obnoxious
- **¡Cómo me cae gordo que me hagan eso!**
  I really hate it when people do that to me!
- **¿Por qué tengo que trabajar con Teodoro? Me cae gordo.**
  Why do I have to work with Teddy? I don't like him.

Slang in Mexico

Cargar(se) el pintor a ☺; llevar(se) el tren a ☺
— To be or get fed up

- **Juan está que se lo carga el pintor.**
  Juan is extremely upset.
- **¡Me lleva el tren! ¡Mira lo que le hicieron a mi coche!**
  God almighty! Look what they did to my car!

Carrerear a ☺
— To pressure ☺ into doing ☺□ really fast

- **Al pobre de Leonardo lo carrerean mucho en el trabajo.**
  They've got poor Leonardo working like a maniac.

Chacotear
— To horse around; to fool around

- **¡No estén chacoteando en clase!**
  Don't fool around in class!

Chanclear (📖 To clump around)
— To dance

- **Esos chavos se han pasado toda la fiesta chancleando.**
  Those kids haven't stopped dancing all night.

Chiquear
— To spoil ☺

- **Si sigues chiqueando a tu sobrino, no va a haber quien lo aguante.**
  If you keep on spoiling your nephew, he's going to be unbearable.

Chivear(se)
— To be overcome by shyness or embarrassment

- **Héctor siempre se chivea cuando llega Alicia.**
  Hector always clams up when Alicia comes into the room.

Chupar (📖 To suck) (see **Ponerse un cuete, inflar**)
— To drink (alcohol)

- **Cuando Abelardo se pone a chupar, a veces desaparece durante una semana.**
  When Abelardo gets to drinking, he sometimes vanishes for as long as a week.
- **Lo único que realmente le gusta a mi hermano es chupar con sus amigotes.**
  The only thing my brother really likes is to drink with his pals.

Clavar(se) □
— To steal □; to pinch □

- **¡Alguien se clavó mi pluma!**
  Someone pinched my pen!

Slang in Mexico

⚐ Colgar los tenis (📖 To put up your tennis shoes because you're not going to need them anymore)
— To die; to kick the bucket; to kick off
- **Me acaban de decir que el viejito que vivía a dos casas colgó los tenis hace un rato.**
  I just found out that the old guy who lived a couple of houses down kicked the bucket just a while ago.

⚐ Cotorrear
— To chat
- **Ponte a trabajar. Llevas toda la mañana cotorreando.**
  Get to work. You have been chatting all morning.

⚐ Cotorrear a ☺
— To pull someone's leg
- **Eso no es cierto. Me estás cotorreando, ¿verdad?**
  That can't be true. You're pulling my leg, aren't you?

⚐ Cuatrapear(sele)
— To get things all mixed up
- **Me hice un lío; se me cuatrapearon las palabras.**
  I made a mess of things; I got the words all mixed up.

♯♯ Dar(se) color
— To realize ❑
- **¡Date color ñeris! Te están viendo la cara.**
  Wake up! They're making fun of you.

Dar(le) cosa a ☺ (see **Dar(le) cus cus a** ☺ and **Dar ñáñaras**)
— To give ☺ the heebee jeebies
- **Siempre que veo una tarántula me da cosa.**
  Tarantulas give me the heebee jeebies.

Dar(le) cus cus a ☺ (📖 To give ☺ the creeps) (see **Dar(le) cosa a** ☺ and **Dar ñáñaras**)
— To be afraid of ☺❑
- **Lo siento, pero no voy a entrar a la caverna con ustedes. Me da cus cus.**
  I'm sorry, but I'm not going into the cave with you. It gives me the creeps.
— To be afraid to do ❑
- **Me da cosa pedirle tu mano a tu papá.**
  I'm afraid to ask your father for your hand in marriage.

Dar(le) duro y tupido
— To do ❑ with all you've got
- **Tenemos muy poco tiempo. ¡Tenemos que darle duro y tupido!**
  We have very little time left. We got to give it our all!

Slang in Mexico

🏵 **Dar el magueyazo** (to fall over from the effects of the **maguey** plant, from which **pulque**, an indigenous alcoholic drink is made in Mexico)
— To fall over drunk
- **Mira cómo va Lorenzo. Está a punto de dar el magueyazo.**
  Look at Lorenzo weaving around. He's about to fall on his face.

Dar el ranazo (📖 To fall like a frog . . . bellyflop)
— To fall heavily
- **¡Iba bajando las escaleras y me di un ranazo tremendo!**
  I was going down the stairs and I fell like a ton of bricks!

Dar el viejazo
— To suddenly become or look old; to lose your youthful looks
- **¿No te parece que Alma está dando el viejazo?**
  Don't you think Alma has aged a lot recently?

Dar entrada; dar jalón
— To flirt; to invite advances
- **¡No le estés dando entrada a todos los muchachos en el baile!**
  Don't be flirting with all the guys at the dance!

Dar jalón (see **Dar entrada**)

🏵 **Dar(le) madruguete a** ☺
— To catch ☺ off-guard
- **El partido de oposición le dio madruguete al partido en el poder.**
  The incumbent party was caught off-guard by the opposition party.

🏵 **Dar mastuerzo** (see **Dar matarile**)

🏵 **Dar matarile a** ☺; 🏵**dar mastuerzo a** ☺; **dar sonaja a** ☺
— To kill; to finish off; to bump off
- **Con su permiso, les voy a tener que dar matarile a los tamales.**
  With your permission, I'm going to have to finish off those tamales.
- **¿Supiste que les dieron mastuerzo a los judiciales que andaban asaltando a la gente?**
  Did you know they bumped off the secret police who were holding people up?

🏵 **Dar(le) ñáñaras a** ☺□ (see **Dar(le) cosa a** ☺□ and **Dar(le) cus cus a** ☺□)
— To give ☺ the creeps or the heebie jeebies
- **No tolero que me pongan inyecciones. Me da ñáñaras**
  I can't stand injections. They give me the creeps.

Dar(se) paquete; ♭dar(se) taco
— To be conceited or snotty
- **Emilio me cae mal, porque se da mucho paquete (taco).**
  I don't like Emilio because he's very conceited.

♭ Dar pendiente (see Estar con el pendiente)

Dar(se) paquete (see Dar(se) taco)

Dar(le) un guamazo a ☺
— To give ☺ a terrific blow
- **Paco me acaba de dar un guamazo sin querer.**
  Paco unintentionally just gave me a terrible whack.

Dar un mal paso
— To get pregnant as a result of an affair; to get knocked up
- **Dio un mal paso cuando era muy joven.**
  She got pregnant when she was a girl.

†† Dar(se) un pasón (see Dar(se) un toque)

†† Dar(se) un pegue (see Dar(se) un toque)

Dar(le) un sablazo a ☺
— To hit ☺ for a loan
- **Sospeché que me iba a dar el sablazo.**
  I knew he was going to hit me for a loan.

♭ Dar sonaja (see Dar matarile)

♭†† Dar(se) un toque; dar(se) un pasón; dar(se) un pegue
— To smoke a joint
- **Esos dos cuates que están en el baño se están dando un toque.**
  Those two guys in the john are smoking a joint.

♭ Dar(le) vuelo a la hilacha
— To really let go and do ❑ uninhibitedly
- **Cuando estuvo en Francia, le dio vuelo a la hilacha.**
  When he was in France, he really went wild.

♭ Desconchinflar(se)
— To go on the blink; to break down
- **Esta porquería de licuadora ya se volvió a desconchinflar.**
  This crumby blender has broken down again.

Slang in Mexico

Deschongar a ☺ (see Agarrar(se) del chongo)
— To rough up ☺ in a brawl
- **A Lola la deschongaron por andar de buscapleitos.**
  Lola got roughed up because she's such a troublemaker.

📖 Despepitar
— To talk; to sing (provide information)
- **Golpearon al reo para que despepitara todo.**
  They beat up the convict to make him talk.

📖 Dormir la mona
— To sleep it off
- **Javier bebió demasiado, y está durmiendo la mona.**
  Javier had too much to drink, and he's sleeping it off.

📖 Echar aguas
— To warn ☺; to tell ☺ when it's OK to move or do ❑
- **Está difícil sacar el coche del garaje en este eje vial tan lleno de tránsito. ¡Échame aguas!**
  It's hard to get the car out of the garage onto this freeway. Let me know when there's a break in the traffic.
- **Voy a clavarme unas de las galletas que dejó ahí Elisa. Échame aguas por si se aparece.**
  I'm going to steal some of the cookies that Elisa left there. Tell me if you see her coming.

Echar ajos y cebollas
— To curse
- **El jefe está furioso; está echando ajos y cebollas.**
  The boss is furious; he's cursing like crazy.

Echar(se) la soga al cuello (📖 To put the noose around your neck)
— Commit to ❑ you can't live up to
- **No prometas terminar el trabajo para mañana; no te eches la soga al cuello.**
  Don't offer to finish the work tomorrow, you know you can't.

📖 Echar(le) la viga a ☺ (📖 To throw the beam at ☺)
— To bawl the hell out of ☺
- **Hoy si me va a echar la viga mi jefe.**
  My boss is really going to bawl the hell out of me today.

📖 Echar(le) los canes a ☺ (see Echar(le) los perros a ☺)

📖 Echar(le) los perros (los canes) a ☺ (📖 To set the dogs on ☺)
— To flirt with ☺; to make a pass at ☺

- **Juan me está echando los perros (los canes) con ganas.**
  Juan is really flirting with (making passes at) me like crazy.

Echar relajo

— To joke around; to fool around noisily; to have a lot of noisy fun

- **Los muchachos de la preparatoria siempre van echando relajo en el camión.**
  The high school kids are always fooling around and making a lot of noise on the bus.
- **A Paula le encanta echar relajo, esté donde esté.**
  Paula loves to joke around, no matter where she is.

⏚ Echar rollo

— To go into a great deal of confusing and roundabout details about ☐, intentionally or not

- **Jorge me estuvo echando rollo durante media hora.**
  George went into a long spiel that lasted half an hour.

⏚ Echar(se) un taco

— To eat ☐ fast

- **No me tardo, voy a echarme un taco y regreso.**
  I won't be long. I'll just have something quick to eat.

⏚ Echar taco de ojo

— To get an eyeful of ☺; to give your eyes a treat

- **Seguramente está en la disco, echando taco de ojo.**
  He'd surely be at the disco, getting an eyeful.

⏚ Echar(se) un farolazo

— To have a shot (a drink); to knock one back

- **Esta cantina es muy pintoresca. Vamos a echarnos un farolazo**
  This cantina is very picturesque. Let's have a shot there.

⏚ Echar un fon (from *phone*)

— To give ☺ a ring (telephone call)

- **Si quieres, en la noche te echo un fon.**
  If you want, I'll give you a ring tonight.

⏚ Echar un torito (📖 To throw a little bull)

— To throw out a hard question

- **Me echaron un torito que no pude contestar.**
  They threw me a question I couldn't answer.

⏚ Echar(se) un trompo a la uña (📖 To make a top spin on your fingernail)

— To do ☐ really difficult

Slang in Mexico

- **¡Échate ese trompo a la uña!**
  Let's see what you can do about that (very difficult) problem! or *Figure that one out!*

📖 **Echar vidrio** (📖 To cast an eye; **vidrio** refers to glass marbles, usually blue, which resemble eyeballs)
— To take a look at ☐; to get a load of ☐
- **Nada más échale vidrio a lo que me regaló mi papá.**
  Just take a look at what my father gave me.

📖 **Empacar(se)** (📖 To pack food in); **entrar(le) al pipirín**
— To eat
- **¿Cómo le hiciste para empacarte cuatro tortas gigantes?**
  How in the world did you manage to stuff four large sandwiches into your face?
- **Vamos a entrarle al pipirín. Ya tengo hambre.**
  Let's eat. I'm hungry.

Empinar el codo (📖 To bend your elbow)
— To drink to excess
- **Le encanta empinar el codo.**
  He loves to spend his time drinking.

📖 **Encajar(se)**
— To abuse a relationship with ☺
- **El mecánico se encajó al cobrar la compostura del coche.**
  The mechanic certainly overcharged for the car job.

📖 **Encuetar(se)** (see **Estar cuete** and **Poner(se) un cuete**)
— To get drunk
- **Hijo, no tomes tanto porque te vas a encuetar.**
  Son, don't drink that much, or you'll get drunk.

📖 **Enchinchar**
— To bother ☺; to waste ☺'s time
- **Ese muchacho sólo está enchinchando a mi hija.**
  That young man is simply wasting my daughter's time.

📖 **Enchufar(se)** ☐ (📖 To plug in ☐)
— To eat ☐ hurriedly
- **Voy a enchufarme un par de tacos.**
  I'm going to have a couple of tacos on the run.
— To be well connected
- **Ernesto está bien enchufado en Hacienda.**
  Ernesto is very well connected at the Internal Revenue Service.

⌘ Entrar(le) al pipirín (see Empacar(se))

⌘ Escabechar(se) a ☺

— To kill ☺

- ¿Viste? Este tipo de la foto se escabechó al policía que lo quiso detener.
  Look! The guy in this picture killed the policeman who was trying to arrest him.

Estar (andar) a la cuarta pregunta

— To be totally broke

- Desde la quiebra de su negocio, está a la cuarta pregunta.
  Since his business failed, he's been totally broke.

⌘ Estar abusado(a), estar buso(a) (buso, a corruption of abusado) (see Ser abusado(a))

— To be smart, clever, shrewd, astute

- Hay que estar muy busos para que no nos agarren usando la copiadora del jefe.
  We really have to be on the lookout so we don't get caught using the boss's copy machine.

⌘ Estar a medios chiles

— To be a bit drunk

- Amado se pone muy chistoso cuando está a medios chiles.
  Amado is very funny when he's had a few drinks.

Estar bueno(a) (see Ser un mango)

— To be really very physically attractive

- Esa muchacha está muy buena.
  That girl is luscious (divine).

↓ Estar (andar) cachondo(a) (see Cachondear(se), ser cachondo(a))

— To be horny

- No sé por qué hoy estoy tan cachondo.
  I don't know why I feel so horny today.

⌘ Estar canijo (see Ser canijo)

— To be tough, difficult to deal with

- Este examen está muy canijo.
  It's a very tough test.
- ¿Te quieres ir de aquí a San Antonio en coche sin parar? ¡Está canijo!
  You want to drive from here to San Antonio nonstop? That's going to be tough!

Estar con el pendiente; dar pendiente

— To worry; to concern; to make ☺ nervous

Slang in Mexico

- **Mi hija se fue a Cuernavaca manejando sola. Estoy con el pendiente (me da pendiente).**
  My daughter is driving to Cuernavaca all by herself. I'm really nervous about it!

📖 **Estar crudo(a)** (📖 To be raw)

— To have a hangover
- **No me hables tan fuerte. Estoy un poco crudo.**
  Don't talk so loud. I'm a bit hung over.

📖 **Estar cuete** (see **Poner(se) un cuete**)

— To be drunk
- **Está cuete desde el martes.**
  He's been drunk since Tuesday.

Estar de la cachetada (📖 To be like a slap in the face)

— To be awful
- **Ultimamente el tiempo ha estado de la cachetada.**
  The weather has been awful recently.

📖 **Estar en chino** (see **Estar canijo**)

📖 **Estar en cueros**

— To be (or run around) naked
- **Estoy en cueros. Espérame tantito.**
  Wait a second. I haven't got any clothes on.

Estar (andar) en la baba (📖 To be drooling)

— To be off on a cloud; to be daydreaming
- **Chocaste porque siempre estás en la baba cuando manejas.**
  You wrecked the car because you're always off on a cloud when you drive.

Estar (andar) escamado(a)

— To be burnt, wary
- **Desde el asalto, Edmundo anda muy escamado.**
  Since the mugging, Edmundo has been very wary.

Estar fúrico(a) (see **Estar trabado(a)**)

📖 **Estar hasta atrás** (see **Estar hasta el cepillo**)

📖⬇ **Estar hasta la madre** (see **Estar hasta el cepillo**)

📖 **Estar hasta las manitas** (see **Estar hasta el cepillo**)

ꝑ **Estar hasta el cepillo** (📖 To be full up to the brush (hair) with drink); ꝑ**estar hasta atrás; estar tomado;** ꝑ**estar hasta la madre;** ꝑ**estar hasta las manitas** (see **Poner(se) hasta el cepillo**)

— To be totally drunk (or drugged)

- **No sé por qué Pedro siempre tiene que estar hasta el cepillo los sábados por la noche.**
  I don't understand why Pedro always has to be plastered on Saturday nights.

ꝑ **Estar hecho(a) bolas** (see **Hacer(se) bolas**)

ꝑ **Estar hecho un camote** or **encamotar(se)**

— To be all confused about ☐

- **Te dije que tomaras el curso de computación. Estás hecho un camote (encamotado).**
  I told you! you should take the computer course. Now you're all mixed up.

ꝑ **Estar hecho un cuero** (see **Ser un cuero** and **Ser un mango**. Also see **Estar en cueros.** Be sure not to confuse these expressions!)

— To be absolutely gorgeous (people only)

- **El hijo de Miguel está hecho un cuero.**
  Miguel's son is a hunk of a guy (absolutely gorgeous).

ꝑ **Estar negro(a)** (see **Estar trabado(a)**)

Estar para el arrastre

— To be in a terrible state

- **Después de caminar diez kilómetros, estoy para el arrastre.**
  After walking ten kilometers, I'm fit to be carted away.

ꝑ **Estar pelón (pelona)** (📖 To be bald)

— To be hairless

- **¿Por qué está pelón el niño?**
  Why is that kid bald?

— ꝑTo be difficult

- Speaker A: **¿Crees acabar todo ese trabajo?**
  Think you can finish the job?

  Speaker B: **No estoy seguro. ¡Está pelón!**
  I'm not too sure. It's pretty complicated!

Estar pendiente (de ☐)

— To be on the lookout (for ☐); to be on the alert (for ☐); to keep an eye out for ☐ or on ☐)

- **Van a entregar la tarjeta de crédito mañana. Procura estar pendiente.**
  They're going to deliver the credit card tomorrow. Be on the lookout for it.

Estar plagado(a) de ☺□
— To be full or overrun by ☺□
- **La fiesta estaba plagada de chilangos.**
  The party was crawling with people from Mexico City.
- **Tu carta estaba plagada de errores.**
  Your letter was full of mistakes.

†† Estar super
— To be terrific
- **La fiesta de Paulina estuvo super.**
  Pauline's party was wonderful!

Estar tomado(a) (see Estar hasta el cepillo)

Estar trabado(a)*; estar negro(a); estar fúrico(a)
— To be fit to be tied; to get absolutely furious
- **El director está trabado (negro) de coraje (fúrico).**
  The director is fit to be tied.
Note: **Trabado** is also "very muscular".

♪⇩ Fajar(se) a ☺
— To neck with ☺; to indulge in heavy petting with ☺
- **Mira, ésos en el coche se están fajando.**
  Look, those people in the car are really necking.
- **Pepe se está fajando a Marta.**
  Pepe is really going at it with Marta.

♪ Fajar(se)
— To work really hard
- **Estamos muy atrasados y tendremos que fajarnos duro para terminar el trabajo.**
  We are behind with the work and have to work really hard to catch up.
— To fight really hard
- **Los boxeadores se fajaron en el segundo round.**
  The boxers fought really hard during the second round.

Fajar(se) los pantalones con ☺
— To get strict; to put your foot down; to get tough with ☺
- **Si no te fajas los pantalones con tu hijo, te va a dar muchos problemas.**
  If you don't put your foot down with your son, he's going to become a real problem.

⇩ Fregar a ☺ (see Jorobar)
— To bother ☺
- **¡No estés fregando!**
  Stop bothering me!

Slang in Mexico

⇩ **Fregón** (n.)
— Someone who is the best at ☐ or at everything; also used to refer to someone who is a pest
   ▪ **Alfredo fue el que localizó el teléfono del presidente. ¡Qué fregón!**
     Alfredo found out the President's phone number. He is really good!
   ▪ **¡Ya párale, muchacho fregón!**
     Stop it, you little pest!

🏳 **Frijolear**
— To bawl ☺ out
   ▪ **¡Ora sí, Pancracio, te va a frijolear el patrón!**
     You're really going to get it from the boss this time, Pancracio!

🏳†† **Friquear(se)** (from the English *To freak out*)
— To freak out; to be impressed; to be afraid of ☐ or ☺
   ▪ **Pepe se friqueó cuando vio a los guaruras.**
     Pepe freaked out when he saw the bodyguards.

🏳†† **Grifear**
— To smoke marijuana
   ▪ **No seas tonto. Aquí no podemos grifear.**
     Don't be dumb. We can't have a joint here.

🏳 **Grillear** (see **(La) grilla**)

Gorrear; gorronear (see **De gorra** and **Gorrón**)
— To get ☐ for free; to bum ☐
   ▪ **Vengo a gorrearte un café.**
     I came to bum a cup of coffee off you.

🏳 **Haber cocas en el refri** (see **Haber moros en la costa** in *Common Expressions in Spanish*)

Haber pájaros en el alambre (see **Haber moros en la costa** in *Common Expressions in Spanish*)

Hacer(se) . . . *
— To play dumb
   ▪ **Tú acusaste a Juan. ¡No te hagas!**
     You squealed on Juan. Don't play dumb!
*   Euphemism. The dots represent a rude word, which is usually just left unsaid.

Hacer(se)

— To pee (more rarely to poop; i.e., have a bowel movement) in your pants; to wet your pants; to dirty your pants

- **¡Me estoy haciendo!**
  I'm peeing in my pants.

Hacer(se) bolas; hacerse pelotas

— To get (be) confused; to get (be) mixed up

- **Necesitas repetirme todo. Ya me hice bolas (pelotas).**
  You need to tell me everything all over again. I'm all mixed up.

Hacer(se) del baño; hacer del baño*

— To pee or to poop in your pants

- **El niño se hizo del baño.**
  The kid peed (or pooped) in his pants.

— To go to the bathroom

- **En un rato voy a tener que hacer del baño.**
  I'm going to have to go to the bathroom in a while

* The usual expression for going to the bathroom is **ir al baño**.

Hacer(se) del dos; hacer del dos

— To poop in your pants

- **El bebé se hizo del dos tres veces en la mañana.**
  The baby pooped three times this morning.

— To poop

- **Si no hace del dos, le doy ciruelas pasas.**
  If he doesn't have a bowel movement, I'll give him some prunes.

Hacer(se) del uno; hacer del uno

— To pee

- **Pedrito a veces se hace del uno en la clase.**
  Pedrito sometimes pees in his pants in class.

— To pee

- **Haz del uno antes de irnos.**
  Go pee before we leave.

⌕ Hacer(se) bolas (pelotas)

— To get mixed up, confused

- **Se hizo bolas con los precios.**
  He got all mixed up with the prices.

× **Hacer caca** □ (see **Hacer pinole** □ and see **Caca** under *Not for Polite Society*)

— To destroy □

- **Reparte los naipes. Te voy a hacer caca.**
  Deal the cards. I'm going to destroy you.
- **Hizo caca el coche.**
  He totaled the car.

ᗐ **Hacer(le) de chivo los tamales a** ☺ (▢ To put goat meat in ☺'s tamales)

— To cheat ☺; to give ☺ a raw deal; to be unfaithful to ☺

- **Creo que a Rubén le están haciendo de chivo los tamales.**
  I think Ruben is getting a raw deal.

ᗐ **Hacer(la) de emoción; hacer(la) de tos**

— To overdo or drag □ out too long; to make a big thing of □

- **Ya dale al niño su regalo. No se la hagas de emoción (de tos).**
  Give the kid his present and stop making such a big thing of it.

⇩ **Hacer(se) el buey; hacer(se) el difunto;** ⇩ **hacer(se) el idiota; hacer(se) el (la) loco(a); hacer(se) el (la) menso(a);** ᗐ **hacer(se) el (la)muerto(a);** ᗐ**hacer(se) el(la) occiso(a);** ᗐ **hacer(se) el (la) tarugo(a); hacer(se) el (la)tonto(a);** ᗐ**hacer(se) la mosquita muerta; hacer(se) maje**

— To play dumb, or to pretend you don't know or notice □ because it would go against your interests to do so

- **¡Te estoy hablando! ¡No te hagas el muerto!**
  I'm talking to you! Don't play dumb!
- **Cuando llegó la cuenta, Gildardo se hizo el loco.**
  When they brought the bill, Gildardo pretended he didn't notice.

Note: This expression, in any of its variations, merits the symbol for vulgarity, but note that some of the variations make it quite vulgar.

Hacer(se) el (la)difunto(a) (see **Hacer(se) el buey**)

Hacer(le) el fuchi a ☺□

— To turn up your nose at ☺□

- **Espero que Leticia no le haga el fuchi a este regalo.**
  I hope Leticia doesn't turn up her nose at this present.

⇩ **Hacer(se) el (la) idiota(a)** (see **Hacer(se) el buey**)

Hacer(se) el (la) loco(a) (see **Hacer(se) el buey**)

Hacer(se) el (la) menso(a) (see **Hacer(se) el buey**)

Slang in Mexico

♄ **Hacer(se) el (la) muerto(a)** (see **Hacer(se) el buey**)

♄ **Hacer(se) el (la) occiso(a)** (see **Hacer(se) el buey**)

♄ **Hacer(se) el (la) tarugo(a)** (see **Hacer(se) el buey**)

Hacer(se) el (la) tonto(a) (see **Hacer(se) el buey**)

Hacer(le) el vacío a ☺
— To avoid ☺; to spurn ☺
▪ **Algo pasa con Pepe. Donde quiera que llega, le hacen el vacío.**
There's something wrong with Pepe, because everywhere he goes, people keep away from him.

Hacer(le) la barba a ☺ (see **Barbear**)
— To suck up to ☺
▪ **Raquel siempre le hace la barba al maestro, para sacar buenas calificaciones.**
Rachel is always sucking up to the teacher, just to get good grades.

Hacer(se) la mosquita muerta (see **Hacer(se) el buey**)

Hacer(le) los mandados a ☺ (📖 To do ☺'s errands)
— To be ☺'s inferior; to be a pipsqueak, a nothing
▪ **¿Para qué tengo que pedirle su opinión a mi primo? Ese cuate me hace los mandados.**
Why should I ask my cousin for his opinion? He's a nobody.

Hacer maje a ☺
— To cheat ☺; to pull a fast one on ☺
▪ **Me hicieron maje con el cambio.**
They cheated me with the change.

Hacer(se) maje (see **Hacer(se) el buey**)
— To play dumb
▪ **Todos sabemos que Alberto perdió la llave, pero se hace maje.**
We all know Albert lost the key, but he plays dumb.

Hacer (una) pataleta
— To have a tantrum
▪ **Espero que no hagas tu pataleta como de costumbre.**
I hope you don't throw your usual tantrum.

Hacer(se) pelotas (see **Hacerse bolas**)

Hacer picadillo ☐ (see **Hacer pinole** ☐)

♌ **Hacer pinole** ☐; ✕ **hacer caca** ☐; **hacer picadillo** ☐

— To break ☐ to smithereens; to break ☺'s heart, image or confidence; to beat ☺ at a game

- **La muchacha tiró el jarrón y lo hizo pinole (✕ caca, picadillo).**
  The girl dropped the jar and broke it to smithereens.

- **Jugó muy mal el domingo pasado, y su contrincante lo hizo picadillo.**
  Last Sunday he played very badly, and his opponent beat the crap out of him.

♌ **Hacer su numerito**

— To do ☐ ridiculous

- **Armando está tan borracho, que no tarda en hacer su numerito.**
  Armando is so drunk that it won't be long before he makes a fool of himself.

Hacer sus necesidades (see **Hacer(se))**

— To pee or poop

- **El cochino perro hizo sus necesidades a media sala.**
  The dirty dog peed (and/or pooped) right in the middle of the living room.

♌ **Hacer talacha**

— To change a tire; to do minor car repairs or do minor handyman's jobs around the house

- **Mientras ellos se divierten, aquí me tienen haciendo talacha.**
  While they're out having a good time, I'm here doing the dirty work.

♌†† **Hornear(se)**

— To inhale marijuana smoke in a closed room or place.

- **¡Mira! Aquellos que están en ese coche se están dando una horneada bárbara.**
  Look! Those guys cooped up in the car are breathing pure marijuana smoke.

♌⬇ **Importar una pura y celestial . . .** *

— To not care; To not give a damn

- **Ese asunto me importa una pura y celestial . . .**
  I don't give a damn about all that.

* Euphemism. The dots represent a very rude word, which is usually just left unsaid.

♌⬇ **Inflar** (📖 To inflate yourself) (see **Chupar** and **Poner(se) un cuete**)

— To drink (alcohol)

- **Chano y Pancho se fueron a la cantina a inflar.**
  Chano and Pancho went to the bar to drink.

♌ **Ir(se) con la finta**

— To be taken in by ☺☐; to fall for ☐

- **Hubo el rumor de que se cancelaba la junta. Yo me fui con la finta y fui el único que faltó.**
  There were the rumor that the meeting was canceled. I fell for it and I was the only one missing.

Ir (salir, venir) disparado (see **Ir (salir, venir) hecho la mocha)**

Slang in Mexico

Ir (salir, venir) hecho la mocha; ir (salir, venir) volando; ir (salir, venir) disparado (📖 To go, come, etc., like a shot)
— To come or go in a great hurry
- **¡Vente a mi casa hecho la mocha! Tengo algo que enseñarte.**
  Get over to my place as fast as you can! I have something to show you.
- **Ana se fue volada cuando supo que había barata en Liverpool.**
  Anna went running off to Liverpool (a department store in Mexico) the minute she found out they had a sale.
- **Se me acabó el tiempo. Tendré que salir disparado.**
  I've run out of time. I'll have to run.

Ir (salir, venir) volando (see Ir (salir, venir) hecho la mocha)

Jeringar (📖 To pump a syringe) (see Jorobar)
— To bother ☺ consistently; to pester
- **Ya sabes que Rogelio va a estar jeringándote todo el día hasta que le prestes el coche.**
  You know that Rogelio is going to be pestering you all day till you lend him the car.
- **¡Ya no me estés jeringando!**
  Stop bugging me!

⚑⇓ Jorobar (this is an euphemism for an extremely obscene word) (see Jeringar)
— To bother ☺ constantly; to bug ☺; to pester ☺
- **A Manuel le encanta estar jorobando a su hermanos.**
  Manuel loves to bug his brothers.

Jugar(sela)
— To take a risk or a chance
- **Sé perfectamente que me la estoy jugando.**
  I know perfectly well that I'm taking a chance.

Latir(le)
— To have a hunch; to have a gut feeling
- **Me late que lo hicieron a propósito.**
  I have a hunch they did that on purpose.
- **Este billete de lotería no me late en absoluto.**
  Something tells me this lotto number is not a winner.

Librar(la) (📖 To get around or over an obstacle, such as a hurdle)
— To be successful at ☐; to manage to do ☐
- **No estaba seguro si iba a poder terminar mis estudios universitarios, pero la libré.**
  I wasn't sure if I was going to be able to get my university degree, but I succeeded.

⚑ Llevar(se) el tren a ☺ (see Cargar(se) el pintor a ☺)

🄿 **Madrugar(le) a** ☺ (see **Dar(le) el madruguete a** ☺)
— To pull a fast one on ☺
- **Irene se descuidó y le madrugaron con su bolsa.**
  Irene wasn't paying attention and she had her purse stolen.

Maliciar ☐
— To have a bad hunch about ☐; to smell ☐ fishy
- **Estoy maliciando que hay algo chueco en este asunto.**
  I smell something fishy in this affair.

🄿 **Malorear a** ☺ (see **Ser malora**)
— To bother people; to pick on ☺
- **Ya me cansé de que me estés maloreando.**
  I'm tired of the way you're always bothering me.

🄿 **Mandar por un tubo a** ☺ (📖 To send ☺ down a pipe, presumably the one leading down from the toilet bowl)
— To send ☺ to hell
- **Le pedí el préstamo al gerente, pero me mandó por un tubo.**
  I asked the manager for the loan, but he sent me to hell.

🄿 **Mandar(se)**
— To go too far; to get carried away
- **Sírvete lo que quieras, pero no te mandes.**
  Help yourself to whatever you want, but don't get carried away.

🄿 **Mangonear a** ☺
— To manipulate ☺; to boss ☺ around; to push ☺ around
- **Elvira mangonea a su marido todo el tiempo y él ni por enterado se da.**
  Elvira is always pushing her husband around, and he doesn't even notice.

🄿 **Menear el bote** (📖 To wiggle your bucket); 🄿**mover el bote** (📖 To move your can)
— To dance
- **Ya estuvimos mucho rato sentados. ¡Vamos a menear el bote!**
  We've been sitting down for ages. Let's dance!
- **Pepe es muy bueno para mover el bote.**
  Pepe is a good dancer.

⬇ **Mentar la madre a** ☺ (see *Not for Polite Society*)
— To insult ☺
- **¿Por qué no le pegaste al tipo que te mentó la madre?**
  Why didn't you sock that guy who insulted you?

Slang in Mexico

Meter la pata (see **Regar el tepache)**
— To put your foot in it
  ▪ **Felipe tuvo que meter la pata.**
    Felipe just had to put his foot in it.

🕮 **Mochar a** ☺
— To cut off
  ▪ **Mónica ya no es mi amiga, la moché por gacha.**
    Monica is no longer my friend. I cut her off for being so mean to me.

🕮 **Mochar(se)**
— To share ☐ with ☺
  ▪ **¡Traes dos tortas! Móchate con una, ¿no?**
    You brought two tortas. Share one with me!

Mover(le) el tapete a ☺ (🕮 To move the rug under ☺'s feet)
— To plot against ☺
  ▪ Speaker A :   **¿Crees que Romero dure mucho como líder del sindicato?**
                     Do you think Romero will last long as union leader?
    Speaker B: **¡Quién sabe! Le están moviendo el tapete.**
                     Who knows! They're plotting against him.

Nacer(le) ☐ (see **Tener ganas** in *Common Expressions in Spanish*)
— To feel like doing ☐
  ▪ **Me hice el tatuaje porque me nació, ¿y qué?**
    I had the tattoo done because I felt like it. Want to make something of it?
  ▪ **Francamente no me nace ir a visitarlos.**
    Frankly I don't feel like going to see them.

Navegar con bandera de tonto(a) (🕮**tarugo(a))** (🕮 To sail around flying the "dumb" flag)
— To go through life pretending to be not too bright
  ▪ **El jefe navega con bandera de tonto (tarugo), pero hay que tener cuidado con él.**
    The boss pretends to be a bit dumb, but you've got to be careful with him.

🕮 **Ningunear a** ☺ (from **ninguno**: none or no one)
— To ignore or pay no attention to ☺
  ▪ **La maestra ningunea a mi hija y eso me molesta mucho.**
    The teacher simply ignores my little girl, and that really bothers me.

🕮 **No dar paso sin guarache** (🕮 Not to take a step without a Mexican sandal)
— To not do anything unless there is some kind of advantage to be had
  ▪ **Manuel es muy ventajoso. No da paso sin guarache.**
    Manuel is very self-centered. He does nothing if there isn't something in it for him.

📖 **No hacer(la)** (📖 To not make it)
— To fail to qualify or be up to par
  ▪ **Le pedí a Rosa que me ayudara con la redacción de este artículo, pero nomás no la hace.**
    I asked Rosa to give me a hand with the wording in this article, but she hasn't got what it takes.

📖 **No saber ni a jícama (ni a melón)**
— An expression used to describe ❑ insipid; to be unchallenging
  ▪ **Ya les volvimos a ganar al póker. No nos supieron ni a jícama (ni a melón).**
    We won again at poker. Those guys aren't good enough for us.

No tener caso (📖 To have no case)
— Not to be worth it; to be pointless
  ▪ **Acaban de avisar que no vienen. No tiene caso preparar los canapés.**
    They just advised us they are not coming. There's no point in making the hors d'oeuvres.

No tener chiste
— To be of no interest
  ▪ **Este libro no tiene chiste.**
    This book is not interesting.

📖 **Parar(se) de pestañas** (📖 To stand on your eyelashes)
— To have a fit (of anger)
  ▪ **Espérate a que tu mamá vea lo que hiciste. ¡Se va a parar de pestañas!**
    Wait till your mother sees what you've done. She's going to have a fit!

📖†† **Pasar(se)** (see Tostar(se))

📖†† **Pasar(le) a** ☺
— To like ☺❑
  ▪ **El profe de química me pasa un resto.**
    I like the chemistry teacher a whole lot.

Pasar(sele) las cucharadas a ☺ (📖 To have too many spoonfuls)
— To drink too much; to have one too many
  ▪ **No quiero discutir contigo. Ya se te pasaron las cucharadas.**
    I don't want to argue with you; you've had one too many.

📖 **Pasar una corta** (see **Apoquinar**)
— To fork out some dough; to bribe; to grease ☺'s hand
  ▪ **Vas a tener que pasar una corta si quieres que te arreglen el problema.**
    You're going to have to pay out some money if you want this problem fixed.

Pegar con tubo (📖 To wham with a pipe)
— To be very successful or very impressive.

Slang in Mexico

- **El mariachi no tuvo mucho éxito en Belice, pero en Venezuela pegó con tubo.**
  The mariachi didn't cause much of a stir in Belize, but people went wild over them in Venezuela.
- **Esa chava me pegó con tubo.**
  I fell for that girl like a ton of bricks.

Pegar(le) un grito a ☺
— Let ☺ know; to give ☺ a yell; to give ☺ a holler
- **Si necesitas algo, pégame un grito.**
  If you need anything, give me a yell.

Pescarlas al vuelo (📖 To catch them in the air or in flight)
— To be as bright as a new penny, as sharp as a knife
- **Ni creas que le vas a tomar el pelo. Él siempre las pesca al vuelo.**
  Don't think you're going to fool him. He's as sharp as a knife.

🔈 Petatear(se) (From **petate**, a palm mat used as a bed)
— To kick the bucket
- **Filemón se petateó cuando menos se esperaba.**
  Filemon kicked the bucket quite unexpectedly.

🔈 Pichicatear
— To be stingy; to be a miser
- **Lupe siempre pichicatea la comida.**
  Lupe is very stingy with the food.

🔈⇩ Pintar un violín (Refers to a rude gesture; it doesn't mean the person actually made the gesture)
— To thumb one's nose at ☺; to send ☺ to hell
- **Le dije que terminara el trabajo, pero me pintó un violín.**
  I told him he had to finish the work, but he ignored me.
— To go back (back down) on a promise
- **Pedro prometió llevarme a la ciudad, pero se me hace que me va a pintar un violín.**
  Pedro promised to take me into town, but I bet he's going to break his promise.
— To disregard a debt
- **Tito me está pintando un violín con el dinero que me debe.**
  Tito has no intention of paying back what he owes me.

🔈 Poner(se) a tono con ☺
— To act the same way as ☺
- **No te pongas a tono con esos imbéciles.**
  Don't stoop to the level of those idiots.

🗫 **Poner(se) abusado(a); poner(se) aguzado(a); poner(se) buso(a) (abusado** and **buso** are a corruption of **aguzado:** sharp, alert**)**
— To be on the alert for an opportunity or an eventuality
- **Tienes que ponerte buso (abusado) en la entrevista, si quieres que te den el puesto.**
  You have to really be on the ball during the interview if you want to get the job.

🗫 **Poner(se) aguzado(a)** (see **Poner(se) abusado(a)**)

🗫 **Poner(se) buso(a)** (see **Poner(se) abusado(a)**)

🗫 **Poner(se) hasta atrás** (see **Poner(se) hasta el cepillo**)

🗫↓ **Poner(se) hasta la madre** (see **Poner(se) hasta el cepillo**)

🗫 **Poner(se) hasta las manitas** (see **Poner(se) hasta el cepillo**)

Poner(sele) (a ☺) la carne de gallina (📖 To get chicken skin); **poner(le) (a ☺) los pelos de punta** (📖 To make your hair stand up on end)
— To give ☺ goose bumps; to really scare ☺
- **Aquel grito en la oscuridad nos puso los pelos de punta (la carne de gallina).**
  That scream in the dark really gave us the creeps (goose bumps).

Poner(le) los cuernos a ☺ (📖 To put horns on ☺)
— To be unfaithful to ☺; to cuckold ☺
- **Nunca le he puesto los cuernos a Lucía.**
  I've never been unfaithful to Lucia.

Poner los ojos como platos (📖 To have your eyes get as big as plates)
— To become very surprised or overwhelmed with amazement
- **Cuando la niña vio el árbol de Navidad con todas esas luces y adornos de colores, puso los ojos como platos.**
  When the little girl saw the Christmas tree with all the lights and colored ornaments, she was overcome with awe.

Poner(le) (a ☺) los pelos de punta (see **Poner(le) (a ☺) la carne de gallina**)

🗫 **Poner(se) hasta el cepillo; poner(se) hasta atrás; ↓ poner(se) hasta la madre; poner(se) hasta las manitas; poner(se) un cuete** (see **Chupar** and **Inflar**)
— To get drunk; to tie one on
- **Creo que Adolfo no va a llegar a trabajar hoy. Anoche se puso un cuete tremendo.**
  I don't think Adolfo will be coming in to work today. He drank himself silly last night.

🗫 **Poner(se) un cuete** (see **Poner(se) hasta el cepillo**)

Slang in Mexico

𝄢 **Poner(se) una soba**
— To be worn out (very tired)
- **Necesitamos un par de días de descanso. Nos pusimos una soba con el cambio de casa.**
  We need a couple of days to rest. We are worn out after the move.

𝄢 **Quebrar a** ☺ (Underworld jargon)
— To kill ☺
- **Al Felipe se lo quebraron en medio de la calle.**
  They killed Felipe in the middle of the street.

𝄢 **Quedar de la cachetada** (see **Estar de la cachetada** and **Quedar del cocol**)
— To turn out very badly
- **Adalberto no supervisó la pintura de su casa, y quedó de la cachetada.**
  Adalberto didn't supervise the paint work on his house, and it looks just dreadful.

𝄢 **Quedar del cocol** (see **Quedar de la cachetada**)
— To turn out very badly
- **Con sus malos modos, Chabela quedó del cocol.**
  Chabela made a terrible impression with those awful manners of hers.

𝄢⇩ **Quedar(se) jetón** (📖 To fall into a state where your face is all distorted)
— To fall asleep
- **No sé para qué traigo a Jaime al cine. Ya se quedó jetón.**
  I don't know why I bring Jaime to the movies. He's dropped off to sleep.

𝄢 **Quemar(se)** (📖 To burn yourself)
— To do ☐ that makes a very bad impression
- **Se quemó por sus malos modales para comer.**
  He made a terrible impression with his bad table manners.

𝄢 **Rajar(se)** (📖 To split open)
— To go back on your word
- **Pedro se rajó cuando supo que iba a tener que acompañar a Lidia.**
  When Pedro found out that he would to have to accompany Lidia, he backed out.

Rebotar
— To return; to bounce (checks)
- **Me rebotaron el cheque por falta de fondos.**
  They returned the check for lack of funds.

𝄢⇩ **Refrescar(sela) a** ☺ (📖 To refresh ☺'s memory about ☺'s mother)
— To call ☺ an S.O.B.
- **Si ese tipo me sigue fastidiando, voy a refrescársela.**
  If that guy keeps it up, I'm going to have to tell him what I think of him.

📖 **Regar el tepache** (📖 To spill the **tepache**, a pre-Columbian drink made from fermented pineapple)**; regar(la)** (📖 To spill it); **meter la pata** (📖 To stick your foot in it)

— To put your foot in it; to screw things up

- **Me suponía que Anselmo iba a regar el tepache (a regarla, a meter la pata).**
  I was sure Anselmo was going to screw things up.

—— * Also, to get pregnant without intending to

- **La tonta de Cuca metió la pata con Andrés.**
  That stupid Cuca really put her foot in it (got pregnant) with Andres.

📖 **Regar(la)** (see **Regar el tepache**)

📖 **Repelar**

— To be a grump; to complain

- **No es para tanto. Ya deja de repelar.**
  It's no big deal. Stop grumbling.

📖 **Retachar**

— To send ☺📖 back

- **Retacharon a Luis de la escuela, por no llevar uniforme.**
  They sent Luis home from school because he wasn't wearing his uniform.

📖 **Sacar(le) a 📖**

— To have or get cold feet

- **Jaime le saca a jugar con Luis, porque sabe que va a perder.**
  Jaime is afraid to play with Luis because he knows he will lose.

📖 **Sacar de onda** (📖 To get ☺ off the wavelength)

— To confuse ☺; to throw ☺ for a loop

- **Con lo que dijiste, me sacaste de onda por completo.**
  You confused me completely with what you said.

📖 **Salir bailando** (📖 To end up dancing)

— To get the short end of the stick

- **Es un pésimo negocio del que vamos a salir bailando.**
  It's a terrible business and we're going to get the short end of the stick (lose our shirt).

📖 **Salir con su batea de babas** (📖 To do 📖 in a slobbering way)

— To say or do 📖 stupid (like a child still in the drooling stage)

- **Te pido un favor. En la junta no salgas con tu batea de babas, como de costumbre.**
  Do me a favor. Don't say anything stupid at the meeting, the way you usually do.

Slang in Mexico

Salir(se) del huacal (📖 To get out of the cage (made of sticks, used to take produce and small animals to market))
— To resist authority
  - **Mis hijos se me están queriendo salir del huacal.**
    My children are beginning to resist my authority at home.

Sentir(se) muy sabroso(a) (📖 To feel that you're yummy)
— To feel that you're superior, or very good or unbeatable at ☐ when that is not always the case
  - **Jorge se está sintiendo muy sabroso, pero va a acabar con las narices rotas.**
    Jorge obviously thinks he's hot stuff, but he's going to end up with a bloody nose.

Sentir (oír) pasos en la azotea (📖 To hear steps on the flat rooftop)
— To have a hunch that ☐ is going to happen; to imagine things
  - **Ya siento pasos en la azotea. No tarda en llegar mi jefe y yo no he terminado con el trabajo.**
    I just know the boss will be here any minute, and I haven't finished this work.
  - **Este cuate siente pasos en la azotea.**
    That guy has bats in the belfry.

Ser abusado(a) (see **Estar abusado(a)**)
— To be on the lookout (**abusado** is a corruption of **aguzado**, from **aguzar**: to be sharp, alert)
  - **No sabía que Efrén era tan abusado. El solito le hizo el ajuste a su coche.**
    I didn't know Efrén was so smart. He overhauled his car all by himself.

Ser barbero(a) con ☺
— To suck up to ☺
  - **Ernesto es un barbero con todos los profesores.**
    Ernesto sucks up to all his teachers.

Ser canijo(a) (see **Estar canijo** and **Ser (muy) mula**)
— To be mean
  - **No le pidas nada a Arturo. Es muy canijo.**
    Don't ask Arturo for anything. He's a mean bastard.

Ser cachondo(a) (see **Cachondear(se), estar cachondo(a)**)
— To be sexually attractive; to be hot
  - **Susana es una chava muy cachonda**
    Susana is quite a sexy girl.

Ser chinche
— To waste ☺'s time
  - **Vámonos antes de que llegue Rafael. Es muy chinche.**
    Let's get going before Rafael comes and takes up all our time.

Ser del año de la canica (see **Ser del año del caldo**)

Ser del año del caldo (📖 To date back to the year in which broth was invented)**; Ser del año de la canica** (📖 To date back to the year in which marbles were invented)
— To be as old as the hills
- **¡Esta foto de tus padres es del año del caldo (del año de la canica)!**
  This picture of your folks is as old as the hills!

📖 **Ser encajoso(a)**
— To be pushy or try to take advantage of people
- **Me está usted cobrando mucho. No sea encajoso.**
  You are overcharging me. That's unfair.
- **Armando es muy encajoso. Siempre me está pidiendo prestado el coche.**
  Armando is a pain. He's always wanting to borrow my car.

📖 **Ser (hacer(se)) guaje**
— To be (to pretend to be) stupid
- **¿Tu hermano es guaje, o nomás se hace guaje?**
  Is your brother really stupid, or does he just pretend to be?

📖 **Ser jalador(a)**
— To go along with everything; to cooperate
- **Rodolfo nunca se niega; es muy jalador.**
  Rudolf never says no. He's very cooperative.

Ser largo(a) como la cuaresma (📖 To be as long as Lent)
— To be very long, interminable, very slow to conclude
- **Estaba muy cansada y la clase estuvo larga como la cuaresma.**
  I was very tired and the class dragged on forever.
— To be exaggerated; to tell every single detail; to be a deceiver or a leg-puller
- **No le creas. Este cuate es largo como la cuaresma.**
  Don't pay any attention to him. He is such a leg-puller.

📖 **Ser malora** (see **Malorear**)
— To be ☺ who likes to bother people; to pick on ☺
- **Tu tío es muy malora.**
  Your uncle is a real pest.

📖 **Ser (muy) mariachi** (📖 To be a mariachi)
— To be a wimp
- **¡Cómo eres mariachi! En toda la noche no sacaste a bailar a Laura.**
  You're a real wimp! You never got up the nerve to ask Laura to dance.

Ser (muy) mula (📖 To be a mule) (see **Ser canijo**)
— To be mean
- **Perdona que te lo diga, pero tu hermano ha sido muy mula contigo.**
  Excuse me for saying so, but your brother has been very mean to you .

🕮 Ser nagual
— To act stupid
- **¡Ah, cómo eres nagual!**
  Boy are you dumb!

Ser terco(a) como una mula
— To be stubborn or hardheaded
- **Tengo horas tratando de convencerlo, pero no lo logro. ¡Es terco como una mula!**
  I've been trying to convince him for hours, but I can't. He's really hardheaded.

🕮 Ser un cuero (🕮 To be a piece of hide) (see **Ser un mango**)
— To be handsome or good-looking (both sexes)
- **Esa chava es un auténtico cuero.**
  That girl is knockout.

Ser un hígado (🕮 To be a liver)
— To be totally obnoxious
- **No soporto al novio de Sandra. Es un hígado.**
  I can't stand Sandra's boyfriend. He's unbearable.

Ser un mango (🕮 To be a ripe, luscious, juicy fruit) (see **Ser un cuero**)
— To be gorgeous, a hunk, to be hot; to be very physically attractive (both sexes)
- **El jefe es un mango, ¿no te parece?**
  The boss is a hunk, don't you think?

🕮 Ser una ficha
— To be a shady or crooked character (a cad, scoundrel, swindler, con artist)
- **No me imaginé que Roberto fuera toda una ficha.**
  I never imagined that Roberto was such a crook.

Sudar(le) el copete (see **Sudar la gota gorda**)

Sudar la gota gorda (🕮 To sweat fat drops of perspiration); **sudar(le) el copete** (🕮 To get sweat on your brow); **sudar tinta** (🕮 To sweat ink)
— To have a hard time; to sweat blood; to get in a sweat
- **Con ese examen sudé la gota gorda (me sudó el copete, sudé tinta).**
  I really sweated that test.

Sudar tinta (see **Sudar la gota gorda**)

🕮 Tapar(le) el ojo al macho (🕮 To cover a male animal's eyes so he won't see a female in heat, the implication being that covering his eyes is a useless gesture)
— To make a vain attempt to hide ☐
- **Se van a dar cuenta del faltante. No podremos taparle el ojo al macho.**
  They are sure to find out about the missing tapes. There's no way we can hide the shortage.

🕮 Tatemar (nahuatl)
— To roast lightly

- **Vamos a tatemar esos elotitos.**
  We are going to roast some fresh corn.

ᕤ Tatemar(se) (nahuatl) (see Quemar(se))

— To get burned, or to make a fool of yourself

- **Si haces esa tontería, te vas a tatemar.**
  If you do such a silly thing, you're going to get burned (to make a fool of yourself).

Tener (traer) botado de (la) risa a ☺ (📖 To make ☺ bounce with laughter)

— To have ☺ in stitches

- **Rogelio es muy chistoso. Siempre me trae botada de la risa.**
  Rogelio is really a scream. He always has me in stitches.

Tener su chiste

— To be complicated, tricky or hard to do

- **Tiene su chiste meter la pelotita en el hoyo.**
  It's no easy thing to get the little ball in the hole.

⇩ Tener chorro; tener chorrillo

— To have the trots

- **No puedo comer nada porque tengo chorro (chorrillo).**
  I can't eat anything because I have the trots.

ᕤ Tener(le) tirria a ☺

— To loathe ☺

- **Celia le tiene tirria a Claudia por lo de Rodrigo.**
  Celia loathes Claudia because of what happened with Rodrigo.

ᕤ Tener una movida (📖 To have a move) (see Movida)

— To have a date which is either for sex pure and simple, or will end up in bed (not a romantic date)

- **Tengo una movida hoy en la noche. No puedo cenar contigo.**
  I have a date tonight. I can't have supper with you.

Tener vara alta (📖 To have a high stick)

— To have pull

- **Tu tío tiene vara alta en la Secretaría de Comercio.**
  Your uncle has pull at the Commerce Department.

ᕤ Tirar de a loco(a); tirar de a lucas

— To ignore a ☺

- **Le dije a tu jefe, pero me tiró de a lucas.**
  I told your boss, but he ignored me.

ᕤ Tirar de a lucas a ☺ (see Tirar de a loco a ☺)

Slang in Mexico

♭⇩ Tirar(se) una pluma (📖 To put out a feather)
— To cut the cheese (i.e., pass wind, fart)
- **El mal educado de tu sobrino se tira plumas delante de todos.**
  That bad-mannered nephew of yours farts in front of everyone.

♭ Traer finto(a) a ☺
— To have ☺ all mixed up or overwhelmed; to pick on ☺
- **Hay que entregar 26 pedidos en tres ciudades hoy mismo. Me traen finto.**
  I have to deliver 26 orders in 3 cities today. They've got me dizzy and running in circles.
- **Por ser tan enojón, todos traen finto a Rafael.**
  Rafael is such a grouch that everyone picks on him..
- **No entiendo sus bromas; me trae finto.**
  I don't understand his jokes; he's got me all mixed up.

Traer(le) ganas a ☺
— To want to beat up or kill ☺
- **Amado le trae ganas a Rafael. Va a acabar pegándole.**
  Amado is dying to beat up Rafael.
— To want to get ☺ into bed
- **Creo que Julio le trae ganas a mi hermana.**
  I think Julio is after my sister.

Traer la lengua de corbata (📖 To have your tongue hanging out like a man's tie)
— To be exhausted
- **Después de correr tanto, llegué con la lengua de corbata.**
  I arrived totally worn out after all that running around.

♭ Tragar camote (📖 To swallow yam)
— To be unable to do ☐ difficult; to be unable to cope or handle a situation
- **En lugar de defenderme, te quedaste tragando camote.**
  Instead of defending me, you just stood there looking scared.

♭ Tronar; tronar a ☺; tronar con ☺
— To break up with ☺
- **Meche y Pedro tronaron la semana pasada.**
  Meche and Pedro broke up last week.
- **Lucía tronó a (con) Carlos y está muy triste**
  Lucia broke up with Carlos and she's very sad about it.

♭⇈ Tostar(se); tronar(selas); atizar; quemar; pasar(se)
— To smoke marijuana
- **Se las están tronando desde ayer.**
  They've been smoking marijuana since yesterday.

- **Aquellos muchachos se acaban de tostar; se les nota a leguas.**
  Those guys just smoked a joint; you can tell a mile away.

♫ Tronar(selas) (see Tostar(se))

♫ Tupir(le)

— To do ☐ with all you've got

- **Hay mucho trabajo. No seas flojo. ¡Túpele!**
  There's lots of work to do. Don't be lazy! Give it your all!

Untar(le) la mano a ☺

— To grease ☺'s palm; to bribe ☺

- **Para conseguir la licencia, tendré que untarle la mano al empleado.**
  I'll have to grease the attendant's palm in order to get the license.

Vacilar

— To joke around

- **A tus primas les encanta vacilar.**
  Your cousins love to joke around.

Valer(le) gorro a ☺; valer(le) sombrilla a ☺

— Not to care, not to give a damn

- **Digan lo que digan, a mí me vale gorro.**
  I don't give a damn, no matter what they say.

♫ Valer(le) sombrilla a ☺ (see Valer(le) gorro a ☺)

Ver caballo (burro) y ofrecer(sele) viaje (To see a donkey and decide you he need a ride)

— To see ☺ and immediately think of ☐ you want from ☺

- **Me encontré con Pilar y me puso a subir libros al estudio. Vio caballo (burro) y se le ofreció viaje.**
  I ran into Pilar and she had me take books up to the study. She always thinks of something she needs done whenever she sees me.

Ver(le) la cara a ☺ (📖 To realize from ☺'s face that he/she is easy to fool)

— To fool ☺

- **¿Pagaste 12 mil por este coche? Creo que te vieron la cara.**
  You paid 12 thousand (pesos) for this car? I think you got taken, man.

Volar(se) (📖 To make ☐ fly) (see **Clavar(se)** (do not confuse **Volar(se)** with **Andar volado** (to be very keen on ☺)
— To steal, filch or pinch ☐
- **En las últimas vacaciones, mi hermano se voló las toallas de todos los hoteles.**
  On our last vacation, my brother lifted the towels at all the hotels.

Volar(se) la barda (📖 To leap over a high wall)
— To outdo yourself; to do ☐ quite extraordinary, wonderful or noteworthy
- **Luis se voló la barda. Donó la mitad de su fortuna a un orfanatorio.**
  Luis outdid himself. He gave half his fortune to an orphanage.

2. Slang Expressions Used as Part of a Sentence (Non-Verbs)

A lo bestia (adv.)
— Excessively; in a rough and uncivilized way
- **Hemos estado trabajando a lo bestia.**
  We have been working like crazy.

A grito pelado (📖 In a naked screech)
— In a very loud voice; at the top of your lungs
- **Lo regañó a grito pelado.**
  She scolded him in a very loud voice (at the top of her lungs).

⇩ **A lo idiota** (adv.) **(see A lo tarugo)**

A lo tarugo; a lo tonto; ⇩a lo idiota (offensive), etc., (adv.)
— In not a very bright way
- **Compraste ese programa a lo tarugo (a lo tonto, a lo idiota); no es compatible con tu computadora.**
  You bought that program without thinking; it isn't compatible with your computer.

A lo tonto (adv.) **(see A lo tarugo)**

🏱 **A todo dar** (adj.)
— Great!; terrific!
- **¡Mi nueva oficina está a todo dar!**
  My new office is just terrific!

†† **Acelerado(a)** (adj.)
— Excited; aggressive
- **Luis anda muy acelerado. Va a terminar peleándose.**
  Luis is pretty wound up. He's sure to get into trouble (into a fight).

🏱 **Achichinque** or **achichincle** (n.) (nahuatl)
— ☺ helper (derogatory)
- **No podré arreglar todo el jardín hoy, porque no vino mi achichincle.**
  I won't be able to finish doing the garden today, because my helper didn't show up.

Adiosito (n.)
— Diminutive of **adiós** (expresses a fond goodbye prior to a brief absence)
- **Adiosito. Regreso mañana**
  (Bye, bye) Bye now. I'll be back tomorrow.

Slang in Mexico

₱ **(Los) agachados** (n.)
— A place to eat tacos (**Agachado** means "stooped" or "leaning forward". At these eating places you must lean forward a bit so the tacos don't drip on your clothes when you bite into them.)
  ▪ **En los agachados de la Merced se come muy bien.**
    The food at the La Merced market is really good.

₱†† **Agandallado(a)** (adj.)
— Not a pal; not friendly
  ▪ **No me gusta andar con Marcos. Está muy agandallado últimamente.**
    I don't want to go around with Marcos. He's pretty hostile lately.

₱†† **Agandalle** (n.)
— Unfriendly act
  ▪ **A Marcos le encanta el agandalle.**
    Marcos enjoys being mean (or aggressive).

₱ **Al chas chas** (adv.) (the non-slang term is **"en efectivo"**)
— In cash; cash on the line
  ▪ **Esta mercancía hay que pagarla al chas chas.**
    This merchandise has to be paid for in cash.

₱ **Al chilazo** (adv.) **(see A lo tarugo)**
— Carelessly; without thinking or planning
  ▪ **Siempre haces todo al chilazo y por eso te sale mal.**
    You never take the time to do things properly, so nothing you do ever works out.

₱ **Al puro pelo** (adv.)
— Just perfect
  ▪ **Tu regalo queda al puro pelo en este cuarto.**
    Your present goes just perfectly in this room.

₱ **Alcancía** (n.) (Underworld jargon) (see **Bote**)
— Jail; penitentiary; the clink
  ▪ **A tu carnal lo metieron a la alcancía.**
    They threw your brother in jail.

₱ **Alipús** (n.) (see **Chínguere, pegue, farolazo, chupe,** etc.)
— An alcoholic drink of any kind
  ▪ **Yo tengo ganas de un alipús antes de la comida. ¿Quién me acompaña?**
    I feel like a drink before lunch. Who'll join me?

₱†† **Aliviane** (n.)
— To hang out with friends; to feel that you are liked by a group of friends
  ▪ **¡Me encanta el aliviane!**
    I really like hanging out with my friends.

Slang in Mexico

꒰ **Amuinado(a)** (adj.) (a corruption of **amohinar, estar mohino(a),** to anger or sadden)
— Angry; sad; down in the dumps
  - **¡El jefe está muy amuinado!**
    The boss is in the dumps!

꒰ **Antojitos** (n.)
— Finger food, usually eaten at sidewalk stands without even sitting down
  - **Los antojitos de esta taquería son famosos.**
    The (finger) food at that taco place is famous.

꒰†† **Aplatanado(a)** (adj.) (📖 Like a squishy, overripe banana)
— Slow; sad; depressed; down in the dumps
  - **Te noto muy aplatanado últimamente.**
    You seem very depressed lately.

Aprovechado(a) (n.)
— One who takes advantage of ☺□; a person who will stop at very little to seize an opportunity to benefit himself
  - **Juan es un aprovechado. Va a quedarse con toda la ganancia.**
    Juan is going to take advantage of you and keep all the profit for himself.

꒰ **Argüende** (n.)
— Noisy, gossipy chatter
  - **¿Qué argüende trae Susana?**
    What's Susana chattering about?

꒰ **Asegunes** (n.)
— Circumstances on which □ depends
  - **Lo que me estás planteando tiene sus asegunes.**
    What you are proposing depends on a lot of things.

Aventón (n.) (📖 A throw)
— A ride (the English *ride* is sometimes heard too)
  - **Yo voy para el sur. ¿Quieres un aventón?**
    I'm heading for the south (of the city). Want a ride?

Baboso(a); maje (n.)
— ☺ dumb
  - **¿A poco crees que soy tan baboso (maje)?**
    Do you really think I'm that dumb?

꒰ **Baras** (adj.) (from **barato(a)**)
— Cheap, inexpensive
  - **¿Ves esta pulsera? Me salió bien baras.**
    See this bracelet? It was really inexpensive.

Slang in Mexico

𝄐 **Barco** (n.)
— ☺ who makes everything easy for you
- **La maestra de química es barco. Nadie reprueba sus exámenes.**
  The chemistry teacher makes everything really easy. Nobody ever fails her tests.

𝄐 **Beberecua** (n.)
— A drinking spree
- **Anduvieron toda la noche en la beberecua.**
  They were out on a drinking spree all night.

𝄐 **Blanquillo** (n.) (used to avoid the word **huevos**, which is slang for testicles)
— Egg
- **En algunas regiones de México, a los huevos les llaman blanquillos.**
  In some parts of Mexico they call eggs blanquillos (little white ones).

†† **Billetiza** (see **Luz**)

𝄐 **Birriondo(a)** (adj.)
— In heat or responsive to an animal in heat
- **Ese gato anda de lo más birriondo.**
  That tomcat is really on the prowl.

Bolillo (n.) (📖 A fairly unexciting bread roll of a golden hue) (see **bolillo** under *Mexican Food*)
— A blond foreigner (The inference being that Anglo Saxons are all lacking in color and spice)
- **En esta época del año hay mucho bolillo en México.**
  There are a lot of foreigners (U.S. and European) here at this time of the year.

(Un) Bonche (from bunch); **un chorro; un chorratal; un resto** (n.)
— A lot of □
- **El colchón tenía un chorro de hoyos.**
  The mattress had a whole bunch of holes in it.
- **Tengo un bonche de trabajo.**
  I have a lot of work
- **Amado salió con un chorratal de tonterías.**
  Amado came out with a lot of stupidities.
- **Cecilia fuma un resto.**
  Cecilia smokes a lot.

Boquiflojo(a) (adj.)
— A gossipy loudmouth
- **No se lo digas al boquiflojo de Raúl.**
  Don't go telling that loudmouth Raul.

Slang in Mexico

📖 **Borlote** (n.)
— A big stink
- **Armaron un borlote por algo que no valía la pena.**
  They made a big stink out of something that was really nothing.

Borrego (n.) (📖 Sheep)
— Used to refer to an untrue story or news item told or printed, especially used by newspapermen. Also used to refer to the people who are very easy to manipulate.
- **Echaron el borrego de que había habido un golpe de estado.**
  They circulated the story that there had been a coup d'etat
- **No sabían cuál era el problema, pero fueron con ella de borregos a protestar.**
  They didn't know what the.problem was, but they all went like a flock of sheep to file a complaint.

📖 **Bote** (n.) (📖 Any container, box, bin) (see **Alcancía**)

📖 **Botellón (n.)** (a takeoff of **bote**)
— Jail; the clink; the cooler; the slammer
- **Metieron al bote a la mitad de la gente que armó el relajo en el juego de fut.**
  Half the people who caused the ruckus at the soccer game were thrown into the cooler.

📖 **Bróder; bródi** (n.) (from brother)
— Pal; friend
- **Oye bróder (brodi), dame una mano.**
  Hey friend, give me a hand.

Buscabullas (adj.)
— A noisy troublemaker
- **¡No permito que me grite ningún buscabullas!**
  I will not allow a noisy troublemaker to yell at me!

📖 **Calzonudo(a)** (adj.)
— Stubborn
- **Imposible convencer al calzonudo de Rodolfo.**
  It's impossible to persuade Rodolfo. He is as stubborn as a mule.

📖 **Campechano(a)** (adj.) (see *Mexican Food*)
— Adjective used to describe a nice fellow
- **Don Pepe es un señor muy campechano.**
  Mr. Pepe is a very outgoing person.

📖 **Canchanchán** (n.)
— A step'n fetch-it; gofer; menial worker on a construction site

Slang in Mexico

- **¡Óyeme! No me dejes cargar con todo. ¿Me viste cara de tu canchanchán?**
  Hey! Don't leave everything for me to carry! What do you think I am, your gofer?

⌂†† Cantón; jaula; depa (n.)
— House, home
- **Te busqué en tu depa y no estabas.**
  I went to your apartment, but you weren't home.

⌂ Capulina (n.) (adj.)
— A great, swell life; also, a poisonous spider found in Mexico
- **¡Ah, qué vida tan capulina te das en Acapulco!**
  You're having the time of your life in Acapulco!

Carcacha (n.)
— Jalopy
- **Las carcachas valen ahora muchísimo dinero.**
  Jalopies are now worth a fortune!
- **Tuvimos que irnos a Acapulco en mi carcacha.**
  We had to drive to Acapulco in my jalopy.

⌂†† Carnal (n.)
— Brother
- **Oye, carnal, vamos a hacer el trabajo juntos.**
  Listen, brother, let's do the job together.

⌂†† Carroza (see Nave)

⌂ Casa chica (see Segundo frente)
— The home of a man's mistress, supported by him
- **Nunca sospeché que Emilio tuviera casa chica.**
  I never suspected that Emilio of kept a mistress.

⌂ Cebada (see Cheve)

⌂ Cervatana (see Cheve)

⌂ Chabacano(a) (n.) (📖 Apricot)
— Clumsy; corny; vulgar
- **El líder pronunció un discurso de lo más chabacano.**
  The leader gave a very vulgar speech.

⌂ Cháchara(s) (n.)
— Knick-knacks; trifles
- **En Tepito pueden comprarse chácharas baratas.**
  You can get all kinds of knick-knacks cheap in Tepito.

📖 **Chafa(s)** (adj.)
— Fake or cheap, poorly made
- **El traje que se compró está muy chafa (chafas).**
  The suit he bought is really sleezy.

📖 **Chamaco(a)** (n.)
— Child; kid
- **Ese chamaco es muy mal hablado.**
  That kid uses a lot of bad language.

📖 **Chamagoso(a)** (adj.)
— Tacky; dirty; grubby
- **¿Cómo te atreves a presentarte así de chamagoso?**
  How dare you turn up looking so grubby?

📖 **Chamba** (n.)
— Job; employment
- **Javier consiguió chamba de velador.**
  Javier got a job as a night watchman.

📖 **Chambón(Chambona)** (n.)
— Silly
- **¿Cómo te fuiste a enfermar hoy, chambona?**
  Why did you have to go and get sick today, silly?
- **El chambón de René hizo todo mal.**
  That silly René did everything wrong.

📖 **Chanchullo** (n.)
— A dirty trick, a scam
- **A Manuel le hicieron chanchullo en el negocio en que se metió.**
  They cheated Manuel in that business he got into.

📖 **Changarro** (n.)
— A small business (store, shop, etc.)
- **¡Ya cierra el changarro y vámonos al cine!**
  Close the shop and let's go to the movies.

📖 **Chango(a)** (n.) (📖 Monkey)
— A derogatory way of referring to a person
- **Te busca el chango del taller mecánico.**
  That dude from the car shop is looking for you.

📖 **Chaparro(a)** (adj.)
— Short person
- **Rodolfo es muy chaparrito.**
  Rodolfo is a real shorty.

Slang in Mexico

— Poor luck
- **¡Ah, qué suerte tan chaparra! Por un número no le atiné a la lotería.**
  What bad luck! I just missed the lottery prize.

♪†† **Chaviza** (n.)
— Youth; young people
- **En el concierto de rock había pura chaviza.**
  Everyone at the rock concert was underage.

♪ **Chavo(a)** (n.)
— Boy; girl
- **Adela anda con un chavo peruano.**
  Adela is going out with a Peruvian boy.

♪ **Cheve; cervatana; cebada; helodia; fría; serpentina; serpiente** (n.) (babytalk for beer)
— Beer
- **Pásame una cheve, mano.**
  Pass me a beer, will you pal?
- **Te invito unas frías, ¿quieres venir?**
  I'm buying the beer. Want to come?

♪†† **Chido(a)** (adj.)
— Great; terrific; wonderful
- **La película estaba de lo más chida.**
  The film was terrific.

♪ **Chilango(a)** (n.)
— A derogatory way of referring to natives of Mexico City. Mainly used by people from other places in Mexico
- **Martín me cae bien, aunque sea chilango.**
  I like Martin, regardless of the fact that he is from Mexico City.

♪ **Chilaquiles** (n.) (see *Mexican Food*)

♪ **Chilpayate** (n.) **(**see *Pre-Columbian Words***)**

♪ **Chiluca** (n.) (📖 The name of a hard stone) (see **Coco; Chirimoya; Choya; Maceta; Tatema**)
— Head
- **Roberto tiene la chiluca vacía.**
  Roberto has no brains in his head.

๒ **Chimiscolero(a)** (adj.)

— Busybody; gossip

- **¡No seas chimiscolera! ¡Siempre andas hablando de los demás!**
  Don't be such a gossip! You're always talking about other people.

๒ **Chimistretas (**see **Chunches)**

๒↓ **Chínguere** (n.) (since this sounds like a very rude word (see *Not for Polite Society*), it's best to use it with close friends only) (see **Alipús; chupe; farolazo**)

— A shot of liquor that hits hard, although it can also mean a strong mixed drink, even a long one

- **En cuanto supo la mala noticia, se echó dos chíngueres.**
  As soon as he heard the bad news, he knocked back two strong ones.

๒ **Chípil (**see *Pre-Columbian Words*)

๒ **Chipocludo(a)** (adj.)

— ☺ that is important

- **Tienes unos amigos de lo más chipocludos.**
  You've got some very important friends.

— ❑ that is nice, good, terrific

- **¡Qué casa tan chipocluda!**
  What a great house!

๒ **Chipote** (n.) (see *Pre-Columbian Words*)

๒ **Chirimoya** (n.) (tropical fruit with a mushy white pulp that resembles brains) (see **Coco; Choya; Chiluca; Maceta; Tatema**)

— Head

- **Tienes la chirimoya llena de humo.**
  Your head is full of nonsense.

๒ **(Un) Chirris** (adj.)

— Little; small; tiny; a little

- **Me duele un chirris la cabeza.**
  I have a slight headache.
- **El suéter no te entra porque es muy chirris.**
  The sweater doesn't fit because it's too small.
- **No tengo mucha hambre. Dame nada más un chirris.**
  I'm not very hungry. Just give me a small piece (a bit).

๒ **Chivas (**see **Chunches)**

Slang in Mexico

꠵ **Chocante** (adj.)
— Obnoxious; irritating; unpleasant
  ▪ **El nuevo jefe es de lo más chocante.**
    The new boss is quite obnoxious.

꠵ **Chones** (n.)
— Panties; also men's shorts or jockey underwear
  ▪ **Estos chones me quedan chicos.**
    These panties are too small for me.

꠵ **(Un) Chorratal** (see **(Un) Bonche**)

꠵ **Chorcha** (n.)
— An informal gathering; the gang
  ▪ **A la tarde me puedes encontrar como siempre en la chorcha.**
    In the afternoon you can find me, as usual, gabbing (hanging out) with my friends.

꠵ **Chorreado(a)** (adj.)
— Dirty; sticky; gummy
  ▪ **¡Ay muchacho, otra vez andas todo chorreado!**
    You've made a mess of yourself again, kid!

꠵ **(Un) Chorro** (see **(Un) Bonche**)

꠵ **Choya** (n.) (see **Coco; Chirimoya; Chiluca; Maceta; Tatema**)
— Head
  ▪ **Agacha la choya o te vas a pegar.**
    Duck or you're going to hit your head.

Chucherías (n.)
— Knick-knacks; trifles
  ▪ **Patricia compró un montón de chucherías en esa tienda.**
    Patricia bought a whole bunch of knick-knacks in that store.

꠵ **Chulo(a)** (adj.)
— Lovely; pretty
  ▪ **¡Qué chulo está tu jardín!**
    Your garden is lovely.

Chunches; chimistretas; cochinadas; porquerías; chivas; tiliches (n.)
— Things; thingamajigs; stuff; junk
  ▪ **El desván está lleno de tiliches. ¿Para qué sirve el chunche ese?**
    The attic is full of junk. What is that thingamajig for?

♭♫ Chupe (n.) **(see Alipús; ↓chínguere; farolazo)**
— The act of drinking alcohol; the act of boozing
- **A Pancho le encanta el chupe.**
  Pancho just loves boozing.

Coco (n.) (📖 Coconut) **(see Chirimoya; Choya; Chiluca; Maceta; Tatema)**
— Head
- **No te pegues en el coco.**
  Don't hit your head.

Cochinadas (see Chunches)

Como me la recetó el doctor (adv.)
— Just what the doctor ordered (referring to girls)
- **Esa chava está como me la recetó el doctor.**
  That girl is just what the doctor ordered.

Con la baba caída (adv.) (📖 With drool dripping from your mouth)
— Stupidly; also used when a person is in a daze of admiration for ☺□
- **Ahí está Pedro con la baba caída.**
  There's Pedro with that usual dumb look on his face..
- **Elena está con la baba caída por ese chavo.**
  Elena is dumbstruck over that boy.
- **Estoy con la baba caída por ese reloj.**
  What watch is too gorgeous for words.

♭♯♯ Conecte (n.)
— A friend or connection
- **Tengo un buen conecte en esa fábrica.**
  I have a good contact at that factory.
— Drug pusher
- **¿Tienes algún conecte en la escuela?**
  Do you know who to get drugs from at school?

♭ Coscolino(a) (adj.)
— ☺ of loose morals
- **La secretaria del jefe es una coscolina.**
  The boss's secretary is not very hard to get.

♭ Cotorro(a) (adj.)
— Witty; funny; amusing
- **Vamos a invitar también a Sergio. Es muy cotorro.**
  Let's invite Sergio too. He's a scream.

Slang in Mexico

🔁 **Coyote** (n.) (📖 Cayote)
— A person who handles certain troublesome legal procedures at government agencies (either a civil servant or a friend of an employee), such as registrations, authorizations and permits, for third parties and for a fee, by means of kick-backs and/or bribes.
  ▪ **Sigue habiendo muchos coyotes en las dependencias oficiales.**
    The government offices are still full of bribe-takers.

🔁 **Cuaderno** (see **Cuate**)

🔁 **Cuaralais** (see **Cuate**)

🔁 **Cuatacho** (see **Cuate**)

🔁 **Cuate(a)** (📖 Twin); **cuaralais; cuatacho(a); cuaderno** (n.)
— Friend; pal; guy, dude; buddy
  ▪ **Mira, este es mi cuatacho Pepe.**
    Look, this is my pal Pepe.
  ▪ **Ese cuate me quitó mi lugar de estacionamiento.**
    That guy stole my parking space.

🔁 **Cuelga** (n.)
— Gift given to a person on his birthday or saint's day
  ▪ **¿Ya pensaron qué le van a dar de cuelga a su mamá?**
    Have you decided what to give your mother on her birthday?

De aquí pa'l real * (adv.)
— The rest is duck soup (easy); the rest is a breeze
  ▪ **Ya logramos la parte más difícil; de aquí pa'l real es fácil.**
    We've got the difficult part over with; the rest is duck soup (a breeze).
* **Pa'l** is a contraction of **para el.**

De chiripa (adv.)
— By sheer chance or coincidence
  ▪ **Pasé el examen de chiripa, porque no había estudiado nada.**
    I passed the test by sheer chance, because I didn't study at all.

De golpe (y porrazo) (adv.)
— Suddenly
  ▪ **No vayas a darle la noticia de golpe (de golpe y porrazo).**
    Don't break the news suddenly.

🔁 **De gorra** (adv.) (see **Gorrear** and **Gorrón**)
— Free; without paying
  ▪ **La comida me salió de gorra.**
    I got lunch free.

⚐ **De hoquis** (adv.)
— For free
- **No me pagaron. Trabajé de hoquis.**
  They never paid me. I worked for nothing.

De la patada (adj.) (adv.)
— Very bad; very badly
- **Los informes que preparó están de la patada.**
  The reports he prepared are a disaster.
- **Juan maneja de la patada.**
  Juan drives really badly.

⚐†† **¡De pelos!** (adv.)
— Great!; Terrific!
- **¡El CD está de pelos!**
  The CD is great!

De perdida (de perdis) (adv.)
— At least (if nothing better can be arranged)
- **A ver si de perdida (de perdis) llega mi caballo en tercer lugar.**
  I hope my horse makes at least third place.
- **¿Ya no hay whisky? De perdida (de perdis) dame un ron.**
  There's no more whiskey? Gimme a rum then (it's better than nothing).

⚐ **De plano** (adv.)
— Simply; absolutely; no two ways about it
- **No quiero trabajar con Luis. De plano no lo aguanto.**
  I don't want to work with Luis. I simply can't stand him.

Speaker A:	**¿No te parece que Nadia es fea?**	
	Nadia is quite ugly, isn't she?	
Speaker B:	**Sí, de plano.**	
	She sure is.	
Speaker A:	**¿Por qué no vienes con nosotros?**	
	Why aren't you coming with us?	
Speaker B:	**De plano no puedo.**	
	I just plain can't.	

⚐ **Desempance** (n.)
— A drink to counteract the effects of too much eating or drinking
- **Después de tanta cerveza, se me antoja un desempance.**
  After all that beer, I feel like having a brandy (or some other drink).

Slang in Mexico

📖 **Desgarriate** (n.)
— A mess
  ▪ **La reunión fue un verdadero desgarriate.**
    The get-together turned into a real mess.

📖 **Despiporre** (n.)
— A very noisy party
  ▪ **Esos cuates armaron un despiporre tremendo.**
    Those guys orchestrated a real blast.

📖 **Destape** (n.)
— Disclosure of any candidate for a government position
  ▪ **La próxima semana es el destape del candidato del PRI.**
    Next week is the announcement of the PRI candidate.

Destartalado (adj.)
— Old and the worse for wear; dilapidated
  ▪ **Me tocó volar en un avión muy destartalado.**
    My flight was on an old rattletrap.

Dominguero(a) (adj.)
— Sunday best
  ▪ **Pancho se puso su traje dominguero.**
    Pancho wore his Sunday clothes.
— A high faluting word not always understood by ordinary people
  ▪ **Mi abuelo siempre usa palabras domingueras cuando se echa sus discursos.**
    Grandfather always uses fancy words when he makes his speeches.

Donde el aire da vuelta (📖 Where the wind turns); **Donde San Pedro perdió el guarache** (📖 Where St. Peter lost his sandal) **(see En el fin del mundo)**

Donde San Pedro perdió el guarache (see En el fin del mundo)

📖 **Echador(a)** (adj.)
— Boastful
  ▪ **Allí está Gabriel, tan echador como siempre.**
    There's Gabriel, as boastful as ever.

📖†† **Efectivo(a)***(adj.)
— ☺□ groovy
  ▪ **Acabo de conocer un cuate bien efectivo.**
    I just met a really groovy dude.
* The original meaning is cash

El dueño del gallinero (📖 The owner of the chicken coop)
— The big boss (slightly sarcastic)
  • **Dejé el coche en el taller para que le arreglaran la defensa, pero no me pudieron dar un presupuesto porque no estaba el dueño del gallinero.**
    I left the car for them to fix the bumper, but they couldn't give me an estimate because the big boss wasn't in.

📖 **Empelotado(a); hecho pelotas** (adj.)
— Love sick
  • **Jaime anda muy empelotado con Raquel.**
    Jaime is love sick over Raquel.
— Confused, mixed up
  • **No puedo acabar con mi tarea. Estoy todo empelotado (hecho pelotas).**
    I can't finish my homework. I'm all mixed up.

En casa del diablo (see **En el fin del mundo)**

En el fin del mundo (📖 At the ends of the Earth)**; En el quinto infierno** (📖 In the fifth hell)**; En casa del diablo** (📖 At the Devil's house)
— In the back of beyond; at the ends of the Earth
  • **No me pidas que vaya a la fábrica. Está en el fin del mundo (la casa del diablo, en el quinto infierno).**
    Don't ask me to go to the factory; it's in the back of beyond.

En el quinto infierno (see **En el fin del mundo)**

Entre pitos y flautas
— What with one thing and another
  • **Estoy haciendo cuentas de los gastos de la boda; entre pitos y flautas, va a costar una millonada.**
    I'm figuring out the cost of the wedding; what with one thing and another, it's going to cost a fortune.

📖†† **Erizo(a)** (n.) **(**see **Andar erizo(a))**
— ☺ who is badly in need of a joint
  • **Jorge no pudo conseguir mota y anda bien erizo.**
    Jorge couldn't get his grass and he's badly in need of a fix..

📖 **Escuintle(a)** or **escuincle(a)** (n.) (nahuatl)
— Youngster (from the Nahuatl **Itzcuintle**, small dog of pre-Columbian times)
  • **¡Me las vas a pagar, escuincle desobediente!**
    You'll pay for that, you little brat.

Slang in Mexico

⚑ Faramalla (n.) **(see Borlote)**
— A lot of noise; a big to do
   ▪ **Es mucha faramalla por algo que no vale la pena.**
   It's a big to do about something that isn't worth it.

⚑ Farolazo (see El chupe)

⚑ Fayuca (n.)
— Merchandise smuggled into the country without paying duties
   ▪ **La apertura de fronteras está acabando con la fayuca.**
   The opening up of the border is putting an end to smuggling.

⚑†† Feria (see Luz)

⚑ Feroz (adj.) **(from feo)**
— Ugly
   ▪ **¿Viste al amigo de Roque? Está feroz.**
   Did you see Roque's friend? He's hideous.

⚑ Fresa (adj.)
— A square; a goody-goody; used to describe a proper, clean-cut, kid with no bad habits such as drinking
   ▪ **¿Cómo te puede gustar ese chavo? Es de lo más fresa.**
   How can you like that boy. He's such a square!

⚑ Fría (see Cheve)

⚑ Fufurufo(a) (adj.)
— Elegant; dressed to kill
   ▪ **Mi hermana vive en una zona muy fufurufa.**
   My sister lives in a very elegant neighborhood.
   ▪ **¿Y ahora por qué andas tan fufurufo?**
   What are you all dressed up for?

⚑ Fusca (n.)
— Pistol
   ▪ **¡Vámonos de aquí! Aquel poli ya sacó la fusca.**
   Let's get our of here! That policeman just pulled out his gun.

⚑ Gabacho(a) (n.)
— Any foreigner, especially people from the U. S. (mildly derogatory; originally said of French people)
   ▪ **Cancún está lleno de gabachos. Es raro ver a un mexicano en la playa.**
   Cancun is full of foreigners. You see very few Mexicans on the beach.

♌ **Gacho(a)** (adj.)
— Not nice
  ▪ **¡Qué gacha eres! No viniste a mi boda.**
    What a good friend you are! You didn't show up at my wedding.

♌†† **Gandalla; gandul** (n.)
— ☺ who is not a pal
  ▪ **No te juntes con Pepe. Es un gandalla.**
    Don't go around with Pepe. He's not a good pal (he can't be trusted).

♌†† **Gandul** (see **Gandalla**)

Garigoleado(a) (adj.)
— Overly ornate
  ▪ **No me gusta ese mueble. Está muy garigoleado.**
    I don't like that piece of furniture. It's too ornate.

♌ **Garraleta** (n.)
— An ugly woman
  ▪ **¿Viste a Gerardo con esa garraleta?**
    Did you see Gerardo with that ugly woman?

Gordo(a) (n.)
— Girl; boy; also, an affectionate way of addressing ☺
  ▪ **Van a venir unas gordas que no conoces.**
    Some girls are coming that you haven't met.
  ▪ **¡Gorda! Tengo una sorpresa para ti.**
    Honey! I have a surprise for you.

♌ **Gorrón, gorrona** (n.) (see **De gorra** and **Gorrear; gorronear**)
— Cadger
  ▪ **Lorenzo nunca paga. Es un gorrón.**
    Lorenzo never pays for anything. He's a cadger, always bumming things off people.

♌†† **Grifa** (see **Mota**)

♌ **(La) grilla** (n.)
— Low, intriguing politics
  ▪ **Mi tío es senador ahora, gracias a que le encanta la grilla (le encanta grillear).**
    My uncle loves the world of low politics. Thanks to that, he is now a senator.
  ▪ **Desgraciadamente en esta empresa hay mucha grilla.**
    Unfortunately, there is a lot of office politics at this company.

Gringo(a) (adj.)(n.)
— Person or thing from the U. S.

Slang in Mexico

- **Acabo de leer *Gringo viejo* de Carlos Fuentes.**
  *I've just read **Gringo viejo** by Carlos Fuentes.*

⌘†† **Guacho** (n.) (from **watch**)
— Clock or watch

- **Mi papá me regaló un guacho muy náis.**
  My father gave me a very nice watch.

⌘ **Guango(a)** (adj.)
— Loose

- **No se te ve bien el saco. Te queda muy guango.**
  That jacket doesn't look good on you. It's too loose.

⌘ **Guaguareo; guaraguara** (n.) (see **Güirigüiri**)
— Conversation; chatter

- **Ahí están Lola y Lupe en el guaguareo.**
  Lola and Lupe are deep in conversation.

Guaje (n.)(adj.) (📖 Gourd)
— Fool; nitwit

- **Mira lo que está haciendo León. ¡Qué guaje!**
  Look what Leon is doing. What a nitwit!

⌘ **Güero(a)** (adj.)
— Blond; not dark complexioned

- **Pásele, güerita, ¿qué le servimos?**
  Come on in, blondy. What'll you have?

Güirigüiri (n.) (see **Guaguareo**)
— Gossip and generally senseless talk; to yack

- **¡Ay, manita! A Raquel le encanta el güirigüiri.**
  Gosh! Raquel just loves to yack.

⌘ **Guitarra** (n.) (Underworld jargon)
— Woman

- **Pepe anda con una guitarra buenísima.**
  Pepe is going out with a striking woman.

⌘ **Harto(a)** (adj.)
— A lot

- **Juan tiene hartos libros**
  Juan has a lot of books.

— Fed up

- **Estoy harta de este lugar.**
  I'm sick of this place.

Hasta decir basta (adv.)
— Used when people overdo ☐ or when ☐ is in excess
  ▪ **En el viaje a Europa, vimos museos hasta decir basta.**
    On the trip to Europe, we saw museums until we were blue in the face!

📖 **Hechizo(a)** (adj.) (from **hecho**, made)
— Fake; improvised
  ▪ **Se me hace que es hechiza la carrocería de ese automóvil tan raro.**
    The body of that funny looking car doesn't look factory made to me.

📖 **Helodia** (see **Cheve**)

📖†† **Herraduras** (see **Patines**)

†† **Hijo** (see **Maestro**)

Hijo de papi (see **Junior**)

Hocicón; hocicona (n.) (📖 Having a snout)
— Having a big mouth; boaster or liar
  ▪ **¿Por qué le dijiste a Gloria que fui al cine con Diana, hocicón?**
    Hey big mouth! Why did you go and tell Gloria that I went to the movies with Diane?

Huipil or **hipil** (n.) (see *Pre-Columbian Words*)

Igualado(a) (adj.)
— No sufficiently respectful; too chummy
  ▪ **El nuevo ayudante es muy igualado. Si sigue así, voy a ponerlo en su lugar.**
    The new assistant is far too chummy. If he keeps it up, I'm going to have to put him in his place.

📖 **Incróspido(a)** (adj.) (see **Persa; Pisteado(a); Estar cuete** and **Poner(se) un cuete**)
— Drunk
  ▪ **Te noto raro, ¿andas medio incróspido?**
    You're acting strange. Are you a bit drunk?

📖 **Itacate** (n.) (see *Pre-Columbian Words*)

📖 **Jaula** (n.) (Underworld jargon)
— Prison, cell
  ▪ **El Güero ya lleva un año en la jaula.**
    The "Guero" has been in jail for a year now.

Jefa, jefe (n.)
— Mother, father

Slang in Mexico

- **¡Jefe! La jefa dice que ya está la comida lista.**
  Dad! Mom says dinner's ready.

⌂†† Joi (see Maestro)

†† Junior; hijo de papi (n.)
— A shallow young adult very spoiled by his rich parents
- **Ese carrazo debe ser de algún junior (hijo de papi).**
  That flashy car must belong to some rich kid.

La calidad de la melcocha (adj.)
— ❑ good (used in boasting)
- **Van a ver lo que es la calidad de la melcocha.**
  Now you're going to see what's good!
  Now you're going to see how it's done!

⌂⇓ La chota; la poli (n.)
— Police
- **¡Corran! Ahí viene la chota (la poli).**
  Run for it! Here come the police.

⌂ La chusma; la raza (n.)
— A collective noun used to refer to uneducated (loud, coarse or crass) people as a whole
- **Quiero llegar temprano, antes de que llegue la chusma (la raza).**
  I'd like to arrive early, before the panting crowd gets there.

⌂⇓ La desa (n.)
— A thingamajig; a thingummy; a dohicky; also a euphemism for any plain bad word
- **Desde hace varios días me duele la desa.**
  My thingummy has been hurting for several days.
- **Pásame la desa.**
  Pass me that dohicky.

⌂†† La greña (see La mata)

⌂†† La mata, la greña (n.)
— Hair
- **Voy a alisarme un poco la greña.**
  I'm going to fix up my hair a bit.

⌂ La percha (n.) (📖 The clothes hanger)
— The body or figure of the person who is wearing the piece of clothing in question
- **Me gusta tu vestido nuevo, pero la verdad es que luce más por la percha.**
  I like your new dress very much, but the fact is it looks good on you because you have a good figure.

La poli (see **La chota**)

La raza (see **La chusma**)

♪ **La tartamuda** (n.) (Underworld jargon) (📖 The stutterer)
— Machine gun
- **Todos los agentes traían su tartamuda.**
  All the agents had a machine gun.

La trompa (n.) (📖 Snout)
— Prominent lips; a pout
- **Cuando se enoja Lupe, siempre para la trompa.**
  Lupe always pouts (her lips stick out) when she's angry.

♪†† **La verde (see Mota)**

Lambiscón; lambiscona (adj.) (see **Barbero** and **Hacer la barba**)
— Brown noser; flatterer
- **No te metas a la política si no eres lambiscón.**
  Don't go into politics if you don't know how to brown nose.

♪ **Lámina (see Nave)**

Lana (n.) (📖 Wool) (see **Pachocha**)
— Money: dough; bread
- **¿Tienes lana?**
  Got any money?

♪ **Leperada (n.) (see Peladeces)**
— Bad word; foul language
- **Jaime no puede hablar sin leperadas.**
  Jaime can't talk without foul language.

Locuaz*; lorenzo (adj.) (for **loco,** crazy)
— Crazy
- **¿Te fijaste en lo que hizo Celso? ¡Está re locuaz (lorenzo)!**
  Did you see what Celso did? He's really crazy.
* The original meaning is talkative, loquacious

♪ **Lorenzo(a) (see Locuaz)**

♪†† **Lux (see Luz)**

Slang in Mexico

⚲†† Luz; lux; feria; pachocha; pachochiza; billetiza; papeliza (see **Lana**)
— Money
- **No traigo nada de luz.**
  I don't have any cash at all.

⚲ Maceta (n.) (📖 Flower pot) **(see Coco, Chirimoya, Choya, Chiluca, Tatema)**
— Head
- **¡Chano es un maceta dura!**
  Chano is really hard headed!

⚲ Machincuepa (n.)
— Somersault
- **Si me tomo otro trago, voy a salir dando machincuepas.**
  One more drink and I'll be somersaulting out of here.

⚲†† Maese (see **Maestro(a)**)

†† Maestro(a); maese; master; hijo(a); joi (n.)
— Used when addressing ☺
- **¡Oye maese, te volaste la barda con esa carne asada!**
  Hey pal, your barbecue is great!
- **Yo aquí soy el mero mero. ¿Captas, hijo (joi)?**
  I'm the boss here Sonny. Get it?

Maje (see **Baboso**)

⚲ Mala leche (n.)
— Malice
- **Lo hizo con la más mala leche del mundo.**
  He did it in a totally malicious manner (with malice aforethought).

Mala pata (n.)
— Bad luck
- **¡Qué mala pata! Perdí mi billetera.**
  What bad luck! I lost my wallet

Mango (n.)
— An absolutely gorgeous man or woman (a mango is considered to be a very juicy scrumptious fruit)
- **¿Quién es ese mango?**
  Who's that hunk?

♪ **Manoplas** (n.) (Underworld jargon)
— Hands
- **¡Cuidado! ¡Fíjate dónde metes las manoplas!**
  Careful! Just watch where you're putting your hands!

♪ **Medicina** (n.) (Underworld jargon)
— Drugs
- **En la peni decomisaron harta medicina.**
  They confiscated lots of drugs inside the jail.

♪†† **Master** (see Maestro)

Menso(a) (adj.) (n.)
— Stupid
- **Me parece que ese perro es medio menso. No va por la pelota.**
  I think this dog is a little bit dumb. He won't go for the ball.
— Nitwit
- **Ese menso me tiró el café en mi vestido.**
  That nitwit spilled his coffee all over my dress.

♪ **Milanesa** (n.)
— A thousand
- **Tony perdió una milanesa.**
  Tony lost a thousand bucks.

♪ **Mitote** (n.) (see **Borlote**)
— Noisy goings-on
- **¡Óiganme! ¿Qué clase de mitote es ese?**
  Hey! What kind of noisy goings-on are these?

♪ **Mochilas** (adj.) (see **Mocho**)

♪ **Mocho(a); mochilas; mojigato(a); persignado(a)** (adj.)
— A very pious Catholic (derogatory)
- **Mi tía es muy mocha y no come carne los viernes.**
  My aunt is very religious and doesn't eat meat on Friday.

Mojigato(a) (adj.) (see **Mocho**)

♪ **Molón, molona** (adj.)
— ☺ who is a pain in the neck
- **¡Ya hijo! ya te voy a comprar tus dulces. No seas molón.**
  All right son, I'll get you your candies. Don't be such a pain in the neck.

♪†† **Momiza** (n.) (from **momia**)
— Adult; old people; senior citizens

Slang in Mexico

- **A ese restaurante va pura momiza.**
  Only the older generation goes to that restaurant.

♫ **Monserga** (n.)
— ❑ very annoying; a pain
- **Todo este asunto es una verdadera monserga.**
  All this affair is a real pain.

♫ **Mordelón** (n.) (📖 One who bites; i.e., extorts bribes)
— Traffic policeman
- **Hoy los mordelones andan desatados.**
  The traffic cops are really on the prowl today.

♫ **Mosca** (n.) (📖 Fly) (see **Lana**)
— Money; bread; dough
- **Se nos acabó la mosca sin poder comprar casi nada.**
  We ran out of dough and we hardly bought anything at all!

♫†† **Mota; yerba; grifa; la verde** (n.)
— Marijuana
- **¡Ni modo, ñeros. Ya no tengo mota (yerba, grifa, de la verde)!**
  Too bad my friends. I'm all out of marijuana.

♫ **Movida** (n.)
— A date (both the person and the occasion) but usually ☺ with whom you are having an affair, especially when the affair is simply for the sake of sex and is entirely lacking romanticism
- **¿Por qué tienes tanta prisa? Te está esperando tu movida, ¿verdad?**
  Why are you in such a hurry? Your lover is waiting for you, right?
- **Yo sé que tienes una movida; no te hagas el inocente.**
  I know you're having an affair. Don't look so innocent!

♫†† **Naco(a)** (adj.)
— ☺ who is crass, vulgar, gross, uneducated, ignorant, rude, etc.
- **La fiesta estaba llena de nacos.**
  The party was full of vulgar people.

Nada más (nomás) eso (esto) falta (faltaba) (📖 That's all that's missing)
— When the last straw has not yet happened or when ☺ proposes ❑ outrageously unreasonable: That's the only thing that hasn't happened; that's all we need now
- **Se enfermaron las vacas y luego le cayó plaga a la cosecha. Nada más falta que haya sequía.**
  The cows get sick, and then the crop gets bugs. I hope we don't have a drought. That's all we need!

— When the last straw happens; this was all ☺ needed
- **Te presenté a la muchacha, te presté el coche, te dejé usar mi traje y te regalé esa corbata. ¿Ahora quieres dinero para gasolina? ¡Nada más eso faltaba!**
  I introduced you to the girl, I lent you the car, I let you use my suit and I gave you that tie. Now you want money for gas? Some nerve!
- **¡Caray! Me empapé con la lluvia, se me rompieron las bolsas del super, y ahora no encuentro las llaves. ¡Nomás eso me faltaba!**
  Hell! I got soaked in the rain, the grocery bags tore open, and now I can't find my keys. This is the last straw!

⌂†† **Nave; lámina; tanque; poderoso; carroza** (n.)
— Automobile
- **Se me descompuso la nave aquí a la vuelta.**
  My car broke down around the corner.

⌂†† **(La) Neta**
— The truth
- **Mira ñeris, la neta, yo no te afané tu cartera.**
  Look buddy, I swear I didn't take your wallet.

⌂†† **Ni en cuenta** (from **No tomar en cuenta**)
— To not notice; it is not important
- Speaker A: **¡Susana no te saludó!**
                 Susan didn't say hello to you.
- Speaker B: **¿Crees que me importa? Yo, ni en cuenta.**
                 Do you think I care? I didn't even notice!

⌂↓†† **Ni máiz** (Euphemism for **"ni madre"**)
— Nothing doing!; nothing; zilch
- Speaker A: **¿Le entendiste al profesor?**
                 Did you understand the teacher?
- Speaker B: **Ni máiz.**
                 Not a word.

Ni papa (n.)
— Nothing whatsoever; zilch
- **¿Cómo vas a presentar el examen si no sabes ni papa?**
  How can you take the test if you don't know a darned thing?

Nomás eso faltaba (see **Nada más (nomás) eso (esto) falta (faltaba)**)

⌂†† **No te azotes**
— Don't get carried away; don't be silly
- **La maestra se enfermó, pero no la llevaron al hospital. ¡No te azotes!**
  The teacher got sick, buy she wasn't taken to the hospital . Don't get so upset!

Slang in Mexico

♫†† Ñero(a) (n.) (from **compañero**)
— Pal
- **Ñero, pásate una feria, ¿no?**
  Hey pal. Lend me some dough.

♫†† Oclayo (n.)
— Eye
- **Por andar de hocicón, le pusieron un oclayo moro.**
  He got a black eye for talking too much.

♫†† Onda; patín (n.) (see **Agarrar su patín**)
— The groove
- **¡Ándale! ¡Agarra la onda (tu patín) y vámonos a la fiesta!**
  Come on. Get in the groove. Lets go to the party.

♫†† Oso (n.)
— Trouble; problem; embarrassing situation
- **¡Ay, manita, qué pena! Hice un oso terrible con Jaime.**
  Gosh! How embarrassing! I made a fool of myself with Jaime.

♫ Otro boleto (n.)
— That's ☐ else quite different; another kettle of fish
- Speaker A: **¿Arreglaron también el alternador del coche?**
              Did they also fix the alternator of the car?
- Speaker B: **No, eso ya es otro boleto.**
              No, that's something else again.

♫ Pachocha (pachochiza) (n.) (see **Luz**)
— Bread ($)
- **¿Te fijaste? Emeterio trae harta pachocha (una buena pachochiza).**
  Did you see that? Emeterio has a real bankroll!

♫†† Papeliza (see **Luz**)

♫ Para aventar para arriba (pa'arriba) (adv.) (📖 Enough to fling up into the wind)
— Enough and some to spare
- **Eugenia tiene admiradores para aventar para arriba.**
  Eugenia has tons of admirers.
- **Ese hombre tiene dinero p'aventar p'arriba.**
  That man has loads of money.

♫ Patín (see **Onda** and **Agarrar su patín**)

♫✝✝ Patines; patrullas; herraduras; pezuñas (n.)
— Feet
- **¡Oye, Beto, no pongas las patrullas en la mesa!**
  Hey Bobby. Don't put your feet on the table!

♫✝✝ Patrulla(s) (n.)(see **Patines**)

♫ Peladeces (n.) (see **Leperada**)
— Bad language, swear words
- **Este muchacho majadero dice puras peladeces.**
  This foul-mouthed little brat uses nothing but cuss words.

♫ Pelado(a) (n.)
— ☺ who uses bad language
- **Ese chofer es un pelado**
  That truck driver is really foul-mouthed.

♫ Peor-es-nada (n.) (📖 Better than nothing) (see **Peor-es-nada** under *Common Expressions in Spanish*)
— A girlfriend or boyfriend with practically nothing to offer, or only slightly better than nothing
- **Ahí viene Natalia con su peor-es-nada.**
  There comes Natalie with her better-than-nothing dud boyfriend.

♫ Pericazo (n.) ✝✝
— A snort of cocaine
- **Se me hace que se van a echar un pericazo.**
  I think they're going to have a snort.

♫ Persa (adj.) (see **Incróspido; Pisteado; Estar cuete** and **Poner(se) un cuete)**
— Drunk
- **Armando se puso bien persa en la fiesta de anoche.**
  Armando got plastered at last night's party.

♫✝✝ Pezuñas (see **Patines**)

Persignado(a) (see **Mocho(a)**)

Pichicato(a)
— A stingy person (adj.)
- **Tu primo es pichicato hasta para comprarse ropa.**
  Your cousin is stingy, even when he's buying himself clothes.
— Stingy; miser (n.)

Slang in Mexico

- **El pichicato de mi padrino me dio nomás diez pesos.**
  My mean old godfather gave me only ten pesos.

📖↓ **Pinchurriento(a)** (adj.) (euphemism; *see Not for Polite Society*)
— Crumby
- **Este restaurante es de lo más pinchurriento.**
  This restaurant is totally crumby.

📖 **Pipirín** (n.)
— Food
- **Nos vemos a la hora del pipirín.**
  See you at lunch time.
- **El pipirín está en el refri.**
  The food is in the fridge.

📖 **Pipirisnais; popis** (adj.)
— Of or pertaining to money and social position
- **Mi jefe me invitó a comer en un restaurante muy pipirisnais.**
  My boss took me to lunch at a very posh restaurant.
- **La gente popis casi siempre compra su ropa en los Estados Unidos o en Europa.**
  Chic people almost always buy their clothes in the United States or Europe.

Piquete (n.) (📖 An insect bite)
— A shot of liquor added to a drink which is not usually drunk with alcohol
- **Hace un chorro de frío. Yo quiero mi café con piquete.**
  It's awfully cold. I want a shot of liquor in my coffee.

📖 **Pisteado(a)** (adj.) (see **Incróspido(a); Persa; Estar cuete** and **Poner(se) un cuete**)
— Drunk
- **Ese cuate anda bien pisteado.**
  That guy is pretty tipsy.

📖 **Pistear** (see **Incróspido; Persa; Estar cuete** and **Poner(se) un cuete**)
— To have a drink; to drink
- **Nomás te juntas con tus cuates para pistear.**
  You get together with your pals only to drink.

Pistito; Coyotito (n.)
— Nap
- **Llámale en media hora, se está echando un pistito (se está echando un coyotito).**
  Call him in half an hour. He is having a nap.

Pisto (n.)
— A drink (alcoholic)
- **Voy a echarme un pisto.**
  I'm going to have a drink.

†† **Poderoso(a)** (see **Nave**)

Pompas; pompis; petacas
— Buns; derriere; backside
- **¿Dónde te sentaste? Tienes sucias las pompas.**
  Where did you sit? Your derriere is dirty.

☈ **Popis** (see **Pipirisnais**)

Por las (re)cochinas dudas; por si las moscas
— Just in case
- **Mejor cierra la puerta con llave, por las recochinas dudas (por si las moscas).**
  Better lock the door, just in case.

Por si las moscas (see **Por las (re)cochinas dudas**)

Porquerías (see **Chunches**)

Quedada (adj.)
— An old maid
- **Tengo una tía quedada, con un carácter feroz.**
  One of my aunts is an old maid and is she a grump!

Quejumbres (n.)
— A person who is constantly complaining
- **¿De veras te duele mucho, o eres demasiado quejumbres?**
  Does it really hurt, or are you just griping?

¿Qué tanto(a) . . . ?
— How much?
- **¿Qué tanto hielo le pongo a la limonada?**
  How much ice should I put in the lemonade?

Rajón, rajona (adj.) (see **Rajar(se)**)
— ☺ who backs down on a deal
- **El rajón de Ernesto no cumplió lo ofrecido.**
  Ernesto is a snake. He backed down on the deal.
- **¿Le vas a entrar a los golpes o eres puro rajón?**
  Are you going to put your dukes up, or are you going to chicken out?

Slang in Mexico

▣ **Ranazo** (n.)
— A painful fall
- **Aquel cuate se dio un ranazo bárbaro.**
  That fellow had a terrible fall!

▣ **Rascuache** (adj.)
— Crumby; cheap; tacky
- **La alberca del hotel está muy rascuache.**
  The hotel pool is very crumby.
- **El amigo de Grisel se portó muy rascuache.**
  What Grisel's friend did was pretty tacky.

Rata (n.) (▢ Rat)
— Thief
- **Ese tipo es rata.**
  That guy is a thief.

Ratón (n.)
— Petty thief; pickpocket
- **Aquel que está en esa esquina tiene fama de ratón. ¡Cuídate de él!**
  That guy standing by the corner is known as a pickpocket. Watch out!

Respondón; respondona (adj.)
— Cheeky
- **No entiendo cómo soportas a tu chofer. Es muy respondón.**
  I don't understand why you put up with your driver. He's damned cheeky.

▣ **(Un) Resto** (see **(Un) Bonche**)

▣ **Rollo** (n.) (see **¡Qué rollo!**)
— A convoluted and confusing explanation (often used when giving excuses); a bunch of bull
- **No me vengas con tu rollo de siempre.**
  Don't give me your usual spiel.

▣ **Ruco(a)**
— Old (people only) (adj.)
- **Mi abuelita no quiso salir en su cumpleaños. Ya está muy ruca.**
  My grandmother didn't want to go out on her birthday. She's pretty old.
— An old person; an old geezer (n.)
- **Esa ruca me regañó porque no traigo medias.**
  That old bat bawled me out because I'm not wearing stockings.

📖 **Sangrón(a)** (adj.) (n.) (📖 Bloody)
— Boring or obnoxious (people only); a jerk
  ▪ **Me habían dicho que el papá de Julia era muy sangrón, pero no es cierto.**
    I had heard that Julia's father was obnoxious, but he isn't.

📖 **Sangronada** (n.)
— An obnoxious act
  ▪ **Manuel me hizo la misma sangronada de siempre.**
    Manuel did the same obnoxious thing he always does.

📖 **Segundo frente** (see **Casa chica**)
— Mistress
  ▪ **Ésa no es su esposa, es su segundo frente.**
    That's not his wife. It's his mistress (lover, paramour).

📖 **Serpentina** (see **Cheve**)

📖 **Serpiente** (see **Cheve**)

📖 **Simón** (adv.)
— Yes
  ▪ Speaker A: **¿Vas a lavar el coche?**
                   Are you going to wash the car?
    Speaker B: **Simón.**
                   Yeah.

📖 **Soba** (n.) (📖 A rubbing) (see **Poner(se) una soba**)
— A task or experience that leaves you totally exhausted.
  ▪ **El cambio de casa fue una verdadera soba. Tuve que hacer todo yo solo.**
    The move to the new house was a real drag. I had to do it all by myself.

📖 **Sopapo** (n.)
— A blow; slap; whack
  ▪ **Si no dejas de hacer tanto ruido, te voy a dar un sopapo**
    If you don't stop all that noise, I'm going to give you a whack.

📖 **Su (tu) segura servilleta** (from **Su seguro servidor**)
— Your unconditional servant
  ▪ **No te preocupes, al fin que aquí tienes a tu segura servilleta.**
    Don't worry. After all, your true blue friend (me) is here.

📖 **Tambache** (n.)
— Bundle of clothes or other stuff
  ▪ **No sé dónde guardar este tambache de ropa.**
    I don't know where to put this bundle of clothes.

Slang in Mexico

Tambo; tanque (n.) (📖 Tank) (Underworld jargon) (see **Bote** and **Nave**)
— Jail, the slammer, the cooler
- **Al ratero que trató de robarme, ya lo metieron al tambo (tanque).**
  The punk who tried to rob me is in the slammer.

📖 **Tatema** (n.) (see **Coco; Chirimoya; Choya; Chiluca; Maceta**)
— Head
- **¡Aprende a usar la tatema, tarado!**
  Learn to use your head, stupid!

Tela de donde cortar (n.) (📖 Material to cut from)
— All kinds of possibilities
- **Puedes manejarlo a tu gusto. Hay mucha tela de donde cortar.**
  Handle it anyway you want. There are all kinds of things you can do.

📖 **Tiliches** (n.) (see **Chunches**)
— Junk; ☺'s things
- **A ver si te vas con tus tiliches a otra parte.**
  Go somewhere else with your junk.

📖 **Titipuchal** (n.)
— A whole lot; a bunch
- **¡Qué bárbaro! Tienes un titipuchal de libros.**
  Wow! You sure have a lot of books!

📖 **Torta** (n.) (📖 A fat mouthwatering sandwich)
— Girl
- **¡César se ligó una buena torta!**
  Cesar picked up a real cool chick!

📖 **Tortuga** (n.) (corruption of **torta**, meaning a sandwich) (see *Mexican Food*)

📖 **Trácala** (n.)
— A scam
- **Ese negocio que te propusieron, es una trácala de lo más burda.**
  That business they proposed is nothing but a scam.

📖 **Tracalero** (adj.)
— A crooked person
- **Ramón es muy tracalero. Si lo descubren le va a ir mal.**
  Ramón is really crooked. If he gets caught, he's in trouble.

Tumbaburros (n.)
— A dictionary

- **Te hace mucha falta un buen tumbaburros.**
  You really need a good dictionary.

♉ (Un) Resto (see (Un) Bonche)

Vaciado(a) (adj.)
— Amusing; entertaining; funny
- **Este libro está bien vaciado. Te lo presto.**
  This is a really funny book. You can borrow it.
- **Jorge es un tipo de lo más vaciado.**
  Jorge is a scream.

Vacilón (n.)
— A fun time
- **A tus primas les encanta el vacilón.**
  Your cousins love to have a fun time.

↓ Valemadrina (n.) (corruption of "Me vale madre"; see *Not for Polite Society*)
— A non-existent "medicine" that makes ☺ not care about anything
- **Si sigues preocupándote así, vas a enfermarte. Tómate tus pastillas de "valemadrina".**
  If you keep on worrying like that, you'll get sick. Don't worry! Take it easy! Be happy!.

Vamos bien
— So far, so good
- **Aún no le entra agua a la lancha. Vamos bien.**
  The boat hasn't started leaking yet. So far, so good.

Vivales (adj.)
— A crooked operator
- **Si fuera tú, no haría negocio con Ramón. Tiene fama de vivales.**
  If I were you, I wouldn't do business with Ramon; he is known to be a slick operator.

Zoquete (adj.)
— Nitwit
- **¡No entiendes nada, pedazo de zoquete!**
  You don't understand anything, you nitwit!

3. Stand-alone Slang Expressions

¡A otro perro con ese hueso!
— Who do you think you're fooling?
- Speaker A: **Manuel sacó diez en todas las materias este semestre.**
  Manuel got straight As this semester.
- Speaker B: **¿El flojo de Manuel? ¡A otro perro con ese hueso!**
  That lazy bum? Who do you think you're fooling?

✍ ¡A todo dar!; ¡A todo meter! (adj.)
— Great!; terrific!; cool!; wonderful!
- Speaker A: **¿Cómo te va en tu nuevo trabajo?**
  How are you doing in your new job?

  Speaker B: **¡A todo meter!**
  Great!
- Speaker A: **¿Qué opinas de Leticia?**
  What do you think of Leticia?.

  Speaker B: **¡Es a todo dar!**
  She's really nice!

✍ ¡A todo meter! (see ¡A todo dar!)

✍ ¡Abusado!; ¡Aguzado!; ¡Buso! (adj.)
— Careful!; use your head!; stay on your toes!
- **Está a punto de empezar el examen. ¡Abusados! (¡Busos!)**
  The test is about to begin. Careful! Use your heads!

¡Adió!
— Used as an interjection to express incredulity or doubt
- Speaker A: **¿Ya sabes que Jaime es millonario?**
  Did you know that Jaime is a millionaire?

  Speaker B: **¡Adió!**
  You're kidding!

✍ ¡Aguas! (see Echar aguas)
— Watch out!; careful! (used as a warning of imminent danger)
- **¡Aguas! ¡No vayas a atropellar a esa viejita!**
  Watch out! Don't run down that little old lady!

¡Ah, jijos! (see ¡Hijo!)
— Gosh!; golly!; jeez!; good God!; holy cow!

Slang in Mexico

- **¡Ah jijos! ¡Mira esta foto de Mariela en bikini!**
  Holy Cow! Look at this picture of Mariela in a bikini!

¡Ahí muere!
— Call it quits!; That's enough!

- **Ya no sigan peleando. ¡Ahí muere!**
  Stop fighting and call it quits!

¡Ahí te voy! (frequently pronounced **áy te voy**)
— Watch out!; Here I come!

- Speaker A: **Ya puedes echar el coche para atrás.**
                     You can back the car up now.
- Speaker B: **¡Ahí te voy!**
                     OK, here I come.

†† Antro
— A discotheque

- **No voy a estar en la noche. Me voy al antro.**
  I won't be home tonight. I'm going to a disco.

¡Aquí sólo mis chicharrones suenan! (📖 The only **chicharrones** that make noise here are mine)

- **I am the only one who gives orders around here!**
  No discutas conmigo. Las cosas se harán como te dije. ¡Aquí, sólo mis chicharrones suenan!
  Don't argue with me. Things will be as I ordered. I am the only boss here!

A ver de qué cuero salen más correas (📖 Let's see what hide produces more belts)
— A boast meaning: Let's see who is best at this!

- **Vamos a jugar. A ver de qué cuero salen más correas.**
  Let's play! Then we'll know who's the best.

†† Batear a ☺
— To dump ☺

- **Me ligué un chavo, pero tuve que batearlo, porque luego conocí a su amigo.**
  I met a boy, but I had to dump him 'cause then I met a friend of his I like better.

¡Caifás con la lana!; ¡Cayitos! (see **Caer(se) con la lana**)
— Pay up!; hand over the dough!; fork over the dough!

- **Son 70 pesos por cabeza, y no pienso esperarlos. ¡Caifás con la lana! (¡Cayitos!)**
  That'll be 70 pesos each, and I have no intention of waiting for my money. Pay up!

Slang in Mexico

℞ **¡Calmantes montes!**
— Take it easy!
  - **Speaker A:**   **¡Apúrale, que tengo prisa!**
                     Step on it! I'm in a hurry!
  - **Speaker B:**   **Calmantes montes. Si me apuro, esto sale mal.**
                     Hey, take it easy. If I hurry, this won't turn out well.

℞ **¡Cayitos!** (see **¡Caifás con la lana!**)

℞†† **¡Chale!**
— How awful!; Yaaakk!
  - **Speaker A:**   **Elena fue al día de campo con un vestido de terciopelo con lentejuelas.**
                     Elena wore a velvet dress with sequins to the picnic.
  - **Speaker B:**   **¡Chale!**
                     How awful!

℞ **¡Chócalas! (¡Chócala!)**
— Shake hands!; Give me five! (to seal an agreement, a bet, etc.)
  - **Estoy de acuerdo, ¡chócalas!**
    I agree. Let's shake on that!

℞ **¡Chupó faros!** (see **¡Ya valió gorro!**)

†† **Dar el avión a** ☺
— To let ☺ think you are paying attention when you're not; To let ☺ have his/her own way; to humor ☺
  - **Si viene de malas, no vayas a bronquearte con mi hermano. Nada más dale el avión.**
    If my brother is in a bad mood, don't argue with him. Just humor him.

℞ **¡En la torre!**
— Yikes!
  - **¡En la torre! Se me olvidó la cartera.**
    Yikes! I forgot my wallet.

†† **¡Está cañón!** (euphemism for a rude expression); **¡Está grueso (a)!**
— That's very difficult!; That's great!; said of ☺ who is great
  - **Siempre no voy a entrar al concurso. ¡Está cañón (está grueso) ganarlo! Pero mi hermano sí. ¡El sí está cañón (El sí está grueso)!**
    I'm not going to take part in the contest. It's very difficult to win! But my brother will. He is great!

†† **¡Está de pelos!**
— That's terrific!; That's cool!

Slang in Mexico

- ▪ **¿Ya viste esa bici, güey? ¡Está de pelos!**
  See that bike, pal! It's cool!

†† ¡Está grueso (a)! (see ¡Está cañón!)

↩ ¡Este arroz ya se coció! (see ¡Ya estuvo!)
— †† Hacer el paro a ☺
— To help ☺ out of a bind
- ▪ **Iba a llegar tarde otra vez, pero tu papá me hizo el paro porque me dio un aventón.**
  I was going to be late again, but your dad helped me out 'cause he gave me a ride.

†† Güey
— Pal, friend
- ▪ **No sabes, güey, conocí a un güey guapísimo. Pero venía con mi ex-güey. Traté de hacerme güey, pero ya me había visto.**
  Guess what friend! I met a real cute dude, but he was with my ex. I tried to play dumb, but he had already seen me.

↩†† ¡Hígados! (see ¡Simón!)

¡Hijo!; ¡Híjole! (see ¡Ah, jijos!)
— Gosh!; goodness!; golly!; jeepers!; Christ!; Jesus!; gee whiz!; damn!
- ▪ **¡Hijo! (¡Híjole!) ¡Mira lo que hizo el perro!**
  Gosh! Look what the dog did!

↩†† ¡Is! (see ¡Simón!)

†† Jetear
— To sleep
- ▪ **Ramón se sienta hasta atrás para poder jetearse en clase.**
  Ramon sits at the back so he can sleep during class.

†† Ligar
— To flirt; to give ☺ the come on; to find a date
- ▪ **Esa chava se viste muy fresa, por eso no liga ni un catarro.**
  She's such a prim dresser. That's why she can't get a boyfriend.

†† Llegar(le) a ☺
- ▪ **Tengo que ir muy bonita. Estoy segura de que hoy me llega Héctor.**
  I've got to look great today. I'm sure Hector will ask me to go steady.

¡Mangos! (see ¡Nanai!)
— Hell no!

Slang in Mexico

- **¿Que me tengo que quedar en casa el sábado por la noche? ¡Mangos!**
  You mean I have to stay home on Saturday night? Hell no!

¡Me lleva el tren!
— Confound it!; Damn it to hell!
- **Mira, ya está lloviendo y no tengo limpiadores. ¡Me lleva el tren!**
  Look, it's raining and I have no windshield wipers. Damn, damn, damn!

¡Me vale!; ¡Me vale sombrilla!
— I couldn't care less!; Who cares?
- Speaker A: **Dice Leticia que está muy molesta contigo.**
  Leticia says she's very upset with you.
- Speaker B: **¡Me vale!**
  I couldn't care less!

¡Me vale sombrilla! (see ¡Me vale!)

Mis ojos (📖 My eyes) (see Molcas)
— Used to refer to ☺ who is present, whom you don't want to mention by name
- **Aquí mis ojos está de muy mal humor.**
  You-know-who is really in a bad mood.

Molcas (see Mis ojos)
— Used when you don't want to use ☺'s name
- **No hables de eso delante de molcas.**
  Don't talk about that in front of you-know-who.

†† ¡Nada que ver! (short version of No tener nada que ver)
— Nothing to do with it!
- **Escucha. ¡Esto es música! Lo de hace rato, ¡nada que ver!**
  Listen to this. This is music. What we heard a while ago has nothing to do with it!

¡Nanai!; ¡Naranjas!; ¡Narices! (these are negative simply because they begin with n, same as No) (see ¡Mangos!)
— No!; Nuts to that!; No way!
- Speaker A: **¿Quieres cuidar a los niños mientras voy al cine?**
  Do you want to look after the kids while I go to the movies?
- Speaker B: **¡Nanai!**
  No way!

¡Naranjas (see ¡Nanai!)

¡Narices! (see ¡Nanai!)

⚥†† Nel; Nelazo; Nel pastel; Nelson

— No

- Speaker A: **¿Te tomas otra cuba?**
  Do you want another drink?

  Speaker B: **Nel (Nel pastel).**
  No.

⚥†† Nelazo (see Nel)

⚥†† Nel pastel (see Nel)

⚥†† Nelson (see Nel)

Ni de chiste

— Not on your life!

- Speaker A: **¿Vas a dejar que se queden con el dinero?**
  Are you going to let them keep the money?

  Speaker B: **Ni de chiste.**
  Not on your life!

Ni fu ni fa

— Neither one thing nor the other; very so-so

- Speaker A: **¿Es bonita la novia de Jaime?**
  Is Jaime's girlfriend pretty?

  Speaker B: **Ni fu ni fa.**
  So-so.

¡Ni loco!

— I'd be crazy to do that!

- Speaker A: **¿Quieres escalar el Popo este fin de semana?**
  Do you want to climb the Popo this weekend?

  Speaker B: **¡Ni loco!**
  Are you kidding?

¡No juegues!

— You're joking!

- Speaker A: **¿Sabes que se murió Chepe?**
  Did you know that Chepe passed away?

  Speaker B: **¡No juegues!**
  You're kidding me!

†† ¡No manches! (euphemism for a rude expression)

— Don't get carried away!; Behave yourself! ; That's not nice!; Stop it!

- **¡No manches! Te acabaste las papas tú solo.**
  That's not nice! You hogged all the fries!

Slang in Mexico

¡No seas . . . !

— Don't be mean, a bastard, an SOB, etc.

- **El pobre niño se muere de ganas por el juguete y tú no se lo compras. ¡No seas!**
  The poor kid is dying for that toy, and you won't get it for him. Don't be mean!
- **¿Ahora andas con tres viejas al mismo tiempo? ¡No seas!**
  Do you mean you're now going around with three women at the same time? Don't be a cad!

†† ¡O sea . . . !

— An all purpose phrase meaning: That is . . . !; I mean . . . !

- **Necesitas ir con nosotros de vacaciones. ¡O sea . . . ! Si no vas, no eres nuestra amiga. ¿Captas?**
  You've got to go with us on vacation. I mean . . . If you don't, you are not one of us. Got it!

㋫ ¡Órale!

— The meaning of this expression depends entirely on the circumstances. It can express surprise, approval, disapproval, warning, permission, disbelief and a number of other feelings and attitudes, depending on what's going on and the speaker's expression, tone and gestures.
— If you bump into someone on the sidewalk, and he exclaims angrily **¡Órale!**, it means: *Hey, watch it buster!*
— If you give your boss a case of very expensive French wine for his birthday and he exclaims **¡Órale!** with raised eyebrows, it means: *What a terrific gift!*
— If you're walking down the street with a male friend, when a curvaceous beauty comes into view, and he gives you a poke with his elbow and says **¡Órale!**, he means: *Get a load of that!*
— If you ask your boss for permission to leave half an hour early and he says **¡Órale!**, he means: *Sure, go ahead!*
— If you are watching TV with a friend and he exclaims **¡Órale!** when a magician turns an elephant into a kangaroo right in front of your eyes, he means: *How in the hell did he do that?*

㋫ ¡Pácatelas!

— Gosh!

- **¡Pácatelas! ¿Ya viste que aquí van a hacer un edificio de 90 pisos?**
  Gosh! Did you see that they are going to build a 90-story skyscraper here?

¡Para nada!

— Not at all!; No way!

- Speaker A: **¿Vas a volver con Jorge?**
                Are you going to make up with Jorge?

  Speaker B: **¡Para nada!**
                Not on your life!

- Speaker A: **¿Te molesta el humo?**
                Does the smoke bother you?

  Speaker B: **¡Para nada!**
                Not at all!

¡Paso!

— I pass; Leave me out of it!

- **No me metan en sus líos. ¡Yo paso!**
  Don't involve me in your problems. I pass! (Leave me out of it!)

†† Pelar a ☺

— To pay attention to ☺

- **¡Mamá, hazme caso! Tengo rato hablándote y no me pelas.**
  Hey, Mom! I have been talking to you for a while and you just pay no attention to me.

†† ¡Pinta tu raya!; ¡Tú no juegas!

— Keep out of this!

- **¡Pinta tu raya! (¡Tú no juegas!) La bronca es con ella.**
  Stay out of this! She is the one in trouble.

†† ¡Qué buena onda!

— That's terrific!

- **Hoy van a dejarnos salir temprano. ¡Qué buena onda! ¿no?**
  We're getting out early today. That's terrific, eh?

¡Qué flojera!

— I don't feel like doing that; What a bore!; I'm too tired!

- **Tengo que lavar el coche. ¡Qué flojera!**
  I have to wash the car. What a bore!

- **Otra vez lunes y hay que ir al trabajo. ¡Qué flojera!**
  Another Monday and I've got to go to work. I don't feel like it.

↓ ¡Qué friega!

— What a nuisance!

- **El tráfico está parado en el Periférico. ¡Qué friega!**
  The traffic is backed up on the freeway. What a nuisance!

꛷×†† ¡Qué jalada!; ꛷×†† ¡Eso está muy jalado! (The origin of these expressions is explained in *Not for Polite Society*.)

— That's pretty hard to believe! That's a big exaggeration!

- **Dice Domingo que él solo preparó la conferencia. ¡Qué jalada!**
  Domingo says he prepared the conference all by himself. That's pretty hard to believe!

†† ¡Qué mala onda!

— What a bummer!

- **Daniel no va a venir porque está enfermo. ¡Qué mala onda!**
  Daniel is not coming 'cause he's sick. That's too bad (What a bummer)!

Slang in Mexico

¡Qué mala pata!
— What lousy luck!

- Speaker A: **La línea aérea me perdió las seis maletas que traía de Europa.**
  The airline lost all six bags I was bringing back from Europe.

  Speaker B: **¡Qué mala pata!**
  What lousy luck!

¿Qué onda?
— What's new?; What's going on?; What's up?

- Speaker A: **¿Qué onda, cuates?**
  Hi! What's up?

  Speaker B: **Nada nuevo. Todo tranquilo.**
  Nothing new. Everything's cool.

¡Qué oso!
— What a fuss!; That's an embarrassing situation

- **¡Qué oso! Quise morirme cuando me di cuenta de que mis pantalones estaban manchados.**
  What a fuss! I wanted to die when I realized my pants were stained!

¿Qué panzón? (corruption of ¿Qué pasó?)
— What's up?

- **¿Qué panzón? ¿Qué hacen aquí?**
  What's up? What are you doing here?

¡Qué poca! (euphemism for a rude expression)
— Disgraceful!; Of all the nerve!

- **¡Qué poca! Eugenio le voló la chava a su hermano.**
  Eugenio stole his brother's girlfriend. What a crappy thing to do! (Of all the nerve!) .

¡Qué relajo!
— What a mess!

- **Ya van tres veces que cambian de opinión. ¡Qué relajo!**
  That's the third time they've changed their mind. What a mess!

¡Qué rollo!
— What a nuisance!

- Speaker A: **Parece que Raquel perdió el dinero.**
  It seems Raquel lost the money.

  Speaker B: **¡Pobre, qué rollo!**
  What a nuisance!

— What a spiel!; What a lot of bull!

- Speaker A: **¿Oíste la excusa que dio Marcos?**
  Did you hear Marco's excuse?

  Speaker B: **Sí. ¡Qué rollo!**
  Yeah! What a lot of bull!

Slang in Mexico

✋ **¡Qué padre!; ¡Qué suave!**

— That's cool!; That's great!

  ▪ **¡Qué padre! (¡Qué suave!) Nos van a dar dos postres.**
    Cool! (Great!) We are getting two desserts.

✋ **¡Qué suave! (see ¡Qué padre!)**

✋ **¿Qué te duele? (📖 What's hurting you?)**

— This is a macho expression to be thrown at anyone who scowls at you as if ❐ were hurting

  ▪ **¿Qué te duele, amigo? ¿Quieres bronca?**
    What's up friend? Are you looking for trouble?

✋ **¿Qué (te) traes? (📖 What are you carrying?)**

— What's your problem? What do you want? What do you think you're doing?

  ▪ **¿Quieres bronca? ¿Qué te traes?**
    You want trouble? What's bothering you?

✋ **¡Sácatelas!**

— An exclamation more or less equivalent to *Goodness!* but with much coarser origins.

  ▪ Speaker A: **Emilia se enojó con Mario y lo corrió de la casa.**
                    Emilia got mad at Mario and ran him out of the house.

    Speaker B: **¡Sácatelas!**
                    Good heavens!

¡Sale!; ¡Sale y vale!

— I agree!; It's a deal!; I'm with you on that!; Let's do it!

  ▪ Speaker A: **Yo digo que empecemos por rentar un local.**
                    I say we should start by renting a place.

    Speaker B: **¡Sale y vale!**
                    I agree! Let's do it!

¡Sanseacabó!

— That is the end of that!

  ▪ **Berta, vas a tomarte tu medicina ahora, y ¡sanseacabó!**
    Berta, you will take your medicine now, and that's the end of it!

¡Sepa!; ✋⬇ ¡Sepa la fregada!; 📖¡Sepa la bola!

— God only knows!; How should I know?; Who knows?

  ▪ Speaker A: **¿Dónde está la engrapadora?**
                    Where's the stapler?

    Speaker B: **¡Sepa!**
                    God only knows!

†† **Ser matado(a)**

— To be very studious

Slang in Mexico

- **Mi hermana es muy matada. Yo prefiero irme al antro con mis amigas, a ver qué ligo.**
  Mi sister is very studious, but I prefer to go to the disco with my friends and meet boys.

✝✝ Ser X (equis)
— To be neither one thing nor the other; to be very so-so
- **Me dijiste que tu hermano era X (equis), pero la verdad es que es bien buena onda.**
  You told me your brother was very so-so, but he's actually real cool.

✍✝✝ ¡Simón!; ¡Sincho!; ¡Hígados!; ¡Is!
— Yes
- Speaker A: **¿Ya viste qué buena chava?**
                      Wow! Did you see that girl's figure?
  Speaker B: **¡Simón! (sincho, hígados, is)**
                      I sure did!

✍✝✝ ¡Sincho! (see ¡Simón!)

✝✝ ¡Tú no juegas! (see ¡Pinta tu raya!)

✍ ¡Va de nuez! (for Va de nuevo)
— (Once) again!
- **No le atiné al blanco, ¡va de nuez!**
  I missed! I'll try again!

✝✝ Volar(se) una clase
— To skip class
- **Me volé una clase para poder ver el partido.**
  I skipped a class to go and watch the football match.

✍ (Ya) ☺□ valió gorro; (Ya) ☺□ valió sombrilla; (Ya) ☺□ chupó faros
— ☺□ became useless; ☺□ is finished; ☺ died; □ won't happen
- **No pierdas tu tiempo reparando esa silla, ya valió gorro (ya valió sombrilla, ya chupó faros).**
  Don't waste your time trying to fix that chair. It is beyond repair.
- **Ayer chupó faros mi suegra.**
  My mother-in-law died yesterday.

¡Vaya!
— Well!
- **¡Vaya! Y ahora, después de todo, te enojas conmigo.**
  Well! After all that's happened, you now get mad at me!

¿Y qué?
— So what?; Want to make something of it?

- Speaker A: **Tienes el pelo demasiado largo y tus calcetines no van con tu traje.**
  Your hair is too long and your socks don't match your suit.

  Speaker B: **¿Y qué?**
  So what?

¡Ya caigo!

— Oh, now I get it! (When it has taken you a very long time to catch on to ☐).

- **¡Ya caigo! ¿Sabes por qué Elena está enojada conmigo? ¡Porque se me olvidó su cumpleaños!**
  Now I get it! You know why Helen is mad at me? Because I forgot her birthday!

¡Ya estuvo!; ¡Este arroz ya se coció!

— Ready!; It's finally over; It's finally done

- **Me costó mucho trabajo, pero ¡ya estuvo! (¡este arroz ya se coció!).**
  I wasn't easy, but it's finally done!

¡Ya estuvo bueno!; ¡Ya estuvo suave!

— That's enough!

- **Niños, ¡ya no estén jugando aquí! ¡Ya estuvo bueno! (¡Ya estuvo suave!)**
  Kids, stop playing here! That's enough!

¡Ya vas!

— It's a deal!; OK! (I like your suggestion); Great idea!

- Speaker A: **¿Qué te parece si hoy vamos a comer comida china?**
  How about Chinese for lunch today?

  Speaker B: **¡Ya vas!**
  Great idea!

Yerba (see Mota)

B. Not for Polite Society

To know the naughty and vulgar expressions of a society is to know the society itself. The Spanish picaresque would not be worthy of the name without the salt and pepper of *bad* words. All the fun would be gone.

These words and phrases should become part of your passive vocabulary simply for the purpose of getting a gist of what is being said. Non-native speakers should resist the temptation to use them, not for reasons of prudery, but because only a practiced native speaker can use them with the proper effect.

Contrary to what people might think, the lower classes do not have a monopoly on coarse language. It is to be heard liberally sprinkled throughout the repartee at the most exclusive gatherings at the very pinnacle of society.

Our purpose here is to provide a fairly ample collection of vulgarisms (used mainly in Mexico), with a brief comment as to the meaning of each. Not only vulgarisms are included, but also the common or amusing words that go hand in hand with them.

♬ **Andar jodido** or **andar jólidei** (see **Joder**)

♬ **Buey** or **Güey** (n.)
— Literally, an ox; used to mean dumb or stupid. (**¡Cómo serás buey!** *You stupid ass!*; **¡No te hagas buey!** *Don't play dumb!*) It is very common and often highly offensive, as it carries the implication of castration.

Cabrón (n.)
— A man who has been cuckolded or condones the adultery of his wife. Jokes are numerous: **Pobre de mi hijita, le salió el marido cabrón**. *My poor daughter, her husband turned out to be a cuckold*. It is also used to mean ruffian, evildoer or bastard (**Fulano es un cabrón.** *So-and-so is a bastard*). If you are proud of being a bastard, the word is used in a bragging tone (**¡A cabrón nadie me gana!** *Nobody is as big bastard as I am!*). In the diminutive, it can even take on an affectionate note (**¡Óyeme, cabroncito!** *Hey, you little bastard!*). **¡Está cabrón!** means *It's very difficult!* (hard to believe, to get or to do); **¡está camión!** and **¡está cañón!** are euphemisms that have recently come into use.

Cabronada (n.)
— According to the dictionary, an infamous action against a person's honor, or a serious annoyance. It is generally used to mean a contemptible act. (**¡Qué buena cabronada le hiciste!** *Boy, you really screwed him good!*).

Caca (n.) **(see Mierda)**

Caca grande (n.) (📖 Big shit)
— A big shot. A big cheese

Cagar(la) (v.) (📖 To shit on ☐)
— To shit (used more in Spain than in Latin America)
  ▪ **Me cago en ☐**
    To hell with ☐
— To make a big mistake
  ▪ **¡La cagaste!**
    You really made a big mistake!
  ▪ **¡Ten cuidado! No vayas a cagarla.**
    Be careful. Don't screw things up!

Carajada (n.)
— A mean action (less violent than a **cabronada**). (**¡Esas son carajadas!** *That's a mean thing to do!*)
  Used relatively little.

¡Carajo! (interjection)
— *Hell!* A very common exclamation. Used to express disappointment, anger, etc. (**¡Carajo!** *Shit!*
  Damn! Hell! **¡Vete al carajo!** *Go to hell!*). It is not as rude as other expressions meaning the same
  thing.

📖 **¡Chin!**
— This expression was originally used as a euphemism of **chinga** or **chinga tu madre**, but it is so
  pervasive, even among children, that it no longer means anything but *Oh boy!*; *Oh, my God!* or
  something of that sort.

📖 **Chinga; chingada** (n.)
— These words have endless applications. They are synonyms of nuisance (**¡Esto es una chinga!** *This
  is a pain in the neck!* or **¡Qué chinga!** *What a damn nuisance!*). **Llevarse una chinga de perro
  bailarín** is to go through a great deal of troubles or to work one's head off; this expression comes
  from the misery dogs go through when being trained for circus or street shows. The **chingada** is
  where one is often sent (**¡Te vas a la chingada! ¡Vete a la chingada!** *Go to hell!*). **¡Me lleva la
  chingada!** or **¡Me carga la chingada!** are expressions of great displeasure. **¡Está de la chingada!**
  means this is awfully difficult, extremely bad, and so on.

Chingadera (n.)
— Generally speaking, a despicable act. (**¡Estas son chingaderas!** *This is an awful thing to do!*).

Chingaderita (n.)
— A **chingaderita** is something insignificant, worthless.

Slang in Mexico

Chingar (v.)

— In Mexico this is a conjugated verb whose basic meaning is to screw (someone). According to Octavio Paz, the word **chingar**, with all its multiple half tones, takes up a great part of our lives and classifies our relations with our friends and fellow citizens. For the Mexican, life is a question of **chingar** or being **chingado** (to screw or be screwed). In other words, to humiliate, to punish and offend, or to be victim of these acts. Common people are so attached to this word, that they use it for many other purposes (**¡Ora, chíngale!** *Get going! Move it!*) (**¡Ya me chingó!** *He screwed me . . . got the better of me!*) (**¡Te voy a chingar!** *I'm going to get you!*). (**¡Chingao!** (from **chingado**) *Hell! Damn!*). **Fregar** is used as an euphemism of **chingar**.

¡Chinga tu madre!

— This is a "**mentada de madre**" and one of the worst possible offenses. It is an invitation to screw one's own mother. As an insult, it exists in many other countries, although the tone varies. In some states in Mexico, such as Veracruz, it is so common that it has lost its capacity to offend. (The grammatically correct expression is **Chinga a tu madre**, but the **a** got lost to make it shorter.)

(Un) Chingo (n.)

— Used by young people (and a great many older ones as well) to mean *a whole lot*. It is said quite free of inhibitions, as in **Me dieron un chingo de lápices.** *They gave a whole bunch of pencils.*

Chingón (n.)

— A person who is a **chingón** (almost always male) is someone who is the best at something or at everything in general, in a self-satisfied, big-ego sort of way . . . someone who is so top-of-the-heap that if he were a lion or a horse, he would be the dominant male. **Fregón** is used as an euphemism of **chingón**.

Coger (v.)

— Literally to grasp or to take. But today, **coger** means to fornicate, to screw (and of course the *F* word). That's why people avoid using the word in its original sense, as it leaves you wide open for all kinds of "**albures**". **Tomar** o **agarrar** is used instead. In bullfighting terms it is used when the bullfighter is injured by the horns of the bull and even this use lends itself to play on words.

Cojones (n.)

— Testicles, balls. To have **cojones** is to be the he-man or to be very brave. To lack them is a symptom of cowardice. Used more in Spain. In Latin America, the term **huevos** (balls) which has various connotations, is used instead. **Tompiates**, originally large woven palm basket, is also a word for testicles in Mexico.

Cojonudo(a) (adj.)

— Said of something that is very good, great. (**¡Estuvo cojonuda la fiesta!** *The party was terrific!*) Of course it also implies maleness. (**¿Te sientes muy cojonudo?** *You're pretty hot stuff, eh?*)

Coño (n.)

— The closest literal translation is *pussy* (rel. to the female anatomy), but the closest meaning is S*hit!, Damn!, Hell!*, or something in that vein. It is usually used alone. Used more in Spain than in Latin America.

Culo (n.)

— This is the bad word for the human rear-end. In Spain and other countries, it is relatively mild, but in Mexico it is highly offensive. It is used as a synonym of coward (**¡No seas culo!** *Don't be a coward!*); however, the noun **culero** is more often used (**No cuentes con fulano, es un culero.** *Don't count on So-and-so. He is a coward.*) It is also used as a verb (**¿Se van a culear?** *Are you going to back down like cowards?*) **Culear** can also mean to fornicate. In all its variations, the word is taboo in Mexico.

Huevos or Güevos (n.)

— Testicles, balls. It is applied in various ways. To designate great courage (**Zutano tiene muchos huevos**. *X has a great deal of courage, guts*). When someone abuses another in any way, it is commonly said: **¡Qué huevos!** *What guts!*, or the very picturesque variant **¡Ah, qué huevos tan azules!** *Oh, what blue balls!*, meaning *How can you do that!* or *Don't you dare!* in a mixture of admiration and disapproval. It is also used to refer to a very lazy person (**Te pesan mucho los huevos.** *You are dragging your ass.*) (See **huevón.**) There is, in addition, a sign made with the hand, as if you were holding the balls, to mean the same thing. **Tompiates**, from the Nahuatl for a big woven palm basket, is used as a synonym of **huevos** (**¡Tiene unos tompiatotes!** *He is so brave!*). **A huevo** (adv.) means that something has to be done whether a person likes it or not. There are picturesque sayings: **Cuando las cosas son a huevo, aunque las gallinas no pongan** (*When there is no choice, no matter if hens lay no eggs*; meaning things have to be done). When someone must put up with something unpleasant or do something against one's wishes, he must **morderse un huevo**, *bite one of your balls*, rather than the bullet (a difficult and painful procedure). When something is exceedingly difficult to do or costs a lot, it costs a ball (**Me costó un huevo**). When the difficulty of the price is even greater, it costs one ball and half of the other (**Me costó un huevo y la mitad del otro**). Obviously, the verb **costar** is used in ordinary language to express difficulty (**Me cuesta mucho levantarme temprano.** *It's very hard for me to get up early*). If you are in polite company and you want to say that something was very expensive, you can say: **Me costó un ojo de la cara.**

Echar (la) hueva (v.)

— To loaf. **Pienso pasarme el día echando la hueva**, *I'm going to spend the day loafing.* **Tengo mucha hueva**, *I don't feel like doing anything.*

Echar (se) un palito (v.)

— To have sexual intercourse.

Slang in Mexico

(La) hueva (n.)

— Laziness. The way you feel when you don't feel like doing □

- **Me da mucha hueva meterme a nadar.**
  I don't feel like going in swimming.

Huevón, huevona (n.)

— Lazy. It is never used in the sense of brave or macho. (**¡Ya levántate, huevón!** *Get up you lazy ass!*)

▷ Jalársela (v.) Jalada (n.)

— This is an euphemism for male sexual self gratification, but a **jalada** has come to mean something that doesn't make sense, a crazy idea (**¡Se te ocurre cada jalada!** *You keep getting these crazy ideas!*). **Jalársela** is to get absurd ideas (**A David le encanta jalársela cuando escribe sus poemas**, *David loves to put these nutty things in his poetry*). **Jalársela** also refers to an exaggeration, the idea being that one pulls one's weenie (so to speak) to make it look longer than it actually is (**¡No te la jales!** *Don't exaggerate!*); although it is very frequently used, it is still vulgar.

Joder (v.)

— A synonym of **chingar**. Particularly in Spain, it has the meaning of to harm, to bother, also to rape or simply to fornicate. In its different tenses, its meaning may vary. **Andar jodido** means to be broke. **Estar jodido** can mean to be in a very bad way or to be mistaken (**¡Estás jodido!** *You are wrong!*). Both **Andar** or **Estar jodido** also mean to be in a very bad shape (**Se ve que andas (estás) bien jodido, ¿estás enfermo?** *You really look terrible, are you sick?*) **¡No jodas!** is *Don't bother me!*, or when said in disbelief, *You're kidding?*

Joda (n.)

— Can also be a synonym of **chinga** (**¡Qué joda se llevaron!** *They really got screwed!*). It is used to refer to something very unpleasant, which is a **joda**.

Madre (n.)

— This word is used to mean either something worthless or something great. (**¡Me vale madre!** *I don't give a damn!*) (**¡Vale madre!** *It's useless!*) (**¡Esto está a toda madre!** *This is terrific!)* **¡Tu madre!** is one way to answer an insult. **Tener poca madre** or **No tener madre** is to be a bastard. However, when referring to a thing, it could be the opposite (**¡El guisado está de poca madre!** *This food is fabulous!*). **Madre** is a kind of wild card. **¡En la madre!** is like *Oh, my God!* (but terribly vulgar). **Darle a** ☺ **en la madre** is to beat someone up or kill him, and **Darse en la madre** is to have an accident where you are badly injured, although **Darse en la madre con** ☺ is to have a fistfight with ☺.

Mamar (v.); Mamón (n.); Mamilas (n.); Mamadas (n.)

— **Mamar** is to suck mother's milk (in which case it is not vulgar at all), but also to practice oral sex. However, **No mames** means *Don't bother me!*, *Don't be a nuisance!* or *Don't try to fool* *me!* (perhaps implying that one does not wish to be sucked on). A **mamón**, or its euphemism **mamilas**, is a pest or a nuisance, who tries to take advantage of people or deceive them. **Fulano es bien mamón** (or **mamilas**) is *So-and-so is a real jerk*. **Mamadas** are incredible, crazy or idiotic ideas. **¡Se te ocurre cada mamada!** is *Where do you get these stupid ideas?* **No me vengan con mamadas** is *Don't come to me with those harebrained ideas!* Then, back to the literal meaning, a common saying is: **Está bien que mamen, pero que no muerdan**, which is *If you've got to suck* (act like a damn fool), *at least try not to bite*. A variation to this is: **¡Está bien que mames, pero no te cuelgues!** *(If you've got to suck, try not to hang your whole weight on it)*. There are other euphemisms: **No mameyes en tiempo de melones** *(No mameyes in melon season)*, is used instead of **¡No mames! Quema mucho el sol** *(The sun is really burning)* is used instead of **¡Qué mamón! Mamón** is also a person who says something disagreeable or who is suspected of telling a lie or of exaggerating (**¡No seas mamón!**). This is much used by teenagers, but still very vulgar.

Mayate (n.) (see Puto)

Mear(se) (v.)

— To piss. **¡Te estás meando fuera de la bacinica!** (📖 You're pissing outside the chamber pot.) This means *You're getting it wrong!* or *You're missing the whole point!*

Mierda (n.)

— Shit. This word is used to emphasize how little someone is worth (**¡Vales mierda!** *You mean nothing! You're a nobody!*), and it is one of the best places to send your enemy, or simply someone who is becoming a pain in the ass (**¡Vete a la mierda!** *Screw you! Go to hell!*). **Caca** means the same thing. To be a **Come caca** (or **caquita**) is to be a poor devil, a nothing, nonentity. To be **Comiendo caca** is to be distracted, to be not thinking.

Mono (n.)

— Used to refer to the feminine sexual parts.

Ojete (n.)

— The dictionary meaning is anus, but in gutter language it is used to mean coward, because that part of the anatomy seems to contract when a person is scared. An **ojete** is also a worthless person (an asshole).

Pedo (n.)

— This word means a fart, but also has a great many meanings, and is a part of many *albures*. **¡Está de pedo!** means *That's very difficult!* **¿Para qué tanto pedo?** means *Why complicate something that is not really complicated?* **Hacerla de pedo** is to make something difficult or to make trouble. **Estar o andar de pedo** is to be drunk; **ponerse un pedo** is to get drunk; **andar persa** is used as a euphemism of **andar pedo**. **Echar de pedos** is to scold someone violently (**El patrón está enojadísimo, ¡me va a echar de pedos!** *The boss is furious, he's going to give me hell!*).

Slang in Mexico

Pendejada (n.)

— Foolishness; stupidity (**¡Qué pendejada acabo de hacer!** *What a stupid thing I've just done!*) (**Se te ocurre cada pendejada.** *You think of the stupidest things.*)

Pendejo(a) (n.)

— According to the dictionary, this means hair that grows in the groin. Also used as a synonym of *stupid*, although it may have different meanings, depending on the phrase. **¡Eres un pendejo!** or **¡Cómo serás pendejo!** means *You jerk, moron, idiot!*). On the other hand **¡Te traigo pendejo!** or **¡Eres mi pendejo!** means I can run circles around you, and also implies that you are taking advantage of another's foolishness. It is frequently used when offended, as in **¡A mí no me van a ver la cara de pendejo!** *No one is going to make a fool of me!* Sometimes it has a festive tone: **Está bueno que seas pendejo, pero no abuses.** *It's OK to be a jerk, but don't overdo it.* Or a derogatory tone: **Fulano es un pobre pendejo.** *John Doe is a poor fool.* **Hacerse pendejo** is to pretend not to know something, to play dead, either to the detriment of others or for one's own benefit. **¡Se me hace que te estás haciendo pendejo para no pagar la cuenta!** *It seems to me that you're playing dead to avoid paying the bill!* An amusing saying is **El que no se hace pendejo, no llega a viejo**, roughly *It's very important to know when to play dead*. **Un pendejo con iniciativa** (a person much to be feared because of his proclivity for causing trouble and getting other people into it) is a fool with lots of get-up-and-go.

♫ Pinche (adj.)

— Literally, a kitchen servant. Now used as an adjective to mean crumby, third rate, tacky. (**¡Qué amigo más pinche!** *What a worthless friend!*, **¡Esto está muy pinche!** *This is pretty crumby!* **¿Dónde están las pinches llaves?** *Where are those darned keys?*). Frequently used in conjunction with another adjective: **Pinche cabrón, pinche puto.** A common insult in Mexico is **¡Hijo de tu pinche madre!** *Son of your worthless mother!* **Pinchurriento** is a way of partially disguising the word.

Pito (n.)

— Nowhere in the Spanish speaking world is there a shortage of words to refer to the male member. **Pito** is the most common (also the cutest, as it means *whistle*). Other (very vulgar) are **chile** (green pepper), **camote** (sweet potato), **pinga, verga, riel** (rail), **chafalote, corneta** (bugle), **pizarrín** (chalk), **reata** (rope), etc.

Puta (n.)

— Whore; prostitute. **Hijo de puta** (son of a bitch, son of a whore) is the ultimate in insults, even worse than **hijo de la chingada. Casa de putas** is a whore house. There are sayings: **Puta la madre, puta la hija, puta la manta que la cobija** (*The mother is a whore, the daughter is a whore, and so is the blanket which covers her*). The exclamation **¡Puta madre!** is not aimed at anyone in particular, but is meant to express displeasure at something gone wrong. A very thinly veiled euphemism of **puta** is **uta**.

Puto (n.)

— A male homosexual, although it is also used as a synonym of coward. It has suffixes with festive overtones: **putón, putete, putarrón, putinski** (**Fulano es medio putón.** *So-and-so is somewhat of a queer*). **Mayate** or **mayatón** is the "masculine" male homosexual. **Joto** is a perfectly common word to define a gay male.

🏱 **Tiznada** (n.)

— Euphemism for **chingada**. It can be said without causing an uproar. **Preguntó si al otro también se lo había llevado la tiznada.** (A line from *Corrido*, a short story by Juan José Arreola.)

🏱 **Tompiates** (n.) (see **Cojones**)

C. The Mexican *Albur*

In most languages, words are so versatile that they can often be invested with double meanings that can be subtle and very witty. The humorist uses them to weave a play on words or an amusing phrase that spices the conversation. The greatest writer in the English language, Shakespeare, was not embarrassed to resort to "the lowest form of wit" (the pun) throughout his numerous masterpieces.

In Mexico, the double meaning achieved by hiding naughty words and phrases in a seemingly innocent sentence is an art form requiring great cleverness. It is known as the **albur**. It invariably involves an attack on someone's masculinity or sexual sensitivity, and that someone usually replies with another **albur**, which is likely to elicit still another, and so on, until the loser fails to think up an appropriate reply and is forced to swallow his pride and accept defeat in silence, since one or more of those present (i.e., a female) may have witnessed the entire exchange without catching any of the double meanings so cunningly lurking just under the surface.

The word **albur** is thought to be a corruption of **calambur**, from the French **calembour**, which means *pun* or *play on words*. The **albur** is always mischievous and always sexually offensive. It is a game normally played between or among men (any woman engaging in this type of verbal ping pong would be considered far too vulgar to be treated as a lady . . . the double standard is still alive and well in Latin America), and is prompted by the same instinct that incites the males of a species to have it out with each other in their irresistible need to establish dominance; however, in the case of the Mexican *Homo sapiens*, the sparring often takes the form of this refined but vicious cleverness rather than a brutish frontal attack (often among friends, like a verbal game of tennis).

There are many standard **albures**, which are no longer particularly original, but continue to be used because they are so effective. A typical **albur** would be **Te invito al Bar del Coyote Cojo**, which translates as *Let's have a drink at the Lame Coyote Bar*. However, any Mexican boy over the age of ten will immediately catch the **Yo te cojo** hidden in the sentence, by means of which the speaker is offering to make the listener the object of his baser instincts. The spirit is playful, but the effect is nevertheless humiliating (*Some Special Cases* warns against using the verb **coger** in Mexico, as it can no longer be uttered free of its very rude sexual connotation).

The **albur** is a truly enticing challenge, which ends with one of the fencers being defeated when he can't come up with a suitable answer. Often the tables are turned, and the challenger becomes the victim. The "**coyote cojo**" **albur** is only one of hundreds of possible ways of shooting off a poison-tipped sexual barb. The **albur** is so all-pervasive that most men can't get through a conversation without them, and that applies to the vast majority of the male population of Mexico. Naturally, this is limited to situations involving close friends, or mass confrontation situations such as sports events where large numbers of men are gathered. The **albur** is never used as a weapon against a mere acquaintance or a stranger.

Slang in Mexico

In his novel **Gazapo**, the Mexican writer Gustavo Sainz makes use of a very old **albur**: "**Más largo que un entierro**", which is actually a perfectly good expression meaning that something is longer than a funeral (very long), when it is not used as an **albur**. But here, since the verb **enterrar** means *to stick something into something* (aside from *to bury*), and **el largo** is the equivalent of *the long one,* the reader will have no trouble guessing the intention behind this little gem, to which the opponent might reply: **Ahora sí me agarraste descuidado,** meaning *You caught me off guard* (the intention being *You grabbed me . . .* the reader can imagine where), or **No me toques ese tema** (*Let's not talk about that*), which can be interpreted as *Don't touch my you-know-what.* These effectively send the ball back to the other guy, who must reply in kind or give up in defeat.

Any reference to **huevos**, which means *eggs* but is also used to refer to the testicles, is rife with **albur** possibilities. In fact people are so wary of this word that grocers and their clientele often use the word **blanquillos** when buying or selling eggs, which usually has the effect of making things worse, since no one can pretend they don't know why they're using **blanquillos** instead of **huevos**. In the same vein, it is hardly possible to ask someone at breakfast **¿Cómo quieres tus huevos?** (*How do you like your eggs?*) without someone answering **¡Con toda el alma!** (*With all my heart!*), or **¿Cómo te hago los huevos?** (*How shall I make your eggs?* but also *How shall I move your thingamajigs?* if one wishes to interpret the sentence this way), to which some wise guy might reply **De aquí para allá**; i.e., *with a swinging motion*). In answer to **¿Le pongo salsa a tus huevos?** (*Shall I put sauce on your eggs?*) (breakfast eggs are often served with tomato sauce), you might hear **No, mejor talco** (*I would prefer talcum powder*).

Any of the ordinary words like **petaca**s (*bags*), **teleras** (*bread rolls with a crease down the middle*), **hoyo** (*hole*), **agujero** (*hole*), **el chico** (*the small one*), etc., which are also used to refer to the human rear-end and the orifice there located, are also fertile soil. If one of these is used in an ordinary sentence, the **albur** expert might retort **¿Me prestas unos pesos?** (*Can you lend me a few pesos?* but actually *Can you lend me that particular portion of your anatomy?*).

The possibilities for **albures** are almost endless; however, it is not our purpose to list them here, since explanations require the use of a great many unsavory words, aside from which we definitely do not consider it advisable for a nonmember of the **albur** club to try his (and much less her) hand at this tricky game. The examples provided should provide an ample idea of what an **albur** is and how it works, so that you are not entirely mystified if you ever get caught in the middle of an **albur** barrage. Generally speaking, if a conversation among friends ever becomes inexplicably cryptic, you are witnessing an exchange of **albures**. In fact, you might even hear the verb **alburear,** as in **¿Me estás albureando?** (*Was that comment meant as an **albur***? when someone is not sure whether or not a particular remark is barbed), or **Te están albureando** (*He is teasing you with an **albur*** when it must be pointed out to someone that he has been made the object of an **albur**).

If the **albur** were simply vulgar and shocking, it would hardly be worth mentioning; the redeeming feature that sets it apart from ordinary filth is the lightning cleverness required to come up with just the

Slang in Mexico

right combination of words necessary to insert the offensive tidbit (recognizable only to the initiate) into a commonplace sentence, disguised as a group of perfectly respectable words.

Regardless of anyone's opinion of the Mexican macho type whose mind is stuck irretrievably in a permanent sex rut, there's no denying that most **albures** are downright funny (the feeble translations provided here do not begin to do justice to the real thing). There's something tremendously sharp about the Mexican personality that is almost completely lacking in the people of the rest of Latin America, and nowhere is it more apparent than in the **albur**.

III
FALSE COGNATES
A. Basic False Cognates

According to some scholars (whom we have no reason to doubt) there are no fewer than 5,000 words that are the same in English and Spanish, because they come from the same root (like *actual* and **actual**). Let's suppose that a lot (or most) are technical, i.e., medical, engineering, and so on. That still leaves an awful lot of words for plain everyday speech, which means that before a person has ever even thought of learning Spanish, he or she is already equipped with a long list of words that will never have to be drilled into his or her head (although, as you will see, some might have to be drilled out).

However, learning Spanish wouldn't be as interesting or challenging as it is if it weren't generously spiced with words that are identical or practically the same in the two languages, and which we have every right to assume have the same meaning, only to discover to our horror (sometimes after quite a long time of innocently, even smugly, tossing them into our sentences) that for some obscure reason the Spanish word means something entirely different from the English word, or what's even worse, sometimes means the same thing and sometimes doesn't, depending on different circumstances which seem impossible to distinguish from each other.

With these realizations come flashbacks of moments in bygone conversations when our pronouncements have been met with an embarrassing silence or with the polite but quizzical look of a person who obviously wonders what in the world we're talking about (non-English speakers have no idea why these mistakes are made, since they have no way of knowing the reasoning behind these seemingly inexplicable gaffes).

These same-but-not-the-same words, which are known as false cognates, are too numerous to memorize en masse. The best way to approach them is just to read through this section every now and then. Certain words will stick in your mind at every reading; others will slip into your subconscious and at least send a danger signal to the brain's speech center every time you feel inclined to make use of them in the wrong way. You will gradually learn how to use some of them properly and when to steer clear of the others.

Remember that the Spanish covered here is the Spanish of everyday language, and that the definition(s) provided for each word is (are) for the usual meaning(s) used in normal conversation.

If you go to the dictionary for any of the words that appear in this section, you are bound to find a number of meanings, sometimes long lists of meanings (many of which are strange, to say the least; they have been used by no normal persons in living memory, and can therefore be disregarded in 99 cases out of 100). That is because the purpose of this book differs entirely from that of the dictionary. A very great deal of what makes a dictionary good for pressing leaves and for elevating little Stevie to a height where his nose is above plate level at the grown-up's dinner table is just plain deadwood. The words and usage covered here are very much alive, and sprouting new growth all the time. However, only the most common meanings of these words (as used by the layman) are dealt with here, to avoid this book becoming unwieldy. By the way, if you occasionally feel that this common usage differs from what the dictionary says, you're absolutely right.

There are several sections in this chapter, and you may find a word appearing in more than one section; this simply means that the word in question is appropriate in more than one section, and that you will be doubly or triply protected.

Section 1 has words in Spanish alphabetical order. *Section 2* has words in English alphabetical order.

False Cognates

1. Spanish-English

Acomodar (v.)
— To arrange ◻ neatly
- **Acomodamos los libros en el librero.**
  We arranged the books in the bookcase.

English: (To)accommodate
— **Darle gusto a** ☺
- **Comprendo lo que usted desea, pero no puedo darle gusto.**
  I understand what you want, but I can't accommodate you.
— **Hacer lo que** ☺ **quiere**
- **No siempre puedo hacer lo que todos quieren.**
  I can't always accommodate everyone.

Note: Aside from *neatly arranged*, **acomodado** also means *affluent, moneyed*.

Actual (adj.)
— Present; current; contemporary; existing today.
- **La situación actual no es la misma de hace dos días.**
  The current situation is not the same as it was two days ago.

English: Actual
— **Real; genuino(a); verdadero(a)**
- **José no sabe quién es su verdadero padre.**
  Jose doesn't know who his actual father is.

Actualmente; en la actualidad (adv.)
— Presently; currently; nowadays
- **En la actualidad (actualmente), la inflación es muy alta.**
  Inflation is currently very high.

English: Actually
— **En realidad; verdaderamente**
- **En realidad él es un hombre muy interesante.**
  He is actually a very interesting man.

False Cognates

Advertir (v.)
— To warn
- **Te advertí que esto iba a suceder.**
  I warned you this was going to happen.

English: (To)advertise
— **Anunciar(se)**
- **Esta empresa anuncia sus productos en revistas para hombres.**
  This company advertises its products in men's magazines.

Afección (n.)
— Malady; illness; disease; complaint (health)
- **Esta afección no es nada rara.**
  This malady is not at all unusual.

English: Affection (n.)
— **Cariño; afecto**
- **Abrazó a su hermano con mucho cariño (afecto).**
  He embraced his brother with great affection.

Agonía (n.)
— The throes of death
- **Su agonía fue larga y dolorosa.**
  Her death (the process of dying) was long and painful.

English: Agony
— **Sufrimiento; dolor muy fuerte físico o mental**
- **Sufrió dolores indecibles con la pierna rota. Hubo que sedarla.**
  She was in agony with that broken leg. She had to be sedated.

Agonizar (v.)
— To be in the throes of death
- **Cuando llegué, Rafael ya estaba agonizando.**
  When I got there, Raphael was already at death's door.

English: (To)agonize
— **Angustiar(se); estar angustiado(a)**
- **Estuvo angustiada una semana sin poder decidirse.**
  She agonized over the decision for a week.

False Cognates

Anciano(a) (adj.) (n.)

— Old (adj.) (people only)

- **Mi abuelita es muy anciana.**
  My grandmother is very old.

— An elderly person (n.)

- **Carlota era una anciana cuando murió.**
  Carlotta was an old woman when she died.

English: Ancient (adj. pertaining to antiquity)

- **Antiguo(a); de la antigüedad**
  - **La cultura Olmeca es la más antigua de México.**
    The Olmec culture is the most ancient in Mexico.

(Con) anticipación (n.)

— In advance; ahead of time

- **Hay que reservar mesa con anticipación.**
  You have to reserve a table in advance.

English: Anticipation

- **Expectación**
  - **Había gran expectación de todos.**
    Everyone was on pins and needles with anticipation.

Anticipar (v.)

— To advance money

- **Le anticipamos tres meses de renta.**
  We paid him three months rent in advance.

— To advise someone that something will happen in the future

- **Te anticipo que va a haber cambios en el comité.**
  I'm advising you (right now, before it happens) that there will be changes in the committee.

Note: **Un anticipo** is an advance payment.

English: (To)anticipate

- **Prever**
  - **Preveo ciertas dificultades.**
    I anticipate certain difficulties.
- **Esperar**
  - **No esperábamos esto.**
    We did not anticipate this.

Antiguo(a) (adj.)
— Old (things only) (see **anciano**)
- **Este reloj es muy antiguo; no tiene menos de 150 años.**
  This clock is very old; it's no less than 150 years old.
— Former (people and things)
- **El antiguo gerente no dictaba sus cartas.**
  The former manager didn't dictate his letters.

English: Antique (n.)
— **Antigüedad**
- **Para ser antigüedad, necesita tener más de 100 años.**
  An object must be over 100 years old to be an antique.

Aparente (adj.)
— Said of that which appears to be something else, but in fact is not
- **Su alegría es aparente nada más; en realidad es una persona que sufre depresiones.**
  Her cheerfulness is not genuine; she actually suffers from depression.
Note: However, **aparentemente** is used the same way as *apparently*
— Visible
- **En esa casa toda la tubería es aparente.**
  All the pipes are visible in that house (not hidden in the walls).

English: Apparent
— **Evidente; obvio(a)**
- **Su ignorancia es bastante obvia.**
  His ignorance is quite apparent.

Apreciar (v.)
— To esteem ☺
- **Yo aprecio mucho a esa señora.**
  I esteem that lady a great deal.

English: (To)appreciate
— **Agradecer**
- **Agradezco que venga.**
  I appreciate your coming.
- **Agradeceré que me pague con cheque.**
  I will appreciate your paying by check.
- **Me agradeció mucho el favor.**
  He was very grateful for the favor.
— **Subir de valor; revaluar(se)**
- **Ese terreno va a subir mucho de valor (se va a revaluar).**
  That piece of land is going to appreciate a great deal (in value).

False Cognates

Argumentar (v.)
— To put forth as a reason; to claim
- **Podríamos argumentar que no tenemos dinero.**
  We could claim we have no money.

English: (To)argue
— **Discutir (con ☺)**
- **No quiero discutir contigo.**
  I don't want to argue with you.

Note: However, **discutir** ❑ is to discuss ❑, as in:
- **Discutimos el plan**
  We discussed the plan.

Argumento (n.)
— The plot of a story
- **El argumento de este libro no es original.**
  The plot of this book is not original.

English: Argument
— **Discusión**
- **La discusión casi terminó en golpes.**
  The argument almost ended in a fight.

Asesoramiento (n.)
— Advice (of a legal or business nature)
- **Dice Manuela que no necesita asesoramiento.**
  Manuela says she needs no advice.

English: Assessment
— **Avalúo**
- **El avalúo no fue justo.**
  The assessment was not fair.

Asesorar (v.)
— To advise; to give expert advice
- **Luis me va a asesorar en la compra.**
  Luis is going to advise me on the purchase.

English: (To)assess
— **Valuar, evaluar**
- **Se necesita un perito para evaluar los daños.**
  Only an expert can assess the damage.

Audiencia (n.)*
— A formal hearing
- **Podrás hacer tu declaración en la audiencia preliminar.**
  You can speak at the preliminary hearing.

*When it is used to mean a meeting with a very important person, such as an audience with the president, it is not a false cognate.
- **Rafael logró obtener una audiencia especial con el Papa.**
  Rafael managed to get a special audience with the Pope.

English: Audience
— **Público**
- **El público no entendió la obra.**
  The audience didn't understand the play.
- **El público aplaudió al pianista con mucho entusiasmo.**
  The audience applauded the pianist most enthusiastically.

Bombero (n.)
— Fireman
- **Los bomberos llegaron en sólo diez minutos.**
  The firemen arrived in only ten minutes.

English: Bomber
— **Bombardero**
- **Los bombarderos van a sobrevolar la ciudad durante el desfile.**
  The bombers are going to fly over the city during the parade.

Bravo(a) (adj.)
— Vicious, dangerously aggressive (said of both animals and people)
- **El perro de Sergio es muy bravo.**
  Sergio's dog is kind of vicious.

English: Brave *
— **Valeroso(a); (tener) valor**
- **Se necesita mucho valor para hacer eso.**
  You have to be very brave to do that.

Note: Because of this false cognate, Aldoux Huxley's famous book *Brave New World* is *Un Mundo Feliz* in Spanish, rather than *Un Mundo Bravo*.

Bruto(a) (adj.) *
— Not very bright, dumb, stupid (adj.)
- **No seas bruto; no te salgas de la escuela.**
  Don't be dumb; don't drop out of school.
— A fool; an idiot (n.)
- **Ese tipo es un bruto. Mira cómo escribió esta palabra.**
  That guy is an idiot. Look how he spelled this word.

*In expressions like **producto bruto, peso bruto** and so on, **bruto** means *gross*.

English: Brute
— **Bestia; salvaje**
- **Ese salvaje le pegó a mi hijito.**
  That brute hit my kid.

Calificar (v.)
— To grade a piece of work or performance
- **No me ha dado tiempo de calificar las pruebas.**
  I haven't had time to grade the tests.

English: (To)qualify
— **Reunir los requisitos para** ☐
- **No reuní los requisitos para el equipo olímpico el año pasado.**
  I didn't qualify for the Olympics last year.
— **Ser aceptado(a) para** ☐
- **Espero ser aceptado para el empleo que quiero.**
  I hope to qualify for the job I want.
— **Ser apto(a) para** ☐
- **No es apto para este tipo de trabajo.**
  He doesn't qualify for this type of work.
— **Tener capacidad para** ☐
- **Es el único que tiene capacidad para chofer.**
  He's the only one who qualifies as a driver.
— **Tener los conocimientos o experiencia necesaria para** ☐
- **Ella no tiene experiencia para ser nana.**
  She doesn't qualify to be a nursemaid.

*However, **calificado**(a) is used to mean that a person is qualified for ☐.

Calificación (n.)
— Grade
- **Las calificaciones de matemáticas dejaron mucho que desear.**
  The math grades left a lot to be desired.

English: Qualifications
— **Capacidad; antecedentes**
- **Sus antecedentes son magníficos.**
  His qualifications are very impressive.

Cándido(a) (adj.)
— Ingenue; innocent; dumb
- **Es tan cándida que cree todo lo que le dicen.**
  She is so innocent that she believes everything she hears.

English: Candid
— **Franco(a)**
- **Arturo te dice las cosas como son; es sumamente franco.**
  Arturo says things as they are; he's entirely candid (frank).

Cargo (n.)
— Post; position (n.)
- **Tiene un cargo muy importante en la Secretaría.**
  He has a very important position at the Ministry.
— Charge (n.) (financial)
- **Este cargo que me hicieron en mi estado de cuenta es incorrecto.**
  The charge that appeared in my bank statement is incorrect.
— Charge (n.) (legal)
- **El cargo de fraude es muy grave.**
  Misappropriation of funds is a very serious charge.

English: Cargo
— **Carga**
- **La única carga que lleva esa barco es una locomotora.**
  The only cargo on that ship is a locomotive.

Carpeta (n.)
— Loose-leaf binder; notebook
- **Ya no está la carpeta donde la dejé.**
  My binder isn't where I left it.

English: Carpet
— **Alfombra**
- **Esta alfombra persa fue de mi abuelo.**
  This Persian carpet was my grandfather's.

Casual (adj.)
— By chance; by coincidence
- **El encuentro fue enteramente casual.**
  The meeting was purely by coincidence.

English: Casual*
— **Informal**
- **¡No se te ocurra usar ropa informal para la cena!**
  Don't you dare wear casual clothes to this dinner!

False Cognates

*__Casual__ is now being used, especially by young people. It seeped into the language through advertising for casual clothes, and we now have __ropa casual__, which actually means coincidental clothes (pretty silly, but the vast majority of people simply don't notice the inconsistency).

Casualidad (n.)
— Coincidence
  - ¡Qué casualidad! ¡Mira quién está aquí!
    What a coincidence! Look who's here!

English: Casualty
  — Heridos o muertos
    - Hubo muchos heridos y muertos.
      There were a lot of casualties.

Colegio (n.)
— School (mostly primary)
  - Los hijos de Laura van al mismo colegio que los míos.
    Laura's kids go to the same school as mine do.

English: College
  — Universidad
    - Mi hijo tiene dos títulos universitarios.
      My son has two college degrees.

Complaciente (adj.)
— Obliging; willing to please
  - Abusan de ti por ser tan complaciente.
    People take advantage of you because you are so obliging.

English: Complacent
  — Satisfecho consigo mismo
    - No veo por qué Tomás tenga que sentirse tan satisfecho consigo mismo.
      I don't see what Tomas has to feel so complacent about.

Complexión (n.)
— Type of build (human body)
  - Pedro es de complexión delgada.
    Pedro is slight of build.

English: Complexion
  — Cutis
    - Graciela tiene un cutis perfecto.
      Graciela's complexion is unblemished.

False Cognates

Comprensivo(a) (adj.)

— Understanding; sympathetic
- **Sergio siempre ha sido muy comprensivo.**
  Sergio has always been very understanding.

English: Comprehensive
— **Integral**
- **El estudio del medio ambiente va a ser integral.**
  The environmental study will be comprehensive.

Comprometer(se) (v.)

— To commit
- **Me comprometí a trabajar con el Sr. Aguayo.**
  I committed myself to work for Mr. Aguayo.
— To promise
- **Me comprometí a entregar el pedido en dos semanas.**
  I promised to deliver the order in two weeks.

English: (To)compromise
— **Llegar a un acuerdo** (When <u>two</u> persons compromise on something)
- **Por fin llegamos a un acuerdo sobre el precio.**
  We finally compromised on the price.
— **Optar por** (When <u>one</u> person compromises on something)
- **Opté por comprar el auto compacto en lugar del modelo de lujo.**
  I had to compromise and buy the compact car instead of a luxury model.

Compromiso (n.)

— A commitment
- **No siento ningún compromiso con esa empresa.**
  I feel no commitment to that company.
— An engagement (social or business)
- **Tengo un compromiso para cenar esta noche.**
  I have a dinner engagement for tonight.
— A wedding engagement
- **El anillo de compromiso de Alicia es muy caro.**
  Alice's engagement ring is really expensive.

English: Compromise
— **Un arreglo** (between <u>two</u> people; there is no equivalent for a compromise made by just <u>one</u> person, so a complete explanation of the situation is required)
- **No estoy muy contento con el arreglo al que llegamos.**
  I'm not too happy about the compromise we reached.

False Cognates

Constipado(a) (adj.) (n.)
— Having a stuffed up nose or sinuses; having a head cold
- **Amanecí constipado hoy.**
  My head was all stuffed up when I awoke this morning.

English: Constipated
— **Estreñido(a)**
- **Necesitas comer más fibra si estás estreñida.**
  You should eat more fiber if you are constipated.

Contento(a) (adj.)
— Happy
- **El jefe está contento porque terminamos el informe.**
  The boss is happy because we finished the report.
— Cheerful
- **Está muy contento desde que recibió esa carta.**
  He's been very cheerful since he got that letter.
— In a good mood
- **¿Por qué estás tan contento hoy?**
  Why are you in such a good mood today?

English: Content
— **A gusto**
- **No es la casa que queríamos, pero estamos a gusto aquí.**
  It's not the house we wanted, but we are content here.

Contentar(se) (v.)
— To make up with ☺ (after a fight or disagreement)
- **Creo que esos dos jamás se van a contentar.**
  I think those two are never going to make up.

English: (To)content yourself with ❑
— **Conformar(se)**
- **Pues yo quería un Mercedes Benz, pero me conformo con este compacto.**
  Well, I wanted a Mercedes Benz, but I will have to be content with this compact car.

Conveniente (adj.)
— Advisable
- **No es conveniente que hagas ese viaje ahora.**
  It is not advisable for you to make that trip just now.
— Suitable; desirable
- **Ese matrimonio no es muy conveniente.**
  That marriage is not very desirable.

English: Convenient
— **Ser(le) cómodo(a) a** ☺
  ▪ **Las 9:00 no es una hora cómoda para mí.**
    Nine o'clock is not convenient for me.
— **Quedar bien; quedar mejor**
  ▪ **A las 11:00 me queda mejor.**
    Eleven o'clock is more convenient.

Convenir (v.)

— To agree
  ▪ **Convinimos un precio justo.**
    We agreed on a fair price.
  ▪ **Convinimos en que yo pagaría la mitad.**
    We agreed that I would pay half.
— To be advantageous; to be in ☺'s interest.
  ▪ **No te conviene contestarle así a tu jefe.**
    It's not in your interest to answer your grandfather like that.
  ▪ **Me conviene más pagar a plazos.**
    I would prefer to pay in installments.

English: (To)convene
— **Convocar**
  ▪ **La asamblea se convocó hace dos semanas.**
    The stockholders' meeting was convened two weeks ago.

Coraje (n.)

— Anger; ire
  ▪ **Adela no me esperó. ¡Qué coraje!**
    Adela didn't wait for me. That really makes me mad.
  ▪ **Hice un coraje muy fuerte con mi hijo.**
    I got really mad at my son.

English: Courage
— **Valor**
  ▪ **Se necesita mucho valor para hacer eso.**
    It takes a lot of courage to do that.
Note: Occasionally you will hear that someone has or lacks the **coraje** to do something, which is a Gallicism, and fairly rare.

False Cognates

Decepción (n.)

  Disappointment
- **Fue una gran decepción conocerlo en persona.**
  It was a great disappointment to meet him in person.

English: Deception (n.)
— **Engaño**
  - **Su engaño es imperdonable.**
    Her deception is unforgivable.

Disgustar (v.)

— To dislike; to annoy; to anger; to upset
- **Estoy disgustado con Elisa.**
  I am upset with Elisa.
- **Me disgusta que hagan esto.**
  I don't like them to do this.

English: (To)disgust
— **Dar asco; causar repugnancia**
  - **Ese tipo me da asco.**
    That man disgusts me.

Disgusto (n.)

— Unpleasantness; annoyance; quarrel; argument
- **Tuve un disgusto con mi socio.**
  I had a quarrel with my partner.

English: Disgust
— **Repugnancia; asco**
  - **La repugnancia (El asco) se le notaba en la cara.**
    His disgust was obvious from his expression.

Disponer de ☐ (v.)

— To have ☐ at your disposal; to make use of ☐
- **Puede usted disponer de esta sala cuando lo desee.**
  This room is at your disposal (you may make use of this room) whenever you wish.
— To have ☐
- **No disponemos de suficientes fondos.**
  We don't have sufficient funds.

English: (To)dispose of ☐
— **Desechar ☐**
  - **¿Dónde puedo desechar estos periódicos viejos?**
    Where can I dispose of these old newspapers?

Disponible (adj.)
— Available
- **El salón grande no está disponible en este momento.**
  The large room is not available just now.

English: Disposable
— **Desechable**
- **Estos platos son desechables.**
  These plates are disposable.

Disposición (n.)
— An official rule; regulation or legal provision
- **Las nuevas disposiciones fiscales son difíciles de entender.**
  The new tax provisions are difficult to understand.
— Service
- **Estamos a su disposición, señor.**
  We are at your service, sir.

English: Disposition (n.)
— **Carácter; temperamento**
- **El gerente general no es de temperamento agradable.**
  The general manager does not have a pleasant disposition.

Editor (n.)
— Publisher
- **Mi editor es de trato difícil.**
  My publisher isn't easy to get along with.

English: Editor (n.)
— **Corrector de estilo**
- **Él gana más que otros correctores de estilo.**
  He makes more than other editors do.

Educado(a) (adj.)
— Well bred; well mannered; gentlemanly; polite (see also **gentil**)
- **Juan siempre ha sido muy educado.**
  Juan has always been very well mannered.

English: Educated (uneducated)
— **Culto(a) (inculto(a))**
- **Es un hombre muy culto.**
  He's a very well-educated man.

False Cognates

Educación (n.)
— Good upbringing; good breeding
- **Hoy en día, muy pocos tienen educación.**
  Nowadays, few people are polite (well bred).

English: Education
— **Estudios**
- **Hizo sus estudios en Europa.**
  He got his education in Europe.

Educar (v.)
— Sometimes used to mean <u>to educate</u>, but more commonly meaning <u>to bring up one's children</u>.
- **La Sra. Páez no sabe educar a sus hijos.**
  Mrs. Páez doesn't know how to bring up her kids.

English: (To)educate
— **Hacer estudios**
- **Todos los hijos de la familia Tinoco hicieron sus estudios en Inglaterra.**
  All the Tinoco boys were educated in England.

Elaborar (v.)
— To prepare ☐ (usually intellectual work)
- **Estoy elaborando una explicación de la Fiesta Brava para los anglosajones.**
  I am preparing an explanation of bullfighting for Anglo Saxons.

English: (To)elaborate
— **Explicar con mayor detalle**
- **Tenga la bondad de explicar el programa con mayor detalle.**
  Kindly elaborate on the program.

Embarazada (adj.)
— Pregnant
- **Mi amiga se casó hace diez años, pero nunca ha estado embarazada.**
  My friend has been married for ten years, but she's never been pregnant.

English: Embarrassed
— **Apenado(a)**
- **Desde que me insultó, Juan se siente apenado cuando tiene que verme.**
  Since he insulted me, it really embarrasses Juan to see me.

Embarazar a ☺ (v.)
— To get a girl pregnant
- **Alberto embarazó a su novia, pero no lo quiere aceptar.**
  Alberto got his girlfriend pregnant, but he won't admit it.

Embarazar(se) (v.)
— To get pregnant
- **Lucy no quiere embarazarse todavía.**
  Lucy doesn't want to get pregnant yet.

English: (To)embarrass (v.)
— **Apenar (se); sentir pena** (**pena** is embarrassment, but also sorrow)
- **Toña no sabe lo que es apenarse.**
  Toña doesn't know what it is to be embarrassed.

Estrechar (v.)
— To squeeze; to embrace
- **Me estrechó en sus brazos.**
  He embraced me.

English: (To)stretch
— **Estirar**
- **El suéter se estiró.**
  The sweater stretched.

Eventualmente (adv.)
— Occasionally; once in a while; every now and then
- **Se aparece por aquí muy eventualmente.**
  He turns up here very occasionally.

English: Eventually
— **Con el tiempo; algún día; a la larga**
- **Algún día ella será socia.**
  Eventually, she'll be a partner.

Éxito (n.)
— Success
- **El éxito fue rotundo.**
  It was a complete success.

English: Exit
— **Salida**
- **Hay dos salidas.**
  There are two exits.

False Cognates

Excitante (adj.) (*)
— Exciting

English: Exciting
- **Emocionante**
  - **Fue un momento muy emocionante.**
    It was a very exciting moment.

Excitación (n.) (*)
— Excitement

English: Excitement
- **Emoción, animación**
  - **¡Qué emoción!**
    What excitement! (How exciting!)

Excitar (v.) (*)
— To excite

English: (To)excite
- **Emocionar**
  - **Los desfiles ya no me emocionan.**
    Parades no longer excite me.
- **Despertar** □
  - **No quiero despertar demasiada curiosidad.**
    I don't want to excite too much curiosity.

Excitado(a) (v.) (*)
— Excited

English: Excited
- **Emocionado(a)**
  - **Diana está muy emocionada (emocionadísima) con la llegada de su primer nieto.**
    Diana is very excited about the arrival of her first grandchild.
- **Animado(a)**
  - **Estamos muy animados por el viaje a Londres.**
    We are very excited about the trip to London.

* All these are exact equivalents in English and Spanish, and are commonly used only in connection with sexual excitement (you can make up your own examples). Every now and then you hear someone using these in Spanish as they are used in English, which although correct according to the dictionary, of course leads to double meanings or plain misunderstandings. It's better to *stay away* from these words in Spanish, except as they relate to sex.

Fábrica (n.)
— Factory; plant
- **La fábrica de telas está en Puebla.**
  The textile mill is in Puebla.

English: Fabric
— **Tela**
- **Esta tela es lavable.**
  This fabric is washable.

Fabricación (n.)
— Manufacturing
- **La fabricación de coches es muy compleja.**
  Car manufacturing is very complex.

English: Fabrication
— **Invento; cuento**
- **Todo lo que dijo es puro cuento.**
  Everything he said was a fabrication, pure and simple.

Fabricar (v.)
— To manufacture
- **En México se fabrican muchas marcas de coche.**
  Many makes of car are manufactured in Mexico.

English: (To)fabricate
— **Inventar**
- **Le encanta inventar excusas.**
  He's always fabricating excuses.

Fastidioso(a) (adj.)
— Boring; annoying
- **Este niño es muy fastidioso.**
  This kid is a pain in the neck.
— Tedious
- **Me dieron un trabajo de lo más fastidioso.**
  The work they gave me was very tedious.

English: Fastidious
— **Quisquilloso(a); exigente; delicado(a)**
- **Mi abuelo es muy quisquilloso para comer.**
  My grandfather is a fastidious eater.

Fiscal (adj.)
— Pertaining to taxes (however, **el Fiscal** (n.) is the District Attorney)

False Cognates

- **Esto no es deducible para fines fiscales.**
  This is not deductible for tax purposes.

English: Fiscal
— Regarding the government's fiscal affairs
  - **Los ingresos del gobierno están en desorden.**
    The government's fiscal affairs are in disorder.

Gentil (adj.)
— Gracious; gentlemanly; kind (see **gracioso**)
  - **El gerente del banco es muy gentil.**
    The bank manager is most gracious.

English: Gentle*
— No specific word in Spanish. The idea is conveyed by saying that someone does something **suavemente, suavecito,** or **con suavidad, tiernamente** (tenderly), **despacito**, or that he is not **brusco**.
  - **Mi dentista hace todo con mucha suavidad (no es nada brusco).**
    My dentist does everything gently.
  - **Juan no es nada brusco con los caballos.**
    Juan handles the horses gently.

* *Gentleman* used to be **gentilhombre** in Spanish; *gentle* obviously comes from the same root. *El Burgués Gentilhombre* is the Spanish version of *Le Bourgeois Gentilhomme*, a play by Molière.

Gracioso(a) (adj.)
— Funny
  - **Ese perrito es muy gracioso.**
    That little dog is very funny.
— Amusing
  - **Me contaron un cuento muy gracioso.**
    I heard a very amusing story.

English: Gracious (well bred, well mannered)
— **Fino** (adj.) (for both sexes); **caballeroso** (adj.) (for men only)
  - **Me pareció que es una persona bastante fina.**
    He seemed very well mannered.
— **Educado(a); gentil**
  - **Después de la cena, la gentil anfitriona tocó el piano.**
    After dinner, our gracious hostess played the piano for us.

False Cognates

Grasa (n.)
— Grease
- **Ese guisado tiene mucha grasa.**
  That dish is very greasy.
— Fat
- **Esta receta es baja en grasa.**
  This is a low-fat recipe.
— Shoe polish
- **Voy a que les den grasa a mis zapatos.**
  I'm going to have my shoes shined.

English: Grass
— **Pasto**
- **El pasto se ve precioso.**
  The grass looks lovely.

Gratificación (n.)
— A reward for the return of something lost
- **La gratificación por el portafolios perdido es de $10,000.**
  The reward for the return of the lost briefcase is $10,000.
— A bonus
- **Este año va a haber gratificación para los que produzcan más de 100,000 cajas.**
  This year there will be a bonus for anyone putting out more than 100,000 boxes.

English: Gratification
— **Satisfacción**
- **Hago entrega de este trofeo con gran satisfacción.**
  It is with much gratification that I present this trophy.

Gratificar (v.)
— To give a reward
- **Hay que gratificar a quien encuentre al perro.**
  We must reward whoever finds the dog.

English: (To)gratify
— **Satisfacer**
- **Estoy muy satisfecho con tu rendimiento.**
  I am very gratified with your performance.

Grosero(a) (adj.) (n.)
— Rude, boorish (persons only) (adj.)
- **Miguel es muy grosero con su novia.**
  Miguel is very rude to his girlfriend.

False Cognates

— A rude, boorish person; a lout (n.)
  ▪ **Miguel es un grosero.**
    Miguel is a boor (a lout).

English: Grocer
  — **Abarrotero(a); tendero(a)**
    ▪ **El tendero me fió estas cosas.**
      The grocer gave me these things on credit.

Grosería (n.)
— A rude, boorish or disrespectful act
  ▪ **Miguel me hizo una grosería.**
    Miguel was rude and disrespectful to me.
— Swear word(s), dirty word(s)
  ▪ **Carlos no puede hablar sin groserías.**
    Carlos can only speak with swear words.

English: Grocery (store)
  — **Tienda de abarrotes (**not usually a greengrocer)
    ▪ **Necesito sal, una lata de atún y jabón. ¿Puedes ir a comprarlos a la tienda de abarrotes?**
      I need some salt, a can of tuna fish and some soap. Could you go to the grocery store to buy them form me?

Guardar (v.)
— To put □ away
  ▪ **Guarda todas esas cosas antes de irte.**
    Put all those things away before you leave.
— To keep □
  ▪ **Aquí es donde guardo la escoba.**
    This is where I keep the broom.

English: (To)guard
  — **Proteger; defender; vigilar**
    ▪ **Necesitamos tres personas para vigilar el embarque de plata.**
      We need three people to guard the shipment of silver.

Habitación (n.)
— Room (in a house)
  ▪ **Esta casa tiene por lo menos 15 habitaciones.**
    This house has at least 15 rooms.

English: Habitation (dwelling)
  — **Vivienda**
    ▪ **Esta vivienda es muy humilde.**
      This habitation is very humble.

Honesto(a) (adj.)

— A combination of decent, upright, reasonable, fair and modest

- **Si el Sr. López fuera honesto, no tendría todas esas cuentas de banco en Estados Unidos y Europa.**
  If Mr. Lopez were really decent, he wouldn't have all those bank accounts in the United States and in Europe.

English: Honest
  — **Honrado(a)**
  - **Es cierto que no todos los policías son honrados.**
    It's true not all policemen are honest.

Idioma (n.)

— Language

- **El inglés es el idioma internacional.**
  English is the international language.

English: Idiom
  — **Expresión idiomática; modismo**
  - **Este libro está lleno de modismos.**
    This book is full of idioms.

Ignorar (v.)*

— Presently used in Spanish only to mean *to be uninformed*, or not to know ❑, and then only when the situation is too formal for a simple "I don't know".

- **No me preguntes por qué se fue. Lo ignoro.**
  Don't ask me why he left. I have no idea.

English: (To)ignore
  — **No hacer caso a** ☺*
  - **No le hagas caso. Está tomado.**
    Ignore him. He's drunk.
  — **Hacer caso omiso de** ❑
  - **Haz caso omiso de estas hojas. No vienen al caso.**
    Ignore these pages. They are irrelevant.

Note: Now occasionally also used to mean the same as in English.

Importe (n.)

— The amount of a bill, invoice, check, investment, etc.

- **Me mandó una cuenta por un importe estratosférico.**
  He sent a bill for an exorbitant amount.

English: Import
  — **Importación**
  - **Las importaciones aún pagan impuestos.**
    Imports still pay duties.

False Cognates

Infatuación (n.)
— Excessive love of self; excessive self-satisfaction; conceit
- **La infatuación de Porfirio no le permite hablar más que de sí mismo.**
  Porfirio's conceit makes him talk only of himself.

English: Infatuation
— **Enamoramiento**
- **Le doy dos semanas a tu enamoramiento para que se acabe de muerte natural.**
  I'll give your infatuation two weeks to die a natural death.

Injuria (n.)
— Offense; affront; insult (verbal)
- **Tus injurias son injustificadas.**
  Your insults are unjustified.

English: Injury
— **Herida** (with or without bleeding)
- **Esta herida no es grave.**
  This injury is not serious.
— **Lastimadura** (no bleeding)
- **La lastimadura duele.**
  The injury hurts.
— **Lesión** (usually implies bleeding although there is a bloodless **lesión en el corazón**, and a **lesión cerebral**, where no external bleeding occurs)
- **La lesión tardó años en sanar.**
  It took years for the injury to heal.

Injuriar (v.)
— To insult; to offend verbally
- **De nada sirve injuriarme.**
  It'll do no good to insult me.

English: (To)injure
— **Lastimar**
- **Se lastimó jugando futbol.**
  He injured (hurt) himself playing soccer.
— **Herir**
- **Muchas personas resultaron heridas en el choque del tren.**
  Many people were injured in the train crash.

Inscripción (n.)
— Registration
- **Las inscripciones se cierran el día 31.**
  Registration is only until the 31st.

English: Inscription
— **Leyenda**
- **No logro descifrar la leyenda de la lápida.**
  I can't make out the inscription on the tombstone.

Inscribir(se) (v.)
— To enroll; to register or sign up for □
- **Me inscribí para el próximo semestre.**
  I signed up for next semester.

English: (To)inscribe
— **Grabar**
- **El trofeo tiene algo grabado en alemán.**
  The trophy has something inscribed on it in German.

Intentar (v.) (synonym of **tratar de** + verb)
— To try; to attempt
- **Voy a intentar verlo mañana.**
  I'm going to try to see him tomorrow.

English: (To)intend (or to plan)
— **Pretender**
- **El gobierno pretende congelar los precios.**
  The government intends to freeze prices.

Introducción (n.)*
— The insertion, putting, bringing or taking of □ into □ else
- **Está prohibida la introducción de ganado al país.**
  Bringing cattle into the country is prohibited.

English: Introduction of ☺ to ☺ *
— **Presentación**
- **Hiciste bien todas las presentaciones, excepto que mi mamá no se llama Olivia.**
  You handled all the introductions well, except that my mother's name isn't Olivia.

Note: An exception is **introducción** to a book or subject, which is the same as *introduction*.

Introducir(se) (v.)
— To insert; to put, bring or take □ into □ else; to come, go or get into □
- **Hay que pagar impuesto para introducir esta máquina al país.**
  Duties must be paid for this machine to come into the country.

False Cognates

- **El doctor introdujo el mercapaso en el torax del paciente.**
  The doctor inserted the pacemaker into the patient's chest.
- **Ese sujeto se introdujo sin boleto.**
  This guy got in without a ticket.

English: (To)introduce ☺ to ☺
— **Presentar** ☺ **a** ☺
  - **Siento mucho haberme olvidado de presentarte al anfitrión.**
    I'm sorry I forgot to introduce you to the host.

Jubilación (n.)
— Retirement (from work)
- **Su jubilación no fue lo maravilloso que él esperaba.**
  His retirement wasn't as wonderful as he expected.

English: Jubilation
— **Júbilo**
  - **Hubo júbilo el día que acabó la guerra.**
    There was jubilation the day the war ended.

Labor (n.)
— Work, job
- **Han hecho una excelente labor educativa.**
  They've done excellent educational work.
— Handiwork, usually embroidery and the like, in which case it is used in plural
- **Las labores de las monjitas son bellísimas.**
  The nuns' handiwork is extremely beautiful.

Laboral (adj.)
— Labor
- **Las relaciones laborales son bastante buenas en esta fábrica.**
  Labor relations are pretty good at this factory.

English: Labor
— **Trabajo**
  - **Todo mi trabajo fue en balde.**
    All my labor was wasted.
— **Los trabajadores**
  - **Los trabajadores y la administración simplemente no pueden ponerse de acuerdo en ese asunto.**
    Labor and management just can't agree on that matter.

False Cognates

Ladera (n.)
— The slope of a hill or mountain
- **Las laderas del Popocatépetl están cubiertas de bosque.**
  The sides of the Popocatepetl are covered with forest.

English: Ladder
— **Escalera de mano**
  - **¿Cómo voy a subir sin escalera?**
    How can I get up there without a ladder?

Largo(a) (adj.)
— Long (measurement)
- **Fue un día muy largo y cansado.**
  It was a long, hard day.

English: Large
— **Grande**
  - **Él no tiene una oficina grande.**
    He doesn't have a large office.

Lectura (n.)
— Reading (n.)
- **El maestro les deja mucha lectura de tarea.**
  The teacher gives them a lot of reading for homework.

English: Lecture
— **Conferencia**
  - **Estuvo muy interesante la conferencia de hoy.**
    Today's lecture was very interesting.

Librería (n.)
— Bookstore
- **Todos los libros de texto están rebajados en la librería esta semana.**
  All textbooks are reduced at the bookstore this week.

English: Library
— **Biblioteca**
  - **Los domingos no abre la biblioteca.**
    The library doesn't open on Sunday.

Miserable (n.) (adj.)
— Stingy; ignoble; small minded; petty (adj.)
- **¡No seas miserable!**
  Don't be stingy!

False Cognates

— Miser (n.)
- **El Sr. Pérez es un miserable.**
  Mr. Perez is a miser.

English: Miserable
— **Desdichado(a); infeliz** (very unhappy)
- **Me siento muy desdichado desde que Gloria se fue.**
  I've felt miserable since Gloria left.
— **Espantosamente mal; con mucho dolor** (in great physical discomfort)
- **Necesito otro analgésico. Me siento espantosamente mal con este dolor de cabeza.**
  I need another painkiller. I feel miserable with this headache.
— **Mortificado(a)** (in great moral discomfort)
- **Sé que Eduardo se siente muy mortificado por lo que hizo.**
  I know Eduardo feels miserable about what he did.

Molestar (v.)
— To annoy; to bother
- **Ese ruido me molesta.**
  That noise bothers me.

Molestar(se) (v.)
— To bother
- **No te molestes en hacer eso por favor.**
  Please don't bother to do that.

Molesto(a) (adj.)
— Bothersome; annoying
- **El ruido de la disco de junto es bastante molesto.**
  The noise from the discotheque next door is pretty annoying.
— Upset
- **Juan está muy molesto**
  Juan is very upset.

Molestia (n.)
— A bother
- **Me temo que esto es mucha molestia para usted.**
  I'm afraid this is quite a bother for you.

English: (To)molest
— **Abusar***
- **No creo que Arnulfo haya abusado de esa niña.**
  I don't believe Arnulfo molested that girl.

* However, this verb has no specific sexual connotation. **Abusar** is to abuse in all kinds of ways, including sexual abuse. For example, **abusar de la confianza** is to go too far in taking advantage of someone's kindness.

False Cognates

Oficio (n.)
— Occupation (usually manual); craft; trade
  - **La carpintería es un oficio que no se aprende tan fácilmente.**
    Carpentry is not such an easily learned occupation.
— A ruling (usually issued by the government)
  - **En cuanto llegó el jefe del departamento dictó varios oficios.**
    As soon as he arrived, the chief of the department dictated several rulings.

English: Office
  — **Oficina**
    - **Hoy no voy a estar en mi oficina.**
      I'm not going to be at the office today.

Pariente (n.)
— Relation; relative
  - **No tengo parientes en los Estados Unidos.**
    I have no relatives in the United States.

English: Parent
  — **Padres** (always used in plural; singular parents are **padre** and **madre**)
    - **Mis padres no vinieron a la boda.**
      My parents didn't come to the wedding.

Pretender (v.)
— To intend
  - **El pretende adquirir todas las acciones.**
    He intends to acquire all the shares.

English: (To)pretend
  — **Fingir**
    - **Siempre finge que no me conoce.**
      He always pretends he doesn't know me.

Publicista (n.)
— Advertising man
  - **Mi marido es publicista.**
    My husband is an advertising man.

English: Publisher
  — **Editor(a)** (person) (a publishing house is una **editora**)
    - **¿Quieres conocer a mi editor?**
      Do you want to meet my publisher?

False Cognates

Reclamación (n.)
— Complaint
- **Hice una reclamación formal por la mercancía dañada.**
  I lodged a formal complaint concerning the damaged merchandise.

English: Reclamation
— **Acondicionamiento de tierras inservibles**
- **El acondicionamiento de esa tierra va a costar mucho dinero.**
  Reclamation of that land is going to cost a lot of money.

Reclamar(le) a ☺ (v.) *
— To complain to ☺
- **Pedro les va a reclamar a los vecinos por el escándalo que hicieron anoche. Nadie pudo dormir.**
  Peter is going to complain to the neighbors about all that noise they made last night. Nobody could sleep.

*This verb is not normally used without mentioning the person to whom the complaint is directed. If there is no need or wish to mention that person, **quejar(se)** is normally used, although it can be used with a direct object too, in which case the correct construction is **quejar(se) con** ☺.

English: (To)reclaim (land)
— **Drenar la tierra** (when flooded, except by sea water)
- **Vamos a tratar de drenar estas tierras para cultivarlas.**
  We are going to try to reclaim this land for farming.
— **Acondicionar tierra inservible** (when affected by something other than water)
- **Vamos a tratar de acondicionar estas tierras para el cultivo.**
  We are going to try to reclaim this land for farming.
— **Ganarle tierra al mar** (when covered by sea water)
- **Vamos a tratar de ganarle tierra al mar para el cultivo.**
  *We are going to reclaim this land for **farming**.*

Recordar (v.)
— To remember
- **Recuerdo que dejé aquí la llave.**
  I remember I left the key here.
— To remind
- **Sí, tú me recordaste acerca de la cita.**
  Yes, you reminded me about the appointment.

English: (To)record
— **Registrar** (accounting and other written records)
- **Nunca se registraron los gastos.**
  The expenses were never recorded.
— **Grabar** (sound)
- **Este CD se grabó en Europa.**
  This CD was recorded in Europe.

Refrán (n.)
— Common, popular saying or proverb
- **"Más vale pájaro en mano que cien volando" es un refrán conocido por todos.**
  The saying "A bird in hand is worth two in the bush" is familiar to everyone.

English: Refrain
— **Estribillo**
- **No me sé las estrofas de "Cielito Lindo," pero sí el estribillo.**
  I don't know the verses of "Cielito Lindo," but I do know the refrain.

Relación (n.)
— List
- **Aquí está la relación de partes de camión.**
  Here's the list of spare parts for the truck.
— Love affair
- **Estoy seguro de que Jorge tiene una relación con Dora.**
  I'm sure Jorge is having an affair with Dora.
— Relationship
- **¿Cuál es la relación entre estas dos personas?**
  What's the relationship between these two people?

English: Relation
— **Pariente**
- **Casi todos mis parientes viven en el Perú.**
  Almost all my relations (relatives) live in Peru.
Note: When used to mean the *relation* or *relationship* between two things, this is not a false cognate.

Remarcar (v.)
— To stress; to emphasize
- **Remarcó ese punto varias veces.**
  He emphasized that point several times.

English: (To)remark
— **Hacer un comentario sobre □**
- **De paso hizo un comentario sobre su viaje a Finlandia.**
  He remarked in passing on his trip to Finland.
— **Comentar**
- **Lo comentó tres veces.**
  He remarked on it three times.
— **Mencionar**
- **Olvidé mencionar que Alberto vendrá mañana.**
  I forgot to remark that Albert is coming tomorrow.

English: Remark (n.)
— **Comentario**
- **No me gustó ese comentario.**
  I didn't like that remark.

Requerimiento (n.)*
— Official summons (court or IRS)
- **Me llegó un requerimiento de Hacienda.**
  I got a summons from the Treasury Department (or IRS).
* However, **requerir** is used as *to require.*

English: Requirement
— **Requisito**
- **Es requisito tener 21 años.**
  It's a requirement to be 21 years of age.

Resumen (n.)
— Summary
- **Ayer entregué el resumen.**
  I handed in the summary yesterday.

English: Résumé
— **Curriculum**
- **Anexé su curriculum a su solicitud de empleo.**
  I attached his résumé to his job application.

Resumir (v.)
— To summarize
- **Hay que resumir este informe.**
  This report must be summarized.

English: (To)resume
— **Reanudar**
- **La junta se reanudará en media hora.**
  The meeting will resume in half an hour.

Revisión (n.)
— Review
- **La revisión tardó seis horas.**
  The review took six hours.

English: Revision
— **Modificación; actualización**
- **La actualización del manual es reciente.**
  The revision of the manual is recent.

Revisar (v.)
— To review
- **Se revisarán todos los papeles de trabajo.**
  All the working papers will be reviewed.

English: (To)revise
— **Modificar**
  - **Los procedimientos se modificaron hace poco.**
    The procedures were revised recently.
— **Actualizar**
  - **Esta lista aún no ha sido actualizada.**
    This list has not been revised (updated) yet.

Secuestrar (v.)
— To kidnap
  - **Secuestraron al magnate en el camino a su casa.**
    The magnate was kidnapped on his way home.

English: To sequester
— **Aislar**
  - **Estará aislado mientras dure el juicio.**
    He will be sequestered for the duration of the trial.

Simpático(a) (adj.)
— Charming; nice; likable
  - **Mario no es guapo, pero es muy simpático.**
    Mario isn't good looking, but he's awfully nice.

English: Sympathetic
— **Comprensivo(a)**
  - **Puedes consultarlo con la directora; ella es muy comprensiva en estas cosas.**
    You can ask the principal about that; she's very sympathetic about this kind of thing.

Simpatía (n.)
— Charm
  - **La simpatía no lo es todo en una persona.**
    Charm isn't everything in a person.

English: Sympathy
— **Comprensión**
  - **Comprendo a la perfección tu punto de vista (Comparto tu punto de vista).**
    You have all my sympathy in this matter (I am on your side).
— **Pésame** (condolences)
  - **Mi más sincero pésame.**
    Please accept my sympathy at this sad time.
— **Compasión**
  - **No necesito tu compasión.**
    I don't need your sympathy (I don't need you to feel sorry for me).

False Cognates

Simpatizar con ☺ (v.)
— To have rapport with ☺; to get along with ☺
- **Simplemente no simpatizo con ellos.**
  I just don't get along with them.
— To like ☺.
- **Me simpatizaron muchísimo tus amigos.**
  I really liked your friends.

English: (To)sympathize
— **Comprender**
- **Estoy empezando a comprender al ex-jefe de Amalia. La despidió por inepta.**
  I am beginning to sympathize with Amalia's ex-boss. He fired her for being useless.
— **Compadecer; sentir(lo) por ☺**
- **Lo siento por ti, pobrecita.**
  I sympathize with you, you poor thing.

Suceder (v.)
— To occur; to happen
- **Todo sucedió en ese departamento.**
  Everything happened in that apartment.

English: To succeed (v.)
— **Lograr □; tener éxito**
- **Logré convencerla.**
  I succeeded in convincing her.
- **Lo logramos (tuvimos éxito).**
  We succeeded.

Suceso (n.)
— Event; happening
- **Estos sucesos tuvieron lugar hace mucho tiempo.**
  These events took place a long time ago.

English: Success
— **Éxito**
- **El libro va a tener mucho éxito.**
  The book will be very successful.

False Cognates

Tarjeta (n.)
— Card (any kind)
- **Lo siento mucho, no traigo tarjeta.**
  I'm sorry. I haven't got my card with me.

English: Target
— **Blanco**
  - **No estás apuntando al blanco.**
    You're not pointing at the target.
— **Meta**
  - **Nuestra meta es vender 600,000 unidades.**
    Our target is to sell 600,000 units
— **Objetivo**
  - **No logramos el objetivo.**
    We didn't succeed in reaching the target.

Tutor(a) (n.)
— Guardian
- **Mi tutor no me ha mandado mi pensión este mes.**
  My guardian hasn't sent my allowance this month.

English: Tutor
— **Maestro(a) particular**
  - **A Virginia le tuvieron que poner maestro particular porque tronó matemáticas.**
    Virginia had to have a tutor because she failed math.

Último (adj.)
— Last
- **Acabo de tomarme la última coca.**
  I just drank the last Coke.

English: Ultimate
— Lo máximo **(positive connotation)**
  - **Esta marca es lo máximo en pianos.**
    This brand is the ultimate in pianos.
— Lo máximo **(negative connotation)**
  - **Matar a tus padres tiene que ser el máximo pecado.**
    Killing your parents has to be the ultimate sin.

Últimamente (adv.)
— Lately; recently
- **No he visto a Bernardo últimamente.**
  I haven't seen Bernardo lately.

False Cognates

English: Ultimately
— **Algún día; a la larga**
  ▪ **A la larga, este río va a secarse.**
    Ultimately, this river will run dry.

Vicioso(a) (adj.) (n.)
— A person who has one or more vices involving illegal or immoral practices.
  ▪ **Juan tiene varios amigos viciosos.**
    Juan has several friends who have unsavory vices.
— A person who is **vicioso** (see above)
  ▪ **Juan es un vicioso.**
    Juan has unsavory vices.

English: Vicious
— **Fiero(a), bravo(a)**
  ▪ **Ese perro es muy fiero (o bravo).**
    That dog is really vicious.
— **Sádico(a)** (It also means sadist)
  ▪ **Fue un crimen sádico.**
    It was a vicious crime.

2. English-Spanish

They say forewarned is forearmed, so here's a list of nasty little reefs and shoals that are extremely easy to run afoul of. They are also false cognates, much like the lengthy list provided in the preceding section, except that the danger here is to assume that the Spanish is the same as the English, whereas in the main false cognate section the idea is to guard against assuming that the English is the same as the Spanish. Naturally, there are cases where mistakes can be made in either direction, which is why some words might be found in both sections. If all this is a bit confusing, it doesn't matter. Just go over the following list and make sure you don't stumble into an uncomfortable situation the next time you're tempted to throw in something like **Quiero introducirte a Graciela** which is not *I want to introduce you to Graciela*, but *I want to put Graciela inside you*, which sounds strange to say the least.

You will notice that examples are always given of the Spanish use of the English word that is considered dangerous. When we consider it interesting or instructive to do so, examples are also given of the Spanish false cognate.

Alteration (n.)
— **Ajuste; modificación; arreglo**
  - *This suit is going to need alterations.*
    Este traje necesita ciertos arreglos.
  - *Spanish*: **Alteración**
— Change (negative connotations)
  - *These books are full of jimmied numbers.*
    Estos libros tienen muchas alteraciones.
  - *Spanish*: **Alterar** (v.)
— To change ☐ (negative connotation)
  - *The printer got the colors in the illustrations all screwed up.*
    El impresor alteró todos los colores de las ilustraciones.
— To make changes (of the kind where ☺ monkeys with ☐ for shady reasons)
  - *Someone changed the numbers in these accounting books.*
    Alguien alteró las cifras en estos libros de contabilidad.

Correspondent (n.) (news)
— **Corresponsal**
  - *He's a correspondent for a U.S. television corporation.*
    Él es corresponsal de una televisora estadounidense.
  - *Spanish*: **Correspondiente** (adj.)
— The right ☐
  - *Find the right page in Spanish.*
    Busca la página correspondiente en español.

False Cognates

Chance (n.)
— **Posibilidad**
- *There's a chance I might get that scholarship.*
  Tengo posibilidades de conseguir esa beca.
— **Oportunidad**
- *Please give me a chance!*
  Por favor, ¡dame una oportunidad!

Spanish: **Chance** (n.)
— Could be; maybe
- *Speaker A:*   *Do you think it will rain?*
                   ¿Irá a llover?
- *Speaker B:*   *Could be.*
                   ¡Chance!

Disgraceful (adj.)
— **Vergonzoso(a)**
- *Your behavior is disgraceful.*
  Tu comportamiento es vergonzoso.

Disgrace (n.)
— **Vergüenza**
- *This is a disgrace!*
  ¡Esto es una vergüenza!

Spanish: **Desgracia** (n.)
— Calamity, disaster
- *What a disaster (stroke of bad luck)!*
  ¡Qué desgracia!

(To be) disgraced
— **Desprestigiar(se); ⇩quemar(se)**
- *We were disgraced by my father's bankruptcy.*
  Nos desprestigiamos (nos quemamos) con la quiebra de mi padre.

Spanish: **Desgraciado(a)** (n.)
— Blackguard; bastard
- *That bastard better not set foot in this house again!*
  ¡Mejor que ese desgraciado no vuelva a entrar en esta casa!

Disgusted (adj.)
— **Asqueado(a)** (physically)
- *He was disgusted by the pig skins in green sauce they served at the party.*
  Se sintió asqueado por el chicharrón en salsa verde que sirvieron en la fiesta.

False Cognates

— **Muy molesto(a)** (psychological)
- *I'm disgusted by the things she said in her letter.*
  Estoy muy molesto por las cosas que dijo en su carta.

Spanish: **Disgustado(a)** (adj.)

— Upset
- *I'm upset (or angry).*
  Estoy disgustado.

Disgusting (adj.)

— **Asqueroso(a)** (physical)
- *This pile of garbage is disgusting.*
  Este montón de basura es asqueroso.

— **Despreciable** (psychological)
- *His treatment of that girl is disgusting.*
  Su comportamiento con esa muchacha es despreciable.

Disgust (n.)

— **Asco; repugnancia**
- *My disgust is quite genuine.*
  El asco (la repugnancia) que siento es muy real.

Spanish: **Disgusto** (n.)

— Dislike
- *I feel dislike for that man.*
  Siento disgusto por ese individuo.

— An attack of annoyance or anger
- *I got awfully angry (or upset).*
  Tuve un disgusto tremendo.

To disgust

— **Dar asco, repugnar** (physical)
- *I can't stand pulque. It disgusts me.*
  No soporto el pulque. Me da asco (me repugna).

— **Dar coraje** (psychological)
- *His lies disgust me.*
  Sus mentiras me dan mucho coraje.

Spanish: **Disgustar(se)** (v.)

— To upset ☺
- *What your friend did upset me.*
  Me disgustó lo que hizo tu amigo.

— To dislike ☺☐
- *I dislike having to do this.*
  Me disgusta tener que hacer esto.

False Cognates

— To get upset or angry
- *Father got upset because I was late.*
  Papá se disgustó porque llegué tarde.
— To have a falling out
- *We had a quarrel.*
  Nos disgustamos.

To introduce ☺ to ☺ (v.)
— **Presentar**
- *I'd like to introduce the Merinos to you.*
  Quiero presentarte a los Merino or **Quiero que conozcas a los Merino.**
Spanish: **Introducir ☺ en ⬜**
— To insert
- *Please insert credit card here.*
  Favor de introducir la tarjeta de crédito aquí.
— To get into ⬜
- *We got into the building through the back door.*
  Nos introdujimos al edificio por la puerta de atrás.
— Put
- *I put a hand into the bag.*
  Introduje una mano en la bolsa.

Luxurious (adj.)
— **Lujoso**
- *The luxurious car is the most expensive.*
  El automóvil lujoso es el más costoso.
Spanish: **Lujurioso(a)** (adj.) (n.)
— Pertaining to lust (adj.)*
- *He made lewd gestures at me.*
  Me hizo gestos lujuriosos.
— Greatly given to the pleasures of the flesh (n.)
- *Pablo is not given to lust.*
  Pablo no es una persona lujuriosa.
* Imagine saying *I like Pablo's apartment; it's a den of sin*, when you mean *It's very luxurious.*

Luxury (n.)
— **Lujo**
- *Elsa leads a life of luxury.*
  Elsa tiene una vida llena de lujos.
Spanish: **Lujuria** (n.)
— Lust
- *Lust is a sin.*
  La lujuria es un pecado.

False Cognates

(Bad) manners (n.)
— **(Tener) malos modales; (ser un) malcriado**
 ▪ *That kid has bad manners.*
   Ese niño tiene malos modales (es un malcriado).

(Good) manners (n.)
— **Buenos modales**
 ▪ *That child has very good manners.*
   Esa niña tiene muy buenos modales (es muy educadita).
Spanish: **Manera** (n.)
 — Way (of doing things)
   ▪ *There are several ways of catching a mouse.*
     Hay varias maneras de atrapar un ratón.

(Good) mannered (adj.)
— **Bien educado**
 ▪ *That child is very well mannered.*
   Esa niña es muy educada.
Spanish: **Amanerado** (adj.) *
 — Effeminate
   ▪ *That guy is effeminate.*
     Ese muchacho es amanerado.
* Imagine saying *Your kid is very effeminate*, when you mean *good mannered*.

Presumption (n.)
— **Suposición**
 ▪ *That presumption is mistaken.*
   Esa suposición es errónea.
Spanish: **Presunción** (n.)
 — ☐ that is shown off; ☐ that ☺ feels conceited about
   ▪ *That particular thing that Alejandro feels so smug about is something I really dislike.*
     Esa presunción de Alejandro me cae muy mal.

Presume (v.)
— **Suponer**
 ▪ *I presume (suppose, assume) that the postman won't be coming today; it's a holiday.*
   Supongo que hoy no va a venir el cartero; es día festivo.
Spanish: **Presumir** (v.)
 — To show off

False Cognates

- *Ana was showing off her engagement ring to me.*
  Ana me estuvo presumiendo su anillo de compromiso.

Spanish: **Presumido(a)*** (adj.)
— A stuck-up, conceited person.
  - *The new teacher is really stuck-up.*
    El nuevo maestro es muy presumido.

Note: Most people use **presumido**, but the absolutely correct word is **presuntuoso**.

To qualify for ☐ (v.)
— **Cumplir con los requisitos para ☐**
  - *He doesn't qualify for this position.*
    Él no cumple con los requisitos para el puesto.

Spanish: **Calificar** (v.)
— To grade (work or performance)
  - *I have to grade 70 tests.*
    Tengo que calificar 70 pruebas.

Qualifications for ☐ (n.)
— **Requisitos para ☐; capacidad para ☐**
  - *He has most of the qualifications for the job.*
    Tiene la mayoría de los requisitos para el puesto.

Spanish: **Calificaciones** (n.)
— Grades
  - *I have better grades this semester.*
    Tengo mejores calificaciones este semestre.

To be qualified for ☐ (v.)
— **Estar preparado(a), ser apto(a) para ☐**
  - *She's well qualified.*
    Está bien preparada.

Spanish: **Ser calificado(a)** (v.)
— To be graded
  - *The tests are graded by the professor.*
    Los exámenes son calificados por el profesor.

To realize (to be aware) (v.)
— **Fijar(se); dar(se) cuenta**
  - *I didn't realize Judy had colored her hair.*
    No me había fijado (no me había dado cuenta de) que Judy se había pintado el pelo.
— **Estar consciente (formal)**
  - *Do you realize that the company has lost its entire capital stock?*
    ¿Está usted consciente de que la empresa ha perdido todo su capital social?

Spanish: **Realizar** (v.)
— Currently used only as to realize dreams, etc.
  - *His dreams never came true.*
    Sus sueños nunca se realizaron.
— To carry out
  - *He carried out a very complex study.*
    Realizó un estudio muy complejo.

To be related (v.)
— **Estar emparentado(a)**
  - *Federico is related to Jorge.*
    Federico está emparentado con Jorge.
Spanish: **(Estar) relacionado(a)** (v.)
— To be (well) connected
  - *I have good connections at the IRS.*
    Estoy bien relacionado en Hacienda.

Relatives (n.)
— **Parientes**
  - *My relatives all live in England.*
    Todos mis parientes viven en Inglaterra.

False Cognates

B. More False Cognates

The following words, as they are used in everyday Spanish, mean something other than what they appear to mean. Using them incorrectly is one of the things that can make a speaker of Spanish as a second language sound silly without realizing it, so beware.

1. Spanish-English

Alterar (v.) *is not* To alter (**modificar**), *but*
— To tamper with □
  - **Estas cifras están alteradas.**
    The figures have been tampered with (fixed).

Antiguo(a) (n.) *is not* Antique (ancient, pertaining to antiquity), *but*
— Old; former
  - **Te presento a mi antiguo jefe.**
    I want you to meet my former boss.

Apreciación (adj.) *is not* Appreciation **(agradecimiento)**, *but*
— Perception; way of seeing things
  - **Creo que tienes una apreciación errónea de las cosas.**
    I think your way of seeing things is mistaken.

Bachiller (n.) *is not* Bachelor (**soltero(a)**), *but*
— Graduate of the equivalent of junior college
  - **Obtuvo el grado de bachiller en junio.**
    He got his junior college certificate in June.

Basamento (n.) *is not* Basement (**sótano**), *but*
— Foundation of a building (also, more commonly, **cimentación**)
  - **El basamento del edificio tiene 30 metros de profundidad.**
    The foundation of the building goes down to a depth of 30 meters.

Capa (n.) *is not* Cap (**gorra**), *but*
— Cape
  - **No he usado esta capa desde que hice el papel del Conde de Montecristo.**
    I haven't worn this cape since I played the Count of Montecristo on stage.
— Layer
  - **Primero va una capa de arena y luego una capa de cemento.**
    First there's a layer of sand and then a layer of cement.

Cifras (n.) *is not* Ciphers (**claves**), *but*
— Figures (numbers)
- **Estas cifras son del año pasado.**
  These are last year's figures.

Confidencia (n.) *is not* Confidence (**confianza**), *but*
— Secret
- **Es una confidencia que no te puedo hacer.**
  I can't tell you. It's a secret.

Congelar (v.) *is not* To congeal (**cuajar; coagular**), *but*
— To freeze
- **Con este frío se van a congelar las tuberías.**
  The pipes are going to freeze with this cold.

Contestar (v.) *is not* To contest (**apelar**), *but*
— To answer or reply
- **¡Corre a contestar el teléfono!**
  Run and answer the phone!

Copa (n.) *is not* Cup (**taza**), *but*
— Stem glass
- **¿Te ofrezco una copa de vino?**
  Would you like a glass of wine?

Crudo(a) (adj.) *is not* Crude (**rudo(a)**), *but*
— Raw
- **El pollo todavía está crudo.**
  The chicken is still raw.
— Hungover
- **Está tan crudo que no puede ir a trabajar.**
  He's so hungover that he can't go to work.

Desgracia (n.) *is not* Disgrace (**vergüenza**), *but*
— Calamity
- **¡Qué desgracia! ¡Me robaron el coche!**
  What a calamity! My car has been stolen!

Desgraciadamente (adv.) *is not* Disgracefully (**vergonzosamente**), *but*
— Unfortunately

False Cognates

- **Desgraciadamente, Roberto no obtuvo el puesto que quería.**
  Unfortunately, Robert didn't get the job he wanted.

Desgraciado(a) (n.) *is not* Disgraced **(puesto(a) en vergüenza)**, *but*
— Bastard (n.)
- **Me divorcié de mi ex-marido porque es un desgraciado.**
  I divorced my ex-husband because he's a bastard.

Ducha (n.) *is not* Douche **(irrigación)**, *but*
— Shower
- **Me voy a dar una ducha antes de acostarme.**
  I'm going to have a shower before I go to bed.

Efectivamente (adv.) *is not* Effectively **(de manera efectiva)**, *but*
— That's right; in fact
- **Efectivamente, es una burda copia.**
  Yes, you're right; this is a clumsy imitation. (or This is, in fact, a clumsy imitation.)

Empresa (n.) *is not* Empress **(emperatriz)**, *but*
— Company
- **Esta empresa tiene varias sucursales.**
  This company has several branches.

Entretener *is not* To entertain **(tener invitados, divertir a ☺)**, *but*
— To delay; to keep ☺ waiting; to waste time
- **Siento haberte entretenido.**
  Sorry to have kept you.
(However, **entretener(se)** is to keep busy or have fun doing ❑, and that ❑ that is **entretenido** is fun.)

Establo (n.) *is not* Stable **(caballeriza)**, *but*
— Small dairy farm
- **Tiene un establo y reparte leche a algunas familias de por aquí.**
  He has a small dairy farm and he delivers milk to a few local families.

Estampa (n.) *is not* Stamp **(estampilla)**, *but*
— Religious illustration, usually on a card
- **¡Qué bonita estampa de la virgen!**
  What a pretty card of the virgin!

Exaltar(se) (v.) *is not* To be exalted **(ser** or **estar exaltado)**, *but*
— To get very upset
- **Juan se exalta muy fácilmente.**
  Juan gets upset very easily.

False Cognates

Existencias (n.) *is not* **Existences**, *but*
— Stock, merchandise
  ▪ **Tenemos pocas existencias.**
    We're low on stock.

Expediente (n.) *is not* Expedient **(oportuno(a))**, *but*
— File
  ▪ **Aquí tiene usted el expediente de este enfermo, doctor.**
    Here's the patient's file, doctor.

Filme (n.) *is not* Film **(película)**, *but*
— A movie (you may also find the word "film")
  ▪ **Ese filme (film) ganó un premio en Cannes.**
    That movie won a prize in Cannes.

Formar(se) (v.) *is not* To form yourself , *but*
— To get in line
  ▪ **Si quiere que lo atienda, tiene usted que formarse.**
    If you want me to attend you, you'll have to get in line.

Fundir (v.) *is not* To fund **(financiar)** *or* To found **(fundar)**, *but*
— To melt
  ▪ **Este es un crisol para fundir metales.**
    This is a crucible to melt metals in.

Grapas (n.) *is not* Grapes **(uvas)**, *but*
— Staples
  ▪ **Hay que comprar clips y grapas.**
    We must buy some clips and staples.

Hacer cola (v.) *is not* To make a tail, *but*
— To stand in line
  ▪ **¿Es necesario hacer cola para subir al autobús?**
    Do I have to stand in line to get on the bus?

Incapacitado(a) (adj.) *is not* Incapacitated **(lisiado(a))**, *but*
— On sick leave
  ▪ **Lleva tres meses incapacitado.**
    He's been away on sick leave for three months.

False Cognates

Insolación (n.) *is not* Insulation **(aislante)**, *but*
— Sunstroke
- **Estuvo tanto en la playa que le dio insolación.**
  He was on the beach for so long that he got sunstroke.

Intoxicado(a) (adj.) *is not* Intoxicated **(borracho(a), tomado(a))**, *but*
— (Food) poisoned
- **Ese muchacho parece estar intoxicado.**
  That boy seems to have some kind of food poisoning.

Junta (n.) *is not* Junta, *but*
— Meeting
- **La junta duró hasta la diez de la noche.**
  The meeting lasted until 10:00 p.m.

Legumbre (n.) *is not* Legume **(leguminosa)**, *but*
— Vegetable
- **Las legumbres cuestan menos en este mercado.**
  Vegetables cost less at this market.

Lima (n.) *is not* Lime **(limón)**, *but*
— Sweet lemon (non-acid lemon)
- **El jugo de lima es muy popular en Guadalajara.**
  Sweet lemon juice is very popular in Guadalajara.

Mantel (n.) *is not* Mantel **(repisa de una chimenea)**, *but*
— Tablecloth
- **Leticia está bordando un mantel.**
  Leticia is embroidering a tablecloth.

Nudo (n.) *is not* Nude **(desnudo(a))**, *but*
— Knot
- **Este nudo está muy apretado.**
  This knot is very tight.

Nuevamente (adv.) *is not* Newly **(recién)**, *but*
— Again
- **Van a revisar nuevamente la estufa.**
  They're going to examine the stove again.

False Cognates

Ocurrencia (n.) *is not* Occurrence (**suceso**), *but*
— Crazy idea, funny idea
- **¡Qué ocurrencia! Arturo quiere escalar el Popocatépetl.**
  Arturo wants to climb Popocatepetl. What a crazy idea!

Parcela (n.) *is not* Parcel (**paquete**), *but*
— Piece of communal land
- **Cada campesino recibirá un préstamo para mejorar su parcela.**
  Each peasant will receive a loan to improve his piece of communal land.

Peculiar (adj.) *is not* Peculiar (**raro(a), extraño(a)**), *but*
— Special; unusual; difficult
- **Este platillo tiene un sabor muy peculiar.**
  This dish has a very unusual taste.
- **Pedro tiene una forma muy chistosa de tomar la raqueta.**
  Pedro has a very special (unusual, but effective) way of holding the racket.

Peste (n.) *is not* Pest (**plaga**), *but*
— Very bad smell
- **Julia vive junto a una fábrica de papel y siempre hay una peste horrible en su colonia.**
  Julia lives next to a paper factory and there's always a stink in her neighborhood.
— The plague
- **La peste acabó con millones de personas en la edad media.**
  The plague killed millions of people in the Middle Ages.

Plaga *is not* The plague (**la peste**), *but*
— Plant disease
- **A mi hermoso sauce le cayó una plaga y murió.**
  My beautiful willow got a disease and died.

Plumero (n.) *is not* Plumber (**plomero**), *but*
— Feather duster
- **¿Dónde compraste este plumero?**
  Where did you buy that feather duster?

Portero(a) (n.) *is not* Porter (**cargador**), *but*
— Doorman
- **El portero está solamente hasta las 12 de la noche.**
  The doorman is only on duty till midnight.

Procurador (n.) *is not* Procurer (**↓padrote, alcahuete**), *but*
— District attorney, public prosecutor

False Cognates

- **El Procurador no está enterado de este caso todavía.**
  The District Attorney doesn't know about this case yet.

Promoción (n.) *is not* Work promotion **(ascenso)**, *but*
— Sale; price reduction
- **Toda la ropa de invierno está en promoción.**
  All winter clothing is on sale.

Quieto(a) (adj.) *is not* Quiet **(callado(a))**, *but*
— Still; unmoving
- **¡Estate quieta! Si te estás moviendo, no puedo peinarte.**
  Keep still! I can't comb your hair if you keep moving!

Quitar (v.) *is not* To quit **(renunciar)**, *but*
— To remove
- **Será difícil quitar esta mancha.**
  This spot will be difficult to remove.
— To get out of the way
- **¡Quítate! Voy a pasar.**
  Get out of the way! I'm coming through.

Rentabilidad (n.) *is not* Rentability **(arrendabilidad)**, *but*
— Profitability
- **No estoy seguro de la rentabilidad de ese negocio que me proponen.**
  I'm not sure about the profitability of the business they're proposing to me.

Rentable (adj.) *is not* Rentable **(arrendable)**, *but*
— Profitable
- **No es rentable tener una gasolinera en México.**
  It's not profitable to have a gas station in Mexico.

Semáforo (n.) *is not* Semaphore, *but*
— Stop light (Street light)
- **Los semáforos no están sincronizados.**
  The stop lights are not synchronized.

Sentir(se) en casa *is not* To feel yourself at home **(tocar sus partes privadas)**, *but*
— To make yourself at home
- **Regreso en media hora Por favor, siéntete en tu casa.**
  I'll be back in half an hour. Please make yuourself at home.

False Cognates

Sobrecargo (n.) *is not* Surcharge **(recargo)**, *but*
— Airline steward(ess) or hostess
- **Hay seis sobrecargos en este vuelo.**
  There are six stewards (or stewardesses) on this flight.

Tormenta (n.) *is not* Torment **(tormento)**, *but*
— Storm
- **Se avecina una tormenta.**
  There's a storm coming.

Torta (n.) *is not* Torte **(pay)**, *but*
— Big sandwich made with a **telera** (see *Mexican Food*)
- **Aquí hacen unas tortas calientes de jamón realmente deliciosas.**
  They make really great hot ham sandwiches in Mexican buns here.

Últimamente (adv.) *is not* Ultimately **(a la larga, con el tiempo)**, *but*
— Lately; recently
- **No hemos visto a Ernesto últimamente.**
  We haven't seen Ernesto lately.

Verdura (n.) *is not* Verdure **(vegetación)**, *but*
— Vegetable
- **¿Trajiste suficiente verdura para toda la semana?**
  Did you bring enough vegetables for the whole week?

False Cognates

2. English-Spanish

Bizarre (adj.) is not **Bizarro** (brave), *but*
— **Extraño(a)**
  - *The incident was quite bizarre.*
    El incidente fue muy extraño.

Candid (adj.) *is not* **Cándido(a)** (innocent), *but*
— **Franco(a)**
  - *I can't be candid with my boss.*
    No puedo ser franca con mi jefe.

Complacent (adj.) *is not* **Complaciente** (eager to please), *but*
— **Satisfecho(a) de sí mismo**
  - *Therese has no reason to be complacent with her performance.*
    Teresa no tiene por qué estar satisfecha de su trabajo.

Cup (n.) *is not* **Copa** (glass), *but*
— **Taza**
  - *I need a cup of coffee.*
    Necesito una taza de café.

To entertain (v.) *is not* **Entretener** (to delay), *but*
— **Tener visitas (invitados)**
  - *We don't entertain much.*
    No tenemos visitas (invitados) con frecuencia.
— **Divertir**
  - *Bob entertained us with some magic tricks.*
    Bob nos divirtió con unos trucos de magia.

Figures (numbers) (n.) *is not* **Figuras**, *but*
— **Cifras; números**
  - *I need the figures today.*
    Necesito las cifras hoy.

To gain (weight) (v.) *is not* **Ganar** (to win), *but*
— **Subir de peso**

False Cognates

- *I've gained 10 pounds.*
  He subido cinco kilos.

Infatuated (adj.) *is not* **Infatuado**(a) (conceited), *but*
— **Tontamente enamorado(a)**
  - *Linda is infatuated with Professor Stuart.*
    Linda está enamorada del profesor Stuart como una tonta.

Mantel (n.) *is not* **Mantel** (tablecloth), *but*
— **Repisa de la chimenea**
  - *The clock is on the mantel.*
    El reloj está en la repisa de la chimenea.

Message (n.) *is not* **Mensaje**, *but*
— **Recado**
  - *Would you like to leave a message?*
    ¿Quiere dejar un recado?

Peculiar (adj.) *is not* **Peculiar**, *but*
— **Raro(a), extraño(a)**
  - *This dish has a very peculiar taste.*
    Este platillo tiene un sabor muy raro (extraño).
— **Chistoso(a)** (also means funny or amusing)
  - *Pedro has a very peculiar (strange) way of holding the racket.*
    Pedro tiene una forma muy chistosa de tomar la raqueta.

Pedestrian (n.) *is not* **Pedestre** (adj.), *but*
— **Peatón**
  - *They are building a bridge so that pedestrians can cross.*
    Están construyendo un puente para que crucen los peatones.

Pollution (n.) *is not* **Polución** (see *Some Special Cases*), *but*
— **Contaminación**
  - *Pollution is worse all the time.*
    La contaminación está cada vez peor.

Porter (n.) *is not* **Portero** (doorman), *but*
— **Mozo**

False Cognates

- *There are no porters at this railway station.*
  No hay mozos en esta estación de tren.

Pump (n.) is not Pompa (derriere), but
— **Bomba**
  - *The pumps will not be turned on without a deposit.*
    Las bombas no operan sin introducir dinero en la máquina.

Quiet (adj.) *is not* **Quieto**(a) (still), *but*
— **Callado(a)**
  - *I can't hear the baby. He is very quiet! I guess he finally felt asleep.*
    No oigo al bebé. Está muy callado. Supongo que finalmente se durmió.

To quit (v.) *is not* **Quitar** (to remove), *but*
— **Renunciar**
  - *I quit my job at the insurance company.*
    Renuncié en la compañía de seguros.

To reduce (weight) (v.) *is not* **Reducir** (to diminish), *but*
— **Bajar de peso**
  - *I've lost ten pounds.*
    He bajado cinco kilos.

Resort (n.) *is not* **Resorte** (spring), *but*
— **Conjunto vacacional**
  - *My son is at a resort in Cancun.*
    Mi hijo está en un conjunto vacacional en Cancún.

To take chances (v.) *is not* **Tomar riesgos**, *but*
— **Correr riesgos**
  - *I don't want to take any chances now.*
    No quiero correr riesgos ahorita.

Vicinity (n.) *is not* **Vecindad** (tenement), *but*
— **Los alrededores; las cercanías**
  - *This address is somewhere in the vicinity of the hospital.*
    Esta dirección queda en los alrededores del hospital.

C. Is It or Isn't It?

Each word in this section has two or more meanings, one of which is the obvious one, since the English and Spanish words come from the same root; the other meaning is what makes these words confusing and dangerous.

For example, **asistir**, as you might suspect, means *to assist*; but it is also used to mean *to attend an event of some kind*. If you are not aware of this second meaning, a sentence like **voy a asistir a la conferencia** can stop you dead in your tracks, or worse, be totally misconstrued.

Here is an example of how words appear in this section:

Asistir (v.)
— To assist   *(meaning a)*
  ▪ **Asistí al cirujano en la operación.**
     I assisted the surgeon in the operation.
— To attend an event   *(meaning b)*
  ▪ **Voy a asistir a la conferencia.**
     I am going to attend the lecture.

None of the second meanings in the list are unusual in any way.

When another word would most likely be used in preference to any of the words in this section, that other word is enclosed in brackets like this: [*other word*].

1. Spanish-English

Accidente (n.)
— Accident
- **Oscar tuvo un accidente ayer.**
  Oscar had an accident yesterday.
— A dip, drop, rise, steep slope, gully, ravine or any other sharp feature in otherwise featureless terrain
- **En esa zona, hay un accidente del terreno.**
  There's a dip (etc.) in the land in that zone.
- **Es un terreno muy accidentado.**
  This land has many dips (etc.).

Acción (n.)
— Action
- **No se ha llevado a cabo ninguna acción.**
  No action has been taken.
— A share in corporate stock
- **Voy a tener que vender algunas de mis acciones.**
  I'm going to have to sell some of my shares.

Afecto (n.)
— Affection
- **Le tengo mucho afecto a Flor.**
  I have great affection for Flor.
— To be fond of □ (**Ser afecto a** □); fondness for ☺□
- **Los Rose son muy afectos al teatro frívolo.**
  The Roses are very fond of vaudeville theater.

Agarrar (v.)
— To catch □
- **La oscuridad les impidió agarrar al ladrón.**
  The darkness prevented them from catching the thief.
— To work □ up
- **El camión agarró gran velocidad en la bajada.**
  The bus reached high speed going downhill.

Aislamiento (n.)
— Insulation

False Cognates

- **Se siente frío porque la casa no tiene aislamiento.**
  You feel the cold because the house has no insulation.
- **El aislamiento de esta conexión eléctrica está defectuoso.**
  The insulation on this electrical connection is faulty.
— Isolation
- **El aislamiento me deprime aquí tan lejos de todo.**
  The isolation depresses me out here so far from everything.

Aliento (n.)
— Breath
- **Lástima de Chayo: tan guapa y tiene mal aliento.**
  Too bad about Chayo: such a nice girl, but she has bad breath.
— Encouragement
- **Hay que dar aliento a los muchachos estudiosos.**
  Good students should be given encouragement (or should be encouraged).
— Wind (music)
- **La flauta es un instrumento de aliento.**
  The flute is a wind instrument.

Amparo (n.)
— Girl's name
- **La novia de José Luis se llama Amparo.**
  Jose Luis' girlfriend's name is Amparo.
— Injunction.
- **No pudieron encarcelarlo porque se presentó con un amparo.**
  They were unable to jail him because he got himself an injunction.
- **No pudieron expropiar el terreno porque tenía amparo.**
  They were unable to expropriate that piece of land because he had an injunction.

Apagar (v.)
— To turn off
- **Apaga la tele. Vamos a comer.**
  Turn off the TV. We're going to have lunch
— To muffle
- **Ponle sarape doblado encima al motor, para apagar un poco el ruido.**
  Cover the motor up with a folded blanket, to muffle the noise a bit.

Aprobar (v.)
— To approve
- **Aún no han aprobado el gasto.**
  The expense hasn't been approved yet.

False Cognates

— To pass a test or exam
  - **Aprobé en todo menos en matemáticas.**
    I passed all the exams except math.

Arrancar (v.)
— To yank □ from ☺□
  - **El ladrón me arrancó la bolsa y se fue corriendo.**
    The thief yanked my purse away and fled.
— To start out or off
  - **Los caballos están a punto de arrancar.**
    The horses are about to start off.
— To start
  - **El coche ya no arranca muy bien.**
    The car doesn't start so well anymore.
— To get going (events)
  - **La junta arrancó hasta las diez y media.**
    The meeting didn't get going until 10:30.

Asamblea (n.)
— Assembly
  - **La asamblea de comerciantes fue la primera de este tipo.**
    The assembly of retailers was the first of its kind.
— Stockholders' meeting
  - **No vamos a votar en la asamblea.**
    We are not going to vote at the stockholders' meeting.

Ascender (v.)
— To ascend; to rise
  - **La temperatura ascendió a 42 grados.**
    The temperature rose to 42 degrees.
— To total
  - **La cuenta asciende a 250 dólares.**
    The bill totals 250 dollars.

Asistir (v.)
— To assist; to help
  - **Asistí al cirujano en la operación.**
    I assisted the surgeon at the operation.
  - **El sacerdote vendrá para asistir al moribundo.**
    The priest will come to assist the dying man.
— To attend □
  - **No puedo asistir a la clase esta tarde.**
    I can't go to class this afternoon.

False Cognates

Asistencia (n.)
— Assistance; help
- **El cirujano contó con la invaluable asistencia de su maestro.**
  The surgeon had his teacher's invaluable assistance.
— Attendance
- **La asistencia al concierto fue pésima.**
  Attendance at the concert was very low.

Note: In a sentence like **"Es una institución de asistencia social"**, **asistencia** means *assistance*.

Banco (n.)
— Bank
- **El banco no abre en la tarde.**
  The bank doesn't open in the afternoon.
— Stool or bench
- **Pablo nos regaló un pequeño bar con tres bancos.**
  Pablo gave us a small bar with three stools.

Bomba (n.)
— Pump
- **No funciona la bomba de gasolina.**
  The gasoline pump doesn't work.
— Bomb
- **Cayeron tres bombas en esta casa durante la guerra.**
  Three bombs hit this house during the war.

Borrador (n.)
— Eraser (in Mexico this is only a blackboard eraser; a rubber eraser is a **goma**)
- **El borrador siempre se le cae en clase.**
  He always drops the blackboard eraser in class.
— A rough draft of something
- **Esto es nada más un borrador.**
  This is merely a draft.

Burro(a) (n.)
— Donkey
- **El burro todavía se usa mucho en México.**
  The donkey is still used a lot in Mexico.
— Ironing board; legs for a plank table
- **Cuando termines de planchar, tienes que guardar el burro.**
  When you finish ironing, you have to put the ironing board away.
— Stupid person
- **Te dije que no era así. No seas burro.**
  I told you that was wrong! Don't be dumb.

False Cognates

Cabeza (n.)

— Head (of anything)

- **Se pegó en la cabeza.**
  He hit himself on the head.

— Talent

- **Tiene mucha cabeza para preparar mapas.**
  He has a great deal of talent for making maps.

— Intelligence

- **El ingeniero es una gran cabeza.**
  The engineer is very intelligent.

Calidad (n.)

— Capacity

- **En mi calidad de ciudadano, protesto por esta injusticia.**
  In my capacity as a citizen, I protest this injustice.

— With the status of . . .

- **Llegaron al país en calidad de asilados políticos.**
  They arrived to this country as political refugees.

— In the form of . . .

- **Como no teníamos abrigo, íbamos en calidad de paleta helada.**
  As we had no coat, we were frozen.

Cardiaco(a) (adj.)

— Cardiac

- **Es un paciente cardiaco.**
  He's a cardiac patient.

— Having the quality of a cliffhanger (enough to cause a heart attack)

- **El juego de basquetbol tuvo un final cardiaco.**
  The last few minutes of the basketball game had us on the edge of our seats.

Cámara (n.)

— Camera

- **Mi cámara es japonesa.**
  My camera is Japanese.

— Hall; chamber

- **¿Dónde queda la Cámara de Comercio?**
  Where is the Chamber of Commerce located?

Capa (n.)

— Cape

- **Te pareces a Drácula con esa capa.**
  You look like Dracula in that cape.

False Cognates

— Layer
- **Todo esto tiene una capa de polvo.**
  There is as layer of dust on everything.
- **La capa de ozono está en peligro de desaparecer.**
  The ozone layer is in danger of disappearing.

Cargar (v.)
— To carry
- **Juan siempre carga pistola.**
  Juan always carries a gun.
— To load
- **Hay que cargar el camión antes de las siete.**
  The truck must be loaded before seven.
— To charge ☐ to ☺*
- **Cárguelo a mi cuenta.**
  Charge it to my account.
- **Cárgueselo a mi papá.**
  Charge it to my father.
* To charge ☺ for ☐ is **cobrar**.
- **Me cobró demasiado por arreglar el coche.**
  He charged me too much to fix the car.

Carrera (n.)
— Career
- **Su carrera en el teatro comenzó cuando tenía cinco años.**
  His career in the theater began when he was five.
— University; studies (degree)
- **Él hizo dos carreras pero no practicó ninguna.**
  He has two college degrees but doesn't work in either of the two areas.
— Race
- **La carrera de bicicletas es de 50 kilómetros.**
  The bicycle race is 50 kilometers.

Carta (n.)
— Letter
- **Le voy a escribir una carta a Juan.**
  I'm going to write Juan a letter.
— Menu
- **¿Nos trae la carta por favor?**
  Would you please bring us the menu?

False Cognates

Casco (n.)

— Hoof

- **Este caballo tiene los cascos desgastados.**
  This horse's hooves are worn down.

— Empty pop bottle (returnable)

- **Dame los cascos para ir por los refrescos.**
  Give me the empty pop bottles so I can go for the soft drinks.

— The main house of an **hacienda**

- **Tengo ganas de reconstruir el casco, pero es muy caro.**
  I want to reconstruct the hacienda house, but it's too expensive.

— Helmet

- **No debes usar la moto sin casco.**
  You shouldn't ride the motorcycle without a helmet.

Causar (v.)

— To cause

- **No sabemos qué fue lo que causó el accidente.**
  We don't know what caused the accident.

— To be subject to a tax

- **Este artículo no causa impuesto.**
  This article is not taxed.

Celebrar (v.)

— To celebrate

- **Vamos a tener que celebrar este éxito.**
  We are going to have to celebrate this success.

— To sign or enter into an agreement or contract

- **Este contrato se celebró hace tres años.**
  This contract was signed three years ago.

Chimenea (n.)

— Chimney

- **La chimenea de la fábrica se tiene que reparar.**
  The chimney at the factory has to be repaired.

— Fireplace

- **Qué bonita se ve la chimenea prendida, ¿verdad?**
  The fireplace looks lovely with a fire in it, don't you think?

Chino(a) (adj.) (n.)

— Curly (hair)

- **Javier es el muchacho de pelo chino.**
  Javier is the boy with the curly hair.

False Cognates

— Goose bumps
- **Se me puso el cuerpo chinito (Me puse chinita* or Se me enchinó el cuero).**
  I got goose bumps.

*In this sense, it is always used in diminutive: **chinito(a)**. **Se me puso la carne de gallina** can also be said. All are equally common.

— Chinese (person)
- **Había un japonés y un chino.**
  There was a Japanese and a Chinese.

— Chinese (language)
- **Las instrucciones vienen en chino y en inglés.**
  The instructions are in Chinese and in English.

Cola (n.)

— Tail
- **Le pisé la cola al pobre gato.**
  I stepped on the poor cat's tail.

— Glue (resin used exclusively in carpentry, and now being displaced by over-the-counter products)
- **Necesito un poco de cola para pegar la pata de la mesa.**
  I need a little glue to fix the table leg.

— Bottled soft drink
- **La Cuba libre se hace con ron y refresco de cola.**
  A "Cuba libre" is made with rum and a cola drink.

— Line (that people stand in)
- **¡A la cola!**
  Get in line!

Cólera (n.)

— Cholera
- **Dicen que ya no hay cólera en esta parte del país.**
  They say there's no more cholera in this part of the country.

— Ire; rage
- **Cuando supo lo que hizo Carlos, se llenó de cólera.**
  He got awfully angry when he found out what Carlos had done.

Coma (n.) (v.)

— Comma
- **Nunca pongas una coma después del sujeto de una oración.**
  Never use a comma after the subject of a sentence.

— Coma
- **El pobre lleva tres semanas en coma.**
  The poor thing has been in a coma for three weeks.

False Cognates

— Second person singular subjunctive of **comer**
  ▪ **Es importante que coma muchas verduras y frutas.**
  It's important for him to eat a lot of fruit and vegetables.

Comedia (n.)

— Comedy
  ▪ **Todas estas películas son comedias.**
  All these movies are comedies.
— Soap opera
  ▪ **Graciela no se pierde la comedia de las seis.**
  Graciela never misses the six o'clock soap.

Competencia (n.)

— A competition
  ▪ **La competencia de natación acaba de terminar.**
  The swimming competition just ended.
— The competition
  ▪ **Tenemos mejores precios que nuestra competencia.**
  We have better prices than the competition.
— Capacity
  ▪ **No le da pena su falta de competencia.**
  His lack of capacity does not embarrass him.

Componer (v.)

— To compose
  ▪ **Clara me compuso una canción muy tierna.**
  Clara composed a really sweet song for me.
— To repair; to fix
  ▪ **Prometieron componer el elevador hoy.**
  They promised to fix the elevator today.

Concepto (n.)

— Concept
  ▪ **El concepto de la reencarnación no siempre es fácil de comprender.**
  The concept of reincarnation is not always easy to understand.
— Item
  ▪ **¿Por qué concepto hicieron la factura?**
  What is the invoice for?
  ▪ **Son muchos los conceptos contenidos en la lista.**
  The items on the list are very numerous.

False Cognates

- **No hay impuesto por concepto de regalías.**
  There is no tax on (the item of) royalties.

Conferencia (n.)
— Conference
- **Va a haber una conferencia médica en diciembre.**
  There's going to be a medical conference in December.
— Telephone call (mainly long distance)
- **Me están cobrando de más por la conferencia a Londres.**
  They're overcharging me for the call to London.
— Talk or lecture
- **Pablo va a dar una conferencia sobre las reformas fiscales.**
  Pablo is going to give a talk on the amendments to the tax laws.

Confiar (v.)
— To confide
- **Nunca le confío mis secretos a Claudia.**
  I never confide in Claudia.
— To trust
- **Confío plenamente en Sergio.**
  I trust Sergio completely.

Constancia (n.)
— Constancy
- **La constancia es indispensable si quieres tener éxito.**
  Constancy is indispensable if you want to succeed.
— Certificate; voucher
- **Necesito una constancia de antecedentes penales y otra de solvencia.**
  I need a certificate from the police department showing I have no police record, and another from the bank stating that I'm solvent.

Contacto (n.)
— Contact
- **No tengo contacto con mi primo.**
  I have no contact with my cousin.
— Electric wall plug
- **En esta habitación hay un solo contacto.**
  There's only one plug in this room.

Contaminación (n.)
— Contamination

False Cognates

- **Encontraron contaminación de mercurio en dos mil toneladas de pescado.**
  They found mercury contamination in two thousand tons of fish.
— Pollution *
- **La contaminación en la ciudad es cada vez peor.**
  Pollution in the city is worse all the time.

*See **Some Special Cases**.

Contaminar (v.)
— To contaminate
- **Esas bacterias pueden contaminar la leche.**
  Those bacteria can contaminate the milk.
— To pollute
- **Los detergentes están contaminando los ríos.**
  Detergents are polluting our rivers.

Constitución (n.)
— Constitution
- **La Constitución de México no es igual a la de los Estados Unidos.**
  The Mexican Constitution is not the same as that of the United States.
— Incorporation
- **La constitución de una empresa es un proceso algo complicado.**
  The incorporation of a company is a somewhat complicated process.

Constituir (v.)
— To constitute
- **Esto constituye un delito.**
  This constitutes a felony.
— To incorporate
- **La empresa se constituyó hace tres años.**
  The company was incorporated three years ago.

Contar (v.)
— To count
- **Cuenta tu dinero con cuidado.**
  Count your money carefully.
— To tell (about ❑)
- **Cuéntame lo que pasó mientras estuve de viaje.**
  Tell me what happened while I was away.

Corriente (adj.) (n.)
— Current (adj.)

False Cognates

- **Ésta es una cuenta corriente.**
  This is a current account.
— Electricity (n.)
- **Antes de cortar los cables, desconecta la corriente.**
  Before you cut the wires, disconnect the electricity.
— Common; vulgar; cheap (adj.)
- **Elisa es muy corriente.**
  Elisa is very vulgar.

Cruzar (v.)
— To cross
- **Hay que cruzar la calle solamente en la esquina.**
  You should only cross the street at the corner.
— To mate
- **Voy a cruzar a mi Fifí con el perro del veterinario.**
  I'm going to mate my Fifi with the vet's dog.

Declaración (n.)
— Declaration, statement
- **La Declaración de Independencia se guarda aquí.**
  The Declaration of Independence is kept here.
— Tax return
- **No encuentro mis declaraciones del año pasado.**
  I can't find last year's returns.

Departamento (n.)
— Department
- **El departamento de contabilidad está cerrado.**
  The accounting department is closed.
— Apartment
- **Te invito a comer en mi departamento.**
  Come and have lunch at my apartment.

Demandar (v.)
— To demand [demandar]
- **El país demanda (exige) un proceso de modernización.**
  The country demands a modernization process.
— To sue
- **Si no me cumples, te demando.**
  If you break your promise, I'll sue you.

Demanda (n.)
— A demand [exigencia]

False Cognates

- **La demanda (exigencia) es clara: quieren justicia.**
  The demand is clear: they want justice.
— A law suit
- **Esta demanda va a durar años.**
  This law suit is going to drag on for years.

Dependencia (n.)
— Dependence
- **La dependencia económica es frustrante.**
  Economic dependence is frustrating.
— Government agency
- **En algunos países, casi todas las dependencias de gobierno son ineficientes.**
  In some countries, almost all government agencies are inefficient.

Descomponer (v.)
— To decompose
- **La basura se está descomponiendo.**
  That garbage is decomposing (rotting).
— To break down; to go on the blink
- **El coche se descompuso en el periférico.**
  The car broke down on the freeway.

Destino (n.)
— Destiny
- **Acéptalo sin resistirte. Es tu destino.**
  Don't fight it. It's your destiny.
— Destination
- **¿Dónde están los pasajeros con destino a Bogotá?**
  Where are the passengers bound for Bogota?

Dirección (n.)
— Direction
- **Es en esa dirección.**
  It's in that direction.
— Address
- **Dame tu dirección.**
  Give me your address.
— The act of conducting
- **La dirección de la orquesta dejó mucho que desear.**
  The conducting of the orchestra left a great deal to be desired.
— The office of the director and his staff (school or corporation)
- **La dirección de la escuela fija las cuotas.**
  The principal's office sets the rates.

False Cognates

Discutir (v.)
— To discuss
- **Vamos a discutir la reorganización empresarial.**
  We are going to discuss the corporate reorganization.
— To argue
- **Discutimos acaloradamente por ese malentendido.**
  We had an upsetting argument because of that misunderstanding.
- **No discutas.**
  Don't argue.

Discusión (n.)
— A discussion
- **La discusión del contrato duró hasta las 3:00.**
  The discussion about the contract lasted until 3:00.
— An argument
- **Hubo una discusión que se convirtió en bronca.**
  There was an argument that turned into a fight.

(El) Editorial (n.)
— Editorial
- **El editorial de hoy es muy interesante.**
  Today's editorial is very interesting.

(La) Editorial (n.)
— Publisher; publishing house (feminine)
- **Voy a ver si esta editorial acepta publicar mi libro.**
  I'm going to see if this publishing house is willing to publish my book.

Efectivo (adj.) (n.)
— Effective (adj.) **(efectivo(a))**
- **No creo que el agua fría sea muy efectiva contra las quemaduras.**
  I don't think cold water is very effective for burns.
— Cash (n.)
- **¿Tienes algo de efectivo?**
  Do you have any cash?

Ejercicio (n.)
— Exercise (physical, military, school work, piano, etc.)
- **Ese ejercicio es demasiado difícil para mí.**
  That exercise is too hard for me.
— Fiscal period
- **Tuvimos pérdida en el ejercicio pasado.**
  There was a loss in the last period.

Elemento (n.)
— Element

False Cognates

- **El radio es un elemento radiactivo.**
  Radium is a radioactive element.
— Person
  - **El Sr. Pérez es un buen elemento.**
  Mr. Perez is an asset.
  - **Iban cuatro elementos en la patrulla.**
  There were four persons in the squad car.

Emitir (v.)
— To emit
  - **Esa fábrica emite demasiados tóxicos.**
  That factory emits too many toxic substances.
— To issue ☐
  - **Estos billetes se emitieron hace dos años.**
  These bills (bank notes) were issued two years ago.

Emisión (n.)
— Emission
  - **Según el medidor, no hay emisiones de monóxido dc carbono.**
  According to the gauge, there are no carbon monoxide emissions.
— Issuance or issue
  - **La emisión de los billetes de banco está estrictamente controlada.**
  The issuance of bank notes is very strictly controlled.

Equipo (n.)
— Equipment
  - **El equipo es importado dc Suecia.**
  The equipment is imported from Sweden.
— Team
  - **Mi equipo tiene tres juegos ganados y uno empatado.**
  My team has won three games and tied one.

Erupción (n.)
— Eruption
  - **La última erupción de ese volcán fue en 1928.**
  That volcano's last eruption was in 1928.
— Rash
  - **Tu bebé tiene una erupción en la espaldita.**
  Your baby has a rash on his back.

Escala (n.)
— Scale
  - **¿No sabes a qué escala está este plano?**
  Don't you know what scale this drawing is?

— Stopover
  ▪ **No es un vuelo directo. Hay una escala en Miami.**
    It's not a direct flight. There's a stopover in Miami.

Escándalo (n.)
— Scandal
  ▪ **Su vida fue un escándalo tras otro.**
    His life was one scandal after another.
— Very loud carryings on
  ▪ **No puedo dormir por el escándalo que están haciendo en esa fiesta.**
    I can't sleep with all the noise they're making at that party.

Escape (n.)
— Escape; evasion
  ▪ **Los presos planearon el escape desde hace meses.**
    The prisoners planned the escape for months.
— Exhaust (pipe) (automobile)
  ▪ **Necesito cambiarle el escape a mi auto.**
    I need to change the exhaust pipe.

Estado (n.)
— State
  ▪ **Está en un estado lamentable.**
    He's in a very bad state.
  ▪ **El estado de Veracruz es bello.**
    The state of Veracruz is lovely.
  ▪ **El Estado Mexicano no es muy poderoso.**
    The State is not very powerful in Mexico.
— Statement (banking, finance, accounting, etc.)
  ▪ **Aquí tengo el estado de cuenta.**
    Here is the statement of account.

Estancia (n.)
— Living room
  ▪ **Voy a comprar unos muebles preciosos para la estancia.**
    I'm going to buy some lovely furniture for the living room.
— Stay
  ▪ **Su estancia en Canadá fue más corta de lo proyectado.**
    His stay in Canada was shorter than planned.
— Hacienda (used most in South America)
  ▪ **El Sr. Tinoco tiene una de las estancias más grandes del estado.**
    Mr. Tinoco has one of the biggest haciendas in the state.

False Cognates

Estimar (v.)
— To estimate
  - **Estas cifras son estimadas.**
    These figures are only estimated.
— To esteem
  - **De veras estimo mucho a esos dos profesores.**
    I think the world of those two teachers.

Estímulo (n.)
— Stimulus
  - **El estímulo eléctrico se registra en esta pantalla.**
    The electrical stimulus registers on this screen.
— Incentive
  - **Puse la fábrica en esa región por todos los estímulos fiscales.**
    We decided on this region for the factory because of all the tax incentives.

Evacuar (v.)
— Evacuate
  - **Los lugareños se negaban a evacuar la ciudad.**
    The inhabitants refused to evacuate the city.
— To have a bowel movement (used medically)
  - **Hace dos días que el niño no puede evacuar.**
    The kid hasn't been able to have a bowel movement for two days.

Existencia (n.)
— Existence
  - **Llevaron una miserable existencia.**
    They led an existence of utter poverty.
— Stock (goods)
  - **Tenemos suficiente(s) existencia(s) en bodega.**
    We have enough stock in the warehouse.

Expedición (n.)
— Expedition
  - **La expedición a la Antártida no salió muy bien.**
    The expedition to the Antarctic was not very successful.
— Issuance
  - **La expedición del certificado se va a tardar.**
    Issuance of the certificate will be delayed.

Facilitar (v.)
— To facilitate

- **Este cajero automático facilita mucho mis operaciones bancarias.**
  This automatic teller really facilitates my banking.
— To give or provide
- **El Sr. Góngora me va a facilitar su privado por un par de semanas.**
  Mr. Gongora is going to let me use his private office for a couple of weeks.
- **Facilíteme su pasaporte.**
  Let me have your passport.

Facultad (n.)
— Faculty (*never* used to mean a body of teachers)
- **La facultad de medicina es enorme.**
  The school of medicine is huge.
— Power
- **El capitán del barco tiene facultad (está facultado) para casar a la gente.**
  The ship's captain has the power (or is empowered) to marry people.

Figurar(se) (v.)
— To appear in □; to be present in □
- **El doctor figura en la directiva del hospital.**
  The doctor is on the hospital board.
— To imagine
- **¡Figúrese qué cantidad de gente había!**
  Imagine how many people were there!

Finalmente (adv.)
— Finally
- **Finalmente me aumentaron el sueldo.**
  I finally got a raise.
— Lastly
- **Y finalmente, quiero decirles lo mucho que agradezco lo que se ha hecho por mí.**
  And lastly, I want to tell you how much I appreciate all you've done for me.

Fondo (n.)
— Funds (plural)
- **Regresaron este cheque por falta de fondos.**
  This check was returned because the account has insufficient funds.
— Fund
- **El fondo de pensiones lo maneja el Sr. Pérez**
  Mr. Perez handles the pension fund.
— The bottom of □ (not anatomic)
- **El fondo de la cisterna está sucio.**
  The bottom of the cistern is dirty.

False Cognates

Frontera (n.)
— Frontier
- **La última frontera es el espacio.**
  Space is the last frontier.
— Border
- **Me abrieron las maletas en la frontera.**
  They searched my baggage at the border.

Fusión (n.)
— Fusion
- **La fusión nuclear aún no es una realidad.**
  Nuclear fusion is still not a reality.
— Merger
- **La fusión de las compañías va a permitir un aumento en la productividad.**
  The merger is going to allow an increase in productivity.
— Blend (not used for blends of food, drink, etc.)
- **Ese óleo es una fusión de estilos.**
  That oil painting is a blend of different schools (techniques).

Gata (n.)
— Cat (fem.)
- **A la gata le encanta dormirse en el sofá.**
  The cat loves to sleep on the sofa.
— 🖑⇩ House maid; servant (an insulting word)
- **La gata que corrí el mes pasado me robó dos anillos y un reloj.**
  The maid I fired last month stole two rings and a watch.

Gato (n.)
— Cat (masculine)
- **Ese maldito gato estuvo maullando toda la noche.**
  That damned cat was howling all night.
— 🖑⇩ Any male employee who does menial work or runs ☺'s errands (an insulting word)
- **Deja de gritarme de esa manera. ¿Crees que soy tu gato?**
  Stop ordering me around like that. You think I'm your flunkey?
— Car jack
- **No quiero salir a carretera sin gato.**
  I don't want to go out on the highway without a jack.

Goma (n.)
— Eraser (rubber)
- **Ya me equivoqué. ¿Tienes una goma que me prestes?**
  I made a mistake here. Do you have an eraser you can lend me?

False Cognates

— Glue
  ▪ **No lo pegues con goma. Usa cinta adhesiva (Ⓜ durex).**
    Don't stick it with glue. Use scotch tape.
— Chewing gum (more commonly known as **chicle**)
  ▪ **No me gusta la goma de mascar (el chicle) sabor menta.**
    I don't like mint-flavored chewing gum.

Gracia (n.)
— Grace
  ▪ **¡Qué gracia la de esa gimnasta!**
    What grace that gymnast has!
— (The quality of being) (to be) funny (not derisive) or appealing
  ▪ **Su forma de hablar me hace mucha gracia.**
    The way he talks is very amusing.
  ▪ **Sus cuentos siempre tienen mucha gracia.**
    His jokes are always funny.
  ▪ **Tiene mucha gracia para tocar el piano.**
    She plays the piano in a very appealing way.

Grande (adj.)
— Large; big
  ▪ **El Gran Danés es más grande que el Labrador.**
    The Great Dane is bigger than the Labrador.
— Grand; wonderful
  ▪ **Fue una gran* fiesta.**
    It was a wonderful party.
*Gran is a shorter version of **grande** (used only in singular, before the noun).
— Ⓜ Old
  ▪ **¿Tú sabías que Leticia es más grande que su marido?**
    Did you know that Leticia is older than her husband?

Helado (n.)
— Ice cream
  ▪ **Quiero otro helado.**
    I want another ice cream.
— Very cold; freezing
  ▪ **Este cuarto está helado.**
    This room is freezing.
  ▪ **No hay refrescos helados.**
    There aren't any cold soft drinks.

False Cognates

Ignorar (v.)
— To ignore [**no hacer caso**]
- **Me ignoró. (No me hizo caso.)**
  He ignored me.
— To be ignorant of □; not to know □
- **Lo ignoro.**
  I don't know (that).
- **Se ignoran las causas del accidente.**
  The cause of the accident is not known.

Implantar (v.)
— To implement (*)
- **Este sistema no se va a implantar hasta el año que viene.**
  This system will not be implemented until next year.
(*) The verb **implementar** (an anglicism) is beginning to be heard in Mexico.
— To implant
- **Este riñón será implantado en una niña de seis años.**
  This kidney will be implanted in a six-year-old girl.

Implantación (n.)
— Implementation
- **La implantación del método será gradual.**
  Implementation of the method will be gradual.
— Implantation
- **La implantación de estos órganos no siempre tiene éxito.**
  Implantation of these organs is not always successful.

Independientemente (adv.)
— Independently
- **Él arregla sus cosas muy independientemente.**
  He looks after his affairs quite independently.
— Regardless
- **Quiero que termines hoy, independientemente de lo que diga Jorge.**
  I want you to finish today, regardless of what Jorge says.

Inscripción (n.)
— Inscription; engraving
- **La inscripción en esa lápida está ilegible.**
  The inscription on that tombstone is illegible.

False Cognates

— The act of enrolling or signing up for □; enrollment
- **La inscripción cuesta cien pesos.**
  The enrollment fee is a hundred pesos.

Inversión (n.)
— Inversion
- **La inversión térmica se acabó a las once.**
  The thermal inversion ended at eleven.
— Investment
- **Ya no tengo inversiones en México.**
  I have no more investments in Mexico.

Invertir (v.)
— To invert
- **No importa que inviertas las cifras; el resultado siempre será el mismo.**
  It doesn't matter if you invert the figures; the result will be the same.
— To invest
- **Marcos invirtió todo su dinero en acciones de Telmex.**
  Marcos invested all his money in Telmex shares.

Investigar (v.)
— To investigate
- **El crimen jamás se investigó.**
  The crime was never investigated.
— To research; to do research
- **En este departamento se investiga el valor nutritivo del nopal.**
  This department does research on the nutritional qualities of the cactus plant.

Investigación (n.)
— Investigation (police)
- **La investigación del asesinato no tuvo éxito.**
  The murder investigation was not successful.
— Research
- **Se necesita mayor presupuesto para la investigación en esta universidad.**
  A bigger budget is needed for research at this university.

Lengua (n.)
— Tongue
- **Alberto tiene la lengua blanca.**
  Albert's tongue is white.
— Language
- **La lengua inglesa se habla en todo el mundo.**
  The English language is spoken all over the world.

False Cognates

Letra (n.)

— Letter (of the alphabet)

- **Faltan tres letras en ese letrero.**
  There are three letters missing on that sign.

— Promissory note*

- **Sólo me faltan tres letras para terminar de pagar la deuda.**
  I have only three promissory notes more to go before the debt is paid off.

Note: The full name is **letra de cambio**, but people simply call it a **letra**. This document is very similar to the **Pagaré** (I owe you).

— Lyrics (music)

- **Esa canción tiene bonita letra.**
  The lyrics of that song are nice.

Leyenda (n.)

— Legend

- **La leyenda del Popocatépetl y el Iztaccíhuatl es muy antigua.**
  The legend of Popocatepetl and Iztaccihuatl is ancient.

— Text or inscription (on a thing or article); message (usually printed)

- **La caja tiene una leyenda, pero está ilegible.**
  There's something printed on this box, but it is illegible.

Ligar (v.)

— To link

- **Este organismo está ligado a las Naciones Unidas de alguna manera.**
  This organization is linked to the United Nations somehow.

— ⌂⇩ To make a conquest

- Speaker A: **Esa chava se me quedó viendo.**
                That girl was looking at me.
  Speaker B: **Sí, mano. ¡Te está ligando!**
                Yeah. She's flirting with you.

— ⌂⇩ To succeed in getting ☐

- **Voy a ver si ligo unos bonos de comida en la empresa.**
  I'm going to try to get some meal tickets at the company.

Lima (n.)

— Sweet lime

- **La sopa de lima de Yucatán es famosa.**
  The lime soup of Yucatan is famous.

— File

- **Me rompí una uña y no encuentro una lima.**
  I broke a nail and I can't find a file.

Mantener (v.)

— To maintain; to keep

False Cognates

- **Hay que mantener buenas relaciones con esa gente.**
  We have to maintain good relations with those people.
- **La tenemos que mantener despierta.**
  We have to keep her awake.
— To support a dependant*
- **Ahora voy a tener que mantener también a mi suegra.**
  Now I'm going to have to support my mother-in-law too.

Note: **Manutención**, not **mantenimiento**, is support of a dependant.

Marca (n.)
— Mark
- **El golpe me dejó una marca en el brazo.**
  The blow left a mark on my arm.
— Brand or trade mark
- **Ésta es la mejor marca de jabón.**
  This is the best brand of soap.

Mordida (n.)
— Bite
- **Todavía tengo la cicatriz de la mordida de ese perro.**
  I still have the scar of that dog bite.
— ⚠ Bribe **[soborno]**
- **Lo que quiere ese inspector es una mordida (un soborno).**
  What that inspector wants is a bribe.

Motor (n.)
— Motor
- **El motor del refri se quemó.**
  The refrigerator motor burned out.
— Engine
- **El motor del camión es de diesel.**
  The truck engine runs on diesel.

Oferta (n.)
— Offer
- **No me gustó su oferta.**
  I didn't like his offer.
— Reduced merchandise; bargain
- **Hay muchas ofertas en esa tienda en estos días.**
  There are a lot of bargains at that store just now.

Ordenado(a)
— Ordained (p.p.)

False Cognates

- **El Padre Pedro fue ordenado hace 50 años.**
  Father Peter was ordained 50 years ago.
— Orderly (adj.)
- **Mi hija es muy ordenada en todo.**
  My daughter is very orderly (neat) in everything she does.

Particular (adj.)
— Particular
- **Esta casa en particular es muy atractiva.**
  This particular house is very attractive.
— Private
- **Yo quisiera tener una secretaria particular.**
  I would like to have a private secretary. *
*You may hear **secretario privado** in high-level government as well.

Patrón (n.)*
— Pattern
- **Aquí va apareciendo un patrón de formas y colores.**
  A pattern of colors and forms is beginning to take shape.
— Employer or boss (in tax and labor legislation). There is no equivalent of the word employer. Also used by blue collar workers, farm hands and servants.
- **El patrón debe inscribir a los trabajadores en el Seguro Social.**
  The employer must register workers at the Social Security office.
*Never used to mean *patron*.

Pegar (v.)
— To hit
- **Te voy a pegar si me vuelves a hacer eso.**
  I'm going to hit you if you do that to me again.
— To stick
- **La calcomanía tiene que pegarse en el vidrio de atrás.**
  The decal has to be stuck on the back window.

Percibir (v.)
— To perceive
- **Percibo cierta renuencia de su parte.**
  I perceive a certain reluctance on his part.
— To receive $
- **Percibo la mitad de mis ingresos por traducciones.**
  I get half of my income from translations.

Percepción (n.)
— Perception

- **Su percepción de lo correcto es algo extraña.**
  His perception of what's right is a bit strange.
— Income (always used in plural)
- **Sus percepciones no son cuantiosas.**
  His income is not large.

Permanencia (n.)

— Permanence
- **La pirámide da una sensación de permanencia.**
  The pyramid gives a sense of permanence.
— A stay; the act of remaining somewhere
- **Su permanencia fue más prolongada de lo esperado.**
  His stay was longer than expected.

Pintar (v.)

— To paint
- **Esta casa se tiene que pintar.**
  This house has to be painted.
— To dye
- **Elisa se pintó el pelo y le quedó verdoso.**
  Elisa dyed her hair and it turned out kind of green.
- **Yo creo que estas cortinas no se pueden pintar.**
  I don't think these curtains can be dyed.
— To make up (reflexive)
- **Magda se ve horrible si no se pinta.**
  Magda looks awful if she doesn't put on make-up.

Planta (n.)

— Plant (botanical and manufacturing)
- **La planta que me regalaste ya floreció.**
  The plant you gave me has flowered.
- **Armando trabaja en una planta maquiladora.**
  Armando works at an in-bond jobbing plant.
— Floor, but only to refer to upstairs (**planta alta**) and downstairs (**planta baja**) in a house.
  Planta baja also means ground floor in a building.
- **Mi oficina está en la planta baja.**
  My office is on the ground floor.
— The sole of the foot (the sole of a shoe is **suela**)
- **La planta del pie no tiene pigmentación.**
  There's no pigmentation on the sole of the foot.

False Cognates

Polvo (n.)

— Dust
- **Todos los libros están llenos de polvo.**
  All the books are covered with dust.
— Powder
- **El bicarbonato es un polvo blanco.**
  Bicarbonate is a white powder.

Preferencia (n.)

— Preference
- **No te puedo dar preferencia; compréndelo.**
  I can't give you preference; you must understand that.
— Priority or right of way
- **Un coche que está en movimiento siempre tiene preferencia.**
  A moving car always has the right of way.

(Al) por mayor (n.)

— Wholesale
- **Rigoberto vende casimires al por mayor.**
  Rigoberto sells suit material wholesale.
— In great quantities
- **Aquí los flojos se dan al por mayor.**
  There are loads of lazy people here.

Presentar (v.)

— To present
- **Tengo que presentar este estudio mañana.**
  I have to present this study tomorrow.
— To introduce
- **Te voy a presentar a todos mis amigos.**
  I'm going to introduce you to all my friends, or *You are going to meet all my friends.*

Presente (n.)

— This (letter, note, request, report, etc.)
- **La presente sirve para recomendar al portador.**
  This (letter) serves to recommend the bearer.
— Gift (fairly formal)
- **Te traje un pequeño presente.**
  I brought you a small gift.

False Cognates

— The present
  - **El presente es más importante que el pasado o el futuro.**
    The present is more important than the past or the future.
— Written on an envelope under a person's name when no address is used
  - **Sr. Andrés Calatayud**
    Presente
    Mr. Andres Calatayud
    (to be hand-delivered)

Presumir (v.)
— To show off ☐
  - **Donato anda presumiendo su coche nuevo.**
    Donato is out showing off his new car.
— To assume
  - **Presumen que hay fallas en la estructura.**
    They assume there are defects in the structure.

Pretender (v.)
— To court ☺
  - **Daniel anda pretendiendo a Aurora.**
    Daniel is courting Aurora.
— To intend
  - **Pretendo terminar el proyecto antes de junio.**
    I intend to finish the project before June.

Propiedad (n.)
— Propriety
  - **Mientras esté el Obispo en la casa, trata de comportarte con propiedad.**
    While the Bishop is in the house, try to behave properly.
— Property
  - **La propiedad mide 27 hectáreas.**
    The property is 27 hectares.
— Ownership
  - **Esta casa es de mi propiedad.**
    This house is mine (the ownership is mine).

Propio(a) (adj.)
— Proper; suitable
  - **Ese atuendo no es propio para ir a misa.**
    That outfit is not proper for going to church.
— One's own
  - **Al fin tengo casa propia.**
    I finally have my own home.

False Cognates

Publicidad (n.)
— Publicity
- **Le hicieron muy mala publicidad por su divorcio.**
  He got very bad publicity because of his divorce.
— Advertising
- **Este producto no se vende sin publicidad.**
  This product doesn't sell without advertising.

Puntuación (n.)
— Punctuation
- **Enrique no tiene idea de lo que es la puntuación.**
  Henry has no idea what punctuation is.
— (game) Score
- **¿Cómo va la puntuación? Sólo quedan tres minutos de juego.**
  What's the score? There are only three more minutes of play.

Real (adj.)
— Royal
- **La carroza real se aproximó lentamente.**
  The royal carriage approached slowly.
— Real; actual
- **El costo real es mayor al presupuestado.**
  The actual cost is more than the budgeted cost.

Recuperar (v.)
— To recuperate; to recover
- **María se está recuperando lentamente de su pulmonía.**
  Mary is slowly recovering from her pneumonia.
— To recover ☐
- **Hay que recuperar el dinero perdido.**
  We must recover the lost money.
— To get ☐ back
- **El Sr. Gómez finalmente recuperó su licencia que le quitó el policía.**
  Mr. Gomez finally got back the license that the policeman confiscated.

Recurso (n.)
— Recourse
- **Sé que no quieres molestar a tu papá, pero no tenemos otro recurso.**
  I know you don't want to bother your father, but we have no other recourse.
— Resource or resort
- **No tenemos los recursos necesarios para el proyecto.**
  We lack the resources required for the project.

False Cognates

- **Este es el último recurso.**
  This is the last resort.

Registrar (v.)
— To register
- **Mi empresa aún no se ha registrado en la Cámara de Comercio.**
  My company still hasn't registered at the Chamber of Commerce.
— To record (accounting)
- **No se registraron todos los pagos del mes.**
  Some of the month's payments were not recorded.
— To search
- **El inspector registró todas las maletas minuciosamente.**
  The inspector searched all my suitcases very carefully.
- **Me registraron en la frontera.**
  I was searched at the border.

Registro (n.)
— Registration
- **Esta tarjeta es la constancia de mi registro en Hacienda.**
  This card is proof of my registration at the IRS.
— Registry
- **Hay sólo una oficina de Registro Civil en esta ciudad.**
  There is only one Civil Registry Office in this city.
— An entry or record (accounting)
- **Este registro de gastos es de hace dos años.**
  This record of expenses is from two years ago.
— Manhole
- **Estaba oscuro y por poco caigo en un registro abierto.**
  It was dark and I almost fell into an open manhole.

Reloj (n.)
— Clock
- **En el reloj de la sala son las doce y cuarto.**
  The living room clock says it's twelve fifteen.
— Watch
- **Mi reloj se mojó en la regadera y está lleno de agua.**
  My watch got wet in the shower and is full of water.

Remisión (n.)
— Remission (medical)
- **La remisión del cáncer sólo se logra en sus primeras etapas.**
  Remission in cancer is only possible if diagnosed early.

False Cognates

— Shipment order or delivery slip
  ▪ **Esto no es una factura; es una remisión.**
    This isn't an invoice; it's a shipment order.

Renunciar (v.)

— To renounce
  ▪ **¡Renuncia a Satanás!**
    Renounce the devil!
— To quit; to resign
  ▪ **Renunció hace un mes.**
    He quit a month ago.

Retirar (v.)

— To retire **[jubilar(se)]**
  ▪ **Me voy a retirar (jubilar) a los 60 años.**
    I'm going to retire when I'm 60.
  ▪ **Mi papá no se ha retirado (jubilado) a pesar de su avanzada edad.**
    My father has not retired in spite of his age.
— To withdraw
  ▪ **Nos vamos a retirar de ese mercado.**
    We are going to withdraw from that market.
  ▪ **¿Cuánto retiraste del banco?**
    How much did you withdraw from the bank?
  ▪ **Ya no te necesito, puedes retirarte**
    I don't need you any more. You may withdraw.

Retirado(a) (adj.)

— Retired **[jubilado(a)]**
  ▪ **El médico retirado (jubilado) no sabía qué hacer con su vida.**
    The retired doctor didn't know what to do with his life.
— Far away
  ▪ **El taxi me cobró extra, porque mi casa está en un lugar muy retirado.**
    The taxi charged me extra because I live a long way off.

Rico(a) (adj.)

— Rich
  ▪ **El tío Eduardo es muy rico; heredó todo lo que tiene.**
    Uncle Eduardo is very wealthy; he inherited all his money.
— Delicious
  ▪ **Estas enchiladas están muy ricas.**
    These enchiladas are delicious.

False Cognates

Seguridad (n.)
— Security
- **Desde el robo, han aumentado las medidas de seguridad en el banco.**
  There's been a lot more security at the bank since the robbery.
— Safety
- **Por tu propia seguridad, te aconsejo que no entres a esa casa.**
  For your own safety, I advise you not to enter that house.

Serio(a) (adj.)
— Serious
- **Esto es un problema muy serio.**
  This is a very serious problem.
— Reliable
- **Te recomiendo a mi carpintero; es bastante serio.**
  I recommend my carpenter; he's quite reliable.

Soportar * (v.)
— To support □ (weight)
- **¿Está seguro de que la columna va a soportar todo ese peso?**
  Are you sure this column is going to hold all that weight?
— To tolerate or stand ☺□ (normally used in the negative)
- **Pedro no soporta al maestro.**
  Peter can't stand the teacher.
- **No soporto este calor.**
  I can't stand this heat.

*Soportar is not used to mean support of a dependant; see **Mantener**.

Sueño (n.)
— Dream
- **Anoche tuve un sueño muy extraño.**
  I had a strange dream last night.
— Sleep
- **Estoy cayéndome de sueño.**
  I'm falling asleep in my tracks.

Suma (n.) (adj.)
— Figure; sum (n.)
- **Esta es la suma de lo que debe.**
  This is the sum (or figure) you owe.
— Utmost (adj.)
- **Este informe es de suma importancia.**
  This report is of the utmost importance.

False Cognates

Superior (adj.)
— Superior
  - **Este producto es de calidad superior.**
    This product is of better quality.
— Over (exceeding x amount)
  - **El precio no puede ser superior a los dos mil.**
    The price can't be over two thousand.

Terreno (n.)
— Terrain
  - **El terreno pantanoso se veía inhóspito desde el avión.**
    The swampy terrain looked inhospitable from the plane.
— A piece of land or lot, usually for building on
  - **Tengo dos terrenos chicos en Cancún.**
    I have two small lots in Cancun.

Timbre (n.)
— Timbre
  - **Su voz tiene un timbre muy bello.**
    His voice has a beautiful timbre.
— Doorbell
  - **Alguien está tocando el timbre.**
    Someone is ringing the doorbell.
— Postage stamp
  - **¿Cuántos timbres necesita esta carta?**
    How many stamps does this letter need?

Tipo (n.)
— Type; kind
  - **Me gusta ese tipo de muebles.**
    I like that kind of furniture.
— Fellow; guy (somewhat derogatory) **(tipo(a))**
  - **Ese tipo no me inspira confianza.**
    I don't trust that fellow.

Título (n.)
— Title
  - **No recuerdo el título de la película.**
    I don't remember the title of the film.
— University degree (see **Carrera**)
  - **Él es universitario titulado. Yo vi su título.**
    He's a university graduate; I saw his degree.

False Cognates

— Title to property
- **Tom no puede vender ese terreno. No tiene los títulos de propiedad.**
  Tom can't sell that land. He doesn't have the title to it.

Usar (v.)
— To use
- **No sabe usar la computadora.**
  He doesn't know how to use the computer.
— To wear (clothing)
- **Lilly siempre usa medias negras.**
  Lilly always wears black stockings.

Violar (v.)
— To violate
- **Estamos violando la ley si no declaramos las esmeraldas en la aduana.**
  We are violating the law if we don't declare the emeralds at customs.
— To rape
- **Ella dice que su novio la violó, pero nadie le cree.**
  She says her boyfriend raped her, but no one believes her.

False Cognates

2. English-Spanish

Naturally, confusion works both ways. So here is a list of English words with obvious and not-so-obvious meanings that can disconcert you a great deal if you're not prepared for them.

Affluent (adj.)
— **Afluente**
- *This river is an affluent of the Grijalva.*
  Este río es afluente del Grijalva.
— **Acomodado(a); adinerado(a)**
- *A lot of affluent people live in this part of town.*
  En esta parte de la ciudad vive mucha gente adinerada.

Appearance (n.)
— **Apariencia**
- *His appearance leaves a great deal to be desired.*
  Su apariencia deja mucho que desear.
— **Aparición**
- *Her sudden appearance at the meeting took everyone by surprise.*
  Su repentina aparición en la junta sorprendió a todos.

Balance (n.)
— **Saldo**
- *I've got to get my bank balance.*
  Necesito preguntar el saldo de mi cuenta.
— **Equilibrio**
- *He lost his sense of balance as a result of the accident.*
  Perdió el sentido del equilibrio a raíz del accidente.

Capitalize (v.)
— **Capitalizar**
- *The liability will be capitalized.*
  Se va a capitalizar el pasivo.
— **Escribir con mayúscula**
- *You must learn that names of all countries should be capitalized.*
  Debes aprender que los nombres de los países se escriben con mayúscula.

Corn (n.)
— **Maíz** (dry corn)
- *Mexico began to import corn last year.*
  México empezó a importar maíz el año pasado.

— **Elote** (fresh corn)
  - *They make some fresh corn tamales in Michoacan called **uchepos**.*
    En Michoacán hacen unos tamales de elote que se llaman uchepos.

Character (n.)

— **Personaje** (character in a play or book)
  - *The character played by Rafael is the most difficult of the whole play.*
    A Rafael le tocó representar al personaje más difícil de la comedia.
— **Tipo(a) raro(a); tipo(a) excéntrico** (a real character)
  - *Amado has 15 cats, and they eat at the table with him. He's a real character.*
    Amado tiene 15 gatos, y comen con él en la mesa. Es un tipo excéntrico.
— **Carácter** (temperament)
  - *Luis is unbearable.*
    Luis tiene un carácter insoportable.

Demonstration (n.)

— **Demostración** (commercial)
  - *They gave me a demonstration on how to use the copier.*
    Me hicieron una demostración de cómo usar la copiadora.
— **Manifestación** (public)
  - *There was a rowdy demonstration in front of the American Embassy last night.*
    Hubo una manifestación escandalosa enfrente de la Embajada de Estados Unidos anoche.

Develop (v.)

— **Desarrollar**
  - *The professor develops his subjects very well.*
    El maestro desarrolla muy bien sus temas.
— **Procesar o revelar película**
  - *There is a discount if you develop your film here.*
    Hay una promoción si revelas tu película aquí.

Fresh (adj.)

— **Fresco** (used for produce, air and temperature only)
  - *I need to get out and breathe some fresh air.*
    Necesito salir a respirar aire fresco.
  - *This lettuce isn't very fresh.*
    Esta lechuga no está muy fresca.
  - *It's quite cool at night in winter in San Miguel.*
    De noche en invierno hace bastante fresco en San Miguel.
— **Nuevo(a); otro(a); limpio(a); de nuevo (fresco(a))**
  - *I need a fresh notebook. This one is full.*
    Necesito otra libreta. Ésta ya se llenó.

False Cognates

- *Here's a fresh pencil right out of the box. Yours is too short.*
  Aquí tienes un lápiz nuevo. El tuyo ya está muy cortito.
- *I'm going to make a fresh start.*
  Voy a empezar de nuevo.
- *Gordon is going to need a fresh shirt to go out to dinner.*
  Gordon va a necesitar una camisa limpia para salir a cenar.
— Atrevido(a)
  - *That fellow is really fresh with the pretty girls.*
    Ese tipo es muy atrevido (es un fresco) con las muchachas bonitas.

Glass (n.)
— Vidrio
— Vaso
  - *Don't worry; the glass that broke was made of ordinary glass.*
    No te preocupes; el vaso que se rompió era de vidrio corriente.

Grow (v.)
— Crecer
  - *Your kids have grown a lot in the last few months.*
    Tus hijos han crecido mucho durante los últimos meses.
— Cultivar
  - *He decided to grow tomatoes in Sinaloa.*
    Decidió cultivar jitomate en Sinaloa.

Just (adj.) (adv.)
— Justo(a) (fair) (adj.)
  - *I really don't think he's a just judge.*
    Realmente no lo considero un juez justo.
— Sólo; solamente; nada más (adv.)
  - *It's just you and I here now.*
    Sólo quedamos tú y yo or **Nada más quedamos tú y yo.**
  - *We have just one car.*
    Sólo (solamente) tenemos un coche or **Tenemos un solo coche.**
— Acabar de + verb
  - *We just had breakfast.*
    Acabamos de desayunar.

Official (n.)
— Oficial (military/police)
  - *Those two are Navy officers.*
    Esos dos son oficiales de la Marina.
— Funcionario(a) (corp. and gov.)
  - *Corporate officials are never members of a union.*
    Los funcionarios de una empresa nunca pertenecen a un sindicato.

- *Government officials are hard to get in to see.*
  No es fácil entrevistarse con un funcionario de gobierno.

Period (n.)
— **Periodo**
- *The vacation period is not very long.*
  El periodo de vacaciones no es muy largo.
— **Ejercicio fiscal**
- *We're about to close the present tax period.*
  Estamos por cerrar el presente ejercicio fiscal.
— **Punto**
- *The periods are incorrectly used in that paragraph.*
  Los puntos están mal puestos en ese párrafo.

Question (n.)
— **Cuestión**
- *It's simply a question of time.*
  Es cuestión de tiempo nada más.
— **Pregunta**
- *I'm not going to ask any questions.*
  No voy a hacer preguntas.

To reach (v.)
— **Alcanzar**
- *The mountain climbers couldn't reach the peak.*
  Los alpinistas no pudieron alcanzar la cumbre.
— **Llegar**
- *The temperature will reach 40 degrees today, according to the radio.*
  Según la radio, la temperatura llegará hoy a 40 grados

To save (v.)
— **Salvar**
- *The dogs saved my life.*
  Los perros me salvaron la vida.
— **Ahorrar** (money)
- *I finally managed to save a thousand dollars for the car.*
  Finalmente logré ahorrar mil dólares para el coche.
— **Apartar; guardar**
- *Save a piece of cake for Tom.*
  Guárdale (Apártale) un pedazo de pastel a Tomás.

False Cognates

Sentence (n.)
— **Sentencia** (law)
- *The sentence in that case was a ten-year prison term.*
  La sentencia en ese caso fue de diez años de cárcel.
— **Oración** (grammar)
- *There are ten sentences in this paragraph.*
  Hay diez oraciones en este párrafo.

To spend (v.)
— **Gastar**
— **Pasar tiempo**
- *We spent ten days in Switzerland on our vacations and we had a great time, but we spent too much money.*
  Pasamos diez días en Suiza y la pasamos muy bien, pero gastamos demasiado dinero.

To support (v.)
— **Soportar** (weight)
- *Each column supports five tons.*
  Cada columna soporta cinco toneladas.
— **Mantener** ($)
- *I support my sister; she's blind.*
  Yo mantengo a mi hermana; ella es ciega.

D. Some Special Cases

Altura
— If you are receiving directions for getting to a place, you would say: **¿A qué altura?** to find out *Corner of what street?*, and the answer might be:
- **Insurgentes, a la altura de Río Mixcoac.**
  Insurgentes, corner of Rio Mixcoac.

Aplicar; solicitar
— **Aplicar** means to *apply* ☐ *to* ☐.
- **Esa pintura no se debe aplicar sobre el metal.**
  That paint shouldn't be applied to metal.
— **Aplicación** is the same; it refers to the application of one substance on something, or of a rule or law.
- **La aplicación de esta regla es obligatoria.**
  The application of this rule is obligatory.
— **Aplicar** is never used as *to apply for* ☐. The verb there would be **presentar** (or **mandar**) **una solicitud para** ☐.
- **Ayer presenté mi solicitud para entrar a tres universidades.**
  I applied for admission to three universities yesterday.
— An application for ☐ is a **solicitud**. A **solicitud** is also a *request* for something.
- **Llené la solicitud a máquina.**
  I typed my application.
- **Nunca me llegó tu solicitud para la computadora.**
  I never got your request for the computer.

Articulado(a)
— Does not mean *articulate*, but *articulated*. A person who is *articulate* is **una persona con facilidad de palabra.**

Buró
— A **buró** (from the French word bureau) is not a *bureau* but a *bedside table*.

Cada semana
— For some reason, *weekly* is not **cada siete (7) días** but **cada ocho (8) días**, and *every two weeks* is not **cada catorce (14) días** but **cada quince (15) días** (every fortnight). *A week from today* is **de hoy en ocho**.

Caja
— Means *box*, but also *cashier* or *the place where one pays* in a restaurant, store, office, etc., which in English is a person (cashier), while in Spanish it is a place (desk, counter, cash register, etc.). The person who handles the **caja** is the **cajero** or **cajera**.

False Cognates

Cambiar de . . .

— In Spanish you don't change planes, cars, etc. The expression is **cambiar de avión** or **de coche** or **de casa**, or whatever. **Cambiar casas** or **aviones** just doesn't make any sense.

Campamento

— The English word *camp* can be **campo** or **campamento**. A *camp* for kids or workers is a **campamento**. *To camp* somewhere is **hacer campamento**, and *to go camping* is **ir de campamento**. **El campo** is the *country*, as opposed to the *city*. Golf and football are played on a **campo de golf** and a **campo de futbol**, respectively, and **un campo** is *a field* for planting things. **Un campo** is also *a space*, as in: **házme un campito** (*make a little space for me*).

Cerrar con llave

— There is no real verb *to lock* in Spanish. That word simply never developed when padlocks and things of that sort came into general use. The usual term is **cerrar con llave**, or **echarle llave a** ☐, or **echarle candado a** ☐.

- **¿Cerraste con llave?**
  Did you lock up?
- **¿Le echaste llave a la caja?**
  Did you lock up the box?

Cigarrillo

— In Mexico, a **cigarro** is a *cigarette*, and a *cigar* is a **puro**. In the rest of Latin America **cigarro** and **puro** are both used to mean *cigar*, and a *cigarette* is a **cigarrillo**.

Coger

— In Mexico, always be careful with the verb **coger**, which inevitably brings to mind all kinds of obscene thoughts. Use **tomar** instead.

Colegio

— **¿En qué colegio (escuela) vas?** is often heard instead of **¿A qué colegio (escuela) vas?** It means the same thing, but the first form is incorrect, although it is in general use.

Conocer

— To *meet* ☺ and to *know* ☺ are both **conocer**. **Conocer** is also used for places.

- **Lo conocí hace años.**
  I met him years ago.
- **Lo conozco desde hace años.**
  I've known him for years.
- **Voy a conocer San Francisco.**
  I'm going to visit San Francisco for the first time.

False Cognates

Conserje

— Don't ask for the **conserje** in Latin American hotels, except the ritziest. **Conserje** comes from the French *concierge*, which in France is a combination doorman/superintendent of an apartment building and has nothing to do with hotels. **Conserje** is the exact counterpart in Spanish. The English *concierge* (in international hotel language, a person in a hotel who makes special tour, show, etc., arrangements for guests), evidently comes from that same French word, but somehow got promoted from the door of apartment buildings to the desk of better class hotels (you make your own tour, show, etc., arrangements at less ritzy hotels). So a **conserje**, who can also be called a **portero** (from **puerta** meaning *door*), although this sounds less classy, is strictly for apartment (and sometimes office) buildings. Posh hotels that do have a concierge call them just that, i.e., concierge.

Contaminación

— Some people who have a higher exposure to English use **polución** to mean pollution; this is quite wrong, as in Spanish the word means *involuntary emission of semen*, as in *night emissions*, which is not what is doing so much harm to our air, land and water. The proper word for pollution is **contaminación**.

Cristales; vidrios

— **Cristal** is not always *crystal* but also high quality plate glass. For example, windows in cars are **cristales**. **Vidrio** has come to mean a second rate (thinner) kind of glass.

Cuba libre

— A *rum and coke* is a **Cuba** (not a **ron con coca**) or a **Cuba libre** (the original name). Any kind of a drink is referred to as a **vinito** by some people. A **cuba** can also be a **cubita**.

Chimenea

— The word **chimenea** refers to the combination of *fireplace, mantel* and *chimney*. There is no special word for *fireplace*. The original word was **hogar** (hearth), which now means *home* (in other words, home was where the hearth was—no pun intended).
  ▪ **Vamos a prender la chimenea.**
    Let's light a fire (in the fireplace).

Dar de alta

— To *register* ☺ or ☐ somewhere is usually **dar de alta** ☺☐. To take ☺ or ☐ off the list or registry is **dar de baja** ☺☐.

Delincuente

— Although a *delinquent* (n.) is **un delincuente**, this word is not used in Spanish as an adjective to refer to amounts due and unpaid. The proper adjective is vencido(a).

False Cognates

Demasiado

— You will occasionally hear that someone is **demasiado linda** or **demasiado agradable**. Whereas *too anything* in English is always a negative concept, some people use **demasiado** followed by a positive adjective to mean *very*. This expression is incorrect, although much used.
  - **Tiene un novio demasiado simpático.**
    Her boyfriend is very charming.

Despedir

— **Despedir** can be used as:
— To fire
  - **Voy a despedir a la muchacha.**
    I'm going to fire the maid.
— To say goodbye
  - **Carlos nunca se despide cuando se va.**
    Carlos never says goodbye when he leaves.
— To see off
  - **Voy a despedir a Anita al aeropuerto.**
    I'm going to see Anita off at the airport.
— To see out
  - **Siempre lo despido en la puerta.**
    I always see him out (to the door).

Electricidad

— **La luz** is usually used rather than **electricidad** to mean *electricity or power*. **Se fue la luz** is *The electricity (power) is out* (from the days when electricity was used exclusively for lighting).

Estímulo

— Is normally an incentive, such as an **estímulo fiscal** or tax incentive. A *stimulant* is an **estimulante**.

Gente

— **Gente** is plural, although **gentes** is used even in written Spanish. In Mexico you will hear that ☺ (singular) is **buena gente**, which means that ☺ is *nice* or *good*.

Gustar

— When you want to say that you like someone in a platonic sort of way, do not use ☺ **me gusta** (or **Me gusta** ☺), because that involves liking ☺ in a non-platonic sort of way. Use ☺ **me cae bien**. If you say: **Me gusta** ☺ means you've taken a hormonal shine to him or her.

Importante

— **Importante** is not always *important*. It is very often used to mean *significant*. So you may hear **importante** used in a negative sentence.

False Cognates

- **Ha habido un importante incremento en la tasa del crimen.**
  There has been a significant increase in the crime rate.
- **La pesca accidental del delfín es más importante en Asia que en México.**
  Incidental dolphin deaths in fishing are greater in Asia than in Mexico.

Infarto

— This word sounds very strange when hearing it for the first time. However, this has nothing to do with gas in the bowels. It means *heart attack*. Most medical terms (used both by doctors and the layman) in Spanish come from Latin or Greek and not from the vernacular, as they do in English.

Ir

— *To walk, drive, fly*, etc. somewhere is sometimes **caminar, manejar** or **volar** somewhere, but more often **ir a pie, ir en coche** or **ir en avión**.

Mermelada

— **Mermelada** is not usually *marmalade*, which is practically unknown in Latin America, but *jam*, which is widely used. If you want *marmalade*, you must ask for **mermelada de naranja**, **limón**, etc.

Mudanza

— **Una movida** is not usually *a move*, but an *illicit amatory partner* or *affair*. A *move* to another house is always the act of **mudarse**, which is done in **un camión de mudanza**, *a moving truck*.

Mueble

— A *piece of furniture* is not un **pedazo de mobiliario**, but a **mueble**. A **mueble** can be anything: *a table, a chair, a cupboard*, etc. The word *furniture* (**muebles**) is not indivisible in Spanish as it is in English. This is also true of *information*. You can have **una información** in Spanish, whereas in English this word would be a piece of information.

No importa

— **No importa** means *It doesn't matter*, but **No me importa** means *I don't care* or *I don't give a damn*.

Nostalgia

— The word **nostalgia** is used to mean *homesickness* in most cases. You will seldom hear it as it is used in English.

Oportuno(a)

— **Con oportunidad, de manera oportuna, oportunamente**, has nothing to do with *opportunity*. All three expressions mean *in a timely manner*, *promptly* or something to that effect.

False Cognates

Persona física o moral

— A taxpayer can be either a **persona física** (an individual) or a **persona moral** (a corporation or other business entity). So **a persona moral** is not a person at all, but a company.

Plátano, Banano

— In Mexico, a *banana* is a **plátano** (which includes all types of bananas eaten as fruit). A *plantain* (never eaten raw, the kind used in Cuban cooking, fried or boiled in main dishes) is a **plátano macho** (📖 "he-banana"). In the rest of Latin America, a *banana* is a **banano**.

Precioso(a)

— **Precioso** is not *precious* but *beautiful*, except for expressions like **metal precioso** (*precious metal*) or **piedra preciosa** (*precious stone*).
- **Tu casa está preciosa** or **Tu casa es una preciosidad.**
  Your house is beautiful.

Primer(a)

— **El primer** and **la primera** arc very often used to mean *the most important*, and have nothing to do with numerical order:
- **El primer poeta de Hispanoamérica.**
  The greatest Latin American poet.
- **La primera diva mexicana.**
  The greatest Mexican singer.

Recepción

— The *front desk* of a hotel, etc., is **la recepción**. This goes for offices too.

Recibo

— A *bill* for electricity, water, gas, telephone, etc., is un **recibo**, even when you haven't paid it. These utility companies issue **recibos**, so you would say **tengo que pagar el recibo de luz**, which doesn't make sense in English. It is also a **recibo** after it has been paid. A bill in a restaurant, etc., is **la cuenta**. A bank note is a **billete**.

Re, rete, requete

— In Mexico, a variation of *very* is to use the prefixes **re**, **rete**, and **requete**, which are the equivalent of *very*, *very very* and *extremely*.
- **Lo hice rebién, a pesar de que el examen estuvo requetedifícil.**
  I did it very well, although the test was extremely hard
- **Linda es retebonita.**
  Linda is really pretty.

Risco

— **Un risco** is a *steep rock* not a *risk*, which is **a riesgo**.

False Cognates

Ticket

— A **ticket** (which obviously comes from English, but no longer means the same thing) is usually the *receipt* that comes out of a supermarket cash register, never a *ticket* for a bus, plane, etc., which is a **boleto**.

Tierra

— When people talk about **mi tierra**, they mean their *place of birth*, where the family still lives and has a home; where that person goes back for visits. This is very frequently heard in Mexico City, where most people are natives of some other part of the country.

Tip

— A *tip* (money) is a **propina**; but a *tip* (information) is **un tip** (anglicism).

Único(a)

— Without an article, this means *unique*, but with an article (**el único**), it means *the only* ☺□.
  ▪ **Esta receta es única.**
    This recipe is unique.
  ▪ **Éste es el único alumno que no aprobó el examen.**
    This is the only student who didn't pass the test.

Voy con . . .

— Do not be confused by people saying **voy con el doctor**, **el plomero**, etc. They do not mean they are going somewhere *with* that person, but that they are going to *see* that person.

False Cognates

E. It's Not Always the Same . . .

This section contains words and expressions that for one reason or another do not fit into other sections, and yet sometimes appear in other sections with different meanings and grammatical functions.

These are particular expressions and words with a number of different meanings. Depending on their association with other words or expressions, they form part of still other combinations, or take on other meanings that are sometimes confusing, sometimes picturesque, and sometimes a little risqué. Generally speaking, you will find a number of ways in which the same word or expression can be used.

Altura (n.)
— Altitude (planes and other flying ships)
- **El avión tomó altura muy pronto.**
  The plane gained altitude very quickly.
— Height (things only)
- **¿Qué altura tiene el edificio?**
  How high is the building?
— Expression used to explain the location of a place by providing a point of reference such as a cross street or a landmark
- **¿A qué altura está el banco?**
  What can you give me as a reference so I can find the bank?
- **Está en Reforma, a la altura del cine Diana.**
  It's on Reforma about where the Diana movie theater is.
— Up to par; up to expectations
- **No está a la altura de nuestros deseos.**
  It's not what we wanted.
— Very classy or exclusive
- **Es filosofía de mucha altura.**
  This is a very highbrow philosophy.

Andar (v.)
— To go around
- **Lucía anda por todos lados sola.**
  Lucia goes around everywhere alone.

False Cognates

— To run (machines)
  ▪ **Dejé el coche andando.**
    I left the car running.
— To be after ☺□
  ▪ **Enrique anda tras de Lucía.**
    Enrique is after Lucia.
— To be doing □
  ▪ **Ya me cansé de andar buscando trabajo.**
    I'm tired of looking for work.
— To go (steady) with ☺; (to see ☺)
  ▪ **¿Andas con alguien?**
    Are you going (steady) with anyone?

Apretar (v.)
— To pinch (to be too tight)
  ▪ **Me aprietan los zapatos.**
    My shoes pinch my feet.
— To speed □up
  ▪ **Se hace tarde; tenemos que apretar el paso.**
    It's getting late. We have to speed up (increase our speed).
— To put the squeeze on ☺□; to pressure ☺□
  ▪ **A ver si cuando le apriete el hambre se decide a trabajar.**
    Maybe when hunger puts the squeeze on him he'll decide to get a job.
— To get worse
  ▪ **En la madrugada apretó mucho el frío.**
    The cold got much worse towards dawn.
— To squeeze
  ▪ **Me apretó la mano.**
    He squeezed my hand.

Barrer; barrer(se) (v.)
— To strip (screws)
  ▪ **Ese tornillo ya se barrió.**
    That screw is stripped.
— To beat □ thoroughly (sports)
  ▪ **Los del equipo foráneo nos barrieron en el juego.**
    The out-of-town team gave us a real beating.
— To skid
  ▪ **Se estrelló en la curva porque se le barrió el coche.**
    He crashed at the curve because the car skidded.
— To sweep
  ▪ **Hay que barrer el patio.**
    The patio has to be swept.

False Cognates

Cola (n.)

— Line (of people)

- **Me tardé mucho, porque la cola en el banco estaba muy larga.**

  I took ages because the line at the bank was very long.

— Glue (carpenter's resin)

- **La pata de esa mesa hay que pegarla con cola.**

  The table leg has to be mended with glue

— An additional uninvited guest

- **No invites a Pepe, porque siempre trae cola.**

  Don't invite Pepe because he always brings someone along.

— Strings attached

- **Creo que lo que me dijo Julián trae cola.**

  I think what Julian said has strings attached.

— Tail

- **Le pisé la cola al gato.**

  I stepped on the cat's tail.

Como

— How? (**¿Cómo?**)

- **¿Cómo se dice "ventana" en francés?**

  How do you say "window" in French?

— How (**Como**) (not interrogative)

- **Así es como se hace este platillo.**

  That's how you make this dish

— Like . . . (**Como . . .**)

- **Carmen habla como argentina.**

  Carmen speaks like an Argentinean.

— What! Gosh! Goodness! Really!, etc. (**¡Cómo!**)

- Speaker A: **Sergio se fue hace dos horas.**

  Sergio left two hours ago.

  Speaker B: **¡Cómo!**

  What!!?

— If (**como**)

- **Ya te di ese dinero. Como lo pierdas, no te daré más.**

  I've given you the money. If you lose it, you get no more.

— As if (**como que**)

- **Ahí viene el latoso de Gerardo. Haz como que no lo ves.**

  There comes that nuisance Gerardo. Act as if you don't see him.

False Cognates

— Well, of course (**Como que . . .**)
- Speaker A: **Tu gato está precioso.**
  Your cat is gorgeous.

  Speaker B: **Como que es un buen angora.**
  Well, of course. He's an Angora.

— What do you mean . . . ? (**¡Cómo que . . . !**)
- **Hijo, te bañas ahora mismo . . . ¡Cómo que no!**
  Son, go take a bath right now . . . What do you mean, no?

— How much? ($) (**¿A cómo da . . . ?; ¿A cómo son . . . ?**)
- **¿A cómo da (a cómo son) los jitomates?**
  How much are the tomatoes?

Cuerno(s) (n.)
— Horn(s)
- **Ese toro tiene los cuernos chuecos.**
  That bull's horns are crooked

— Croissant
- **En esa panadería hacen unos cuernos riquísimos.**
  They make delicious croissants at that bakery.

— ☺ (To send ☺ to) hell
- **A Pepe lo mandaron al cuerno por su mal carácter.**
  They sent Pepe to hell because of his bad temper.

— ☺ Not on your life!
- **¿Pensaste que ya había aceptado? ¡Cuernos!**
  You thought I had agreed? Not on your life!

— (To be) unfaithful to ☺   (see under *Slang in Mexico* **Poner(le) los cuernos a** ☺)
- **Me late que Lola le pone cuernos a Beto.**
  I suspect that Lola is unfaithful to Beto.

Chocar; chocante
— To crash or have a car accident.
- **Esteban ha chocado tres veces.**
  Esteban has crashed three times.

— Shake! (**Chócalas!**)
- **Finalmente llegamos a un acuerdo. ¡Chócalas!**
  We have finally reached an agreement. Let's shake on it!

— To dislike
- **Me choca tener que ir a ese tipo de fiesta.**
  I dislike having to go to that kind of party.

— (To be) unpleasant

False Cognates

- **Manuel es un tipo muy chocante.**
  Manuel is a very unpleasant person.
— To clash or be incompatible.
  - **Juan y Emma no deben trabajar juntos porque chocan constantemente.**
    Juan and Emma shouldn't work together because they constantly get in each other's hair.

Dar; dar(se) (v.)
— To grow and thrive (**dar(se)**)
  - **Tus azaleas se están dando muy bonitas, pero las rosas no se dan en este clima.**
    Your azaleas are doing very nicely, but roses doesn't do well in this climate.
— Said when an opportunity arises
  - **No se dará otra oportunidad igual.**
    There won't be another opportunity like this one.
— To succumb to ☺'s sexual advances
  - **Ivonne es de cascos muy ligeros. Se da al primero que se le acerca.**
    Morals are not Ivonne's strong point. She leaps into bed with the first guy that comes along.
— To sell ❑ at X price
  - **Dan la manzana a diez pesos kilo.**
    Apples are (they sell apples at) ten pesos a kilo.

Dejar (v.)
— To leave ❑ somewhere
  - **Dejé el coche en el taller.**
    I left the car at the shop.
— To depart
  - **Dejaron el hotel hace una hora.**
    They left the hotel an hour ago.
— To allow or to let ☺ do ❑
  - **Su mamá no la deja salir de noche.**
    Her mother doesn't allow her to go out at night.
— To stop ❑
  - **Ya deja de hacer tonterías** or **Ya déjate de tonterías.**
    Stop that nonsense.
— To leave ☺
  - **Mi papá nos dejó cuando yo tenía tres años.**
    My father left us when I was three.
— To let ☺ abuse you or get the better of you (**dejar(se)**).
  - **Su esposa lo obliga a lavar los platos, ¡y él se deja!**
    His wife makes him wash the dishes, and he just lets her!

Echar; echar(se)
— To throw ❑

- ▪ **Échame ese desarmador**
  Throw me that screwdriver.
— To drop or put ❑ in ❑
  - ▪ **¿Qué le echaste a esta sopa?**
    What did you put in this soup?
— To lie down (**echar(se)**)
  - ▪ **Me voy a echar un rato.**
    I'm going to lie down for a while.
— To have ☺ turn on you (**echar(se) a ☺**)
  - ▪ **Por intrigante se echó encima a todos sus compañeros.**
    All his friends turned on him as a result of his intrigues.
— You can tell (**echar de ver**)
  - ▪ **Luego luego se echa de ver que tiene mucho dinero.**
    You can tell right away that the man is wealthy.
— To miss ☺❑ (**echar de menos**)
  - ▪ **Echo de menos aquellos días felices.**
    I miss those happy days.
— To keep an eye on ☺❑ (**echar un ojo a ☺❑**)
  - ▪ **Mi casa se queda sola. Por favor échale un ojo.**
    There'll be no one at home for a few days. Please keep an eye on the house for me.
— To disprove ☺❑ (**echar por tierra**)
  - ▪ **Echó por tierra todas las teorías anteriores.**
    He disproved all previous theories.

Embarcar; embarcar(se)
— To board a ship
  - ▪ **Nos embarcamos en Nueva York.**
    We boarded the ship in New York.
— To ship ❑
  - ▪ **La mercancía fue embarcada hace dos días por ferrocarril.**
    The merchandise was shipped two days ago by rail.
— To get involved with or in ☺❑ (**embarcar(se) con ☺❑**)
  - ▪ **Cómo me arrepiento de haberme embarcado en ese negocio tan malo.**
    I really regret getting involved in this terrible business.
— To involve ☺ in ❑ (usually without ☺ knowing that the venture is doomed to failure)
  - ▪ **Me embarcaron en una empresa casi quebrada.**
    They conned me into getting involved in an almost bankrupt company.

Embargo
— However (**sin embargo**)
  - ▪ **Te has comportado muy mal. Sin embargo, tus calificaciones son buenas.**
    You have behaved very badly. However, your grades are good.

False Cognates

— A lien (from **embargar**: to put a lien on ❒)
  - **Le dolió mucho el embargo de su casa.**
    The lien they put on his home really got to him.

Feria (n.)
— A fair
  - **Tengo muchas ganas de ir a la Feria de las Flores.**
    I really want to go to the flower fair.
— Change ($)
  - **Creo que hay feria en esa caja.**
    I think there's some change in that box.
— To have an unpleasant experience (**ir(le) como en feria**)
  - **No me preguntes por mi cita con el dentista. Me fue como en feria.**
    Don't even ask me about my dentist appointment. I had an awful time.
— ℗ Money
  - **Evaristo está muy amolado. Hay que pasarle una feria.**
    Evaristo is really badly off. We should give him some money.

Lucir
— To look (good or bad)
  - **Luces muy bien.**
    You look very good.
— To shine
  - **Esa estrella luce a mitad del firmamento.**
    That star is shining in the middle of the night sky.
— To be productive
  - **Me lució mucho la mañana.**
    That was a most productive morning (I got a lot done).
— To call attention by doing something awful (or wonderful)
  - **Ya tiraste toda la champaña. ¡Te luciste!**
    You've spilled all the champagne! Brilliant!
  - **Te salió magnífica la fiesta. ¡Te luciste!**
    The party was great! You were brilliant!
— To show off
  - **Andaba luciendo su nuevo coche.**
    He was showing off his new car.

Mano
— Ease in handling ☺ or ❒ (**tener mano izquierda**) (from the left-handed bullfighting pass)
  - **Maneja muy bien las situaciones difíciles. Tiene mucha mano izquierda.**
    He's good at these difficult situations. He knows how to handle people.
— Great quantities (**a manos llenas**)

False Cognates

- **Le han dado dinero a manos llenas.**
  He's been given great gobs of money.
— In my power **(en mi(s) mano(s))**
  - **Siento que no esté en mi mano resolverlo.**
    I'm sorry it's not in my power to fix things.
— Tied **(a mano)**
  - **Después de jugar tanto tiempo, quedamos a mano.**
    After playing so long, we ended up in a tie.
— Thief **(mano larga)**
  - **Cuidado con Rafael. Es mano larga.**
    Careful with Rafael. He steals things (he's a thief).
— ☺ who is prone to beating people up **(Ser un mano larga** or **Tener la mano larga)**.
  - **Tiene que hacer algo al respecto. José volvió a pegarle a la maestra. Es un mano larga (Tiene la mano muy larga).**
    You have to do something about it. Joe hit his teacher again. He really likes beating people up.
— To grease ☺'s palm; to bribe **(untar la mano de ☺)**
  - **Tendré que untarle la mano al inspector.**
    I'll have to grease the inspector's palm.
— To be good at ❑ **(tener buena mano)**
  - **Tu restaurante siempre está lleno. Tienes buena mano para los negocios.**
    Your restaurant is always crowded. You're really good at doing business.

Mar; mares
— Endlessly complicated **(haber mar de fondo)**
  - **En ese problema hay mar de fondo.**
    This problem is tremendously complex.
— In a flood of tears **(llorar a mares)**
  - **Mi tía estaba hecha un mar de lágrimas.**
    My aunt was in a flood of tears.
— To cry rivers
  - **Mi tía estaba llorando a mares.**
    My aunt was crying rivers.
— Sea
  - **El mar está picado**
    The sea is choppy.

Medir; medida
— To do ❑ to excess **(no medir(se))**
  - **¡Mira qué quemada de sol! No te mediste.**
    Boy! Look at that sunburn! You really got carried away!
— To take ☺ on **(medir(se) con ☺)**
  - **Me gustaría que ese boxeador se midiera con uno de su nivel.**
    I'd like that boxer to take on someone of his own size.

False Cognates

— To have ☺ pegged (**tomar(le) la medida a** ☺)
- **Están abusando de ti. ¡Ya te tomaron la medida!**
  They are taking advantage of you. They've got you pegged.
— To measure
- **Mañana me van a medir para mi traje de bodas.**
  I'm getting measured for my wedding dress tomorrow.

Menos

— Exactly (**ni más, ni menos**)
- **Pagué mil pesos, ni más ni menos.**
  I paid exactly one thousand pesos.
— No less (**ni más, ni menos**)
- **Demetrio llegó a coronel, ni más ni menos.**
  Demetrio rose to the rank of colonel, no less.
— To miss (**echar de menos**)
- **Echamos de menos a Conchita.**
  We miss Conchita.
— To underrate (**hacer menos**)
- **No tienen por qué hacerte menos.**
  They have no reason to look down on you.
— To leave (**hacer(se) menos**)
- **Ya es muy tarde. Vámonos haciendo menos.**
  It's very late. Let's leave.
— Less; fewer
- **Cada día tengo menos pelo.**
  I have less hair every day.

Menudo

— What a..!
- **Menudo susto nos dio Chepe al caerse de la moto.**
  What a fright Chepe gave us when he fell off the motorcycle!
— Quite a..!
- **En menudo lío te has metido.**
  You've got yourself into quite a mess!
— Very fine (small)
- **Está cayendo una lluvia menudita.**
  There's a very fine rain falling.
- **Olga es una niña muy menudita.**
  Olga is a very slender, small-boned girl.
— Often (**a menudo**)
- **Ya no vienen tan a menudo como antes.**
  They don't come as often as they used to.

False Cognates

— Tripe (beef stomach)
- **¡Qué sabroso está el menudo!** (see *Mexican Food*)
  This is really good **menudo***!*

𝄞 Mole

— A very popular Mexican sauce (see *Mexican Food*)
- **Este mole no pica.**
  This mole isn't hot.
— ❏ ☺ is really good at (**mi mero mole**)
- **Este trabajo es mi mero mole.**
  This work is exactly what I do best.
— Blood
- **Le pegaron en la nariz y le sacaron el mole.**
  They socked him on the nose and drew blood.

Nota

— To do ❏ crumby (**dar la nota**)
- **Emilio dio la nota con su mala educación.**
  Emilio spoiled things with his bad manners.
— Grade (homework or test)
- **Al niño le pusieron una nota mala en clase.**
  The boy got a bad grade in class.
— House of ill repute (**casa de mala nota**)
- **Cerraron la casa de mala nota que había enfrente.**
  The house of ill repute across the street was closed down

Ojo(s)

— To have it in for ☺ (**traer a ☺ entre ojos**)
- **Esa vieja malvada me trae entre ojos.**
  That nasty old bitch has it in for me.
— To shrink up and disappear; to beat it (**hacer(se) ojo de hormiga**) (📖 To become the size of an ant's eye)
- **Juan se hizo ojo de hormiga.**
  Juan vanished.
— To cost an arm and a leg (**costar un ojo de la cara**)
- **Me costó un ojo de la cara, pero vale la pena.**
  It cost an arm and a leg, but it's worth it.
— To put the evil eye on ☺ (**echar(le), hacer(le) a ☺ mal de ojo**)
- **Todo me sale chueco. ¿Me habrán echado (hecho) mal de ojo?**
  Everything I do goes wrong. Did someone put the evil eye on me?

False Cognates

⛢ **Onda; ondón**

— Wave
  - **En este pueblo apenas se reciben las ondas de radio.**
    This town barely receives any radio waves.
— What's up?; What do you want?; What's going on?; What is it? (**¿Qué onda?**)
  - **¿Qué onda?**
    What's up?
— Get with it! (**¡Agarra la onda!**)
  - **Agarra la onda.**
    Get with it!
— To be with it (**estar en onda**)
  - **Estás fuera de onda.**
    You're not with it (You don't really get the picture).
— To be a great guy (or gal) (**ser buena onda**)
  - **Este cuate es muy buena onda.**
    This fellow is a great guy!
— How great (**¡Qué buena onda!**)
  - **¡Mira! ¡Es James Bond! ¡Qué buena onda!**
    Look! It's James bond! Terrific! (Cool!)
— What a drag! What a disaster! What a bore! (**¡Qué mala onda!**)
  - **¡Ay mano, qué mala onda!**
    Good Lord! What a mess!
— A ball (**ondón**)
  - **Esos chavos traen un ondón que no veas.**
    Those kids are having a ball.

Pasar

— To pass; to go by a place
  - **Pasé por casa de Juan el viernes.**
    I went by Juan's house on Friday.
  - **Creo que Mari no va a pasar el examen.**
    I don't think Mari is going to pass the exam.
— ⛢ To swallow (**pasar(se)** ☐)
  - **Me cuesta trabajo pasarme las aspirinas.**
    I have trouble swallowing aspirin.
— ⛢ To overstep the limits (**pasar(se) de la raya**)
  - **Te estás pasando de la raya y te va a ir mal.**
    You're overstepping the limits, and you're going to get into trouble.
  - **El pesado de Ricardo se pasó de la raya.**
    That nerd Ricardo overdid it.
— To drink too much (**pasar(se) de copas**)
  - **Ramón está muy pasado de copas.**
    Ramón is really drunk.

False Cognates

— Drugged (**pasado**)

- **Ese ñeri anda bien pasado.**
  That dude is really wasted.

Pastel

— Cake

- **El pastel costó 100 pesos.**
  The cake cost 100 pesos.

— The thing that is causing the trouble; the reason for the problem (**el pastel**)

- **Cuando entraron en la casa, descubrieron el pastel.**
  When they entered the house, they found the cause of the trouble.

— All for himself (**todo el pastel**)

- **No quiero hacer negocios contigo. Eres muy abusivo. Siempre quieres quedarte con todo el pastel.**
  I don't want to go into business with you. You always want everything for yourself.

Perro(a)

— Dog

- **Me encantan los perros.**
  I love dogs.

— Feeling quite depressed (**andar como perro sin dueño**)

- **Desde que lo dejó Gilda, Rómulo anda como perro sin dueño.**
  Since Gilda left him, Romulo has been quite depressed.

— Tiger; merciless; ruthless

- **Es muy buena gente, pero como abogado es un perro.**
  He's a nice guy, but ruthless as a lawyer.

Picar

— To sting

- **Me picó una abeja.**
  A bee stung me.

— To chop (food)

- **Hay que picar la cebolla bien finita.**
  The onion has to be chopped fine.

— To chip stone

- **Esos presos deberían estar picando piedra.**
  Those prisoners should be chipping stone.

— To munch on something that you spear on toothpicks or just pick up in your fingers

- **De botana pusimos unos cuadritos de queso para picar.**
  We put out some cheese for people to munch on.

— To take the bait (**picar el anzuelo**)

- **No es ningún tonto. No picó el anzuelo.**
  We couldn't fool him. He didn't take the bait.

False Cognates

— To set two people against each other
   - **Si sigues picándolos, acabarán por pelearse.**
     If you keep on setting them against each other, they'll end up by having a fight.

Picar(se)
— To do ☐ you can't stop; to get hooked on ☐
   - **Me dormí hasta las cuatro, porque me piqué leyendo este libro.**
     I fell asleep at four in the morning 'cause I got hooked on this book

Pie*
— Foot
   - **No tiene pies bonitos.**
     She doesn't have pretty feet.
— To lose control (**ir(sele) los pies**)
   - **Sospecho que ahora sí se te fueron los pies.**
     I suspect you really screwed things up this time.
— To suffer from the same weakness (**cojear del mismo pie**)
   - **Volví a encontrarme a tus amigas apostando en Las Vegas. Esas dos hermanitas cojean del mismo pie.**
     I ran into your friends gambling in Las Vegas again. Those two sisters suffer from the same weakness.

* If you see this on a menu, don't panic, it means *pie*, as in English; more often, it is written **pay** and pronounced as in English.

Plana
— The VIPs (**la plana mayor**)
   - **En la mesa principal estaba toda la plana mayor.**
     All the important people were at the main table.
— To have the bad habit of always trying to be one up on ☺ (**Enmendar(le) la plana a** ☺)
   - **Benjamín quiere enmendarle la plana a todo el mundo. Nunca falla.**
     Benjamin is always trying to get one up on everybody. It never fails.

Plancha
— Iron
   - **Me quemó el pantalón con la plancha.**
     She burnt my pants with the iron.
— A slab (as of marble)
   - **Quiero una plancha de mármol aquí en la entrada.**
     I want a slab of marble here in the entrance.
— To have ☐ work out just the opposite of what you had planned or expected (**tirar(se) una plancha**)
   - **Me tiré una plancha terrible con esa muchacha.**
     I was really terribly wrong about that girl liking me.

False Cognates

— To stand ☺ up (**pegar una plancha**)
  ▪ **No vayas a pegarme una plancha.**
    Please don't stand me up.
— Dolt; moron
  ▪ **Ciriaco es una auténtica plancha.**
    Ciriaco is a total moron.

Subir

— To go up or rise
  ▪ **Voy a subir a mi cuarto por la caja.**
    I'm going up to my room for the box.
  ▪ **El globo sube porque tiene helio.**
    The balloon rises because it's full of helium.
— To put ❑ up; raise
  ▪ **Si quieren ir, ¡suban la mano!**
    If you want to go, raise your hand!
— To get up or climb up ❑ or onto ❑
  ▪ **Se me subió el gato a las piernas y me llenó de pelos.**
    The cat climbed up on my lap and got me full of hair.
— To go to ☺'s head
  ▪ **Ya se le subió su nuevo puesto.**
    His new position has gone to his head.
— To intoxicate
  ▪ **A Rogelio se le subieron las copas.**
    The drinks have gone to Rogelio's head.

Suerte

— Luck
  ▪ **¡Qué suerte tiene Mario! Se sacó la lotería.**
    What luck Mario has! He won the lottery!
— So that; in such a way that . . . (**de suerte que . . .**)
  ▪ **Hay que colocarlo de suerte que quede al centro.**
    It has to be placed so that it's in the center.
— Fortunately; luckily (**por suerte . . .**)
  ▪ **Por suerte no te vio el profesor.**
    Fortunately, the teacher didn't see you.
— To die at the moment of sexual climax (**quedar(se) en la suerte**)
  ▪ **Bedoya se quedó en la suerte.**
    Bedoya died while in bed with a woman.
— ☺'s fortune (as told by a fortune teller) (**la suerte**)
  ▪ **Voy a que me digan la suerte.**
    I'm going to have my fortune told.

False Cognates

Tablas

— Wooden boards
- **Llévate esas tablas a la bodega.**
  Take those boards to the storehouse.
— The tablets received by Moses with the ten commandments
- **Moisés recibió las tablas de la ley.**
  Moses received the tablets with the ten commandments.
— The multiplication tables
- **No se sabe las tablas de multiplicar.**
  He doesn't know the multiplication tables.
— Tied (even score)
- **Después de tanto jugar, quedamos tablas.**
  After all those games, we were tied.
— Of great experience (having stood on many platforms to perform)
- **Es un orador con muchas tablas.**
  As a speaker, he has a great deal of experience.

Taco

— Taco
- **Mi taco está sabrosísimo.**
  My taco is delicious.
— To curl up (hacer(se) taco)
- **Tengo tanto frío, que me haré taco en la cobija.**
  I'm so cold! I'll just roll up in this blanket.
— A billiard cue
- **No pudimos jugar billar, porque no había ni un taco.**
  We couldn't play pool because there wasn't a single cue.
— ♭ To put on airs (**dar(se) taco**)
- **A Rebeca le gusta darse taco.**
  Rebecca likes to put on airs.
— To get an eyeful (**dar(se) un taco de ojo; echar taco de ojo**)
- **Fernando está afuera echando taco de ojo, viendo pasar a las muchachas.**
  Fernando is outside, getting an eyeful, watching the girls go by.

Tal

— Said of two people who complement each other (derogatory) (**tal para cual**)
- **Chano y Chon están tal para cual.**
  Chano and Chon were meant for each other (are two of a kind; are as alike as two peas in a pod, etc.)
— A bastard; a disagreeable, nasty and/or crooked person; an S.O.B. (**tal por cual**)
- **El vecino resultó ser un tal por cual.**
  The neighbor turned out to be an S.O.B.

False Cognates

— Just as ☺☐ is (are) (**tal cual**)

  ▪ **No le cambies nada. Déjalo tal cual.**
   Don't change a thing. Leave it just as it is.

— As long as; on the condition that; provided that (**con tal de que**)

  ▪ **Te lo doy, con tal de que dejes de llorar.**
   Yes, you can have it, as long as you stop crying.

— So + adj.

  ▪ **Hace tal frío, que no arranca el motor de mi coche.**
   It's so cold that my car engine won't start.

Tamaño

— Size

  ▪ **¿De qué tamaño es el patio?**
   What size is the patio?

— Great; big

  ▪ **Iba caminando, y me salió tamaño perrote.**
   I was walking along when this great big dog jumped out at me.

— Serious

  ▪ **¡Tamaño problema tienes!**
   That's a serious problem you have there.

— Guts (**tamaños**)

  ▪ **Le faltan tamaños para enfrentarse a su suegra.**
   He hasn't got the guts to face up to his mother-in-law.

Tantear

— To fool; to swindle; to pull a fast one on ☺

  ▪ **Te están queriendo tantear.**
   They're trying to swindle you.

— A dirty trick (**tanteada**)

  ▪ **Le hicieron una buena tanteada.**
   They pulled a dirty trick on him.

— To feel ☺☐ out

  ▪ **Tantea a tu papá, a ver qué le parece la idea.**
   Feel your father out to see what he thinks of the idea.

  ▪ **Es conveniente tantear el terreno.**
   It's advisable to feel out the terrain.

— To make a guess at ☐; to make a rough estimate (**calcular al tanteo**; **hablar al tanteo**)

  ▪ **Me dio el costo al tanteo.**
   He made a guess at the cost.

  ▪ **¿Me sabes algo, o me hablas al tanteo?**
   You really know something about me, or you are just gessing?

False Cognates

Tardar; tardar(se)

— To be away or gone for long
- **No te vayas a tardar.**
  Don't be long. (Come back soon.)
- **Me voy a tardar en el centro.**
  My trip downtown is going to take a while.

— At the latest (**a más tardar**)
- **Lo necesito para el jueves a más tardar.**
  I need it by Thursday at the latest.

— I'm surprised it took you so long to . . . (sarcastic) (**te tardaste en . . .**)
- **Te tardaste mucho en decir algo desagradable.**
  I'm surprised it took you so long to say something disagreeable.

— To take a long time to do ☐
- **Tardan mucho en hacer los análisis.**
  They take ages to do the analysis.

Terminar; terminar(se)

— To finish ☐
- **Ya voy a terminar mi trabajo.**
  I'm going to finish my work.

— To end up . . . ing (**terminar . . . ndo** or **terminar por . . .**)
- **Terminó dando clases en una escuela de gobierno.**
  He ended up giving classes at a government school.
- **Voy a terminar por despedir a Rodríguez.**
  I'm going to end up firing Rodríguez.

— To run out of ☐ (**terminar(selc)**)
- **El dinero se nos terminó.**
  We ran out of money.

Tirar; tirar(se)

— To throw ☐ out or away
- **Ve a tirar la basura.**
  Go and throw out the garbage.

— To do target practice (**tirar al blanco**)
- **Fuimos a tirar al blanco.**
  We went to do some target practice.

— To be all dressed up and looking terrific (**estar echando tiros**)
- **¡Ay mamita, vienes tirando tiros!**
  Gosh! You look like a million dollars!

— No way (with negatives only) (**ni a tiros**)
- **No lo vas a lograr ni a tiros.**
  There's no way you'll be able to do it.

— Within reach; close by (**tener □ a tiro**)
  - **¿Por qué no aprovechas ahora que lo tienes a tiro?**
    Why don't you do it now that you're really close by?
— To seduce ☺ in a very unromantic way (**↓ tirar(se) a ☺**)
  - **El muy bárbaro se tiró a la enfermera.**
    The bastard had his way with the nurse.
— To throw yourself down somewhere (**tirar(se)**)
  - **Cuando se oyeron los disparos, todos se tiraron al suelo.**
    When the shots were heard, everyone threw themselves to the ground.
— To pull (a synonym of **jalar**)
  - **La carroza iba tirada por seis caballos blancos.**
    The carriage was pulled by six white horses.
— To spill; to drip; to waste (usually water from a tap or faucet) (**tirar(se)**)
  - **Hay que arreglar el excusado, porque se está tirando mucha agua.**
    The toilet has to be fixed; it's constantly dripping.
— Absolutely; beyond a doubt; just plain + adj. (**de a tiro**)
  - **Hoy está el jefe de a tiro imposible.**
    The boss is just plain impossible today.

Tocar

— To play a musical instrument
  - **Le gusta mucho tocar el piano.**
    He loves to play the piano.
— To ring a bell or buzzer
  - **Hay que tocar el timbre varias veces.**
    You have to ring the bell several times.
— To mention a particular subject
  - **Cuando estés hablando con él, no vayas a tocarle ese punto.**
    Don't bring that subject up when you're talking to him.
— To be ☺'s turn to play or to do □ (**tocar(le)**)
  - **Te toca jugar.**
    It's your turn to play.
— To get □ in a draw or similar distribution of □
  - **Le tocó el premio mayor.**
    He won the main prize in the lottery.
— To play the radio, record player, cassette player, etc.
  - **El radio está tocando, pero no hay nadie.**
    The radio is playing away, but there's no one here.
— To touch
  - **No toques la plancha, está muy caliente.**
    Don't touch the iron. It's very hot.

False Cognates

— To be nuts (**estar tocado**)
  ▪ **El maestro está medio tocado.**
    The teacher is nuts.

Todo(a)
— All of everything
  ▪ **Tienes que comerte toda la sopa.**
    You have to eat all the soup.
— All kinds of things; everything (a wide variety) (**de todo**)
  ▪ **En esta tienda venden de todo.**
    They sell all kind of things in this store.
— A free-for-all (**todos contra todos**)
  ▪ **Se pusieron todos contra todos.**
    It developed into a free-for-all.
— In spite of everything (**a pesar de todo** or **con todo y todo**)
  ▪ **Con todo y todo (a pesar de todo), no estuvo tan mal la fiesta.**
    It wasn't such a bad party, in spite of everything.
— In a great hurry (**a toda prisa**)
  ▪ **Estuvo aquí un minuto, a toda prisa.**
    He dropped in for a minute in a terrific hurry.
— Great!; Terrific!, etc. (**a todo meter**)
  ▪ **Tu nueva casa está a todo meter.**
    Your new house is terrific.

Traer
— To bring
  ▪ **Ve a traer unas cervezas.**
    Go get some beer.
— ☞ To be on ☺'s case; to bug ☺ (**traer de encargo a ☺**)
  ▪ **Estoy harto de que Tomás me traiga de encargo.**
    I'm fed up with Tomas; he's always after me (bugging me).
— To have ❒ on you (money, ID, a weapon, etc.)
  ▪ **¿Traes dinero?**
    Do you have any money with you?
— To have a spell of bad luck (**traer(la) chueca**)
  ▪ **Volví a perder al póker. La traigo chueca.**
    I lost at poker again. I'm having rotten luck.
— What's eating you? What do you want with me?
  ▪ **¿Qué traes? ¿Por qué me miras así?**
    What's eating you? Why are you looking at me like that?

False Cognates

Tratar; trata

— To be about ☐

- **Ese libro trata de las guerras mundiales.**
  The book is about the two World Wars.

— To treat ☺ (well or badly)

- **Tere trata muy mal a su servidumbre.**
  Tere treats her servants very badly.

— To try; to attempt

- **Ahora trata de abrir la puerta desde afuera.**
  Now try to open the door from the outside.

— White slavery (**trata de blancas**)

- **Se dedican a la trata de blancas.**
  They deal in white slavery.

— To deal with ☺; to have to do with ☺

- **Yo no trato a esa gente.**
  I don't deal with (have nothing to do with) those people.

Tren

— Train

- **Por poco pierde el tren.**
  He almost missed the train.

— Landing gear

- **Se descompuso el tren de aterrizaje.**
  The landing gear stopped working.

— The speed and intensity at which ☺ leads his or her life

- **¿Podrás sostener ese tren de vida?**
  Will you be able to keep up the pace (at which you are living your life at present)?

— ⚑ Hell! Damn!, etc. (**¡Me lleva el tren!**)

- **¡Me lleva el tren! ¡No me dieron el aumento!**
  Hell and damn! I didn't get the raise!

Triste

— Sad

- **Está muy triste Irma porque la dejó su novio.**
  Irma is very blue because her boyfriend dumped her.

— Bleak

- **En esta zona el paisaje es bastante triste.**
  The landscape is pretty bleak around here.

— Miserable

- **Le dieron cien tristes pesos.**
  She was given a hundred miserable pesos.

False Cognates

Tronar

— To thunder
- **Estuvo tronando toda la noche.**
  There was thunder all night long.

— To fail (a test, etc.)
- **Víctor tronó el examen de química.**
  Victor flunked the chemistry test.

— To go bankrupt and close down
- **Ya tronó la panadería de la esquina.**
  The bakery on the corner just went belly up.

— To break up with ☺
- **Vicente tronó con su novia.**
  Vicente broke up with his girlfriend.

— To be furious with ☺
- **Mi papá está que truena contra su socio.**
  My father is furious with his partner.

— To smoke marijuana **(tronar(selas))**
- **Huele a mariguana. ¿Quién se las está tronando?**
  It smells like grass. Who's smoking marijuana?

— ⌨A Mexican saying meaning: I'm a number one around here.
- **Aquí sólo mis chicharrones truenan.**
  I'm the boss around here.

— To crack; to break (under excessive weight)
- **La viga se tronó.**
  The beam cracked.

Trucha

— Trout
- **La trucha azul es muy sabrosa.**
  Blue trout is really delicious.

— ⌨ Astute
- **Valerio es muy trucha para los negocios.**
  Valerio is really clever at business.

— ⌨ To be on the alert; to stay on your toes **(poner(se) trucha)**
- **¡Ponte trucha! No te vayan a transar.**
  Keep on the alert. They might try to trick you.

Valer; vale

— To be good; to be worthy
- **Este muchacho vale mucho.**
  He is a very worthy boy.

— ▷ To be no good; to be worthless (**¡Vale! ¡Vale sombrilla!**)
  - **Tu gran tocadiscos ya valió sombrilla.**
    Your super record player is no good (has broken down, won't work).
— A receipt or voucher (**vale**)
  - **Fírmame un vale por este dinero.**
    Sign a receipt for this money.
— Chum; buddy; pal, etc. (**vale** or **valedor** ☺)
  - **Hazme caso, vale, no te azotes.**
    Take my advise, chum. Don't get carried away.
  - **Buenos días, mis valedores.**
    Good morning, fellas!
— ▷ I don't give a damn! (**¡Me vale!**)
  - **¡Me vale! (↓¡Me vale madre(s)!)**
    I don't care! (I don't give a #?&!)
— To use ☺□ (**valer(se) de** ☺□)
  - **Se está valiendo de Alicia para sus intrigas.**
    He's using Alicia to carry out his intrigues.
— If you know what I mean . . . (**valga la expresión**)
  - **Rogelio no es el próximo Premio Nobel, valga la expresión.**
    Rogelio isn't the next Nobel prize winner, if you know what I mean.
— My goodness! Goodness gracious! (**¡Válgame Dios!**)
  - **¡Válgame Dios! ¡Es tardísimo!**
    Good Lord! It's awfully late!

Vela

— Candle
  - **¿Ya compraron la vela de primera comunión?**
    Have you bought the first communion candle yet?
— Sail
  - **Este yate tiene tres velas.**
    This yacht has three sails.
— To have nothing to do with □; to have no say in □ (**no tener vela en ese entierro**)
  - **A mí no me preguntes. Yo no tengo vela en ese entierro.**
    Don't ask me. I have no say in this business.
— If one thing doesn't work out, there's always something else you can try (**si una vela se apaga, otra te queda encendida**)
  - **No te preocupes, Mario. Si una vela se te apaga, otra te queda encendida.**
    Don't worry Mario. If one thing doesn't work, you can always try something else.
— A piece of snot that has formed like an icicle on ☺'s nose
  - **Al chamaco le está colgando una vela.**
    That kid has a snotty nose.
— Awake; without sleeping (at night when people normally sleep)

False Cognates

- **Pasé la noche entera en vela.**
  I was up or awake the entire night.

Velar
— To have the body of a recently deceased relative lying in its coffin at home or in a funeral parlor for friends and relatives to pay their respects to, which usually involves spending the night with the body until it is buried or otherwise disposed of the next day; the act of visiting the family of the deceased and staying up with the body all night or part of the night (**velar a** ☺)
- **Velaron al abuelo en su casa.**
  They had the grandfather's wake at home.
— To become fuzzy, blurred or veiled (photo) (**velar(se)**)
- **Le entró luz a la cámara y las fotos se velaron un poco.**
  Light got into the camera and the pictures have a yellow overtone.

Vencer
— To win; to conquer; to beat
- **César venció en las Galias.**
  Caesar conquered Gaul.
- **El tenista australiano venció al canadiense.**
  The Australian tennis player beat the Canadian.
— To expire; to fall due or mature
- **Ya venció tu permiso para manejar.**
  Your driving permit has expired.
— To sag; to give in (said of a beam, bridge or anything designed to support weight) (**vencer(se)**)
- **La cimbra se venció.**
  The formwork gave in.
— Arm wrestling (**jugar vencidas**)
- **Te juego unas vencidas.**
  Let's do some arm wrestling.

Vestir
— To dress; to get dressed (**vestir(se)**)
- **Me voy a vestir en un momento.**
  I'll be getting dressed in just a minute.
— Dress (adj.) (**de vestir**)
- **Eso es demasiado informal. Quiero un traje de vestir.**
  That's too informal. I want a dress suit.
— To enhance; to make ☺☐ look good
- **Es un puesto que viste mucho.**
  That job is rather glamorous (prestigious).

False Cognates

Vida

— To live an easy and comfortable life (**dar(se) buena vida**)
- **¡Qué (buena) vida se da Santiago!**
  Santiago certainly lives an easy life!

— A life of vice (**la mala vida**)
- **Parece que te gusta la mala vida.**
  You seem to like everything that's crooked, low and tacky.

— To turn to prostitution to make a living (**dar(se) a la mala vida**)
- **La pobre Rebeca se dio a la mala vida.**
  Poor Rebecca turned to prostitution to make ends meet.

— To get through life from one day to the next (**ir(la) pasando**)
- **Así vamos pasando la vida.**
  We live life like this (one day at a time).

— To be at death's door (**estar con la vida en un hilo**)
- **Hace un mes que está con la vida en un hilo.**
  He's teetering between life and death for a month now.

— Darling; sweetheart (**mi vida**)
- **Qué bonita estás, mi vida.**
  How pretty you look, darling.

Viento

— Wind
- **No me gusta jugar cuando hay viento.**
  I don't like to play when the wind is blowing.

— Said of ❐ that is going very well (**viento en popa**) (📖 With the wind from behind)
- **Su empresa va viento en popa.**
  His business is doing very well.

— Come hell or high water (**contra viento y marea**) (📖 Against wind and tide)
- **Lo vamos a lograr, contra viento y marea.**
  We're going to achieve it come hell or high water.

— Said of ❐ that is made known to everyone (**a los cuatro vientos**) (📖 To the four winds)
- **Lo anda diciendo a los cuatro vientos.**
  She's going around telling everyone about it.

Vista

— Sight
- **Su vista no es buena.**
  His sight isn't good.

— View
- **Hay una bonita vista desde aquí.**
  There's a nice view from here.

— To lose sight of ☺❐ (**perder de vista**)
- **No pierdas de vista al cargador.**
  Don't lose sight of the porter (or don't let the porter out of your sight).

False Cognates

— With the naked eye (**a simple vista**)
  - **Se ven las larvas a simple vista.**
    The larvae are visible to the naked eye.
— To pretend you don't see or notice (**hacer(se) de la vista gorda**)
  - **No te alteres, hazte de la vista gorda.**
    Don't get upset. Just pretend you don't see anything.
— To be obvious (**saltar a la vista**)
  - **Por más que disimules, salta a la vista.**
    It doesn't matter how much you try to cover it up; it's obvious.
— In view of; in view of the fact that . . . (**en vista de que . . .**)
  - **En vista de que no llegan, nos vamos sin ellos.**
    In view of the fact that they haven't arrived, we're leaving without them.
— In plain view (**a la vista de todos**)
  - **Le metió un tiro al muchacho a la vista de todos.**
    He shot the boy in plain view of everyone.
— See you! (**¡Hasta la vista¡**)
  - **Ya se me hizo tarde, tengo que irme. ¡Hasta la vista!**
    It's late. I've got to go. See you!
— Ho! (as in land ho!) (**tierra a la vista**)
  - **¡Tierra a la vista!**
    Land ho!

Volar
— To fly (in a plane)
  - **A Gilda no le gusta volar.**
    Gilda doesn't like to fly.
— To fly (as birds)
  - **Es agradable ver volar a las golondrinas.**
    It's lovely to watch the swallows fly.
— To steal (**volar(se)**)
  - **Salvador se voló ese cenicero del hotel.**
    Salvador stole that ashtray from the hotel.
— Said of something that is being written very fast (**a vuela pluma**)
  - **Escribió la carta a vuela pluma.**
    He dashed off the letter.
— To blow up (with explosives)
  - **Los guerrilleros volaron el edificio.**
    The guerrillas blew up the building.
— To cantilever ❐
  - **Los balcones están volados.**
    The balconies are cantilevered.

False Cognates

— To do ❐ at stop speed (**volar a . . .** or **. . . de volada**)
- **Voló a hacer lo que ella le ordenó.**
  He flew to do her bidding.
- **Hizo los sandwiches de volada.**
  She made the sandwiches in a flash.
— To do ❐ brilliantly; to hit home run (**volar(se) la barda**)
- **Luis acertó todas las respuestas. ¡Se voló la barda!**
  Luis got every single answer right! He was brilliant!

Volver
— To return; to go back or come back to a place
- **Quiero volver a París el año entrante.**
  I want to return to Paris next year.
— To regain consciousness (**volver en sí**)
- **Tardó mucho en volver en sí.**
  It took a long time for him to regain consciousness.
— To vomit; to throw up (**volver el estómago**)
- **Le cayó mal la comida y fue a volver el estómago.**
  His lunch upset his stomach and he went to throw up.
— To go crazy (**volver(se) loco**); to drive ☺ crazy (**volver loco a ☺**)
- **La situación es para volverse loco.**
  This situation would drive anyone crazy.
- **Lidia está volviendo loca a su mamá.**
  Lydia is driving her mother crazy.
— To turn into ❐ else (**volver(se) ☺❐**)
- **. . . y el príncipe se volvió sapo.**
  . . . and the prince turned into a frog.
— To do ❐ again (**volver a . . .**)
- **Volvió a cometer el mismo error.**
  He made the same mistake again.

Voz
— Voice
- **Berta tiene muy bella voz.**
  Bertha has a beautiful voice.
— To give the orders (**llevar la voz cantante**)
- **Siempre le gusta llevar la voz cantante.**
  He always likes to be the one to give the orders.
— To spread the word; to get around (news) (**correr la voz**)
- **Me pidió que corriéramos la voz.**
  He asked me to spread the word.
- **Se corrió la voz del accidente.**
  Word of the accident got around fast.

False Cognates

— To raise your voice (**levantar la voz**)
  ▪ **¡No me levante la voz!**
    Don't raise your voice with me!
— To not be entitled to express an opinion; to be unable to do anything about a given situation; to have no say in the matter (**no tener ni voz, ni voto**)
  ▪ **No tiene ni voz ni voto.**
    He has no say in the matter (or there's nothing he can do about it).

Vuelta
— To go to many different places in search of □ (**dar muchas vueltas**)
  ▪ **Hay que dar muchas vueltas para encontrar estacionamiento.**
    It's hard to find a place to park there (you have to go round and round to find a place to park there).
— To avoid ☺□ (**sacar la vuelta**)
  ▪ **Creo que te sacaron la vuelta.**
    I think they avoided you.
— To be extremely simply or obvious (**no tener vuelta de hoja**)
  ▪ **Eso no tiene vuelta de hoja.**
    This is pretty straightforward.
— To go for a ride or a walk (**dar una vuelta**)
  ▪ **¡Vamos a dar una vuelta!**
    Let's go for a ride (or a walk)!
— Until you come back, or until next time (**¡Hasta la vuelta!**)
  ▪ **¡Adiós! ¡Hasta la vuelta!**
    See you next time!
— Once more; again (**de vuelta**)
  ▪ **¿Ya estás aquí de vuelta?**
    Are you back here again?
— To think □ over and over (**dar(le) vueltas a □**)
  ▪ **No le des tantas vueltas al asunto.**
Don't mull over the matter so much.

Ya que
— As soon as . . .
  ▪ **Ya que termines te lo diré.**
    As soon as you are finished, I'll tell you.
— Since; as; in view of . . .
  ▪ **Ya que me ofreces ayuda, te la acepto.**
    Since you are offering help, I'll accept it.
— What choice do I have?
  ▪ **¡Ya qué me queda!**
    What alternative is left to me?

False Cognates

IV
GRAMMAR HINTS

A. SER and ESTAR

Here is something else that thoughtful Spanish scholars might never have allowed into their language if they had had any idea of the trouble it would cause generation after generation of English speakers struggling to get some kind of a grasp on a distinction quite foreign to their sense of logic.

Whereas in English the verb *to be* is used to denote both essence and accidental or temporary condition, in Spanish the verb **ser** denotes essence and the verb **estar** is generally used to refer to an accidental or temporary condition. This chapter contains formulas which should pretty well do away with confusion concerning this traditionally awkward problem of choosing between **ser** and **estar**.

Ser is used to signify an inherent (usually permanent) characteristic or essential quality, as in: **La piedra es dura** *(Stone is hard)*; **Soy mujer** *(I'm a woman)*; **Juana es bonita** *(Juana is pretty)* and **¿Cómo es?** *(What is it like?)*. An essential condition of the subject is referred to in all these sentences. All stones are invariably hard, or they would cease to be stone, as in the case of molten stone, which becomes lava. In the second sentence not only is the specification of sex implied, but also its metaphysical essence. In the case of **Juana es bonita**, the speaker refers to a woman who has the quality of beauty, regardless of passing circumstances, although such beauty may be fleeting. When asking **¿Cómo es?**, we are attempting to determine the good and bad qualities inherent in the subject; if referring to a person, we are trying to determine if he or she is tall, short, beautiful, good, evil, and so forth; if speaking of a house, we want to know whether it is small or large, and so on.

Estar is generally used when the quality ascribed to the subject is accidental or temporary in nature. For example: **El cielo está nublado** *(The sky is cloudy)*; **Estoy furioso** *(I'm furious)*; **¡Qué bonita estás!** *(How pretty you look!)*; **¿Cómo está usted?** *(How are you?)*. These are changeable conditions, which as a rule do not alter the essence of the subject. Whether or not there are clouds in the sky does nothing to change the sky itself. A man may be of a peaceful nature, but at a given moment he might become infuriated, and then regain his usual composure. When you tell a woman that she looks pretty, you mean that she looks pretty just at the moment, the implication being that this is not always the case. *How are you?* obviously refers only to the present time.

Because the concepts of the Spanish verbs **ser** and **estar** differ widely, they cannot be interchanged without altering the meaning of the sentence. In some cases, the use of the wrong verb results in a meaningless sentence; in other cases, the result is ambiguous or just laughable.

In some cases, the condition attributed to the subject may be of long (although temporary) duration. Youth passes by, beauty may disappear, wealth comes and goes, but in the meantime, they characterize the subject. In such cases, either verb (**ser** or **estar**), may be used. However, the phrase may acquire a different nuance with the use of one rather than the other.

We can say: **Soy joven** or **Estoy joven**, (*I'm young*) but in the second case, the fact that our youth will come to an end (perhaps very soon) is recognized. On the other hand, by saying **Soy joven**, the speaker implies a sort of eagerness to prolong his youth.

If we say of someone **Está bonita** (*She's pretty*), we mean that she is pretty at a given moment only, maybe because she dressed up and used a hair-do or make-up that makes her look pretty. If we say of someone **Es bella** or **bonita**, we are speaking of beauty that somehow transcends age and circumstance.

When we say of a rich man **Es rico**, we are implying that he has been wealthy for a long time and probably will continue to be so; but if we say **Está rico**, we suggest that he has recently become rich and is not likely to remain that way for long.

In other cases, the accident that has befallen the subject is of a definite and permanent nature. One must say: **Está muerto**, because such a condition is the result of dying and does not imply an essential characteristic of the subject. The person who died had been alive, but dead or alive, he is or has been essentially a human being.

If a door is kept closed, you say: **Esa puerta siempre está cerrada** (*That door is always closed*). But you cannot say: **Esa puerta es cerrada**, because there is always the possibility that some day it will be opened, aside from which the sentence is in passive voice, meaning the door is closed (by someone).

Grammar Hints

In general terms, the verb **SER** is used as a state-of-being verb:

— When the predicate is a noun or an infinitive:
- **La música es un arte.**
  Music is an art.
- **Pedro es pintor.**
  Peter is a painter.
- **Eso es perder el tiempo.**
  That is a waste of time.

— When the predicate is a qualifying adjective that expresses a permanent quality:
- **Dios es bueno.**
  God is good.
- **Ese joven es peruano.**
  That young man is Peruvian.

— When the predicate is a qualifying adjective, a possessive pronoun or a noun in a phrase wherein property, origin, etc., are substituted or understood:
- **Su riqueza es mucha.**
  His wealth is great.
- **El libro es mío.**
  The book is mine.
- **El reloj es de Juan.**
  The watch is Juan's.
- **Estas naranjas son de California.**
  These oranges are from California.

— As an auxiliary when used to form the passive voice of transitive verbs:
- **El hijo bueno es amado por sus padres.**
  A good son is loved by his parents.

— As an impersonal verb, it is used only in the third-person singular of each tense, without an expressed subject:
- **Es temprano.**
  It's early.
- **Era de noche.**
  It was dark.
- **Será tarde.**
  It will be late.

The verb **estar** is used:

— Between two nouns when the second one follows a preposition:

- **Mi hermano estaba de pie.**
  My brother was standing.
- **Mi padre estaba con calentura.**
  My father was feverish.

— When it implies being in a place:
  - **Estaré en México el próximo lunes.**
    I will be in Mexico next Sunday.
  - **Estuve en Lima dos semanas.**
    I was in Lima for two weeks.

— When it is followed by a present participle and denotes a more or less sustained act:
  - **Estuve escribiendo.**
    I was writing.

The following examples show the clear difference between **ser** and **estar**:

SER	ESTAR
▪ **Luis es colérico** *Luis is prone to anger.* Refers to his disposition	▪ **Luis está colérico.** *Luis is angry.* Because he became angry; ❑ or ☺ infuriated him
▪ **Luis es blanco.** *He has fair skin.*	▪ **Luis está blanco.** *Luis is white.* Very pale, probably from fright or illness
▪ **Luis es frío.** *Luis is a cold person.* By temperament	▪ **Luis está frío.** *Luis became cold.*
▪ **Luis es gordo.** *Luis is a fat person.* He has always been fat.	▪ **Luis está gordo.** *Luis became fat.* He has gotten fat lately.

The student should take note of the following differences:

SER	ESTAR
▪ **Ser callado(a).** Is said of ☺ who never speaks	▪ **Estar callado(a).** Is said of ☺ who is silent at the moment
▪ **Ser tranquilo(a).** Is said of ☺ who is peaceful by nature	▪ **Estar tranquilo(a).** Is said of ☺ who is calm just at present
▪ **Ser cojo(a).** Is said of ☺ who was born lame	▪ **Estar cojo(a).** Is said of ☺ who is temporarily lame (perhaps due to gout, arthritis or a fracture)

Grammar Hints

SER	ESTAR
▪ **Ser loco(a).** Is said of ☺ who is insane	▪ **Estar loco(a).** Is said of ☺ who is temporarily crazy about ☐ or ☺
▪ **Ser malo(a).** Is said of ☺ who is bad	▪ **Estar malo(a).** Is said of ☺ who is ill
▪ **Ser delicado(a).** Is said of ☺ who is gentle, delicate, fastidious	▪ **Estar delicado(a).** Is said of ☺ who is in bad health at present
▪ **Ser sordo(a).** Is said of ☺ who is born deaf	▪ **Estar sordo(a).** Is said of ☺ who has lost his hearing, whether temporarily or permanently
▪ **Ser serio(a).** Is said of ☺ who is a serious, earnest, dignified person	▪ **Estar serio(a).** Is said of ☺ who is in a serious mood at present
▪ **Ser alegre.** Is said of ☺ with a cheerful disposition	▪ **Estar alegre.** Is said of ☺ who is in a cheerful mood
▪ **Ser alto(a).** Is said of ☺ who is tall	▪ **Estar alto(a).** Is said of ☺ (a boy or girl) who was not as tall as now; ☺ who has grown lately
▪ **Ser empleado(a).** Is said of ☺ who is an employee	▪ **Estar empleado(a).** Is said of ☺ who is employed

Correct

☑ **Estoy contento(a).**
☑ **Es de usted.**
☑ **Está lloviendo.**
☑ **Es cobarde.**
☑ **Es suficiente.**
☑ **Es lógico(a).**
☑ **Es un(a) perro(a).**
☑ **Está dormido(a).**

Incorrect

☒ **Soy contento(a).**
☒ **Está de usted.**
☒ **Es lloviendo.**
☒ **Está cobarde.**
☒ **Está suficiente.**
☒ **Está lógico(a).**
☒ **Está un(a) perro(a).**
☒ **Es dormido(a).**

There are words that in some countries have two different connotations and change their meaning with the auxiliary verb.

Grammar Hints

Estoy vivo means *I am alive*; but **Soy vivo** means *I am bright*. You may say **Tu hermana es muy buena**, meaning *your sister is a very good person,* but if you were to say **Tu hermana está muy buena**, you are likely to acquire a black eye, since this means *your sister is very well stacked*, or something in that vein.

If you say of or to an elderly man **Está verde**, it means that he is looking ill (his skin has taken on a greenish hue); but if you say **Es verde**, you mean that he is a dirty old man.

Juan es borracho means that John is a drunkard; but **Juan está borracho** means he is drunk.

Are you decent? would mean both **¿Estás visible (vestido(a))?** or **¿Eres (una persona) decente?** This is an example of the importance of using **ser/estar** properly.

Exercise

Translate the following sentences into Spanish. The answers are on the following page (no cheating!).

1. *The man is not really a coward; he is sick.*

2. *She is a very busy woman.*

3. *I have been so busy today.*

4. *They found out that their baby is deaf.*

5. *They say John was drunk at the party.*

6. *All the girls are in love with him.*

7. *Her family is not wealthy.*

8. *She used to come often, but she can't now that she's ill.*

9. *He is a fine teacher.*

10. *It is raining.*

Grammar Hints

Answers

1. El hombre no es un cobarde; está enfermo.

2. Es una mujer muy ocupada.

3. ¡He estado tan ocupada hoy!

4. Se enteraron de que su bebé es sordo.

5. Dicen que Juan estaba borracho en la fiesta.

6. Todas las muchachas están enamoradas de él.

7. Su familia no es rica.

8. Ella venía con frecuencia, pero ahora que está enferma no puede.

9. Es un magnífico profesor.

10. Está lloviendo.

Grammar Hints

B. PARA and POR; PERO and SINO

O f the Spanish prepositions, **para** and **por** need special attention. The uses of **para** and **por** (different forms of *for*) are as confusing to the English speaking student as those of **pero** and **sino** (different forms of *but*), which is why they are presented together here. Once the precise meaning of the two prepositions and the two conjunctions is understood, using them should not be too difficult.

1. PARA and POR *(for)*

The meanings of the prepositions **para** and **por** are as follows:

PARA expresses:	If you use **POR** instead:
— Destination	
▪ **Voy para Veracruz.** *I am going to (headed for) Veracruz* or *I am going towards Veracruz.*	▪ **Voy por Veracruz** *I am going somewhere in the vicinity of Veracruz.* ▪ **Voy al Sureste por Veracruz.** *I'm going to Southeast Mexico through Veracruz.*
— Purpose	
▪ **Esto es para escribir.** *This is for writing.*	The sentence becomes meaningless.
— In relation to:	
▪ **Esto es malo para la salud.** *This is bad for your health.*	The sentence becomes meaningless.
— As *for*:	
▪ **Para mí es inútil** or **Para mí no sirve.** *For me it is useless.*	The sentence becomes meaningless.
— Period of time:	
▪ **Tengo trabajo para un año.** *I have work for a year.*	▪ **Tengo trabajo por un año.** *I have been hired (I have a contract) for a year.*
— Use or purpose of an action or thing:	

Grammar Hints

PARA expresses:	If you use **POR** instead:
▪ **Esto es para él.** *This is for him.*	▪ **Esto es por él.** *This is by him.* Referring to something written, composed or made by him.
▪ **Estos microscopios para el laboratorio son muy caros.** *These microscopes for the lab are very expensive.*	The sentence becomes meaningless.
— In comparison ▪ **Para mi gusto, el cuadro es mediocre.** *In my opinion (for my taste) the picture is mediocre.*	The sentence becomes meaningless.
— As a synonym of **en**: ▪ **Iré para Pascua.** *I will go during Easter.*	▪ **Iré por Pascua.** *I will go around Easter.*
— To investigate a purpose: ▪ **¿Para qué viniste?** *What did you come for?* ▪ **Para terminar el trabajo.** *To finish the job*	▪ **¿Por qué viniste?** *Why did you come?* ▪ **Porque quise.** *Because I wanted to.*
— For the purpose of: ▪ **Para terminar, diré mi opinión.** *To finish up, I'll give my opinion.*	The sentence becomes meaningless.
— In favor of: ▪ **Pedir para los pobres.** *To ask alms for the poor.*	▪ **Pedir por los pobres.** *To pray for the poor.*
— Use to which things are put: ▪ **Este vaso es para vino.** *This glass is for wine. This is a wine glass.*	The sentence becomes meaningless.

POR indicates:	If you use **PARA** instead:
— Cause: ▪ **Hacer algo por necesidad.** *To do something due to necessity.* ▪ **Arruinado por la lluvia.** *Ruined by the rain.*	The sentence becomes meaningless.
— Across; along: ▪ **Caminar por el campo.** *To walk through the country.*	The sentence becomes meaningless.
— As a synonym of **como** (as): ▪ **¿La aceptas por esposa?** *Do you take her as your wife?*	If you use **para** instead, it is incorrect, but understandable.

Grammar Hints

POR indicates:	If you use **PARA** instead:
— Manner:	
• **Me hice entender por (medio de) señas.** *I made myself understood in sign language.* • **Hablar por teléfono.** *To speak by phone.* • **Viajar por avión** *To travel by plane.*	The sentence becomes meaningless.
— Cost:	
• **Compró el terreno por 500 mil pesos.** *He (she) bought the lot for 500 thousand pesos.*	The sentence becomes meaningless.
— Instead of another; in substitution of:	
• **Firmaré por tí.** *I'll sign for you.*	The sentence becomes meaningless.
— Approximate place:	
• **Vivo por Chapultepec.** *I live by (near) Chapultepec.*	The sentence becomes meaningless.
— Equivalence:	
• **Vale por cien.** *It is worth one hundred.*	The sentence becomes meaningless.
— In search of:	
• **Voy por pan.** *I am going to get some bread.*	The sentence becomes meaningless.
— Multiplication:	
• **Dos por dos, cuatro.** *Two by two is four.*	The sentence becomes meaningless.

2. PERO and SINO (but)

The conjunctions **sino** and **pero** differ in nuance. **Pero** is an adversative corrective conjunction as it compares by limiting (**Viejo pero fuerte.** *Old but strong.*); whereas **sino** is an exclusive adversative conjunction because it opposes without allowing coexistence. (**No es verde, sino azul.** *It is not green, but blue.*)

In English *but* is used for both of these ideas, which is why Spanish speakers learning English usually cast about for the English equivalent of **sino**, since nothing in their experience even remotely suggests that **pero** and **sino** have anything at all in common; by the same token, English speakers learning Spanish who are unaware of this trap invariably throw in **pero** when they mean **sino**, having no reason to suspect that anything as simple as *but* could be broken down into two quite different forms.

Generally speaking, **sino** is used for the English *but* when the first part of the sentence is negative, and the second part expresses something that is or occurs *rather than* what is or occurs in the first part, as in **No fue Pedro, sino Juan** (*It was not Peter, but John*); **No me gustan las peras, sino las manzanas** (*I don't like pears, but apples*). Note that the second part of these sentences explains or corroborates the negative element. The novice might translate *He is not poor, but rich* as **No es pobre, pero rico**, which of course should be **No es pobre, sino rico.**

The following examples will help make this point clear:

- **Es agradable, pero presume demasiado.**
  He is nice, but shows off too much.

- **No soy fuerte, pero soy saludable.**
  I'm not strong, but I am healthy.

Note that in the first example the first part is affirmative, while in the second example it is negative. In neither case does the second part offer an explanation or a corroboration, nor is it contradictory. In these cases *but* must be translated as **pero**. A useful tip is that **pero** is always followed by a verb.

C. Dual Words

During the development of Romance languages, most words were formed from a single Latin expression. Words came from both the Classical Latin and the Vulgar Latin and eventually developed different connotations. Below is a short list of these, for those who are curious about this sort of thing.

Acre (adj.)
— Acrid; harsh; pungent; mordant; bitter; caustic
  - **Despide un olor acre muy desagradable.**
    It gives off a nasty acrid smell.

Agrio(a) (adj.)
— Sour; acid (food); disagreeable (said of a person)
  - **Este pepino está demasiado agrio.**
    This pickle is too sour.

Ánima (n.)
— Soul; spirit; soul in pain or purgatory
  - **Rezo por las ánimas del purgatorio.**
    I pray for the souls in purgatory.

Alma (n.)
— Soul; spirit; heart; liveliness; vigor; energy
  - **Le vendió el alma al Diablo.**
    He sold his soul to the Devil.
  - **Ponía toda el alma en lo que tocaba.**
    He put his whole soul into what he was playing.

Atónito(a) (adj.)
— Astonished; amazed; astounded
  - **Al ver aquello me quedé atónito.**
    I was astounded at what I saw.

Tonto(a) (adj.)
— Silly; foolish; "dumb" (adj.); fool (n.)
  - **Julio es un tonto de capirote.**
    Julio is a total fool.

Grammar Hints

Cripta (n.)
— Crypt; vault
- **Bajo el templo construyeron una cripta.**
  They built a crypt under the temple.

Gruta (n.)
— Grotto; cave; cavern; subterranean galleries
- **En las grutas hay estalactitas y estalagmitas.**
  There are stalactites and stalagmites in the caves.

Fastidio (n.)
— Annoyance; irritation; bother; nuisance; weariness; boredom; tedium
- **¡Qué tipo más fastidioso!**
  What an annoying fellow!

Hastío (n.)
— Ennui; boredom; tedium; revulsion (towards food)
- **Llegué al hastío por no hacer nada por tanto tiempo.**
  I'm bored to tears of doing nothing for so long.

Íntegro(a) (adj.)
— Whole; complete; integral; honest; upright; honorable
- **Ernesto es un hombre muy íntegro.**
  Ernesto is a man of great integrity.
- **Me devolvieron íntegra la cantidad.**
  They reimbursed the entire amount.

Entero(a) (adj.)
— Whole; entire; complete; upright; just; straight; robust; strong; healthy; pure; virginal
- **Con la catástrofe se conmovió el mundo entero.**
  The whole world was moved by the catastrophe.
- **A pesar de su edad se le ve muy entero.**
  He looks very healthy, in spite of his age.
- **¿Quieres una salchicha entera?**
  Do you want a whole sausage?

Lucrar (v.)

— To earn; obtain; profit; make a profit; fill one's pockets

- **No es malo lucrar, cuando se hace con moderación.**
  It's not wrong to make a profit, if it is done in moderation.

Lograr (v.)

— To achieve; attain; obtain; get; possess; enjoy; be succesful; manage to + verb

- **Con su carácter tan firme, siempre logra lo que quiere.**
  With that strength of character, he always gets what he wants.
- **¿Finalmente lograste vender toda esa mercancía obsoleta?**
  Did you ever manage to sell all that obsolete merchandise?

Mácula (n.)

— Stain; spot; blot; blemish

- **La Virgen María no tuvo mácula (es inmaculada).**
  The Virgin Mary was completely unstained (pure).

Mancha (n.)

— Stain; spot; blot; smudge; patch

- **Tienes una mancha horrible en tu falda.**
  You have an awful stain on your skirt.

Masticar (v.)

— To masticate; chew (used with food in general)

- **Para nutrirte debes masticar bien lo que comes.**
  For good nutrition, you should chew your food well.

Mascar (v.)

— To masticate; to chew (used with non-nutrients)

- **No hagas tanto ruido al mascar chicle.**
  Don't make so much noise when you chew gum.

Testificar (v.)

— To testify; attest; bear witness to

- **¿Crees que tenga el valor de testificar en el juicio?**
  Do you think he's got the courage to testify at the trial?

Atestiguar (v.)

— To witness; attest; testify

- **Nadie hubo para atestiguar los hechos.**
  There was no one there to witness the events.

Grammar Hints

Tímpano (n.)
— Eardrum; tympanum
- **Para resolver su infección del oído, tuvieron que perforarle el tímpano.**
  They had to pierce her eardrum in order to cure her ear infection.

Timbre (n.)
— Stamp; seal; tax stamp; doorbell; buzzer; quality or tone of voice or instrument (timbre)
- **Están tocando el timbre de la puerta principal.**
  They're ringing the buzzer (bell) at the main door.
- **Era el timbre más raro de su colección.**
  It was the rarest stamp in his collection.
- **La soprano tiene un bellísimo timbre de voz.**
  The timbre of the soprano's voice is exquisite.

Verificar (v.)
— To verify; confirm; check; examine; inspect; carry out; fulfill; prove true
- **Debemos verificar lo que nos han dicho.**
  We must confirm what they have told us.

Averiguar (v.)
— To ascertain; find out; inquire into; investigate
- **Están averiguando las causas de su despido.**
  They are investigating the reasons for his dismissal.

D. Some Dubious Accents

People commit countless errors in Spanish, as people do in every language. Some of these mistakes occur so often and are so generalized that they become habitual and collective. These are the most dangerous in learning a language properly. Any foreigner who is constantly seeing and hearing spelling and pronunciation mistakes can get very confused. Below is a list of words which are most often written or pronounced incorrectly by native speakers. Reference to verbs includes all endings.

Right:		**Wrong:**
☑ **Adecua**	*He (she) makes ☐ agree with ☐ else*	☒ **Adecúa**
☑ **Espécimen**	*Specimen*	☒ **Especímen**
☑ **Periodo**	*Period*	☒ **Período or periódo**
☑ **Negocia**	*He (she) negotiates*	☒ **Negocía(n)**
☑ **Financia**	*He (she) finances*	☒ **Financía**
☑ **Espacia**	*He (she) spaces*	☒ **Espacía**
☑ **Alineo**	*I align*	☒ **Alíneo or alinéo**
☑ **Delineo**	*I sketch, I outline*	☒ **Delinéo**

— With an accent, the meaning is:

- **Lástima** (adj.)
  Too bad!

- **Líquido** (n.)
  Liquid

- **Fórmula** (n.)
  Formula

- **Íntimo** (adj.)
  Intimate

— With no accent, the meaning is:

- **Lastima**
  He (she, it) damages or hurts ☺☐

- **Liquido**
  I liquidate

- **Formula**
  He (she) formulates

- **Intimo**
  I become intimate with ☺

Grammar Hints

E. The Diminutive in Spanish

The diminutive in Spanish has very special significance. It is one of the most characteristic features of the language, and arises from a sensitivity common to Spanish speaking people (with regional variations). Diminutive endings in Spanish are quaint and revealing. Here is a selection of samples which will provide an overview of usage.

In Spanish, not only nouns can be made diminutive, but also adjectives, adverbs and even some verb forms, such as the past participle.

For example, **El señor estaba parado** is by no means the same as **El señor estaba paradito**; the first refers to a man of normal height, while the second probably refers to someone on the short side. There is also a considerable difference between **La niña estaba sentada** and **La niña estaba sentadita**. In the second case, the diminutive does not refer to the size of the girl, but conveys the speaker's fondness for her, and perhaps also indicates that the girl was sitting in a very self-possessed and ladylike way.

The diminutive in Spanish is often an expression of affection. A mother may call her son **hijito**, not because he is small (he could be 50 years of age and 6 foot 6), but because she loves him so much.

However the diminutive can also be used to offend (very effectively). A wealthy lady referring to the home of a "friend" with a smaller bankroll might say **Tienes una casita muy agradable**, which does not mean that the house is small, but that it is not really worthy of note.

If someone says **El jefe es muy especial** (see False Cognates), he is suggesting that his boss is of strong character, or arbitrary, mean, and so on, but **El jefe es muy especialito** puts his masculinity in doubt. **Graciela es mensa** means Graciela is not too bright, but **Graciela es mensita** injects affection and therefore somehow softens the judgment.

When we ask someone to give a book or report **una leída**, we mean that he should read it fairly conscientiously, but if we ask him to give it **una leidita**, we mean that he should just go over it more or less superficially. While in English you can be invited to *have a smoke* or *a cigarette*, in Spanish you can hear: **¿Nos echamos una fumadita?**, which accentuates the pleasure of the moment.

Pasadas las cuatro de la tarde means some time after four o'clock, whereas **pasaditas las cuatro** implies just a couple of minutes after four.

According to the dictionary, the adjective **mero** means pure or simple. For example, you can say **La mera intuición lo hizo cuidarse** (*Pure intuition made him cautious*). But in Mexico, **mero** is used differently. **Aquí mero** is *right here*; **ya mero** is *in just a minute*. And, of course, it is used in the diminutive, as in **Aquí merito** (*right in this exact place*) and **ya merito** (*in just a few seconds*), these two imply a greater degree of accurancy as regards place, and a shorter lapse of time.

Grammar Hints

The same relationship exists (pretty much) between **apenas** and **apenitas**. Something that **apenas asoma** is sticking out farther that something that **apenitas asoma**.

An interesting diminutive is **adiosito** instead of **adiós**, especially used by women; this gives the impression that the parting will be only a brief one. You may also hear **hasta lueguito** (from **hasta luego**), which implies an even briefer parting.

Here is a short list of names that in Mexico and other Spanish-speaking countries have indeterminable variations, many of them diminutives.

— **Francisco**
  ▪ **Paco, Paquito, Paquillo, Pacorro, Pancho, Cisco, Quico, Pancholín, Francis**
— **Carlos**
  ▪ **Carlitos, Carlillos, Carlangas, Carloncho, Charly**
— **Luis**
  ▪ **Luisito, Luisillo, Luisín, Luisón, Güicho**
— **Ramón**
  ▪ **Ramoncito, Ramoncillo, Ramonín, Moncho**

All these variations are nicknames.

Practically anything can be made a diminutive: Some interesting diminutives having to do with age are **jovencito**, which is not a short **joven**, but:
— a very young boy,
— a term showing affection for a boy or young man, or
— a sarcastic term for a boy or young man.

As concerns time, if someone says they're going to do something **temprano**, it simply means *early* (in the morning, afternoon, etc.). But **tempranito** always means *first thing in the morning*.

Ahora means *now*. **Ahorita** evidently means *right now* or *right away*, although it should not always be taken too literally. **Ahorita voy** does not invariably mean *I'm coming this very instant.* As with *I'll be right with you,* it could mean *I'll be with you as soon as I'm finished with this more important matter.*

Juan Rulfo's use of **tantito** in **"Desviviéndose por conocer aunque sea tantito de la vida"** means *just a bit* of life.

To walk **de puntas** is on toe shoes, as in ballet. But **de puntitas** is on tip toes.

The examples could go on indefinitely, but these will do to get the idea across. Just remember to avoid saying things like **el pequeño niño** and **la silla chica** when you can say **el niñito** and **la sillita.**

Grammar Hints

F. Abbreviations

As in many other languages, there are a a lot of abbreviations in written Spanish, which are often similar or identical to those used in other languages, but in other cases are quite different. Below is a fairly ample sampling of the most commonly used abbreviations in Spanish.

a.C.
— **Antes de Cristo**
Before Christ

A.C.
— **Asociación Civil**
Civil Association; used after the name of a non-profit, tax exempt, service organization, usually charitable)

a/C
— **a cuenta**
on account (an advance payment or down payment).

afmo.
— **Afectísimo**
most affectionately (seldom used now to sign off letters)

atte.
— **Atentamente**
attentively (very much used to sign off letters)

atto.
— **atento**
with full attention

c.c.
— **centímetro cúbico**
cubic centimeter

Cía.
— **compañía**
company

cl.
— **centilitro**
centiliter

cm.
— **centímetro**
centimeter

col.
— **columna**
  column

D.; Dn.
— **Don**
  respectful way of addressing a gentleman

D.m.
— **Dios mediante**
  God willing ("I will be there in April, God willing").

Da., Dña.
— **Doña**
  respectful way of addressing a lady.

Dr.
— **Doctor**
  Doctor

E.
— **este**
  east

ed.
— **edición**
  edition

etc.
— **etcétera**
  et cetera

Excmo. (a)
— **Excelentísimo (a)**
  Most excellent (to address a bishop, embassador, etc.)

F.C.; FF.CC.
— **ferrocarril(es)**
  railroad

Fr.
— **Fray**
  Brother; used before the name of clergy in religious orders

gr.
— **gramo (s)**
  gram

Gral.
— **General**
  (Army) General

Grammar Hints

ib.; ibid.
— **ibidem**
in the same place

izq.
— **izquierda**
left

kg.
— **kilogramo**
kilogram

km.
— **kilómetro**
kilometer

Lic.
— **Licenciado**
*Persons with a bachelor's degree or lawyer are **licenciados**, and use the title before their names.*

m.
— **metro**
meter

M.N.
— **Moneda nacional**
Mexican pesos, as opposed to foreign currency

mg.
— **miligramo**
milligram

mm.
— **milímetro**
millimeter

Mons.
— **Monseñor**
Monsegnor

Mtro.
— **Maestro**
used before the name of school teachers and orchestra conductors

N.; Nte.
— **norte**
north

N.E.
— **noreste**
northeast

N.O.
— noroeste
  northwest

N.S.
— Nuestro Señor
  Our Lord

No.
— número
  number

núm.
— número
  number

O.
— Oeste
  west

P.; pág.
— página
  page

P.p.
— páginas
  pages

P.D.
— postdata
  (the equivalent of PS in English, which is also used in Spanish on occasions)

p.ej.
— por ejemplo
  for example

p.p.
— por poder
  used only when signing for someone else

P.S.
— post scriptum (Latin)
  Post script

Pbro.
— presbítero
  used before the name of a Roman Catholic priest

Pdo.
— pasado
  past

Grammar Hints

Prof.
— **profesor**
  professor

prol.
— **prólogo o prolongación**
  prologue or prolongation

q.e.p.d.
— **que en paz descanse**
  rest in peace

R.I.P.
— **Requiescat in pace** (latin)
  rest in peace

Rev.
— **Reverendo**
  Reverend

S.A.
— **Sociedad Anónima**
  the equivalent of Ltd. or Inc.

S.A. de C.V.
— **Sociedad Anónima de Capital Variable**
  same as S.A., except that additional capital contributions can be made during the lifetime of the company

S.C.
— **Sociedad Civil**
  used after the name of a professional service organization or partnership

S.E.
— **Su excelencia**
  His (Her, Your) Excellency

S.M.
— **Su Majestad**
  His (Her, Your) Majesty

S.O.
— **Sudoeste**
  southwest

S.S.
— **Su Santidad**
  Your Holiness; used preceding the Pope's name

s.s.
— **seguro servidor**
  your certain servant

Grammar Hints

sig. (s).
— siguiente (s)
  following

Smo.
— Santísimo
  Holy

Sr. (a)
— Señor (a)
  Mister

Srita.
— Señorita
  Miss

Sto. (a).
— Santo (a)
  Saint

su afmo. y s.s.
— su afectísimo y seguro servidor
  your devoted and unfailing servant

T.; t.
— tomo
  book

Ud. (s)
— usted/es
  you

V.gr.
— verbigracia
  for example, such as

Vda.
— viuda
  widow

Vo.Bo.
— Visto Bueno
  approval or authorization; used just before a signature okaying something

Vol. (s)
— volumen (volúmenes)
  volumes

Grammar Hints

The abbreviation for **Estados Unidos** (United States) is **E.E.U.U.** or just **E.U.** The abbreviations of the Mexican states might also prove useful, as they are seldom familiar to English speakers.

STATE	Abbreviation
Aguascalientes	Ags.
Baja California Norte	B.C.N.
Baja California Sur	B.C.S.
Campeche	Camp.
Coahuila	Coah.
Chiapas	Chis.
Chihuahua	Chih.
Distrito Federal	D.F.
Durango	Dgo.
Guanajuato	Gto.
Guerrero	Gro.
Hidalgo	Hgo.
Jalisco	Jal.
México	Mex.
Michoacán	Mich.
Morelos	Mor.
Nayarit	Nay.
Nuevo León	N.L.
Oaxaca	Oax.
Puebla	Pue.
Querétaro	Qro.
Quintana Roo	Q.R.
San Luis Potosí	S.L.P.
Sinaloa	Sin.
Sonora	Son.
Tabasco	Tab.
Tamaulipas	Tamps.
Tlaxcala	Tlax.
Veracruz	Ver.
Yucatán	Yuc.
Zacatecas	Zac.

THE NAMES OF THE LETTERS

It is rather important to know the names of the letters and to be able to use them easily, as you will often find it necessary to spell words (especially your name).

a	**a**
b	**be (or be labial)**
c	**ce**
d	**de**
e	**e**
f	**efe**
g	**ge**
h	**hache**
i	**i**
j	**jota**
k	**ka**
l	**ele**
m	**eme**
n	**ene**
ñ	**eñe**
o	**o**
p	**pe**
q	**cu**
r	**ere**
s	**ese**
t	**te**
u	**u**
v	**ve (or ve labiodental)**
w	**doble ve or doble u**
x	**equis**
y	**i griega**
z	**zeta**

Grammar Hints

G. Latin Words in Spanish

A s in many other languages, certain Latin words or phrases are used in everyday speaking or writing, either in their original form, or adapted to Spanish, for the simple reason that there is no good version of the word or phrase in Spanish. Here is a list; some of these are used the same as in English.

A fortiori (pronounced "a forsiori")
— Obligatory; whether you like it or not
- **La junta de las 11:00 no es opcional. Es a fortiori.**
  The eleven o'clock meeting is not optional. You've got to go.

Agenda
— A list of things to be done
- **El ministro tiene su agenda llena.**
  The minister's agenda is full.
— A little notebook
- **Mi jefe no encuentra su agenda.**
  My boss can't find his notebook.

Alias
— Otherwise named (same as in English); also known as
- **Este es mi hermano Tomás, alias El Tigre.**
  This is my brother Tom, alias The Tiger.

Bis
— Used after a number which is repeated to distinguish one from the other
- **Trajiste el expediente 210. Pedí el 210 bis.**
  You brought file number 210. I asked for 210 bis.

Déficit
— Deficit (same as in English)
- **El déficit está creciendo.**
  The deficit is growing.

Errata
— An error; a list of errors, followed by the correct version
- **Este error (esta errata) no está en la fe de erratas.**
  This mistake is not in the list at the end of the book.

Grammar Hints

Ex abrupto
— Something said or done inconveniently, suddenly or unexpectedly
  - **Su ex abrupto arruinó la cordial conversación.**
    His unexpected outburst spoiled the cordial conversation.

Ex profeso
— Suitable or made for a specific purpose
  - **Este cuarto fue construido ex profeso para oír música.**
    This room was specifically built for listening to music.

(A) grosso modo
— In general; without going into details
  - **Hicimos un plan a grosso modo.**
    We made a rough plan.

In fraganti
— In the act; red-handed
  - **Los sorprendieron in fraganti, abriendo la caja fuerte.**
    They were caught in the act of opening the safe.

Ipso facto
— Immediately; right away
  - **Hay que hacer esto ipso facto.**
    This has to be done immediately.

Lapsus
— A momentary loss of memory
  - **Tuve un lapsus y se me olvidó el nombre del director.**
    My mind went blank and I forgot the director's name.

Memorándum*
— Note to assist the memory (same as in English).
  - **Este memorándum llegó ayer.**
    This memorandum arrived yesterday.

*The word is usually pluralized as **memorándums** in Spanish.

Modus vivendi
— The means of making a living
  - **El deporte es su modus vivendi.**
    Sports is his way of making a living.

Grammar Hints

Non plus ultra
— Something unsurpassable (used as a noun)
- **Este coche es el non plus ultra de los coches de carreras.**
  This car is the ultimate in racing cars.

Peccata minuta
— Minor fault or mistake
- **No te preocupes, lo que hiciste es peccata minuta.**
  Don't worry. What you did it's just an unimportant fault.

Per se
— By itself (same as in English)
- **Nada más lee esta página. El libro per se no es importante.**
  Just read this page. The book itself is not important.

Post mortem
— After death; following the event
- **Le dieron el premio post mortem.**
  He was awarded the prize posthumously.

Prorrata; prorratear (from Pro rata)
— Proportionately
- **Los gastos van a ser prorrateados (a prorrata).**
  The expenses are to be paid proportionately.

Quórum
— The number of members of a body (committee, board, panel, etc.) (same as in English)
- **No hubo junta, porque no hubo quórum.**
  There was no meeting because there was no quorum.

Superávit
— Surplus, as concerns money matters
- **El superávit por revaluación es considerable.**
  The restatement surplus is significant.

H. The Use of Prepositions

U se of the wrong preposition accounts for a large number of common errors. Of course, this is because the student thinks in English and translates literally.

A sangre fría (not Con sangre fría or En sangre fría)
— In cold blood

- **Lo mató a sangre fría.**
  He killed him in cold blood.
- **No puede matar un animal a sangre fría.**
  She cannot kill an animal in cold blood.

A veces (not En veces)
— Sometimes

- **A veces viajamos en autobús.**
  We sometimes travel by bus.
- **El ferrocarril se retrasa a veces.**
  The train is sometimes late.

Acordar(se) de (not Recordar(se) de)
— To remember

- **Siempre se acuerda de mi cumpleaños.**
  He always remembers my birthday.
- **Tu hermana no se acuerda de mí.**
  Your sister doesn't remember me.

Al contrario (not En contrario)
— On the contrary

- **No estoy enojado. Al contrario, estoy feliz.**
  I am not angry. On the contrary, I am delighted.
- **Al contrario de lo que pensé, él sí compró la casa.**
  Contrary to what I believed, he did buy the house.

Grammar Hints

De la misma manera (not En la misma manera)
— In the same way
- **Hazlo de la misma manera.**
  Do it the same way.
- **Siempre actúa de la misma manera.**
  He always acts the same way.

Del mismo modo (not En el mismo modo)
— In the same way
- **Hazlo del mismo modo.**
  Do it the same way.
- **Lo hizo del mismo modo.**
  She did it the same way.

Distinto del (de la) (not Distinto que el)
— Different from
- **Este es distinto del que te di.**
  This one is different from the one I gave you.
- **Esta tela es distinta de la que te vendí.**
  This fabric is different from the one I sold you.

En forma de (not En la forma de)
— In the shape of
- **Es un pastel en forma de corazón.**
  It's a cake in the shape of a heart.
- **Está construido en forma de arco.**
  It's built in the shape of a bow.

Ocupar(se) en; ocupar(se) de (not Ocuparse con)
— To busy yourself with
- **Ocúpate de tus cosas.**
  Look after your own affairs.
- **No tengo tiempo para ocuparme en esas cosas.**
  I have no time to think about (take care of) such things.

However:
- **Estoy ocupado con esto.**
  I am busy (working) with this.

Grammar Hints

Pensar en (not Pensar de)
— To think of

- **Pienso en ti siempre.**
  I think of you always.
- **No hay que pensar en lo malo, sino en lo bueno.**
  One must not think of the bad (things), but of the good.

However:

- **¿Qué piensas del matrimonio?**
  What do you think about marriage?

I. Homophones

These are words that sound the same but are spelled differently, like *bear* and *bare*, which just add to the other quite numerous complications of learning a language, but must nevertheless be borne (not born), as they are part of the language and there's no way of getting around them. Some of these exist on the fringes of the language (and can be safely stowed away on the hardest-to-reach shelves of the mind), but others are very much a part of everyday speech and have to be grappled with. You will know which are which as you go over the list.

Words that are usually encountered in normal everyday spoken Spanish are preceded by a tick (✓). You need those; they are indispensable tools. But you may safely assume that the others will appear only at extremely rare moments, and then more often than not only in highbrow or technical written Spanish. Naturally, the thing to look out for is cases where both homophones are ticked. More common or equally common synonyms are given.

Whenever verbs are homophones, the different conjugations of those verbs are also homophones, unless one or the other is irregular. Only infinitives are provided.

In some places, homophones involving the letters **c**, **s** and **z**, are not actually homophones. In Spain for example, where the **z** and the **c** are lisped, they do not sound the same as the **s**, as they do in most of Latin America.

(✓)Abrasar (v.)
— To burn to ashes.
- **En cualquier momento se habría podido abrasar su casa.**
  His house could have gone up in flames at any moment.

(✓)Abrazar (v.)
— To hold, to embrace, to hug a person or other embraceable thing or being; involves both of the holder's or embracer's arms. This word is not used for just holding a thing in one's hand
- **Sueño con abrazarla.**
  I dreamed of embracing her.

(✓)Acechar (v.)
— To watch a person or animal with a view to pouncing on or catching him, her or it; to stalk
- **Los soldados tuvieron que acechar al enemigo dos días.**
  The soldiers had to stalk the enemy for two days.

Asechar (v.)
— To trick; to deceive
- **El demonio no cesa de asechar al hombre.**
  The devil never ceases to deceive man.

Acerbo(a) (adj.)
— Sour; bitter; cruel; severe (said of a person; the common, garden word for this is **amargado**; a sour taste is **agrio**, and bitter **amargo**)
- **Aquél fue el más acerbo dolor que había sentido.**
  That was the most severe pain I had ever felt.

(✓)Acervo (n.)
— An accumulation of things, most often of cultural values or knowledge
- **El acervo cultural de la nación mexicana es muy grande.**
  Mexico's cultural heritage is very ample.

(✓)Aprehender (v.)
— To catch, to capture (a person)
- **No tardan en aprehender al criminal.**
  It won't be long before they catch the criminal.

(✓) Aprender (v.)
— To learn
- **Cuanto más puedas aprender, mejor para ti.**
  The more you learn, the better.

(✓) Aprehensión (n.)
— Capture
- **Su aprehensión fue muy difícil.**
  His capture was very difficult.

Aprensión (n.)
— A feeling of fearful foreboding; apprehension
- **Jorge sufre la aprensión de las enfermedades.**
  Jorge has apprehension about getting sick.

(✓) Arrollo (v.)
— First-person singular of the verb **arrollar:** to hit; to run over
- **Por poco arrollo a ese muchacho descuidado.**
  I was about to run down that careless boy.

(✓) Arroyo (n.)
— Stream; brook; bed of a stream (also *street*, but rarely used this way)
- **El arroyo es cristalino.**
  The brook is crystal clear.

(✓) As (n.)
— Ace
- **El as es la primera carta de la baraja.**
  The ace is the first card in the deck

(✓) **Has** (v.)
— Second-person singular of the auxiliary verb **haber**
- **No has comido todavía.**
  You haven't had lunch yet.

(✓) **Haz** (v.) (n.)
— Singular imperative of the verb **hacer**
- **Haz lo que te digo.**
  Do as I say.
— Bundle; bunch; a beam of light (this meaning is rarely used)
- **Un haz de luz muy intenso brillaba por la ventana.**
  A very bright ray of light was shining through the window.

(✓) **Asar** (v.)
— To roast
- **Ya es hora de asar la carne.**
  It's time to roast the meat.

Azahar (n.)
— Orange, lemon or citron blossom
- **Cualquier ramo de azahar me recuerda mi boda.**
  Any bunch of orange blossoms reminds me of my wedding.

(✓) **Azar** (n.)
— Random; chance; hazard; misfortune; mischance
- **Tomó un naipe al azar.**
  He took a card at random.

(✓) **Ascenso** (n.)
— Job promotion
- **Luis obtuvo un buen ascenso.**
  Luis got a good promotion.

Asenso (n.)
— From the verb **asentir**: To agree; to assent
- **Teníamos todo listo. Sólo esperábamos el asenso de la mesa directiva.**
  We had everything ready. We were just awaiting the consent of the Board of Directors.

Asta (n.)
— Animal horn (**asta bandera**: flagstaff)

(✓) **Hasta** (conj.)
— Until
- **Le limaron el asta, hasta dejarla inofensiva.**
  They filed down its horn until it was rendered harmless.

Barón (n.)
— Baron (title of nobility)
- **El Barón era déspota con la servidumbre.**
  The Baron was a despot with his servants.

(✓) Varón (n.)
— Male (Used only to distinguish sex of newborns or school age children. Used for humans only; a male animal is **macho**. Otherwise, sex distinctions are **masculino** and **femenino**).
- **Un varón era siempre preferido en las familias coloniales.**
  A male was always preferred in colonial families.

(✓) Basta (v.)
— Third-person singular of the verb **bastar**: To suffice; to be enough.
- **Basta de caminar hoy por esta vasta planicie.**
  That's enough for today of walking across this vast plain.

(✓) Vasta(a) (adj.)
— Vast; huge
- **Se inundó una vasta región del estado.**
  A vast region of the state was flooded.

Basto(a) (adj.)
— Rough; coarse
- **De un tipo grosero se dice que es un hombre basto.**
  A lout is said to be coarse.

(✓) Vasto(a) (adj.)
— Vast, huge
- **Su conocimiento es vasto.**
  His knowledge is vast.

(✓) Bate (v.) (n.)
— Third-person singular of the verb **batir**: To beat, whip, mix (used in cooking); also a baseball bat.

Vate (n.)
— Poet; bard
- **Ya van dos veces que el vate se bate en un duelo a muerte.**
  The poet has twice been in a duel to the death.

(✓) Bello(a) (adj.)
— Beautiful (synonym: **hermoso**)

(✓) Vello (n.)
— Soft human hair
- **No es nada bello tener exceso de vello.**
  There is nothing beautiful about excess hair.

Grammar Hints

(✓) **Bota** (n.)
— Leather container from which wine is drunk; boot
- **Mientras me quito las botas, ve por la bota de vino.**
  While I get the boots off, go for the wine skin.

(✓) **Vota** (v.)
— Third-person singular of the verb **votar**: To vote
- **El pueblo vota cada cuatro años.**
  The people vote every four years.

(✓) **Botar** (v.)
— To launch a ship
- **Mañana van a botar el nuevo barco.**
  The new ship will be launched tomorrow.
— To throw (away) or get rid of
- **No botes tu ropa por todo el cuarto.**
  Don't throw your clothes all over the room.
— To bounce (a ball)
- **Esta pelota ya no bota bien.**
  This ball doesn't bounce properly.

(✓) **Votar** (v.)
— To vote
- **No voy a votar por el candidato socialista.**
  I'm not going to vote for the socialist candidate.

(✓) **Bracero** (n.)
— Farm laborer
- **Se fue de bracero a trabajar en Texas.**
  He went to work as a farmhand in Texas.

Brasero (n.)
— Brazier; fire-pan; hearth; fireplace (for cooking)
- **Estamos usando el brasero porque nos cortaron la luz.**
  We are using the brazier (to cook on) because our electricity was cut off.

(✓)**Callo** (n.)
— Corn; callous (derm.)
- **Por suerte no tengo ningún callo.**
  Luckily I have no corns.

(✓) **Callo** (v.)
— First-person singular present tense of the verb **callar**: To remain quiet
- **Si lo deseas, callo todo lo que sé.**
  If you wish, I won't say a word about what I know.

Cayo (n.)
— Cay; key; islet
- **El faro del cayo estaba descompuesto.**
  The lighthouse on the key was out of order.

(✓) Calló (v.)
— Third-person singular past tense of the verb **callar**: To remain quiet
(✓) Cayó (v.)
— Third-person singular past tense of the verb **caer**, to fall
- **Rafael calló las razones por las que cayó de las escaleras.**
  Rafael said nothing about why he fell down the stairs.

(✓)Casa (n.)
— House
(✓) Caza (n.)
— The hunt
- **Salí de casa muy temprano para irme de caza.**
  I left the house very early to go hunting.

(✓)Casado(a) (v.) (adj.)
— Past participle of **casar(se)**: To get married; married
- **Estoy casado con la hermana de Lupita.**
  I'm married to Lupita's sister.
(✓) Cazado (v.)
— Past participle of **cazar**: To hunt
- **Nunca he cazado un jabalí.**
  I have never hunted a wild boar.

(✓) Cause (v.)
— Singular present tense subjunctive of the verb **causar**: To cause
- **Es probable que esta lluvia cause ciertos daños.**
  This rain will probably cause a certain amount of damage.
(✓) Cauce (n.)
— River bed
- **Vamos a tener que dragar el cauce del río.**
  We are going to have to drag the river bed.

Cebo (n.)
— Primer charge; bait
- **Espero que a los peces les atraiga este cebo.**
  I hope the fish are attracted by the bait.

Grammar Hints

Sebo (n.)
— Fat; grease (from beef)
  - **Esa carne tiene demasiado sebo.**
    This meat has too much fat.

(✓)Cesión (n.)
— From the verb **ceder**: To waive; to cede; to hand over
(✓)Sesión (n.)
— Meeting; session
  - **Durante la sesión hicieron la cesión de sus derechos.**
    They ceded their rights during the meeting.

(✓)Cede (v.)
— Third-person singular of the verb **ceder**: To waive, to cede
(✓) Sede (n.)
— Seat; headquarters; location of an event like the Olympic Games or a convention
  - **Ningún país cede fácilmente la sede olímpica.**
    No country will willingly give up its rights to host the Olympic Games.

Cegar (v.)
— To blind; to fill in (a well)
  - **Cuidado porque esa luz te puede cegar.**
    Be careful, because this light can blind you.
Segar (v.)
— To reap; mow; cut
  - **Conviene segar el trigo a tiempo.**
    The wheat should be reaped (with a sickle) on time.

(✓)Cien (n.)
— One hundred
  - **Hay por lo menos cien alumnos.**
    There are at least a hundred students.
(✓) Sien (n.)
— Temple (anatomic)
  - **Es peligroso un golpe en la sien.**
    A blow to the temple is dangerous.

Ciervo (n.)
— Deer (poetic use, the usual word is **venado**)
  - **El ciervo tenía unas astas muy hermosas.**
    The deer had very beautiful horns.

Siervo(a) (n.)
— Serf; servant; slave (not used much since the end of the feudal system)
- **El sacerdote es un buen siervo del Señor.**
  The priest is a good servant of God.

(✓)Cierra (v.)
— Third-person singular of the verb **cerrar**, to close
(✓) Sierra (n.)
— Jagged mountain range
- **Cierra esa puerta, porque se mete el frío viento de la sierra.**
  Close the door because the cold air from the mountains gets in.
— Saw (for sawing wood)
- **Ya es necesario afilar la sierra**
  The saw has to be sharpened.
— Swordfish
- **La sierra frita estaba muy sabrosa.**
  The fried swordfish was very good.

(✓)Cima (n.)
— The tip (as of a mountain)
Sima (n.)
— Chasm; abyss
- **Es muy largo el camino desde la cima del monte hasta la sima del barranco.**
  It's a long way from the peak of the mountain to the bottom of the gorge.

Cirio (n.)
— Large beeswax church candle
- **Ese cirio echa demasiado humo.**
  That big candle is smoking too much.
Sirio(a) (adj.)
— Syrian
- **El comerciante sirio tenía rostro cetrino.**
  The Syrian merchant had a swarthy complexion.

(✓) Cocer (v.)
— To cook
(✓) Coser (v.)
— To sew
- **Cuando terminó de cocer la carne, se puso a coser mi camisa.**
  When she was through cooking the meat, she began to sew my shirt.

Grammar Hints

(✓) Cocido(a) (v.)

— Past participle of the verb **cocer**: To cook; also a regional Spanish dish

- **Este pescado está muy mal cocido.**
  This fish is very badly cooked.

(✓) Cosido(a) (v.)

— Past participle of the verb **coser**, to sew

- **Aquel pantalón está bien cosido.**
  That pair of pants is well sewn.

Concejo (n.)

— Town council; board of aldermen

(✓)Consejo (n.)

— A piece of advice; some advice

- **Los miembros del concejo no quieren oír ningún consejo.**
  The members of the town council refuse to listen to any advice.

(✓) Desecho (n.) (v.)

— Cast-off; residue; also first-person singular of the verb **desechar**: To dispose of or get rid of, thus also waste, trash, rubbish

- **Es un lamentable desecho humano.**
  He's a sorry human cast-off.

(✓) Deshecho (v.)

— Past participle of the verb **deshacer**, to undo

- **¿No has deshecho aún ese absurdo trato?**
  Haven't you undone that silly deal yet?

Desolló (v.)

— Past tense, third-person singular of the verb **desollar**: To skin; flay (not used much in today's world)

- **La infame tribu desolló vivo al misionero cristiano.**
  The ghastly tribe flayed the Christian missionary alive.

(✓) Desoyó (v.)

— Past tense, third-person singular of the verb **desoír**: Not to pay attention; to ignore; the usual term is **no hacer caso**

- **Desoyó todas las advertencias que le hicieron.**
  He ignored all the warnings they gave him.

(✓) Echa/echo

— Third-person singular/first-person singular of the verb **echar**: To throw; to toss

- **Luis, echa esa basura en el mismo bote donde yo la echo.**
  Luis, throw out that garbage in the same can I throw it in.

Grammar Hints

(✓) Hecha/hecho
— Feminine / masculine past participle of the verb **hacer**: To do or to make
- **Esa escultura está bien hecha; en cambio, aquel cuadro está muy mal hecho.**
  That sculpture is well done; however, that painting is very badly done.

Encausar (v.)
— To prosecute
- **Lo van a encausar por el robo que cometió.**
  He's going to be prosecuted for the robbery he committed.

(✓) Encauzar (v.)
— To channel; to guide
- **Es conveniente encauzar a los jóvenes por el buen camino.**
  Young people should be guided along the straight and narrow path.

(✓) Errar (v.)
— To err; to miss; to wander
- **Hay que cuidarse de no errar el camino.**
  One must be careful not to lose one's way.

Herrar (v.)
— To shoe a horse; to bind with iron
- **Van a herrar a ese caballo.**
  That horse is going to be shoed.

(✓) Grabar (v.)
— To engrave; to etch
- **Se dedica a grabar en acero; es un verdadero artista.**
  He etches on steel; he's a real artist.
— To record
- **Voy a grabar esta canción.**
  I am going to record this song.

(✓) Gravar (v.)
— To tax; to impose a tax
- **¿Las llamadas de teléfono están gravadas?**
  Is there a tax on telephone calls?

(✓) Hallamos (v.)
— Third-person plural of the present and past tense of the verb **hallar**: To find, to discover

(✓) Hayamos (v.)
— First-person plural or perfect tenses of the auxiliary verb **haber**: to have
- **Estaremos tranquilos cuando hayamos encontrado los datos que no hallamos.**
  We'll be able to relax when we hit on the data we can't find.

Grammar Hints

(✓) **Honda (adj.)**
— Deep
- **Estas albercas no son muy hondas.**
  These pools aren't very deep.

Onda (n.)
— Wave (water, light, electric, sound and air)
- **Las ondas de sonido son comparativamente largas.**
  Sound waves are comparatively long.

Losa (n.)
— Slab; stone

(✓) **Loza** (n.)
— Crockery, chinaware
- **Se rompió la loza al caer sobre la losa.**
  The china broke when it fell on the stone floor.

(✓) **Masa** (n.)
— Dough
- **Las tortillas se hacen con masa de maíz, pero también de trigo.**
  Tortillas are made with corn or wheat dough.

Maza (n.)
— Mace (Medieval weapon)
- **Le descargó un terrible golpe de maza.**
  He gave his opponent a dreadful blow with his mace.

Mecías (v.)
— Past tense second-person singular of the verb **mecer**: To rock; to swing; to sway
- **Mientras te mecías en el columpio se fueron tus amiguitos.**
  Your little friends left while you were swinging on the swing.

(✓) **Mesías** (n.)
— Messiah
- **Los judíos aún esperan al Mesías.**
  The Jews are still awaiting the Messiah.

(✓) **Peces** (n.)
— Plural for **pez**, fish
- **El Caribe está poblado por bellos peces.**
  The Caribbean is full of beautiful fishes.

(✓) **Peses** (v.)
— Second-person singular present subjunctive of the verb **pesar**: To weigh
- **Más vale que peses los bultos uno por uno.**
  You better weigh the packages one by one.

(✓) **Ralla** (v.)

— Third-person singular, present tense of the verb **rallar**: To grate

- **Con este aparato se ralla muy bien el queso.**
  This thing grates cheese very well.

(✓) **Raya** (n.) (v.)

— Line

- **Esa raya que trazaste no está derecha.**
  The line you drew is not straight.

— Scratch (on the surface of something)

- **Con esta vieja aguja es seguro que el disco se raya.**
  The record is sure to get scratched with this old needle.

— To verge on

- **Este poema raya en lo ridículo.**
  This poem verges on the ridiculous.

(✓) **Rallar** (v.)

— To grate

- **Voy a rallar un poco de zanahoria.**
  I'm going to grate a bit of carrot.

(✓) **Rayar** (v.)

— To draw lines or to scratch (the surface of something): To verge on

- **Con esa fibra puedes rayar el vidrio.**
  You might scratch the glass with that steel wool.

Rasa (adj.)

— Level (as in level teaspoon)

- **Ponle una cucharadita rasa de polvo de hornear.**
  Add a level teaspoon of baking powder.

(✓) **Rebelar(se)** (v.)

— To rebel; to revolt; to resist

(✓) **Revelar** (v.)

— To reveal; to develop (film)

- **Al rebelarse estos jóvenes, lo que hacen es revelar un problema social.**
  What these young people do when they rebel is to reveal a social problem.

Rebosar (v.)
— To overflow
- **Lupe se ve muy bien. Rebosa alegría.**
  Lupe looks wonderful. She's brimming over with cheerfulness.

Rebozar (v.)
— To muffle; wrap; cover; dip in batter and fry
- **Un buen cocinero sabe como rebozar mejor el pescado.**
  A good cook knows the best way to dip fish in batter for frying.

(✓) **Reciente** (adj.)
— Recent

(✓) **Resiente** (v.)
— Third-person singular, present tense of the verb **resentir**: To resent, begin to weaken, to feel the effects of a wound or injury
- **Manuel resiente todavía los efectos de su reciente enfermedad.**
  Manuel is still feeling the effects of his recent illness.

(✓) **Ribera** (n.)
— Bank; shore; beach
- **La ribera del Papaloapan es muy fértil.**
  The banks of the Papaloapan River are very fertile.

Rivera (n.)
— Brook; stream; creek
- **Una estrecha rivera cruzaba el sembradío.**
  A brook crossed the planted field.

(✓) **Sabia** (adj.)
— Wise; learned

Savia (n.)
— Sap of a plant
- **Los investigadores tomaron la sabia decisión de aprovechar la savia del arbusto.**
  The researchers took the wise decision to make use of the bush's sap.

(✓) **Tasa** (n.)
— Rate (as of interest)
- **La tasa anual de esos bonos ha subido mucho.**
  The yearly rate of those bonds has risen a lot.

(✓) **Taza** (n.)
— Cup
- **Voy a servirme una taza de café.**
  I'm going to serve myself a cup of coffee.

(✓) Tubo (n.)

— Tube or pipe

- **El tubo se rompió y el agua se está saliendo.**
  The pipe broke and the water is running out.

(✓) Tuvo (v.)

— Third-person singular, past tense of the verb **tener**: To have

- **Raquel tuvo que aceptar su equivocación.**
  Raquel had to accept her mistake.

- **Mi abuelo tuvo una gran fortuna que luego perdió.**
  My grandfather had a great fortune, which he later lost.

(✓) Ves (v.)

— Second-person singular, present tense of the verb **ver**: To see

- **El ojo que ves no es**
  ojo porque tú lo veas,
  es ojo porque te ve.
  The eye you see is not
  an eye because you see it,
  but because it sees you.
  (Poem by Antonio Machado)

(✓) Vez (n.)

— Time (this time, every time, etc.)

- **Cada vez que tose el enfermo, se pone muy pálido.**
  Every time the patient coughs, he gets very pale.

Grammar Hints

J. Pronunciation

If your pronunciation is still shaky, here is an approximation of the sound of Spanish letters. It is the key to all pronunciation. As from very recently, double consonants in Spanish are no longer considered as separate letters. That is the case of **Ch** and **Ll**, which we are including here for phonetic purposes only.

1. Consonants

B

— Only in Yucatan is the *b* pronounced as in English, and all non-Yucatecans think this pronunciation is most amusing; imitations of Yucatecans speaking with their heavy *b* are usually greeted with gales of laughter; the general *b* sound is as if you were going to say the English *b* sound, but were too lazy to actually close your lips . . . the result is an *almost-b,* with air escaping between the almost closed lips. The *v* usually sounds the same.

bar	*bar*
barba	*beard*
carbón	*coal*
sobar	*to rub*
vámonos	*let's go*
viga	*beam (wood)*
guayabera	*type of shirt worn in the tropics*

C

— Pronounced exactly like a *k* before consonants, as well as before *a, o* and *u*. Pronounced like an *s* before *e* and *i*.

clavo	*nail*
acné	*acne*
ocre	*ochre*
octavo	*eighth*
cama	*bed*
costal	*bag*
curioso	*curious*
cenicero	*ashtray*
cisterna	*cistern*

Grammar Hints

CH

— This was a separate letter in Spanish. It is always pronounced as in *china*, never the sound *k* as in *chemist* and *architect*.

chamaco	*boy*
hacha	*ax or hatchet*
chivo	*goat*
chango	*monkey*
gancho	*hook or hanger*
arrachera	*fajita*

D

— This is one of the letters that differ the most from the way it is pronounced in English. Generally speaking, when a word begins with a *d*, it is pronounced as in English.

día	*day*
dedo	*finger*
distinto	*different*
Daniel	*Daniel*
domingo	*Sunday*
dentro	*inside*

However, when it appears in any of the subsequent syllables of a word, is softens so much that it sounds more like an English *th* than a *d* (the sonorous *th*, as in *though* and *then*, not the mute version as in *thing* or *thistle*).

sábado	*Saturday*
montada	*mounted*
orquídea	*orchid*
tiroide	*thyroid*
agridulce	*sweet-and-sour*
variadísimo	*very varied*
amada	*beloved*
comida	*food*
dedal	*thimble*
didáctico	*didactic*

F

— Same as in English.

G

— As in *guy*, before *a*, *o* and *u*, and before *ue* and *ui*.

gamuza	*suede*
gordo	*fat*
gula	*gluttony*
guerra	*war*
Guillermo	*William*

Grammar Hints

As the *h* in home, before *e* and *i*.

gemela	*twin*
giro	*turn*

H
— Always mute as in *honor*.

huérfano	*orphan*
hijo	*son*
hazlo	*do it!*
humor	*humor*
hecho	*fact*

J
— Always like the *h* in *home*.

jabón	*soap*
jerga	*floor rag*
jitomate	*tomato*
jorongo	*poncho*
jugo	*juice*

K
— Always as in English.

kilo	*kilo*
kilómetro	*kilometer*

L
— Same as in English.

LL
— In most Latin American countries, especially in South America, like the *sh* in *shave*, the *g* in *ingenue* or the *g* in *gene*; in Mexico, like the *y* in *young*.

lleva	*takes*
lleno	*full*
llave	*key*
lluvia	*rain*
llovía	*rained*

M
— Same as in English.

N
— With the tongue, as in the English *never*, before vowels and all consonants except *c*, g, *q* and *j*.

no	*no*
nada	*nothing*
negro	*black*
ninguno	*none*
nulo	*null*

Grammar Hints

In the throat, as in the English *sang*, before *c*, *g*, *q* and *j*

ancla	*anchor*
tango	*tango*
tanque	*tank*
naranja	*orange*

Ñ

— There is no equivalent sound in the ordinary English. Like *gn* in *poignant*. If you don't know how to pronounce *poignant*, ask someone who does. The dictionary isn't likely to help.

P

— Same as in English. In Spanish there is no *ph* combination (as in *phone*).

Q

— As a *k*. The *u* in words like **querer** and **química** is never pronounced; a few other words coming unchanged from the original Latin pronunciation (**quorum**) are an exception.

R

— Like a child's imitation of a car engine, when it's the first letter in a word

Rodrigo	*Rodrigo*
rama	*branch*
rústico	*rustic*
ronco	*hoarse*
rico	*rich*
reno	*reindeer*

Like the *r* in *through* when it is *not* the first letter in a word (this is the biggest pronunciation problem for English speaking people), or like the *t* in *later* (when later is pronounced as in American English). Before you try to pronounce this sound in Spanish, say these English words several times in good Americanese, to get the feel of the sound . . . the tongue barely touches the roof of the mouth *once*, *not* like the rolling double *r* or the single *r* at the beginning of words. Remember, it is the *t* in these words that sounds like the Spanish *r*.

Peter	*alligator*	*letter*	*better*
setter	*fatter*	*beautiful*	

Also like the *d* in:

ladder	*had her*	*madder*	*gladder*

You must feel your tongue touching the roof of your mouth, and remember that feeling, so you can transpose it to Spanish. Now, try these words in Spanish:

Grammar Hints

aro	hoop
toro	bull
quiero	I want
para	for
Lara	Lara
mora	blackberry
María	María
moronga	blood sausage

It gets more difficult when it comes before a consonant, but the sound is the same.

alarma	alarm
aparte	apart
perla	pearl
charla	talk
parto	birth
tarjeta	card

It is also hard to handle when it comes after a consonant, as in:

patria	homeland
agrio	sour
atrio	atrium
trigo	wheat
ebrio	drunk
trepar	to climb
cromo	chrome
pronto	soon
tráfico	traffic
trusa	men's jockey underpants
tres	three

The *double r* (the famous rolling r), as in the following words, has no counterpart in English, but sounds the same as the single r in the first letter of a word (like a child's imitation of a car engine . . . without making it too long).

error	error
ferrocarril *	train
carro	car
parra **	grape vine
gorro	cap
tierra	earth
derrota	defeat
Mediterráneo	Mediterranean
Monterrey	Monterey
hierro	iron
desarrollo	development
irrisorio	negligible

As in the following tongue-twisters:

*   **Rr con rr cigarro, rr con rr barril; rápido ruedan los carros, los carros rodando del ferrocarril.**

**   **En la Barranca de Ibarra vivían Guerra y Parra; Parra tenía una perra y Guerra tenía una parra . . . mióse la perra de Parra en la parra de Guerra y Guerra dióle de palos a la perra.**

S

— Same as in English.

T

— Same as in English in words like *toy*.

V

— In normal Spanish, there is usually no noticeable difference between the pronunciation of *b* and *v*. Certainly no ones takes the trouble to put upper teeth against lower lip as the correct pronunciation requires . . . the result is that uneducated people have no idea whether words are spelled with *b* or with *v*; the *v* usually sounds like a soft *b* (whereas the *b* usually sounds like a hard *v* . . . i.e., they sound the same). See **B**.

visa	*visa*
verbo	*verb*
vainilla	*vanilla*

You will probably notice that **voy** usually sounds like **boy** and **vengo** like **bengo**, etc.

W

— Not a letter in the Spanish alphabet. Appears only in words adopted from other languages (mostly English), such as *watt*, *watercloset*, *whiskey* and *water polo*. It can have two sounds:

▪   like the Spanish **u** when it comes from the English (*watt*)
▪   like the Spanish **v** when it comes from German (*Wenceslao*)

Y

— Same as for the **LL**.

Z

— In the New World, nobody lisps the *z*, and if you try, you will get some very strange looks, so you are advised to stay away from it; the *z* simply sounds like an ordinary *s*.

Grammar Hints

2. The Pronunciation of Vowels . . . Most Important

Whereas English is a language of consonants, Spanish is a language of vowels. There is hardly a consonant that is not accompanied by a vowel, so it is important to be able to pronounce them properly. In general terms, English speaking people tend to pronounce vowels in Spanish the way they pronounce them in English words, which usually leaves the listener wondering just what the speaker is trying to say.

Vowels in Spanish all have a <u>single sound</u>, not a double sound as most vowels in English:

English		Spanish	
a	ey	**a**	ah
e	ee	**e**	eh
i	ai	**i**	eeh
o	ou	**o**	oh
u	you	**u**	ooh

Grammar Hints

K. Spelling

The most common mistakes in spelling occur with words that are written somewhat alike in both languages. Following is a short list of words often misspelled.

WRONG		RIGHT
accelerar	—	**acelerar**
acceptar	—	**aceptar**
acquirir	—	**adquirir**
acquisición	—	**adquisición**
harmonía	—	**armonía**
architecto	—	**arquitecto**
automóbil	—	**automóvil**
Brazil	—	**Brasil**
cemeterio	—	**cementerio**
zero	—	**cero**
sciencia	—	**ciencia**
circumstancias	—	**circunstancias**
comparasión	—	**comparación**
complexo	—	**complejo**
consequencia	—	**consecuencia**
choro	—	**coro**
questión	—	**cuestión**
demonstración	—	**demostración**
demonstrar	—	**demostrar**
distincto	—	**distinto**
dozena	—	**docena**
efficiente	—	**eficiente**
émfasis	—	**énfasis**
emeralda	—	**esmeralda**
euphoria	—	**euforia**
exhonerar	—	**exonerar**
frequente	—	**frecuente**
govierno	—	**gobierno**
abilidad	—	**habilidad**
illegible	—	**ilegible**
immediatamente	—	**inmediatamente**
immediato	—	**inmediato**
immenso	—	**inmenso**
innocencia	—	**inocencia**
major	—	**mayor**
objectivo	—	**objetivo**
orchesta	—	**orquesta**
pamfleto	—	**panfleto**
prisón	—	**prisión**
punctuación	—	**puntuación**
responsibilidad	—	**responsabilidad**
serape	—	**sarape**
subjectivo	—	**subjetivo**
subsequente	—	**subsecuente**
teléphono	—	**teléfono**

Grammar Hints

— Nouns and adjectives ending in *z* drop this letter and take on *ces* to form the plural.

nuez	**nueces**	(not **nuezes**)
juez	**jueces**	(not **juezes**)
faz	**faces**	(not **fazes**)
haz	**haces**	(not **hazes**)

— Proper names are written with a capital letter, but not the adjective (**gentilicio**) derived from the name, as in the case of countries and nationalities. **Francia** is written with a capital letter, but not **francés**; **Inglaterra**, but not **inglés**; **China**, but not **chinos**; **Japón**, but not **japonés**.

— The days of the week and the months of the year are not written with capital letters: **lunes**, **martes**, **enero**, **febrero**, etc.

— A **CH** that sounds **K** in English words is **QU** in Spanish words:

arCHitect	**arQUitecto**
orCHestra	**orQUesta**

— A **PH** that sounds **F** in English words is **F** in Spanish words:

PHilosoPHy	**FilosoFía**
bibliograPHy	**bibliograFía**

— The ending **TION** in English is **CIÓN** in Spanish:

naTION	**naCIÓN**
condiTION	**condiCIÓN**

— Most English endings **CTION** are **CCIÓN** in Spanish. Connection (**conexión**) is an exception:

proteCTION	**proteCCIÓN**
aCTION	**aCCIÓN**

L. The Infamous Subjunctive

Verbs constitute one of the greatest challenges in mastering a language. For English speaking students in general, Spanish verbs are not too difficult, except for the subjunctive trap. First of all, you should know that the English subjunctive and the Spanish subjunctive are two very different things. In English, the subjunctive exists more as a concept than as a grammatical reality. Although it is much used, as its forms differ from the indicative only in the third-person singular and in some irregular verbs, it presents no problem whatsoever. Not so in Spanish. To learn the use of this mood, you must think exclusively in Spanish (no translating from the English).

The subjunctive is not based on certainties or facts (not black is black and white is white) like the indicative. It has a certain subjectivity, a definite lack of reality. It is subservient to or contingent upon a governing idea expressed in an independent clause, and appears in the subordinate clause.

In English, the infinitive forms are used for the present subjunctive without adding **s** to the third-person singular, with the exception of the verb *to be*, which becomes *were* in all persons of the past subjunctive. But in Spanish, if you say: **Dios te bendice**, you are stating *God blesses you*, and not imploring *God bless you!* The correct form is **¡Dios te BENDIGA!**

It is interesting to note that the singular of the subjunctive is identical to the **usted** form of the imperative.

- **Es posible que VENGA.**
  He may come.
- **¡VENGA usted enseguida!**
  Come here right away!

In Spanish the subjunctive is used as follows: (examples presented in approximate order of importance)

After expressions involving a *degree of possibility*.

- **Es posible que este niño GANE el certamen.**
  This child may win the contest.
- **No sé si VENGA Carlos hoy.**
  I don't know if Carlos will come today.
- **¿Crees que Gloria TENGA novio?**
  Do you think Gloria has a boyfriend?
- **Quizá TENGAMOS que rentar la casa.**
  We might have to rent the house.
- **Ojalá que VENGAN hoy.**
  I hope they come today.

Grammar Hints

When the main clause expresses *doubt*, *denial*, *belief* or *understanding*. In interrogative, the subjunctive is used in the subordinate clause.

- **Mi hermano duda que yo lo QUIERA tanto.**
  My brother doubts that I love him so much.
- **El ladrón negó que HUBIERA robado la joya.**
  The thief denied having stolen (that he had stolen) the jewel.
- **¿Cree usted que el presidente HAYA dado la orden?**
  Do you believe that the president gave the order?

After adverbial conjunctions that express indefinite *future time*, *purpose*, *supposition*, *provision*, *result* and *concession*, such as:

Suponiendo que
— In the event that . . . ; supposing that . . . (Supposition)
- **Suponiendo que CONSIGA el dinero, ésta es una buena compra para él.**
  Assuming he gets the money, this is a bargain for him.

Mientras
— While (Provision)
- **Mientras yo ESTÉ aquí, no corres peligro.**
  While I'm here, you're in no danger.

En caso de que
— In the event that (Purpose)
- **En caso de que FALTE comida, podemos usar estas latas.**
  In the event that there's not enough food, we can use these tins (cans).

Siempre que . . . ; siempre y cuando . . . ; con tal de que . . .
— Provided that . . . ; as long as . . . ; on the condition that . . . (Provision)
- **Estuvo de acuerdo en hacerlo, siempre y cuando Pepe no lo SEPA.**
  He agreed to do it, as long as Pepe doesn't find out.

Tan pronto . . . ; en cuanto . . .
— As soon as . . . (Purpose)
- **En cuanto LLEGUE Ifigenio, nos iremos.**
  As soon as Ifigenio gets here, we'll leave.

Antes de que . . .
— Before . . . (Purpose)
- **Antes de que te DUERMAS, apaga la luz.**
  Before you go to sleep, turn off the light.

De manera que; para que
— So that (Result)
- **Déjalo ahí, de manera que yo SEPA donde está.**
  Leave it there, so I'll know where it is.

A pesar de que
— In spite of (the fact that) . . . ; even if . . . (Concession)
- **No voy a preocuparme, a pesar de que me AMENACEN.**
  I refuse to worry, even if they threaten me.

A menos (de) que . . .
— Unless
- **Mañana habrá día de campo, a menos que LLUEVA.**
  There'll be a picnic tomorrow, unless it rains.

Para cuando . . .
— When, by the time (Purpose)
- **Si la casa no está lista para cuando me CASE, rentaré un departamento.**
  If the house isn't ready by the time I get married, I'll take an apartment.

Cuando . . .
— When . . . (Purpose)
- **Cuando LLEGUE el bebé, su cuarto estará listo.**
  When the baby arrives, his room will be ready.

Para que . . .
— So . . . (Purpose)
- **Me voy para que PUEDAS estudiar.**
  I'll leave now so you can study.

In the subordinate clause, when the main clause expresses *emotion* or *feeling* (*regret*, *pity*, *fear*, *hope*, *surprise*).

Siento que . . .
— I'm sorry (that) . . .
- **Siento que no HAYAS visto a Pedro.**
  I'm sorry you didn't see Pedro.

Lástima que . . . ; qué pena que . . .
— It's a shame (that) . . . ; too bad (that) . . .
- **¡Qué pena que ESTÉS en esas condiciones!**
  It's a shame you're in such bad shape!

Grammar Hints

Temo que . . .
— I'm afraid (that) . . .

- **Temo que SEA muy tarde.**
  I'm afraid it might be too late.

Espero que . . . ; ojalá que . . .
— I hope (that) . . .

- **Esperamos que ustedes TENGAN un feliz año.**
  We hope you have a happy year.

Me sorprende que . . .
— I'm surprised (that) . . .

- **Me va a sorprender mucho que LLEGUEN a tiempo.**
  I'm going to be very much surprised if they arrive on time.

In the indirect or implied command.

- **Quiero que todos VAYAN a mi casa.**
  I want everybody to go to my house.
- **Te suplico que me CONTESTES.**
  I beg you to answer me.
- **No permito que me HABLEN así.**
  I do not allow people to speak to me in that manner.

If one of the following verbs is used in the main clause and involves an indirect or implied command, and is followed by **que**:

Decir que . . .
— To say/tell that . . .

- **Le dijo a Oscar que se FUERA.**
  She told Oscar to leave.

Ordenar que . . .
— To order that . . .

- **El general les ordenó que ATACARAN.**
  The general ordered them to attack.

Mandar que . . .
— To order that . . .

- **Ella me mandó que me FUERA.**
  She ordered me to leave.

Grammar Hints

Pedir que . . .

— To ask that . . .

- **No hemos pedido que nos TRAIGAN el coche.**
  We have not asked for the car.

Rogar que . . .

— To beg ☺ to + verb

- **Le ruego que me ESCUCHE.**
  I beg you to listen to me.

Querer que . . .

— To want ☺ to + verb

- **Mi padre no quiere que nos VAYAMOS.**
  My father does not want us to go.

After the following expressions:

Conviene que . . . ; es conveniente que . . .

— It is advisable that . . . ; ☺ had better . . .

- **Conviene que LEAS esto.**
  You had better read this.

Es preferible que

— It is preferable that . . . ; ☺ had better . . .

- **Es preferible que no VENGAS.**
  You had better not come.

Es mejor que

— It is better that . . . ; ☺ had better . . .

- **Es mejor que DEVUELVAN el dinero.**
  They had better return the money.

Más vale que . . .

— It would better; ☺ had better . . .

- **Más vale que ESPEREMOS.**
  We had better wait.

Urge que . . . ; es urgente que . . .

— It is urgent that . . .

- **Urge que me TRAIGAS los papeles.**
  It is urgent that you bring me the papers.

Grammar Hints

Es importante que . . .
— It is important that . . .

- **Es importante que se ENTREGUEN los documentos a tiempo.**
  It is important that the documents be delivered on time.

When the subordinate clause precedes the main clause and begins with **que** or **el que**.

- **Que tú ESTÉS aquí no es culpa de ellos.**
  The fact that you are here is not their fault.
- **El que no VENGAN es increíble.**
  Their not coming is incredible (unbelievable).

1. Simple Tenses

Present

The present subjunctive is formed by adding the endings **e, es, e, emos, en, en** to the stem of the first-person singular of the present indicative of verbs ending in **AR**; by adding **a, as, a, amos, an, an** to the stem of the first-person singular of verbs ending in **ER**; by adding **a, as, a, amos, an, an** to those ending in **IR**.

	CANTAR	COMER	SUBIR
que yo	cante	coma	suba
que tú	cantes	comas	subas
que él o ella	cante	coma	suba
que nosotros	cantemos	comamos	subamos
que ustedes	canten	coman	suban
que ellos	canten	coman	suban

Imperfect Tense

The imperfect subjunctive has two forms. The most commonly used form adds **ara, aras, ara, aramos, aran, aran** to the stem of the third-person plural of the preterite indicative of verbs ending in **AR**; and **iera, ieras, iera, ieramos, ieran, ieran** to the stem of third-person plural of the preterite indicative of verbs ending in **ER** and **IR**.

	CANTAR	COMER	ESCRIBIR
que yo	cantara	comiera	escribiera
que tú	cantaras	comieras	escribieras
que él o ella	cantara	comiera	escribiera
que nosotros	cantáramos	comiéramos	escribiéramos
que ustedes	cantaran	comieran	escribieran
que ellos	cantaran	comieran	escribieran

The second form is sometimes used in written Spanish, but is hardly ever heard in everyday Spanish anymore, and most students will be able to get through life quite comfortably without ever running into it or being called upon to use it. However, for purposes of information, **ase, ases, asemos, asen, asen** are added to the stem of the third-person plural of verbs ending in **AR; iese, ieses, iese, iesemos, iesen** are added to the stem of the third-person plural of verbs ending in **ER** and **IR**, thus:

	HABLAR	VENDER	SUBIR
que yo	hablase	vendiese	subiese
que tú	hablases	vendieses	subieses
que él o ella	hablase	vendiese	subiese
que nosotros	hablásemos	vendiésemos	subiésemos
que ustedes	hablasen	vendiesen	subiesen
que ellos	hablasen	vendiesen	subiesen

2. Compound Tenses

As in the case of most compound tenses, those of the subjunctive are formed by conjugating the auxiliary verb **HABER** in the corresponding tense, and then adding the past participle, which carries the meaning.

For the present perfect subjunctive, the present subjunctive of **HABER** is placed before the past participle of the main verb.

	HABLAR	COMER	ESCRIBIR
que yo	haya hablado	haya comido	haya escrito
que tú	hayas hablado	hayas comido	hayas escrito
que él	haya hablado	haya comido	haya escrito
que nosotros	hayamos hablado	hayamos comido	hayamos escrito
que ustedes	hayan hablado	hayan comido	hayan escrito
que ellos	hayan hablado	hayan comido	hayan escrito

3. Pluperfect Subjunctive

For the pluperfect subjunctive, the imperfect subjunctive of **HABER** is used. Below is the commonly used form, followed by the practically-never-heard form.

	HABLAR	COMER	ESCRIBIR
que yo	hubiera hablado	hubiera comido	hubiera escrito
que tú	hubieras hablado	hubieras comido	hubieras escrito
que él	hubiera hablado	hubiera comido	hubiera escrito
que nosotros	hubiéramos hablado	hubiéramos comido	hubiéramos escrito
que ustedes	hubieran hablado	hubieran comido	hubieran escrito
que ellos	hubieran hablado	hubieran comido	hubieran escrito

	HABLAR	COMER	ESCRIBIR
que yo	hubiese hablado	hubiese comido	hubiese escrito
que tú	hubieses hablado	hubieses comido	hubieses escrito
que él	hubiese hablado	hubiese comido	hubiese escrito
que nosotros	hubiésemos hablado	hubiésemos comido	hubiésemos escrito
que ustedes	hubiesen hablado	hubiesen comido	hubiesen escrito
que ellos	hubiesen hablado	hubiesen comido	hubiesen escrito

A good way to discover the right forms:

For the present subjunctive, ask yourself in Spanish, for instance **¿Es necesario que yo VAYA?** (Is it necessary that I go?), **¿Es necesario que yo COMA, que yo TENGA, que yo ESPERE . . . ?** etc. (Is it necessary that I eat, that I have, that I wait?).

For the past subjunctive, ask yourself: **¿Era necesario que yo . . . ?** and add the form that would come to your mind with a little practice: **¿Era necesario que yo ESCRIBIERA, TUVIERA, COMIERA?**

The future subjunctive expresses the fact or act as contingent: **Si FUERE necesario, se hará** (*Should it be necessary, it will be done*). **Si VINIERE, háblenle** (*If he should come, speak to him*). This tense is practically never used in the spoken language, and little in the written language. The present indicative is generally used instead: **Si viene, háblenle** (instead of the subjunctive **VINIERE**).

Grammar Hints

Exercise A

Translate the following sentences.

1. Nuestra maestra quiere que aprendamos el subjuntivo.

2. El presidente manda que paguemos los impuestos.

3. La mamá de María no le permitirá que vaya.

4. Me dijo que sentía que yo hubiera estado enfermo.

5. Espero que ustedes aprendan buen español.

6. Los alumnos se alegraron de que el profesor les diera el día libre.

7. Es una lástima que no hayan comprado la casa.

8. ¡Ojalá puedan hacer el viaje!

9. Es probable que sí lo hagan.

10. ¡Ojalá cese la guerra!

11. Ella no quiere que la vea su mamá aquí.

12. Es una lástima que no hayan podido asistir al concierto.

13. Quiero que comas esa fruta.

14. Mi hermano quería que fuéramos al cine hoy.

15. El niño tenía miedo de que se perdiera su pelota.

16. Debieron venir antes de que Enrique se fuera.

17. Hubiéramos ido con mucho gusto.

18. Deseo que pases un feliz cumpleaños.

19. ¡Que tengas un feliz año nuevo!

20. Me sorprende que no hayan venido.

21. Es increíble que tarden tanto en llegar.

Grammar Hints

22.   Sería penoso que te viera en esas fachas.

23.   ¿Crees que venga? Espero que sí venga, pero dudo que lo haga.

24.   Salieron sin que los viera el policía.

25.   Es preciso que lo tomes con calma.

26.   Es necesario que compres un coche nuevo.

27.   No creo que le den el empleo.

28.   Es difícil que lleguen a tiempo.

Exercise B

Translate the following sentences. Check the translation on the following page.

1. Don't believe everything you hear.

2. The business may have failed.

3. They will wait until we go.

4. They would have waited until we arrived, if they had known.

5. We are leaving next week, unless there is too much work to do.

6. The plane will land at 6:00, unless the weather is bad.

7. The children would go to the park, if they were given permission.

8. Would you go back to France if you had the opportunity?

9. I would go gladly, but I would prefer to visit another country.

10. If she had asked you, would you have told her the truth?

11. Mr. López would have closed the deal if he had had the money.

12. I doubt that he left when he said he did.

13. I am surprised this political party has remained in power for so long.

14. We don't want you to sell that property.

15. He promised to do what he could for her.

Answers to Exercise A

1. Our teacher wants us to learn the subjunctive.
2. The president orders that we pay taxes.
3. Mary's mother will not allow her to go.
4. He (she) told me that he (she) was sorry that I had been ill.
5. I hope you learn correct Spanish.
6. The students were glad that the professor allowed them a free day.
7. It's a pity that they did not buy the house.
8. I hope they can make the trip.
9. They will probably do that.
10. I hope the war comes to an end.
11. She doesn't want her mother to see her here.
12. It's a pity they couldn't attend the concert.
13. I want you to eat that fruit.
14. My brother wanted us to go the movies today.
15. The child was afraid that his ball would be lost.
16. They should have come before Enrique left.
17. We would have gone gladly.
18. I hope you have a happy birthday.
19. May you have a happy new year!
20. I am surprised that they have not come.
21. It's unbelievable that they are taking so long to arrive.
22. It would be a shame if he saw you in those clothes.
23. Do you believe he will come? I hope he does, but I doubt it.
24. They left without the policeman seeing them.
25. You must take it easy.
26. You need to buy a new car.
27. I don't believe they will give him the job.
28. It is unlikely that they will arrive on time.

Grammar Hints

Answers to Exercise B

1. No crea todo lo que oye. (No creas todo lo que oyes.)
2. Es posible que el negocio haya fracasado.
3. Esperarán hasta que nosotros nos vayamos.
4. Habrían esperado hasta que llegáramos, si hubieran sabido.
5. Saldremos la semana entrante, a menos que haya exceso de trabajo.
6. El avión aterrizará a las 6:00, a menos que haya mal tiempo.
7. Los niños irían al parque si les dieran permiso.
8. ¿Volvería usted a Francia si tuviera la oportunidad? (¿Volverías a Francia si tuvieras la oportunidad?)
9. Iría con gusto, pero preferiría visitar otro país.
10. Si ella le hubiera preguntado, ¿le habría dicho usted la verdad? (¿Si ella te hubiera preguntado, ¿le habrías dicho la verdad?)
11. El Sr. López habría cerrado el trato si hubiera tenido el dinero.
12. Dudo que se fuera cuando dijo.
13. Me extraña que este partido haya durado tanto en el poder.
14. No quisiéramos que vendieras esa propiedad.
15. Prometió hacer lo que pudiera por ella.

V

LIVING IN MEXICO

A. Polite Phrases

---

1. Introductions

If you must introduce two people, you address the most important one first; failing that, the eldest one. If neither importance nor age is a factor, then address a lady rather than a man. If both introductees are of the same importance, age and sex, then address the person who is less well known to you.

Let's assume that you must introduce Juan to Mrs. Martinez (the latter being a person of considerable hierarchy, for whatever reason).

You turn to her and say:

- **Sra. Martínez, permítame presentarle a mi amigo (colega, compañero de clase**, or whatever**) Juan.**

You then turn to Juan and say:

- **Juan, la Sra. Martínez . . .** (and if necessary, you explain who Mrs. Martinez is).

There are more elaborate ways of introducing people formally, but elaborateness is beloved of uneducated people. Better-educated ones are dropping formality because looking and acting more at ease makes them seem more confident and sure of themselves. So the speaker of Spanish as a second language will do well to stay cool and keep it simple (but *polite*).

If the situation is not so formal, and you must introduce two people in a business or social situation, you turn to the one you have decided deserves more deference and say:

- **Sr. Camacho, le presento a Jorge Ortíz . . .**

. . . and you add whatever is appropriate in the way of identification; but keep it short so you can also turn to the other person and say:

- **Jorge, el Sr. Camacho**

. . . so that Jorge can shake hands and say the equivalent of *How do you do?* or words to that effect.

In a very informal, social situation, where last names don't count, you might just say:

- **Arturo, éste es Pancho**

. . . and leave it at that.

Latin Americans almost always shake hands. Touching doesn't make anyone nervous south of the Rio Grande (which of course is the **Río Bravo** to Latins) as long as the touching in question is from the catalog of standard, clear-cut movements known to all.

If you are being introduced, you can say:

- **Mucho gusto** or **Encantado(a).**
  Nice to meet you; Pleased to meet you; How do you do?

Encantado(a) doesn't sound affected like *charmed* or *enchanted* in English. It is normally used by ladies, in which case it would be **encantada**, or by men when meeting a lady, but it is perfectly fine for anyone to use anywhere.

- **Es un placer** (*It's a pleasure*) (a tiny bit stiff).

- **¿Cómo está usted?** or **¿Cómo estás?** (*How are you?*)

Of course you don't normally use **tú** with someone you're only just meeting, except when the person you're meeting is a child, or is a young person of your own age.

Those are the usual responses, but you may also hear phrases like:

- **¡Hola!**
  Hi!

- **¡Quihubo!**
  How ya doing!

- **¡Qué onda!**
  What's up!, etc.

Hola is OK as a greeting once you have already met someone, as long as the relationship is fairly informal. The other two are slang and best left to native speakers, unless you consider yourself a real pro.

2. Greetings

With all the following expressions, it is up to you whether to use them in the **tú** or the **usted** form. Once you have met a person, or once you already know someone, saying *Hello!* or *Hi!* goes like this:

People you are not friendly with but must greet:

- **¡Buenos días!**
  Good morning!

- **¡Buenas tardes!**
  Good afternoon!

- **¡Buenas noches!**
  Good evening! Good night!

Once you have greeted someone on a particular day, you can't keep saying **¡Buenos días!** or any of the above greetings every time you run into him or her (at school or office or some other place where you're likely to keep seeing the same people over and over), so you just say **¡Hola!** to your Latin American friends or friendly acquaintances; they feel hurt if you don't at least nod or smile or wave or acknowledge their presence in some way when you meet by chance. You could also say:

- **¿Qué tal?** (familiar)

- **¿Qué hubo?** (very familiar, pronounced **Quiubo**) or

- **¿Qué húbole?** (also very familiar, pronounced **Quiúbole**)

A lot of people in Mexico will say **¡Hola!, ¿Cómo estás?** (*How are you?*), which is not really practical if you're just saying Hi! in passing, because if you say **Bien, gracias** (*Fine, thanks*, the standard response) you feel it's only decent to say **¿Y tú?** (*And how are you?*), which means you either have to stop and take this exchange of pleasantries through to a natural conclusion, or raise your voice quite a lot so you can hear each other across the distance you have covered by the time you get to the end of all this exchange of information.

In the case of someone you haven't seen for quite some time, you could say:

- **¡Tanto gusto de verlo(a) (verte)!**
  So nice to see you!

3. Leave-taking

On taking leave of a person or place, **¡Adiós!** is usually used if you are not returning or if you plan to be away for some time (taking a trip perhaps). If you'll be back the next day, the usual phrase is **¡Hasta mañana!**, although you can say **¡Buenas noches!** if the sun has gone down. If you have six hours before you have to leave for the airport, you will hear: **¡Que descanses!** (Have a good rest!), or else if you have a Spanish speaking guest at home, you can say: **Yo apago la luz. ¡Que duermas bien!** (I'll turn the light out as I leave. Sleep well!).

¡Adiós! is sometimes used to greet someone you bump into in the street but are not going to stop to chat with. If you see the person in question only occasionally, you say **¡Hasta pronto!** when taking your leave. **¡Hasta luego!** is used only when you are pretty sure you'll be seeing this person again the same day, so don't use it when saying good bye for the day or for good.

¡Hasta la vista! is not used nearly as much as movies and television films about Latins would have you believe, but **¡Hasta la próxima!** is common when leaving any periodic or regularly scheduled event at which people get together for an specific purpose, such as a Rotary meeting or choir practice.

¡Nos vemos! is used familiarly only, but it is a good, standard sort of goodbye, because it doesn't imply anything except that you (or the other person) is leaving. You can also use this in response to a person who says goodbye, to avoid always repeating the same thing the other person says (as long as it's an informal leave-taking; it can't be said to anyone you would consider an **usted**, or whom you don't know well).

If you are leaving a social gathering, any of the above is OK to use on friends or acquaintances. If you're taking your leave from someone you just met on a not so informal occasion and you didn't get a chance to get too friendly with, you'll have to be a little more formal and say something like **Ha sido un placer** or **Tuve mucho gusto en conocerlo.**

¡Que te (le) vaya bien! (*May things go well with you*) is a pleasant reply to anyone saying goodbye in any circumstances (except when it's goodbye for good).

4. Other Politenesses

If you want to ask someone for something (the salt, some keys, a signature, etc.) the standard phrase is: **¿Lo (la) molesto con las llaves** (or whatever)**?**, which sounds like *Shall I molest you with the keys?* but of course just means *Would you be kind enough to give me the keys?* You can also use **¿Me permite las llaves por favor?** If the situation is quite formal, a person could say for example: **Tenga la bondad de firmar aquí** (*Please be kind enough to sign here*).

— Then the other person (upon doing whatever it is he/she is being requested to do) will say:

- **No es molestia.**
  It's no bother

- **Con gusto.**
  With pleasure

- **Aquí tiene** (when handing you □).
  Here you are.

- **Claro que sí.**
  Of course.

- **Por supuesto.**
  Of course.

- **¡Cómo no!**
  Naturally!

To thank someone, you can say **¡Gracias! ¡Muchas gracias! ¡Muchísimas gracias! ¡Mil gracias! ¡Muy agradecido! ¡Le agradezco mucho** (or **muchísimo**)**!** depending on the degree of gratitude involved.

The person being thanked usually says:

— Standard:

- **¡De nada!**

- **¡No hay de qué!**

- **¡No tiene por qué!**

— Formal:

- **¡Es un placer!**

- **¡A sus órdenes!**

When someone offers to help you, opens the door for you, picks up something you dropped or does something of that sort, you would ordinarily say: **No se moleste** (*Don't bother*)**.** The other person normally replies **No es molestia** (*It's no bother*); you can then say *thank you* in any of the ways listed above.

In a situation where you need to say something like *Please allow me . . .* you would say: **Perdón** (*Sorry*). This, of course, is used as an apology. However, it is very common to hear it before a question, as in **Perdón, ¿qué calle es ésta?** (*Excuse me. What street is this?*), in which case **Perdón** is included as an apology for inconveniencing or interrupting someone.

Other common apologies are:

- **Lo siento.**
- **Lo siento mucho.**
- **Disculpe.**

Replies to an apology would be:

- **No tiene por qué disculparse.**
- **No tenga cuidado.**
- **No se preocupe.**
- **No hay por qué.**

If someone calls you from another room, you say **¡Voy!** (📖 I'm going, meaning: *Coming!*). Face to face you say **¡Diga!** or **¡Dígame!** (*What can I do for you?*). Lower class and old fashioned people say **¡Mande!** (*Order me!*) at a distance or close up.

The usual toast when having a drink is **¡Salud!** (*Cheers! To your health!*) It is also used when someone sneezes.

B. Modes of Address

Always address a woman as **Señorita**, unless you know that she is married, in which case say **Señora**. Market and street vendors, as well as servants, often shorten the word to **Seño**.

In Spain, young men are sometimes addressed as **Señorito,** while in Mexico the word **Joven** is the most commonly used. **Jovenazo** is a slang form used quite a lot by waiters in low-price cafes and bars. A man, regardless of his age, may be addressed as **Señor** or **Caballero**, the latter being very formal.

In Spanish a gentleman may say **mi esposa, mi señora** or **mi mujer** when speaking of his wife, and **su esposa**, **su señora** or **su mujer** when referring to someone else's wife. A lady would refer to her husband only as **mi esposo** or **mi marido**. In some areas of Mexico, she would refer to him as **mi señor**. When speaking of someone else's husband, she would say **su esposo** or **su marido**.

Servants usually refer to the people they work for as: **la señora, el señor, el joven** and **la señorita** or **la niña**. **La niña** is sometimes used to refer to the daughter of the family, regardless of her age.

A physician is addressed as **Doctor**, which is sometimes shortened to **Doc**, when the physician is a friend. **Doctorcito** is used by people of the lower classes. An attorney is formally addressed as **señor licenciado, abogado** or simply **licenciado**. In a friendly relationship, he may be called **Lic** (pronounced *leek*).

Ingeniero or **señor ingeniero** are used when addressing an engineer; and **arquitecto** or **señor arquitecto** for an architect. When writing, **ingeniero** is shortened to **Ing.** and **arquitecto** to **Arq.** Recently, the people working for them have shortened these words to **Inge** (En-he) and **Arqui** (Ar-ki), but only when speaking.

The feminine of **doctor** is **doctora**; of **arquitecto**, **arquitecta**; of **abogado** and **licenciado**, **abogada** and **licenciada**; of **ingeniero**, **ingeniera**.

Political officials are addressed much as in English: **Señor Presidente**, **Señora Presidenta**; **Señor Gobernador**, **Señorita (Señora) Gobernadora**; **Señor Senador**, **Señorita (Señora) Senadora**; **Señor Diputado**, **Señorita (Señora) Diputada**; **Señor Juez**, **Señorita (Señora) Juez**. In the case of the military, the possessive pronoun "my" is usually placed before the rank: **mi general**, **mi coronel** and **mi capitán**.

The clergy:

Su Santidad for the Pope

Su Eminencia for a cardinal

Su Excelencia for a bishop or archbishop

Su Reverencia is used by nuns and priests among themselves

Reverenda Madre addressing a mother superior or prioress

Sor, hermana addressing a nun or sister

Padre addressing a priest or father

Maestro, which means master or teacher, is used to denote respect for talent and learning. A distinguished painter, musician, architect, writer, physician, and so on, is often addressed this way. In Mexico, this is also used to address artisans and workers such as plumbers, carpenters, electricians, and so on. It is quite common to hear them called **maestro** and referred to as **el maestro López**, **el maestro carpintero**, and so on. In this case the word is often pronounced **máistro**.

Profesor is often shortened to **Profe**, but the feminine **Profesora** is not shortened.

Don and **Doña** are used to denote respect and are placed before the first name or the full name. You may address or refer to **Tomás Bravo** as **Don Tomás** or as **Don Tomás Bravo**, but not as **Don Bravo** although in some regions of Mexico this is commonly used as a respectful way to address someone (in southern Veracruz you will hear **Don García**). The same holds true for the feminine **Doña**, regardless of whether she is a married or an unmarried woman. **María Martínez** may be called **Doña María** or **Doña María Martínez**; **Ana Robles de Guzmán** is **Doña Ana** or **Doña Ana Robles de Guzmán**.

C. On the Telephone

On answering the telephone, you may say:
- **¿Bueno?; (¿Diga?); (¿Sí..?); (Aló)**

Sometimes the person answering the telephone may say:
- **Casa del Sr. Martínez . . . (Casa del Dr. Bravo).**

It is common (although discourteous) for the person calling to ask:
- **¿Con quién hablo?**
  Who is speaking?

A more polite way is:
- **¿Con quién tengo el gusto?**
  May I know to whom I have the pleasure of speaking?

A better way may be:
- **Habla la señorita Muñoz. ¿Está la señora Robles?**
  This is Miss Muñoz speaking. Is Mrs. Robles at home?

If the caller doesn't identify him or herself, the person answering the telephone would ask:
- **¿De parte de quién?**
  Who is calling? or May I say who is calling?

If the person called is not available, the person answering the telephone would say:
- **No está (en este momento) ¿Gusta dejar algún recado?**
  He's not in. Do you want to leave a message?

Although, you will sometimes hear the <u>incorrect</u> forms:
- **No se encuentra**
  She's not in.
- **¿Quiere dejar un mensaje?**
  Do you want to leave a message? (anglicism).

The person calling might then ask:
- **¿A qué hora la encuentro? (¿A qué hora la espera?)**
  When should I call back? (When do you expect her?)
- **¿Puedo dejar un recado?**
  May I leave a message?

If you get a wrong number, you will be told:
- **Está equivocado.**
  Wrong number.

You then proceed to apologize:
- **Usted perdone. (Disculpe.)**
  I'm sorry.

because of real or imaginary allergies. Organized animal hunting, which has been difficult to eradicate, is an old British custom and fishing continues to be a "civilized" habit throughout the world.

However, foreigners are horrified in Latin America when they see famished street dogs, who are mistreated by everyone and either succumb to disease or meet their death under the wheels of a vehicle of some sort. These people are also offended at the sight of a watch dog stuck on a rooftop to do his duty by barking at strangers, or chained up all day to be set loose only at night.

They are also scandalized by the idea of bullfights, although a lot of them make sure they get ringside seats, so they can comfortably faint on the next person's shoulder the minute the blood starts to flow.

All of these are cultural issues. They have nothing to do with social strata or with levels of education. It is not unusual to see a wealthy man from the right side of the tracks shamelessly kicking a dog, or a beggar sharing his pitiful scraps of food with a street dog.

If you feel offended by the Latin American treatment of animals, try not to make it a personal crusade, which would be futile. Attitudes are changing and the situation will without a doubt improve.

3. Manners Matter

Manners are as important in Latin American as in any other part of the world, except that the former have certain peculiarities. An English-speaking tourist finds Latin saccharin politeness annoying the same way that a Spanish-speaking person feels resentful of the bluntness and harshness with which people treat each other in the rest of the world. Parisians are famous for their rudeness, just as Latin Americans are famous for being polite.

When in Rome, do as the Romans do, and if you want to fit in and be accepted, it is important to remember the following:

— Say **por favor** when asking for things or services, and if possible, work in a smile.

— Say **gracias** in a polite way once you have received what you asked for.

4. ¡Buen Provecho!

People wish each other **Buen provecho** before, during or after a meal (mostly the noonday meal). It is the equivalent of the French (Bon appétit) . . . an old fashioned politeness. The reply is **Gracias. Igualmente**.

Living in Mexico

5. Meal Times

Mealtimes are rather different in Mexico (and Spain) from what they are in other countries. Breakfast, of course, is eaten before going to work, as best as anyone can, but lunch, which is the heavy meal of the day (because digestion is difficult at night at certain altitudes, especially Mexico City) is usually from 2:00 to 3:00.

Among office people, the later you go out to lunch and longer you linger over it, the more important you are in the office hierarchy. As for supper, most people, except maybe the kiddies, wouldn't think of eating anything at 6:00. Supper comes at least a couple of hours later, when all the members of the family have arrived home for the day. However, meals can be had at any time of the day (and most of the night) at fast service eating places, where no one thinks ill of anyone's eating habits.

6. El Abrazo

The **abrazo** is universal. It is a means of expressing congratulations or affection. The warm Latin **abrazo**, perhaps originating in Spain, is an everyday occurrence, most particularly at birthdays, weddings, graduations and funerals. In Mexico, friends embrace each other whenever they meet after a few days of not seeing each other. People embrace all their friends and acquaintances (sometimes dozens and dozens of them) when wishing them a happy new year.

7. Dress

Conventions as concerns dress have changed throughout the world. Tourists distinguish themselves everywhere by the way they dress. If you are a tourist in Latin America, by all means wear sneakers to walk all day, but wear shoes for dinner, and a tie if the place is formal. You and those around you will feel better.

Proper dress (all the time, not just at dinner) is a sign of respect for others, and a way of earning respect back in return. Shorts, bare skin and loud skirts, except at tourist resorts, cannot lead to anything good.

8. ¡Planta Baja!, Por Favor

If you get onto one of the few manned elevators left and ask for the first floor when what you really mean is the ground floor, you will have to take the stairs down from what for English speakers is the second floor. In Latin America, the ground floor is the **planta baja** (marked **PB**) and the floor above that is the first floor. Also, since 13 is not an unlucky number in Latin America, numbers don't jump from 12 to 14.

In a house, the ground floor is the **planta baja**, and the upper floor is the **planta alta**.

9. Say It with Your Hands

There is a worldwide language of the hands, sometimes exclusive to countries or regions, sometimes shared internationally. Specialists such as Desmond Morris have reported on the ample repertoire of hand expressions worldwide.

One that you see all the time in Mexico is the right hand held up in front of your face, palm towards you, and moved a few inches away and towards you again several times in quick succession. This means "thank you" and is very commonly used in situations where a verbal thank you is not feasible, and even sometimes when a person is within earshot. It also means "no, thank you" when something is being offered that you do not wish to accept. Another is the gesture used to show the height of an animal; this is done not with the palm facing down, but perpendicular to the ground. However, to show the height of a child, the palm faces down.

10. The Greasing of the Palm

La mordida, the bite, bribery (part of the worldwide epidemic) is very much a part of everyday life in Latin America. Some things can't be done without it. In fact, although people realize it is basically "not right", it is simply taken for granted in many situations. So, what are the situations in which it's better just to grease a palm, or a few palms, than to get involved in a never-ending morass of procedures that only lead to a dead-end? Well, that is somewhat subjective, but if you are stopped for some real or imaginary traffic violation, everyone knows that you pull out a bill and discreetly slip it in with your license as you hand it to the cop, if you don't want to get stuck in a non-stop argument designed to exasperate you to the point where you'll give in and pay him off anyway.

A bribe is sometimes called for to streamline any kind of government or official procedure, such as the issuance of a building permit, arranging an electricity contract, getting a telephone line to work properly, securing a driver's license, and so on.

Living in Mexico

¿Cómo lo podemos arreglar? is the cue for the person posing the difficulty to name his/her price as to how the impasse can be overcome or the procedure expedited.

However, it takes some experience and skill to carry this off properly, and a failed attempt at bribery can be very nasty, so your best bet is to arrange for a native friend or contact of some kind to handle this sort of thing. Always find out from a native how a particular situation should be handled before taking things into your own hands.

11. ¡Compadre!

The **compadre** and the **comadre** are a time-honored institution. The greatest honor a person can do a friend is to ask him or her to be his child's godparent. The person who is receiving the honor feels immensely gratified, and those two persons are henceforth **compadres** or **comadres** or a combination thereof. The name bestows special standing to a person and it is assumed that the **comadres** or **compadres** will be bosom buddies forever (they probably have been since childhood).

The compadre of the parent of the child is the child's **padrino** or **madrina**, and the child is the **padrino** or **madrina**'s **ahijado** or **ahijada**, which is also a very strong bond, as it is said: **a falta de padre, padrino** (*if you have no father, a godfather is the next best thing*). People who are **compadres** and **comadres** call each other by those names.

12. Bargaining

Bargaining, which is an international custom, is another thing that is expected in many places. Unless the price of a thing or a service is formally or officially established on a price list or price tag, bargaining is de rigueur, especially when dealing with market vendors, artisans or any kind of home maintenance people such as plumbers, carpenters, electricians, and so on. If you don't at least give it a stab, you are considered rather dim, so don't just take the first price quoted as the last word. It is a good idea to get to know the standard price of different items that are important in your life, and use them as a reference so that you'll know how hard to bargain without going too far and being insulting. On the other hand, remember that once you let a person overcharge you and get away with it, he or she will not only continue to do so (on an escalating scale), but the word could get out to other people with whom you must deal, and everyone else will try to overcharge you as well.

Although bargaining is not applicable at the professional level (doctors, lawyers, dentist, architects, etc.), knowing market prices will help you to ensure that you are not dealing with unscrupulous professionals.

Living in Mexico

13. Measurements

Since there is no world system of weights and measures, any traveler must become familiar with the system used in the country visited. All of Latin America uses the metric system, and always has. To speak of acres, yards, quarts, miles or pounds can give rise to confusion similar to that which would arise if a Spanish speaker used terms such as "a kilometer", "two kilos", and so on in the United States. Basic equivalencies are as follows:

a. Length	
1 centimeter	0.3937 inch
1 meter	1.0936 yards (almost the same)
1 kilometer	0.6214 mile

b. Area	
1 square meter	10.764 square feet or
	1.196 square yards
1 square kilometer	0.386 square mile
1 hectare	2.471 acres
1 liter	1.0567 U.S. liquid quarts

c. Mass or Weight	
1 gram	0.0322 troy ounce
1 kilogram	2.2046 pounds
1 metric ton	2,204.6 pounds

14. Surnames

As most people know, Latin Americans have two surnames: the father's family name and the mother's maiden surname. So, if your name is Robert, your father's surname is Weston and your mother's maiden name was Brown, your official name in Latin America is Robert Weston Brown (whether you like it or not). This is used on all official documents, such as passport, license, correspondence, and so on.

Informally, many people just use their name and one surname (their father's), as people do in English speaking countries, but a lot of people use both surnames, especially when the second is less mundane or common than the first. For example, **Pedro Pérez Borbón** will probably always use both surnames, because **Pedro Pérez** sounds so very ordinary (while **Borbón** has a distinctly aristocratic ring to it), aside from which, the second surname helps to place and distinguish him from other people whose first surname is **Pérez**. The important thing for the foreigner to remember is not to refer to **Pedro Pérez Borbón** as **Sr. Pérez** or **Sr. Borbón**. The custom is to use these as compound surnames, as those of Mexican Presidents **López Mateos** and **Díaz Ordaz**.

Living in Mexico

And talking of surnames, these are not pluralized in Spanish. You do not speak of a couple called "**los Merinos**", but "**los Merino**".

15. ¿Tú or Usted?

Choosing between **tú** and **usted** to address people has always been a problem for English speaking foreigners, but it need not be. Generally speaking, everyone except a bosom pal is spoken to as **usted**. It is considered socially unacceptable to use **tú** to someone who has not invited you or given you permission to do so. Amongst Latins, the older person is the one who says: **Háblame de tú** (or **No me hables de usted**). If you are the older person, someone might ask: **¿Puedo hablarle de tú?,** which more or less forces you to agree, but not necessarily. So, to keep things simple and manageable, just use **usted** on everyone, except intimate friends. If a person uses **tú** on you when you have not invited him/her to do so, just continue to speak to that person with **usted** and pretend you haven't noticed that he/she is getting overly familiar. It is important to point out that it is now very common to use **tú** right from the start, especially among young people.

Perhaps the most difficult part of this is the conjugations. Just remember that verbs used with **tú** in the present tense end in **S**, while those used with usted do not. This is also true of the auxiliary verbs used with future (**vas/va**), present perfect (**has/ha**), present progressive (**estás/está**), past progressive (**estabas/estaba**), as well as simple future (**tomarás/tomará**), etc.

16. Driving

Large Mexican cities (Mexico City, Guadalajara, Monterrey), and even the smaller ones (like Puebla, Cuernavaca or Xalapa), are different regarding driving. Do not take anything for granted while behind the wheel south of the Rio Bravo. When you have a green light, make sure to look carefully before going ahead and taking the intersection, as it is part of driving reality in Mexico that cars keep going through a light for several seconds after it has turned red, on the supposition that the cars getting the green light will take a while to start up and get going. This is sometimes carried to extremes at large intersections, so don't just look at the light… look at what might hit you.

When it's a question of yielding, some people will let you go first, but a lot won't, and if you don't push your way through, the people behind you will get upheaved about you holding up the flow of traffic. The trick is to look as though you don't see the guy you're about to collide with (look a little dumb perhaps) and just go (while actually checking things out of the corner of your eye or the side of your head). Of course, other people use this tactic too, so it takes a lot of nerve. Be ready to slam the breaks on.

Caution is also called for on highways, where you must remember that some drivers make up their own rules and are capable of some very strange moves without ever realizing they are doing anything wrong.

Should you have an incident with another driver, never argue. In many countries, an argument may just involve a lot of vociferous sabre rattling, but in Mexico, people can get carried away and become violent, so it might be advisable to assume an expression denoting that you are confused and don't want a fight.

17. Christmas

Christmas in Latin America is losing more and more of its original flavor as the American commercial notion of Christmas is none too gently pushed down people's throats by every radio, TV, magazine and newspaper in the land. And since Latins in general are eager to embrace American style modernity and consumerism in their effort to put the "old ways" behind them and imitate the habits of the "first world", Christmas trees and jingle bells, Santa Claus and his sled and reindeer, lots of artificial snow, all the English carols and all kinds of other alien and little understood symbols are becoming the norm… replacing all the very colorful local Christmas customs which have come down through the ages. But the customs of one's ancestors are passed down in the genes, and in spite of all these foreign imports, Christmas is still very different from what it is in northern countries.

In Mexico, Christmas season begins on December 16 with the first **posada** (there is one every might up to December 24) which is supposed to be a kind of reenactment of Mary and Joseph seeking accommodation at different inns, being turned away and then finally being taken in and lodged in a stable. The script is set to music, with the people seeking admittance and those on the other side of the door denying it and then finally granting it (half the partygoers on one side and half on the other). The words are sung from memory or from printed cards. Once that has been done, there is a lot of drinking of **ponche** (from punch) (see *Mexican Food*), one or more **piñatas** are broken, and a very good time is had by all, although many people consider these festivities to be simply an excuse to drink too much. These **posadas** transcend all class lines, and can be seen and heard in open-air court yards from the poorest **barrios** to the poshest mansions and clubs.

Christmas itself is celebrated on Christmas Eve, not Christmas Day. Families generally gather at the home of the oldest generation for Christmas dinner. This traditionally consists of several courses such as fruit salad before the main attractions, usually **romeritos** (a green leafy affair in **mulato** chili sauce with shrimp fritters) or **balacao** (salt cod) preferably Norwegian (see *Mexican Food*). Although these two dishes are not particularly inexpensive to produce, especially the cod, which is imported and very pricey, people with a bit more money (or pretensions) than the average serve turkey, or a suckling pig (head and all), or a whole ham, and/or some other large and impressive cut of meat. All this is prepared not only for Christmas dinner, but in sufficient quantities to last for several days, since the **recalentado** (warmed-up leftovers) are even better than the main meal, and close friends and relatives who drop in with Christmas wishes usually expect to partake of these delights. Families with sufficient resources exchange gifts, wear evening clothes, drink fine wines and generally "do" Christmas in the European fashion.

The "**nacimiento**" is a representation of the nativity scene using small colored figures made of clay. The tradition of setting the **nacimiento** is slowly being lost. People have turned to Christmas trees and Santa Claus instead. The eve of January 6th, Mexicans traditionally celebrate the visit of **los Tres Reyes Magos** (the three wise men), by serving up the **rosca de reyes** (sweet bread in the form of a wreath) and hot chocolate. Kids expect presents both at Christmas (from baby Jesus or Santa) and on **Reyes**, brought by the three wise men.

18. The Mexican Attitude Towards Death

Mexicans are very concerned about death. They have coined not one, but many words for it. Possibly no other people in the world have the same idea of death. "In Mexico" —said Paul Westheim, the famous historian— "death is not the devilish adversary of man; it is presented as a good friend or as a pal with whom one may even joke around". This attitude seems to be the result of two traditional ideas about death, that of the natives and that of the Spaniards, with all the resulting philosophical and religious implications.

a. The concept of death in pre-Hispanic Mexico

According to specialists, in pre-Hispanic Mexico, death had a symbolic religious value. It represented a destructive power in one or another deity, as well as an individual's hope of becoming a sort of messenger sent to that deity and united to it by death.

This duality corresponds to a complete system of thought within which death represents rebirth. Such a concept helps to understand that for pre-Hispanic Mexicans, death by human sacrifice was a privilege. Fray Bernardino de Sahagún tells us of a theatrical performance among the Aztecs in which the actors played, the role of one of the gods in an almost mystic manner. At the climax, the dramatic fiction became reality when the actor was sent to join the god he was representing.

Theogenic dualism, as well as the idea of a future life more perfect than the present one, are elements that seem to lead to such familiarity with death that Westheim points out the possibility that the skull (so widely used by the natives as a decorative motif) "might actually be a symbol of life".

The indigenous heritage, not only of indifference, but of a certain wish to die "because death is the beginning of a new existence, the true one", seems a likely component of the psychological attitude towards death in the Mexico of today.

b. The concept of death in Spain

Our first thought would be that Spain represents the opposite of the common pre-Hispanic Mexican attitude towards death. Cultural and religious reasons would lead one to believe that the **mestizo**[1] of Mexico received, through his Spanish heritage, a fear of another world, based mostly on the idea of an inexorable God always ready to condemn for all eternity those who die without his friendship, which is guaranteed only by confession. However, we can extract eloquent testimonials, especially from

---

[1] The average Mexican of today; i.e., a mixture of indigenous and Spanish blood

literature (it must not be forgotten that literature is the most direct expression of popular feeling) of the Spaniards' attitude towards death, which, if not like the natives' indifference, does not conform to the terror implanted by a sometimes ignorant clergy. The Spaniards do not take death so seriously. The theatre of the Middle Ages included the famous *dances of death*, wherein the performer had a dialogue with Death in a performance not far removed from the burlesque. Again, in the *Romancero*, one finds examples of this type of camaraderie with death (Romance of the Man in love and Death) in which death warns the Man that his own death will occur soon, and the man replies in a very friendly informal tone:

¡Ay muerte tan rigorosa	*Oh, so rigorous death*
Déjame vivir un día!	*Let me live but one day!*

c. The Mexican approach to death

With these elements, perhaps too schematic, we may arrive at the conclusion that pre-Conquest Mexicans seem not to have known the fear of death, but looked upon it as an easy step from one life to another, and perhaps for this reason, in Mexico, even today, as poet Xavier Villaurrutia observed, "death is easily accepted, and the greater percentage of Indigenous blood coursing in our veins, the greater the acceptance".

How does the Spanish influence modify the indigenous indifference to death? Is there really such an indifference? Let us consider other points of view. According to Antonio Alatorre, the philologist "If the Mexican appears to strive to give the impression that he does not fear death, the very abundance of expressions and the continuing coining of new ones show that he is concerned with death".

What we might call the Mexican approach to death seems to correspond to a psychological complex wherein contradictory elements may be found: the indigenous indifference and the Spanish fear. We have already stated that neither of these attitudes is completely clear and unquestionable.

The fact is that the Mexican approach to death is something predominantly humorous. Whether this Mexican attitude is motivated by contempt or by just the opposite is uncertain. Octavio Paz holds that "in the Mexican's attitude there is perhaps as much fear as is shown by others", while Gaarder states "It is not that in Mexico there is not the fear of death found in other countries; on the contrary, the average Mexican will attribute these manifestations to an eagerness to convert the terror that the unknown inspires in him into a farce. From this viewpoint, one might believe that the Mexican today really laughs at death because it is expected of brave men, or that he tries to face death with courage, which he attempts to prove by a show of contempt".

Be that as it may, the Mexican approach to death is manifest in characteristic expressions peculiar to the Mexican people, and these expressions correspond to a philosophy belonging to the lowest social strata, as well as to the highest manifestations of art and culture. In popular songs and **corridos** we hear:

Yo no soy de los cobardes	*I'm not one of the cowards*
Que le temen a la muerte;	*Who fear death;*
La muerte no mata a nadie,	*Death doesn't kill anyone,*
La matadora es la suerte.	*The killer is Fate.*

Or again:

Si me han de matar mañana,	*If I'm to be killed tomorrow,*
¡Que me maten de una vez!	*Why not kill me right away?*

d. The idea of death as expressed by Mexicans today

Such an attitude gives rise to a popular vocabulary, at times vulgar, at others admirably philosophical, but always picturesque and interesting. We hope the following will help the student understand more fully the Mexican approach to death, as well as the varied vocabulary regarding it. As these expressions are very numerous, only the most commonly used are listed below, with a brief explanation as to their literal meaning.

— The following all mean *to die*:

- **Alzar** (or **colgar**) **los tenis** (📖 To lift up the tennis shoes)
- **Apagar(sele) el motor a** ☺   (📖 To have ☺´s motor die)
- **Azotar como chango viejo** (📖 To drop like an old monkey)
- **Cargar** (📖 To carry)
- **Cerrar los ojitos** (📖 To close the little eyes)
- **Chupar faros** (📖 To suck on **Faros**, a very inexpensive brand of cigarettes)
- **Clavar el pico** (📖 To lower or drop the beak)
- **Dar el changazo** (📖 To flop down like a monkey)
- **Dejar el pellejo** (📖 To leave your skin behind)
- **Desbielar(se)** (📖 To break down due to an overheated tie rod)
- **Doblar los remos** (📖 To fold the oars)
- **Enfriar(se)** or **quedar(se) frío** (📖 To become cold)
- **Entregar el equipo** (📖 To hand in the equipment)
- **Estirar la pata** (📖 To stretch out the paw)
- **Ir(se) al hoyo** (📖 To go into the hole)
- **Ir(se) al otro barrio** (📖 To go to the other neighborhood)

- **Levantar los huaraches** (📖 To lift up the **huaraches**)
- **Llevar(selo) patas de catre** (📖 To be taken away by cot legs)
- **Liar el petate** (📖 To fold up the **petate**)
- **Palmar**
- **Pelar(se)** (📖 To peel or skin)
- **Petatear(se)** (📖 From **petate**)
- **Quebrar(se)** (📖 To break)
- **Quedar(se) patitieso** (📖 Said when ☺'s legs get stiff)
- **Restirar(se)** (📖 To stretch out)
- **Cafetear a** ☺ (📖 To drink coffee at ☺'s wake)

— To accompany the family of a recently deceased person while the body is at a funeral home, or lying in state at the family home

— The following words mean *death*:

- **Flaca** (📖 Skinny)
- **La huesuda** (📖 The bony one)
- **Calaca** (📖 Skeleton)
- **Candinga** is another word for the *devil*

E. Pre-Columbian Words

It is only natural for Spanish in Mexico, especially in central and southern Mexico where most of the pre-Columbian population was (and is) found, to be peppered with pre-Columbian words, mostly from the **Nahuatl**. This is a list of some of the words commonly heard in everyday conversation in Mexico.

Achichinque or achichincle

— Helper (slightly derogatory).

Acocil

— A fresh water shrimp.

Aguacate

— Avocado.

Ahuehuete

— Very large and voluminous tree; the wood is similar to cypress. The famous tree in Santa Maria del Tule, in Oaxaca, is 40 meters tall, and over 200 years old.

Amate

— A tree and the bark of that tree, which is used to make a kind of parchment used to write or paint on.

Atole

— A hot drink made of ground corn.

Cacahuate

— Peanut. In Cuba and other Latin American countries, it is called **maní**.

Cacahuazintle

— A special kind of corn with large, white grains, much prized for making **tortillas** and **pozole**.

Calpulli

— Aztec clan based on common ancestors; also a piece of community land.

Camote

— Sweet potato. Also a desert prepared with sweet potato and sugar, made into a paste, cut into bars, wrapped in India paper and packed in small boxes (see *Not for Polite Society*).

Capulín

— Wild cherry tree and the fruit thereof.

Cempasúchitl

— Marigold. Also called "flower of the dead", bright yellow or orange, and very much used to decorate graves. Marigolds are native of Mexico.

Comal

— Flat pan, earthenware or iron, set over a fire to toast grains and cook or reheat tortillas.

Coyote

— The cayote or prairie wolf. Also a person who provides his services (**coyotaje**) to third parties to get certain troublesome legal procedures done by means of kick-backs.

Cuitlacoche (frequently spelled **huitlacoche**)

— Edible grayish black fungus that grows on corn cobs; considered a delicacy, and quite expensive.

Chachalaca

— A tropical bird common to southern Mexico noted for its peculiar song.

Chagüistle or **chahuistle**

— Non-edible disease of corn and wheat plants (see in *Slang in Mexico* **Caer(le) el chahuistle . . .**).

Chamaco(a)

— Child, infant.

Chapopote

— Tar.

Chapulín

— Grasshopper.

Chapultepec

— In Nahuatl this means "Hill of the Grasshopper", which is the beautiful park in Mexico City that takes its name from the hill within the park, once the site of the Aztec rulers' dwelling, later a castle, which housed the Emperor Maximilian and Empress Carlota, and subsequently the residence of a number of Presidents up to and including Porfirio Diaz.

Chayote

— A pear-shaped, prickly form of squash used in salads and stews.

↓ Chiche or chichi (chichigua: foster nurse)

— A vulgar term for the feminine breast.

Chichicuilote

— Grey edible, almost extinct bird.

Chile

— Chili (hot pepper); refers to all varieties. Called **ají** in South America (see *Not for Polite Society*).

Chilpayate

— Child, infant.

Chinampa

— Small floating garden found currently only in Xochimilco, which is now part of Mexico City. Xochimilco is a lake formed by channels surrounding the floating gardens, which include the houses and little farms of the inhabitants.

Chípil

— From the Nahuatl *tzipitl*; used when referring to a spoiled child or a cry-baby; said of a sickly, irritating, annoying child whose mother is pregnant (also used when a husband acts thus).

Chipote

— A lump (usually on the head) resulting from a blow.

Chipotle or chilpotle

— A smoked **chile**, most delicious and used in many dishes.

Chiquihuite or chiquigüite

— A woven palm basket without handles, generally used for tortillas.

Ejote

— String bean.

Elote

— Fresh corn.

Epazote

— Herb (grows wild) used in folk medicine and to spice food.

Equipal

— Chair, the seat of which is made of leather with the back and arms of reed, native of the State of Jalisco.

Escuintle or escuincle

— Youngster (from the Nahuatl **Itzcuintle**, meaning small dog), also used to refer to a pre-Columbian dog.

Guacamole

— A spread made of mashed avocado, seasoned or spiced (see *Mexican Food*).

Guaje

— A gourd (from which the pulp has been removed) used as a container/receptacle. Also a slang expression meaning *foolish*, *dumb* (see **Ser (Hacer(se) guaje)** under *Slang in Mexico*).

Guajolote

— Turkey.

Henequén (Mayan and West Indian roots)

— Variety of the agave or sisal (the fiber and the plant).

Huacal

— A sort of crate used to transport chickens and produce to market.

Living in Mexico

Huachinango

— Red snapper.

Huapango

— Melody and dance of southern Mexico.

Huarache or guarache

— Sandal used by most Indians.

Huehuenche or güegüenche

— Old Indian, leader of a group of Indian dancers on a pilgrimage.

Huipil or hipil

— Long loose sleeveless tunic worn by women, mainly in the South (specially Yucatan) but also in other parts of Mexico.

Huisache or huizach

— Thorny desert bush; sap used to make ink.

Hule

— Rubber tree and rubber itself.

Itacate

— A supply of food to take on a trip, originally wrapped in a large cotton handkerchief (hobo style), now carried in a bag or basket.

Jacal

— Hut.

Jícama

— Edible root vegetable, with white flesh, eaten raw with lemon juice and chili.

Jícara

— A type of dried gourd, used as a bowl or container.

Jitomate

— Tomato. Not to be confused with the (green) **tomate**, which is a different vegetable. (See **tomate**.)

Maguey (Caribbean word)

— Cactaceous plant with large broad leaves edged with thorns, common to arid terrain; from the different kinds of **maguey** plant **pulque**, **mezcal** and **tequila** are made.

Maíz

— Dried corn (maize).

Malacate

— Hoisting machine; also an archeological piece.

Mayate

— Beetle (see *Not for Polite Society*).

Mecapal

— A strip of leather placed across the forehead to which a load carried on the back is attached with strong cord. The strip can also be made of some resistant fabrics, as is usually the case in Mexico City.

Mecapalero

— A porter that uses a **mecapal**.

Mecate

— String made from agave fiber.

Memela

— An oblong **tortilla**, thicker than the ordinary type. In Honduras it is sweet.

Metate

— A slab of flat, porous stone used to grind corn with a stone rolling pin. (See *To be (way) overdressed* under *Common Expressions in English*.)

Living in Mexico

Mezcal

— An alcoholic drink made from different types of **agave** plant.

Mezquite or mesquite

— A tree. The juice is used in ophthalmology.

Milpa

— A cornfield.

Molcajete

— A mortar made of stone in which to mash and grind food with a stone pestle known as a **tejolote**.

Mole

— A thick sauce made of several kinds of dried peppers and other ingredients (see *Mexican Food*).

Nopal

— The traditional cactus plant, with flat paddle shaped edible leaves. Its fruit, the **tuna** (prickly pear) is also eaten.

Ocote

— A type of pine tree rich in resin; the wood is used in construction and small pieces are used as tinder.

Olote

— Corn husk.

Paliacate

— Large printed cotton bandana, usually red.

Petate

— A woven palm mat used as a bed by peasants.

Peyote

— A hallucinogenic plant found in the northern part of Mexico (*Lophophora williamsii*).

Pilmama

— Nursemaid.

Pinole

— Roasted, ground corn, sweetened and flavored, usually with cinnamon.

Popote

— A type of straw for making brooms; also a drinking straw.

Pulque

— The fermented juice of the agave. In the Pyramid at Cholula (Puebla), there is a fresco which has been named "Pulque drinkers".

Quelite

— A plant that grows wild, eaten when tender.

Quetzal

— A bright-plumed, long-tailed bird of the jungles of Southern Mexico and Central America.

Quexquémetl

— A colorful overblouse used by Indian women.

Sinsonte or centzontle (📖 400 voices)

— Bird with a beautiful song.

Tamal

— Corn dough mixed with lard and bits of chicken or pork, then steamed in banana or corn leaves.

Tecolote

— A kind of owl.

Tejocote

— Fruit which ripens in December. A drink called **ponche** (from punch), which is served during Christmas festivities, is made by boiling certain fruits such as sugar cane, prunes, **tejocotes**, sugar, cinnamon and guavas, with and without alcohol.

Living in Mexico

Temazcal

— A small chamber made of adobe brick used as a steam room; the steam is produced by pouring water on heated stones.

Tenate or tanate

— A woven palm basket used to carry food.

Tepache

— A drink made from fermented pineapple juice.

Tezontle

— A highly porous, maroon colored volcanic rock used in Mexican colonial-type buildings.

Tepetate

— Yellowish clay rock used in construction; also yellowish clay soil.

Teponaxtle

— A type of drum.

Tequesquite

— Salt formed on a dry lake bed, used in cooking.

Tequila

— A gin-like drink made with the juice of a certain type of agave. This alcoholic drink, together with **mezcal**, are the best known Mexican drinks.

Tianguis

— An Indian market.

Tlacuache

— A marsupial resembling a mole.

Tlapalería

— A small store selling paint, nails, screws, light bulbs, turpentine, etc., not as sophisticated as a hardware store. (From the Nahuatl **tlapalli**, meaning colors.)

Tomate verde

— A slightly sour fruit resembling the tomato but smaller, green rather than red, and concealed inside an outer husk; used to make the cooked or raw sauces found on every Mexican table.

Tompiate

— Large woven palm basket (see *Not for Polite Society*).

Totopo

— Tortilla cut into wedges and fried or toasted until crunchy; eaten with beans, guacamole, etc.

Zacate

— Grass used as forage for cattle; also a luffa like vegetable fiber used for bathing and washing dishes.

Zapote

— Sapodilla tree and fruit.

Zopilote

— Buzzard; vulture.

However, aside from these words (mostly nouns), thousands of place and street names are also pre-Columbian and part of every day life. There are too many to list here, but are usually long and awkward for non-Mexicans. Examples are **Popocatépetl, Iztaccíhuatl, Nezahualcóyotl, Tlalpan, Tlalnepantla, Tlaxcalantongo, Cocoyoc, Tlaxcala, Tepozotlán . . .** and so on.

F. Mexican Food

Reading a menu, especially in Mexico can often be a frustrating business. This section includes descriptions of certain of the most often encountered dishes and food which might cause confusion for people coming across them for the first time. Quite a few of these dishes predate the Spanish conquest, but still form part of the everyday diet. Some items in this section are simply definitions.

Adobo

— Looks like **mole**, but is drier and less hot. Used with pork.

Agua de limón, naranja, tamarindo, etc.

— Lemonade, orangeade and so on, made with a large variety of fruits. Also known as **aguas frescas**.

Arrachera

— This grilled meat has recently become very popular in the northern part of Mexico, as well as in the southern United States, where they call it **fajitas**. This cut is taken from the diaphragm of the steer.

A la plancha

— A method of cooking whereby a piece of meat, chicken, fish, etc., is grilled on a very hot metal surface (not ridged, and not exposed to direct flame or embers).

A la veracruzana

— A way of cooking and serving fish in a tomato sauce with onion, olives, capers, and **chiles largos**.

Alegrías

— These look and taste something like rice cakes, but are made with amaranth (**amaranto**). They are not found in restaurants but are mostly peddled on street corners or where candied fruit is sold.

Atole

— A hot breakfast drink made from ground corn and flavored with vanilla, chocolate, strawberry, etc., or served unflavored. It is usually available where tamales are sold (e.g., street stands early in the morning).

Bacalao

— This is a salt cod dish brought to Mexico by the Spaniards. The two variations are **A la vizcaína** and **A la sevillana** (from Vizcaya and from Seville), the main difference being that in the former, the fish is in large pieces and in the latter, the fish is flaked. In both cases, it is cooked with potatoes, olives, almonds, tomatoes (optional) and pimento peppers. The salt cod must be Norwegian, as there is no such fish native to Mexico. Salty but very tasty. Prepared mostly around Christmastime.

Barbacoa

— This word sounds like barbecue, but is actually a whole sheep (sometimes goat) cooked slowly with hot stones in a covered pit. A side product is the **consomé**, which drips from the meat into a container while cooking. The taste is very strong, but delicious. Barbacoa is eaten with hot tortillas and **salsa borracha**.

Birria

— Goat served with reddish broth, not very hot. This is a typical dish of Tlaquepaque, an area of Guadalajara, in Jalisco, and in general, the central part of Mexico.

Bolillo

— Non-sweet, chewy roll with a crisp crust. Usually served in a basket on restaurant tables. Sometimes used as a substitute of a **telera** to make **tortas**. Very good.

Cabrito

— Roasted kid, prepared in a special kind of oven. You may also find **cabrito al pastor**, which is the kid roasted over direct flames. Found mostly in the northern part of Mexico.

Camote

— A sweet potato. Both the white and the yellow kind are common. In Puebla, the famous **camotes**, are made from this sweet potato (candied and wrapped in paper). The ideal dessert if you have a sweet tooth.

Campechano(a)

— A **campechano** is a person born in the State of Campeche. It is also an adjective meaning half-and-half, or mixed. For example, a **Cuba campechana** is rum and coke watered down with soda water; oyster and shrimp cocktail; pale and strong beer, etc.

Living in Mexico

Carnitas

— A favorite in Mexico. A pig is cooked in a huge cauldron in its own fat, stirred with a wooden paddle for hours on end. People then can order their favorite part of the pig, usually the leaner parts of the meat, but there is also a nose, ear, etc., which are eaten with hot fresh **tortillas**, topped off with **salsa mexicana**, **salsa verde** or **guacamole**, coriander, chopped onion, etc.

Chalupas or chalupitas

— Finger food. **Tortilla** dough is worked into a small flat round shape, fried, spread with green or red hot sauce, shredded meat and sometimes crumbled white cheese and chopped onion. There are four or five **chalupitas** per order.

Chayote

— Green vegetable shaped a bit like a pear, with a delicate flavor. Not eaten raw.

Chilaquiles (never used in singular)

— A dish made from torn up **tortillas** (usually a way of using **tortillas** that are no longer fresh), fried golden crispy and cooked with strips of chicken or eggs, sauce (**mexicana, verde**, etc.) and topped with thick cream, onion rings and crumbled white cheese. **Chilaquiles** are very hot, which is why they are supposed to be useful in curing a hangover. There is also the not-so-hot version of **chilaquiles** for tourists.

Chile

— There is an enormous variety of **chiles**. There are fresh and dry (some have one name when they are fresh, and another when they are dry, as **chile poblano**, fresh and **chile ancho**, dry). They are prepared in sauces to be eaten alone or as part of other dishes; they can also be prepared with oil and vinegar **en escabeche** (pickled), or as a paste, like all the different types of **moles** and **adobos**, or in powder form.

You can find very mild **chiles** and others that are really dangerous (**habanero**). In general any given **chile** can be very tolerable today, and very hot another occasion. It would be a tough task to name them all, so we list the most common: **ancho** (mild to semi-hot), **cera** (mild to semi-hot), **chilaca** (mild), **chipotle** (mild to hot), **cuaresmeño** (semi-hot), **de árbol** (hot), **guajillo** (mild to semi-hot), **habanero** (extremely dangerous), **jalapeño** (semi-hot), **largo** or **güero** (mild), **manzano** (very hot), **morita** (mild to semi-hot), **pasilla** (mild to semi-hot), **piquín** (very hot), **poblano** (mild to semi-hot), **serrano** (hot). Of course, this classification is strictly from a Mexican point of view.

Chiles en nogada

— A dish made the same way as **chiles rellenos**, but stuffed with spiced minced meat (**picadillo**) and covered with a sauce made with ground walnuts (**nuez de Castilla**, which is an off-white color).

This is then sprinkled with pomegranate seeds. The result is green, white and red (the colors of the Mexican flag). Nuts and pomegranates are seasonal and only available around August. This dish was first prepared for Agustín de Iturbide, Mexican emperor, in 1822.

Chiles rellenos

— **Chiles poblanos** which have been roasted, peeled and stuffed with ground beef, cheese, tuna fish, refried beans, etc. They are then dipped in frothy beaten eggs, and fried in oil. This process is called **capear**. Then, they are served as is, or with cooked tomato sauce. A classic.

Chicharrón

— This is the crunchy skin of the pig, the way it gets when cooked with **carnitas**. It is either eaten as it is or in some kind of sauce, usually **salsa verde**, with fresh hot **tortillas**. Very tasty.

Chongos (zamoranos)

— Even though the **chongo** is a hair-do involving a bun at the nape of the neck, the **chongos** of Zamora, a town in the state of Michoacan, are a sweet made from milk.

Chorizo

— Pork sausage made with paprika and other spices. Very strong flavor. Must be cooked, usually crumbled. Usually served with eggs and made into **tacos**. This "sausage" as originally Spanish- There are differen versions, depending on the region.

Cochinita pibil

— This is the prime regional dish of Yucatan, but is very popular all over Mexico. It is made with shredded cooked pork, prepared with sour oranges, in an **achiote** sauce and eaten with freshly made **tortillas** and garnished with special kind of purple onion (**cebolla morada**) prepared with oil and vinegar. If you are offered sauce made with **chile habanero**, bear in mind it is extremely hot. You may find **pollo pibil** or **pollo en achiote**, which would be the same dish, but made with chicken instead of pork.

Enchiladas

— These are always a good bet. The dish consists of strips of chicken wrapped up in a **tortilla**, bathed mainly in **salsa verde** or **mole** sauce (both included in this section) and topped with grated cheese, thick cream and raw onion rings. Filling and tasty. Again, there are different versions of **enchiladas**, depending upon the region. The **enchiladas potosinas**, for instance, are small (4" in diameter), folded, with cheese; they are found not only in San Luis Potosi, but also frozen in some super markets.

Enchiladas suizas

— Enchiladas cooked with cream, tomato sauce (with no **chile**), and cheese and made *au gratin* in the oven. You can consider these **enchiladas** the "tourist version" of the previous ones. These are completely unknown in Switzerland.

Filete

— This can be either meat or fish. In either case, it is a top quality cut (free of fat and gristle in the case of meat, free of bones in the case of fish). If meat, it is usually grilled, but there are several popular ways of preparing **filete de pescado** (see **mojo de ajo**, **empanizado**, **a la plancha**).

Flauta

— These are called **flautas** due to their resemblance to a flute. They are big, flat **tortillas**, filled with shredded meat (beef, pork, chicken), rolled up tight and then fried. Served with salsa verde or salsa mexicana, chopped onion, crumbled white cheese, chopped lettuce, and sometimes, light cream.

Frijoles

— Beans. **Frijoles de la olla** are just beans boiled with onion, garlic and a bit of pork fat. **Frijoles refritos** are refried beans; i.e., cooked till they are soft, then mashed while simmered with a few spoonfuls of oil or pork fat, until most of the liquid evaporates and a *puree* remains. **Frijoles charros** are **frijoles de la olla** cooked with pork and **chicharrón**.

Garnachas

— Finger food. **Tortilla** dough is worked into a flat round shape, then spread with green or red hot sauce, crumbled white cheese and chopped onion.

Gorditas

— These are not fat girls, but finger food. **Tortilla** dough is mixed with beans, **chicharrón**, etc., or just the dough worked into a thick round shape, then fried, and served with hot sauce. There are also sweet **gorditas** made with brown sugar.

Guacamole

— Avocado mashed with bits of tomato, onion and **chile serrano**, used as a garnish or eaten with **tortillas** or **totopos** (see **Totopos**).

Guisado (n.)

— A main lunch dish involving some kind of meat in a sauce, and usually eaten with tortillas.

Huaraches (📖 Leather sandals)

— Also finger food. **Tortilla** dough is worked into a flat oblong shape, with a little ridge around the edge and then fried, spread with refried beans, topped with almost anything (shredded lettuce, crumbled white cheese, chopped onion and so on), on which a hot sauce is usually drizzled.

Licuado

— A drink made by running fruit through a blender and adding milk (not water). Bananas, mango, berries (only strawberries and blackberries are in plentiful supply in Mexico), are the most common fruits used.

Lima

— Not a lime or a lemon. It looks like a lemon, but the taste is entirely different . . . sweet instead of sour, and quite mild. There are no lemons in Mexico; only limes, which are called **limones**. The **lima** juice is delicious.

Manchamanteles (📖 spot-the-tablecloth)

— The fact that the tablecloth ends up rather soiled gives an idea of the nature of this dish, which is one of the *haute cuisine* specialties of Puebla, based on pork and chicken in **adobo** sauce, to which fruit (pear, peach) is added.

Memelas

— Very similar to the **huaraches** described above.

Menudo

— A dish made of beef tripe, usually very spicy. A hot dish, good in the early morning for a big hangover.

Milanesa (📖 A girl from Milano, Italy)

— A veal cutlet which has been pounded flat, then breaded and fried. You may also ask for a **milanesa de puerco** (pork) or a **milanesa de pollo** (chicken).

Mixiote

— A stew of sliced lamb, rabbit or chicken in **adobo** sauce, encased in **maguey** leaves (tied at the top) and steamed.

Mojo de ajo

— A way of serving fish and other seafood. A handful of finely chopped garlic is slowly browned in oil or butter. The fish or seafood is then fried and dressed with the garlic and oil. To people not used to large quantities of garlic, this may sound overpowering, but the dish is really very tasty.

Living in Mexico

Mole

— When properly made in the traditional manner, **mole poblano** is one of the jewels of Mexican cuisine. It is a sauce made from different types of ground dried **chiles** (**mulato**, **ancho**, **pasilla** and **chipotle**), almonds, sesame seeds, toasted **tortillas**, chocolate (not sweet), and an array of spices. All this is toasted and ground up together on a **metate** (see **Metate** in *Pre-Columbian Words*). Broth is added to achieve the desired consistency. The color of this rich sauce is a dark reddish brown. It can be quite hot. This is then cooked with pieces of chicken, pork or turkey; then served with Mexican rice (sometimes) and **tortillas**.

There are many versions of **mole**, depending on the region. In Oaxaca you can find **mole negro** together with five other kinds of **mole**, all in the same place.

Mole de olla

— A dish prepared with broth, onion, garlic, pieces of beef, **chile ancho** and vegetables, including pieces of corn and a special kind of **tuna** called **xoconostle**, which gives the stew a unique flavor.

Mole verde or pipián

— It is made like **mole poblano**, but the main ingredients are squash seeds. The resulting color is light green. This tasty dish is served with chicken, pork or turkey, accompanied by rice and **tortillas**.

Molletes

— A **bolillo** is split, then spread with refried beans (**frijoles refritos**) and topped with grated cheese. This is grilled in the oven until the cheese melts, and is served immediately with **salsa mexicana**.

Nachos

— **Totopos** topped with melt cheese and **chile jalapeño**.

Nopal

— The leaf from the common cactus plant. **Nopalitos** is a dish made from these leaves, either roasted, diced and served with tomato and onion, or boiled, diced and cooked with scrambled eggs. Reputed to have many natural healing properties. This dish goes way back to before the Spanish conquest.

Pambazos

— A pambazo is a soft, oval non-sweet roll, bathed in a hot **chile** sauce, then fried and stuffed with potatoes fried with **chorizo**. This creation is then topped with shredded lettuce and crumbled white cheese. They are usually found at sidewalk stands, but also in first class restaurants as one of their specialties.

Living in Mexico

Pancita

— A dish prepared in different ways from beef tripe. Used mainly as a breakfast dish.

Pan dulce

— This refers to an assortment of sweet bread or rolls eaten daily at breakfast or supper and sold in all bakeries in Mexico. Mexico is the only country with such a wide variety of bread. Each type (there are many), has a colorful name such as: **alamares**, **besos**, **bigotes**, **campechanas**, **chilindrinas**, **cocoles**, **conchas**, **magdalenas**, **nueves**, **ochos**, **orejas**, **picones**, **piedras**, **polvorones**, **gendarmes**, etc.

Panucho

— Finger food from Yucatan. **Tortilla** dough is worked into a small flat round shape, fried, topped with **cochinita pibil** (not-so-traditional **panuchos** may have shredded chicken, or other meat), **cebolla morada** (chopped purple onion), and **chile habanero** sauce.

Pepito

— This is a steak (always **filete**) sandwich made with a **bolillo** instead of sandwich bread.

Pipián (see **Mole verde**)

Ponche

— This obviously comes from the English *punch*. It is made from different combinations of liquors, but the classical **ponche** served (hot) at the **posadas** (pre-Christmas celebrations) contains rum, a drink made from hibiscus flowers, cinnamon, and fruits in season, which always include chunks of peeled sugar cane and **tejocotes** (a small local plum-like fruit).

Pozole

— A special dish made with fresh **cacahuazintle** corn (hominy) and pork, and seasoned depending on the region of Mexico in question. The result is either pinkish, colorless or greenish. It is spiced with lemon, oregano, chopped lettuce, **chile piquín** and eaten with toasted **tortillas**. It tastes a lot better than it sounds.

Quesadilla

— A **tortilla** filled with almost anything (cheese, beans, squash flower, **cuitlacoche**, mushrooms, any meat, etc.). The **tortilla** is folded once and either heated on a grill or browned in oil.

Rajas

— A popular side dish consisting of chiles poblanos, roasted, peeled, cut in strips and cooked with onion and cream.

Romeritos

— **Romeritos** are small leafy plants that grow on the banks of lakes on the Mexican highland plateau, or are grown commercially. They are cooked with **mulato** chile, diced potatoes and small fritters made with dry ground shrimp. These fritters were previously made with **aguaucle**, the eggs of flies living around the lakes. This may not sound very appetizing, but is truly delicious. The dish was originally very popular during Lent, but is now seen most at the Christmas dinner table.

Ropa vieja (📖 Old clothes)

— A dish made of shredded cooked pork seasoned with olives, capers, chiles largos and vinegar in tomato sauce, which is boiled together until almost dry.

Salpicón

— A dish made of shredded cooked beef (the part of the beef used is called **falda** (📖 skirt), mixed with raw onion, radishes, lettuce, avocado, tomato, **chipotle**, dressed with olive oil and vinegar, and eaten cold.

Salsa mexicana

— A sauce made by finely chopping raw tomato, onion, **chile serrano** and coriander. Served on practically anything.

Salsa verde

— A sauce made of **tomate verde**. The sauce is made by cooking the **tomates** with **chiles serranos** and onion, then making a mush in a mortar and pestle (nowadays most people use a blender). This is the sauce in which **chicharrón** is cooked to prepare **chicharrón en salsa verde**.

Sesos

— Brains, usually beef, commonly eaten in **quesadillas**.

Sincronizadas

— Ham and cheese on a wheat **tortilla**, folded, or between two **tortillas** like a sandwich, and grilled. Eaten with **guacamole**, **salsa verde** or any other sauce.

Sopa

— In Mexico there is **sopa seca** (dry soup) and **sopa aguada** (watery soup). The former includes rice and noodles, and the latter is a soup as known everywhere.

Sopa de médula

— A soup made of the beef spinal chord.

Sope

— Finger food, sometimes eaten as an appetizer. **Tortilla** dough is worked into a thick round shape, usually with a ridge around the edge, then spread with refried beans, topped with chicken, **chorizo**, pork or beef meat, sliced tomato, shredded lettuce, crumbled white cheese, chopped onion and so on, on which a **chile** sauce is usually drizzled.

Tacos

— These hardly need an explanation. Basically a taco is anything wrapped in a hot **tortilla**. There are many variations, and the **tortilla** is fresh made, or fried and browned once the filling is in. Fillings include all kinds of meats (see **Carnitas**), sausage (**chorizo**), vegetables (potatoes, beans, guacamole, etc.) or a combination thereof. There are also **tacos de guisados**, which are filled with almost any Mexican dry dish.

Tacos al pastor

— We don't know what shepherds have to do with this type of taco. Thin slices of pork are skewered, and spread with **adobo**. The skewer then rotates over an open flame. Usually small **tortillas** warmed using the fat from the meat are used to wrap around the meat, parsley, chopped onion, little pieces of pineapple and sauce.

Tamales

— There are a good many types of **tamales**. The most common type found throughout Mexico and other countries of Latin America are made of ground corn, spiced and filled with chicken or pork, wrapped in banana leaves or corn husks and steamed slowly. There are also sweet **tamales**.

Tampiqueña

— This is grilled meat, accompanied with an **enchilada**, refried beans, **rajas**, cream and **aguacate**. Several restaurants and chefs claim to have invented it.

Telera

— A chewy roll, slightly larger and flatter than a **bolillo**. **Teleras** are used to make **tortas**.

Tinga

— Pork stew prepared with **chorizo**, onion, tomato, **tomate verde** and seasoned with **chipotle**. Traditionally served with just-made **tortillas**.

Tomate verde

— A native of Mexico not usually found anywhere else in the world. It is a small, tomato-like vegetable which never turns red and is the basis for many Mexican dishes and sauces.

Torta

— This is not a *torte*, but a sandwich-type arrangement usually made with a **telera** (sometimes a **bolillo** is used instead), spread with mayonnaise or butter and stuffed with one or several of the following: ham, chorizo, baked leg or pork, **milanesa**, egg omelet, cheese, chicken, etc., plus refried beans, sliced tomato, avocado, hot sauce or any kind of **chiles** and shredded lettuce. **Tortas** are often made hot on a grill. They are sold almost anywhere, including at sidewalk stands where passersby can have a quick pick-me-up. Some people make **torta de tamal**, i.e., a **bolillo** filled with a **tamal**, which contains enough calories to keep you going for several days.

Tostada

— A **tortilla** either toasted hard or fried until hard, then topped with **frijoles refritos**, meat or chicken, shredded lettuce, onion rings, a dollop of heavy cream and crumbled white cheese. There are certain variations of this, although the classic is the **tostada de pata**, made with **pata de puerco en escabeche** (pickled pigs' feet).

Totopos

— **Tortilla** quarters fried until hard and used to scoop up food, usually **frijoles refritos** and **guacamole**.

Tuna

— This has nothing to do with any fish. It is the fruit of the **nopal**. Eaten just as any other fruit. Over consumption of **tunas** may cause constipation. (see **Al nopal . . .** under *Proverbs and Sayings in Spanish*).

G. Where Are You From?

Like people all over the world, people in Mexico are proud of their native city and their home state, but are quick to make up jokes (some fairly offensive) about other people's place of origin. Some nouns denoting a person's place of origin are downright insulting. Below there is a list (of the non-insulting variety) for Mexican states, plus a list of Latin American countries. Some variations are also included. Note that none of these words is capitalized.

A person is	If he was born in
aguascalentense	Aguascalientes
bajacaliforniano (a)	Northern Baja California
campechano(a)	Campeche
coahuilense	Coahuila
colimense	Colima
chiapaneco(a)	Chiapas
chihuahuense	Chihuahua
duranguense or durangueño(a)	Durango
guanajuatense	Guanajuato
guerrerense	Guerrero
hidalguense	Hidalgo
jalisciense	Jalisco
mexiquense	the state of México
michoacano(a)	Michoacán
morelense	Morelos
nayarita	Nayarit
neoleonés	Nuevo León
oaxaqueño(a)	Oaxaca
poblano(a)	Puebla
potosino(a)	San Luis Potosí
queretano(a)	Querétaro
quintanarroense	Quintana Roo
sinaloense	Sinaloa
sonorense	Sonora
sudcaliforniano(a)	Southern Baja California
tabasqueño(a)	Tabasco
tamaulipeco(a)	Tamaulipas
tlaxcalteca	Tlaxcala
veracruzano(a)	Veracruz
yucateco(a)	Yucatán
zacatecano(a)	Zacatecas

A person is	If he was born in
argentino(a)	**Argentina**
boliviano(a)	**Bolivia**
brasileño(a)	**Brazil**
colombiano(a)	**Colombia**
costarricense	**Costa Rica**
cubano(a)	**Cuba**
chileno(a)	**Chile**
dominicano(a)	**Dominican Republic**
ecuatoriano(a)	**Ecuador**
guatemalteco(a)	**Guatemala**
haitiano(a)	**Haití**
hondureño(a)	**Honduras**
nicaragüense	**Nicaragua**
panameño(a)	**Panamá**
paraguayo(a)	**Paraguay**
peruano(a)	**Perú**
puertorriqueño(a) (*)	**Puerto Rico**
salvadoreño(a)	**El Salvador**
uruguayo(a)	**Uruguay**
venezolano(a)	**Venezuela**

*Usually misspelled **portorriqueño**.

Care should be taken with the endings of these words to avoid mistakes like **queretense** (the correct noun is **queretano(a)**), and **chihuahueño(a)**, which is a breed of dogs (the correct noun is **chihuahuense**).

A native of the Federal District (**Distrito Federal**) (Mexico City) is never called a "**distrito federaleño**". People from the capital city are sometimes called **capitalinos(as)**, or more derogatively **chilangos(as)**. The latter is mostly used by people who are not from Mexico City. In that same vein is the word **jalisquillos(as)** referring to natives of **Jalisco**, alluding to their machismo which arose from the movies of half a century ago in which the **charro** (the higher class landowner) became established as a model of great virtue (backed up by a pistol). People from San Luis Potosí are sometimes called **tuneros(as)** (from **tuna**, which is Spanish for pickly pear).

Certain other of these nouns, such as **chapín** for Guatemalan, **nica** for Nicaraguan, **tico(a)** for Costa Rican, **charrúa** for Uruguayan and **borinque** for Portorican, are half endearment and half mocking.

Living in Mexico

VI
Latin American Construction Vocabulary

It's interesting to note the differences between construction methods in Mexico and in the United States. Obviously, this is due to differences in culture rather than to differences in climate and topography. Otherwise, homes would look the same in desert areas in both countries, and in tropical areas in both countries and so on. But they do not.

A house or building is usually very obviously Mexican or very obviously American at the very first glance. The buildings, churches and homes built by the Spaniards in early California and the U.S. southwest (many of which are still standing, as they were built to last . . . such as the Alamo and the California missions) ceased to be built as soon as that area fell into other hands, because the Spaniards were no longer the brains behind construction in those areas.

Wooden homes began going up in their place, because that was the way newcomers from the East were used to building. They came from areas covered with forest, where wood was free for the taking and easy to handle, although prone to disappearing in a fire, tornado or hurricane, as we are constantly reminded on the news broadcasts (you'd think people would put on their thinking caps while standing on the piles of smoking debris or mountains of shattered wood which are the remains of the homes and build slightly sturdier edifices after that . . . but they don't seem to do that . . . they just build the exact same house all over again).

In Northern Mexico, homes were originally flat roofed (practically no rain in those parts) and made of whatever was at hand, like adobe (which provides great insulation from the heat), stone and clay brick, usually around a central courtyard called a *patio*, which is an Arab design adopted from the Moors who ruled Spain for 400 years and brought the design from their blisteringly hot desert homelands.

In the rest of Mexico, the Spanish style prevailed, which usually involves homes being surrounded, not by picket fences, but by high walls of stone or adobe to provide security. In other words, construction style depends on who is doing the constructing. An alien from outer space would have no trouble figuring out that the Spaniards dominated everything from Northern Mexico to Tierra del Fuego (with a few insignificant exceptions), and yet an American or European would be unable to tell whether an adobe or cinderblock house in a photograph is in Mexico, Guatemala, Nicaragua, Colombia, Ecuador . . . you get the picture, because the mentality behind all those houses is quite the same.

Nevertheless, throughout history, construction concepts and methods have changed from one country or area to another. It is hard to speak of "construction in Mexico" or "construction in the United States". What we have here is the vocabulary used by construction workers in the main cities, without mentioning differences from region to region, which would result in an entire book.

We are aware that many readers could very well reply: "Where I live we build in a different way". In general terms, the vocabulary contained here applies to Latin American tradition used as from the second half of 20th century in most cities in Mexico and Latin America. We have not included vocabulary used in construction systems in the United States, which in many cases can be called assembly rather than construction.

The variety of differences between today's architecture, materials and building methods in Latin America and the United States and Canada makes it very difficult to draw up a comprehensive glossary of terms. We have tried, and these are the results.

In order to provide a broader picture of construction in Latin America, we have included two small entries, i.e., one on the Day of the Holy Cross, and a paragraph from the play **Los Albañiles** by the renowned Mexican writer, Vicente Leñero.

LA SANTA CRUZ

La Santa Cruz (the Holy Cross) is celebrated on May 3, mainly by construction workers in Mexico. It goes back to the Emperor Constantine in his search for the cross on which Jesus was crucified and possibly a celebration by the initial Franciscan missionaries, who took up a pre-Hispanic custom having to do with a petition to the gods of good harvests.

The fact is that present-day construction workers, in spite of the change to the liturgical calendar by Pope John XXIII, which was later retracted, have celebrated the Santa Cruz for centuries (partly religious and partly pagan). A wooden cross decorated with flowers and tissue paper is placed on the highest point of the building-in-process in hopes that the gods will smile on the project (and prevent it from collapsing). This is then followed by a large meal and copious amounts of liquor (beer, tequila and pulque) provided by the owner of the new edifice for the construction workers and their families, all of which is enjoyed to the accompaniment of deafening firecrackers, usually until no one is left standing.

Los Albañiles (fragment)

by Vicente Leñero

La obra necesita comer para ir formando su cuerpo, ingeniero, como la gente. Se come el tabique, se come el cemento y las varillas y la arena. ¡Mire qué grandote se ve ya nuestro edificio!, hasta parece un gigante . . . Me gusta ir viendo crecer las obras; desde que son un mugroso terreno lleno de basura y de miados de perro. Luego se limpia y se arregla, como se arregla a una novia para que le hágamos un hijo. Y se los hacemos, ¡cómo de que no! Los edificios son como los hijos. Por eso me gusta trabajar en esto de la construcción. Y más me gustaría si las obras nunca se acabaran. Mientras un edificio está así, creciendo, es de usted y mío y de todo nosotros; se le ve nuestro sudor, nuestro trabajo, hasta nuestra sangre. Ya terminado ya qué. Es de otra gente que no vio crecer a ese hijo y que no puede quererlo como nosotros, que le fuimos dando la vida pedazo a pedazo.

A construction project needs to eat in order to build up its body, just like people do. It eats up bricks, and it eats cement and steel rods and sand. Look how big our building looks! It looks huge! I like to watch a building grow, from the time it's a dirty old lot full of trash and dog shit. Then the lot is cleaned out and fixed up, the way we fix up a bride ready to produce a child. And we produce it; we sure as hell do! Buildings are like your children. That's why I like to work in construction. And I would really love it if buildings were never finished! As long as building is like that . . . growing, it's yours and mine and ours . . . it belongs to all of us. You can see our sweat on it, our work, even our blood. Once it's finished, what the hell! It's someone else's . . . someone who didn't watch that child grow, someone who can't love it the way we love it, we who gave it life little by little.

Commonly Used Construction Terms

Note: Latin American construction workers often rely on phonetics when writing, and sometimes don't distinguish between *s* and *c* and *z* and between *b* and *v*.

Latin American Construction Vocabulary

Commonly Used Construction Terms

Spanish	English
a escuadra	straight (at a 90 degree angle)
a espejo	mirror image
a la mitad	half full; half way
a plomo	plumb; vertical; straight up and down
abatible	collapsible
acabado	finishing
acanalada	corrugated (used for roofing sheets)
accesorios	accessories
acero	steel
acero inoxidable	stainless steel
acometida	the point at which utilities (power, drainage, water, telephone, etc.) are connected to a new building or home.
aglomerado	pressboard
aguarrás	turpentine
agujerar	to make holes
ahogado	placed inside poured concrete or under plaster so that it is no longer visible
aislar	to insulate
al hilo	in a straight line
al ras	evenly or flush
alacena	pantry
alambre	wire
alambrón	wire rod
albañil	mason
alberca; piscina	swimming pool
alcantarilla	sewer
alfombra	wall-to-wall carpet
aluminio	aluminum
alzar	to lift; to raise
amacizar	to make something fast and rigid (unmovable)
amarrar	to tie
anclas	anchors; the metal pieces sticking out from a steel or iron window frame that serve to anchor the frame into the concrete or brick wall opening
andamio	scaffolding
ángulo	a length of metal in an "l" shape
antecomedor	breakfast nook
antiderrapante	slip proof
apagador	light switch
aparente	visible (not hidden, like pipes and conduits running along a wall)
apilar	to stack
aplanado	to level, to grade, to smooth up, to float (usually refers to cement mixture or plaster on walls, etc.)
aplanar	to plaster (wall, ceiling, etc.) with cement
apretado	tight; tightly screwed in or on
apuntalar	to shore; to brace; to prop
arco	hacksaw frame

Latin American Construction Vocabulary

Spanish	English
arena	sand
argollas	rings (wood or metal)
armella	eyebolt
aserrín	sawdust & wood shavings
atornillar	to screw
azotea	a flat (not slanting) roof edged with a low parapet
azulejo	hand made tile
bajar	to lower; to go down
bajo alfombra	the layer of stuff that goes under carpeting
bajo llave	under lock & key
balcón	balcony
barandal	a railing
barniz	varnish
barnizar	to varnish
barra	a bar; a counter (kitchen)
barrer	to sweep
barreta	crowbar
barro	earthen (n.); made of clay
berbiquí	ratchet brace for drilling
bidón; tambo	an empty oil drum
bisagra	hinge
block	block
boiler	water heater
bomba	pump
bombear	to pump
botaguas	a length of metal or plastic fixed to the bottom edge of a door or window to keep rainwater out
bote	a bucket
bréiker	breaker (electrical)
brilloso	shiny
broca	drill bit
brocha	paint brush
buldozer	bulldozer
bulto (de cemento, de cal, etc.)	a sack or bag (of cement, etc.)
cable	electric cable or wire
cablear	to install electric cabling
cadena	chain; a girder or reinforced concrete beam at floor level (see **trabe**)
cajón	drawer; also an individual parking space
cal; calhidra, preparado de cal	lime (used in mixing cement)
calentador	heater (water or space)
cámara	inner tube; chamber
camión	truck; bus
camión materialista	a truck that delivers building materials
canaleta	gutter (on roof)
cancel	partition (usually of lightweight material)
candado	padlock
caoba	mahogany
capa; mano	a coat or layer of something like paint or cement

Latin American Construction Vocabulary

Spanish	English
cargar	to load; to charge
carpintería	carpentry; carpentry shop
carpintero	carpenter
carretilla	wheelbarrow
cartón	cardboard
cascajo	rubble from a construction site (usually when there has been some demolishing) (see **escombro**)
casco	hard hat
castillo	a heavy, thick reinforced concrete column poured at the corners of a room
cedazo	a screen for sifting (sand, etc.)
cedro	cedar
celosía	lattice on a window; Venetian blind
cemento	cement
cepas	trenches dug for stone foundations to be built in
cepillar	to plane (carpentry)
cepillo	brush; plane (carpentry)
cerca	close, closeby, near, nearby (adj.); fence (n.)
cernidor	a screen for sifting (sand, etc.)
cero fino	a white artificial sand used in cement mixtures (thinner than **cero grueso**)
cero grueso	a white artificial sand used in cement mixtures (thicker than **cero fino**)
céspol	a gooseneck water trap under a sink
chaflán	cant; a length of outward slanting cement mixture at ground or floor level, usually to keep rain water flowing away from a wall
chalán	a mason's assistant
chamba	work; job
chapa	lock (on a door)
chapopote	tar
chorrear	to dribble
chueco	bent; crooked (said or people as well)
cielo raso	a ceiling made of lacquered or whitewashed sailcloth and attached to wooden beams (no longer used in building, but still in existence in many homes)
cimbra	form (for pouring concrete)
cimbrar	to place wooden formwork for pouring concrete
cimiento	foundation
cisterna	cistern
claro	said of light colors; of course!; a span from x to x
clavar	to nail
clavo	nail
closet	closet
cobre	copper
cocina	kitchen
codo	elbow (plumbing or electrical)
coladera	drain hole in floor or shower with a drain cover
(el) colado	an expanse of poured concrete
colar	to pour concrete
colgar	to hang

Latin American Construction Vocabulary

Spanish	English
colocar	to put; to place
color liso	solid color (no print)
comedor	dining room
componer	to repair
conducto	conduit (as for cable)
conexiones	plumbing or electrical connections
confitillo	a very fine gravel
contacto	a wall plug (for plugging electric appliances into)
contrafuerte	pillar of masonry serving to support a wall
cordón	string
corredizo	sliding (adj.)
correr	to fire (slang); to slide open or closed, like a sliding door; to move or push a little way
cortina	curtain
cortinero	curtain rod or equivalent
cristal	good quality glass (windows, tabletops, etc.) (see **vidrio**)
cuadrado	square
cuadro	picture or square shape
cuate	pal
cubeta	bucket
cubo	a bucket or similar container; a square space left in the interior of a house or building to provide light and air
cubrir	to cover (as with a tarp or cloth)
cuchara	trowel
cuña	a wedge, but also any flat piece of metal (with or without a wooden handle) with a fairly sharp edge, used to scrape paint or uneven surfaces (cement, etc.)
cúpula	a dome (concrete, usually covered with tile)
curar	to cure (watering a cement mixture)
cúter	cutter
dala	a crosswise reinforcement halfway between floor and ceiling
dar(se) una vuelta	to drop in to inspect or visit
dar(le) vuelta	to turn (like a handle or crank)
demoler	to knock down or demolish
desagüe	drain
desarmador	screwdriver
desatornillar	to unscrew
descanso	a rest; a landing in a staircase
descargar	to unload; to remove a charge
descimbrar	to remove wooden formwork after poured concrete has hardened
descomponer	to break or otherwise mess up a device so that it no longer works
descompuesto	out of order
desechar	to dispose of
desenroscar	to unscrew a cap, hose, etc.
desenvolver	to unwrap
deslizar	to slide
despedir	to fire; to give off (like an odor or gas)
despegar	to unstick; to unglue
desván	attic
dibujos; planos	drawings; blueprints

Latin American Construction Vocabulary

Spanish	English
dintel	upper part of a door or window frame
diseño	design
doblado	bent
doblar	to bend
domo	a skylight (usually acrylic or glass in a frame of some kind)
drenaje	drainage
drenar	to drain
ducto	a duct; usually black or orange hose through which electric cables are run when cabling a house or building; also air conditioning duct
duelas	floor boards
duro	hard, difficult (adj.)
emboquillar	to prepare a door or window space (in stucco, brick, concrete etc. building) in preparation to installing the frame
empaque	rubber washer (for hoses etc.)
emparejar	to even out; to make even
empotrado	built-in (adj.), like a built-in oven or bookcase
empujar	to push
en línea recta	in a straight line
encalar	to apply a coat of lime dissolved in water
enchufar	to plug in
enchufe	a plug (that is plugged into the wall)
endurecer	to harden
engrasado	greased
enroscar	to screw on a cap, hose, etc.
entrega	delivery
entregar	to deliver
entrepaño	a shelf (as in a bookcase, usually wood)
envolver	to wrap
equipo	equipment or a set of tools
escalera	ladder or steps or a stairway
escalera de caracol	spiral staircase
escalera de mano	ladder
escalón	step
escoba	broom
escombro	rubble resulting from construction work (not usually including rubble from demolishing) (see **cascajo**)
espejo	mirror
esquina	corner (exterior)
estacionamiento	parking place
estante	shelves in a piece of furniture (not necessarily wood)
estibar	to stack
estufa	stove
excavar	to dig
excusado	toilet
extender	to roll out; to spread out
exterior	outside; outdoor (adj.)
extractor	an extractor
fijar	to fix (as in repair); to make rigid something that is loose
filo	sharp edge or just edge
filoso	sharp

Latin American Construction Vocabulary

Spanish	English
firme	a slab of poured concrete
flojo	loose
forrar	to line
forro	lining
fosa séptica	septic tank
fraguar	to harden (usually cement after it has been poured)
¡fuera abajo!	look out below!
fuga	leak (out) (see **gotera**)
fundir	to melt
fusible de seguridad	fuse
galvanizado(a)	galvanized
galvanizar	to galvanize
gancho	hook
gato	jack
gogles	goggles or eye protectors
golpear	to strike (a blow); to beat; to beat up
gotera	a leak in a roof
gotero	a hanging section (about 1 inch high) along the edge of a roof to prevent rainwater from running up the inside of the eaves and down the wall
gradas	stone or concrete steps (usually outdoors)
grava	gravel
grúa	crane
grueso	thick (for solid items and for paint or semi liquid mixtures like cement mix)
gualdra	a large beam placed across the top of a fireplace
hacer mezcla	to make a cement mix (with sand, gravel and water, and sometimes lime)
harnear	to sift; to screen
harnero	a screen for sifting (sand, etc.)
herrería	iron work; shop where iron work is done
hierro	iron
hierro forjado	wrought iron
hierro fundido	cast iron
hilada	a row of bricks
hilo	thread; also thread as in pipes that screw into each other; plumb line
hondo	deep
hoyo	hole
hueco	hole (n.); hollow (adj.)
huella	the depth of a step in a staircase
iluminación	lighting
iluminar	to light something
impermeabilizante	waterproofing (material) (n.)
impermeabilizar	to waterproof
impermeable	waterproof (adj.)
incapacidad	sick leave
inodoro	toilet
inspección	inspection
inspector	inspector
interior	inside (adj.)

Latin American Construction Vocabulary

Spanish	English
invertir	to turn upside-down; to invert
jardín	yard; garden
jardinera	planter (gardening)
junta	joint (between tiles)
junta con silicón o cemento blanco	caulking
ladrillo	a thin brick 1 and 2 inches thick
lámina de acero	steel sheeting
lámina de asbesto	asbestos sheeting (for roofing . . . no longer used)
laminado	laminate; laminated
lámpara	lamp (any kind)
latón	brass (n.)
lavamanos, lavabo	bathroom sink
lavar	to wash
lechada	a mixture of very thin water and white cement
lechadear	to apply a mixture of very thin water and white cement just enough to cover a surface, or to fill in small spaces in floor a wall tile joints
lija (papel de lija)	sandpaper
lijar	to sand (carpentry)
lima	file (for filing metal)
limar	to file (metal)
liso	smooth
listón	ribbon
llave	key; water tap (kitchen or bathroom)
llave mezcladora	water tap designed to blend hot and cold water
llave "alen"	allen key
llave de paso	stopcock
llave en mano	a turnkey project
llave "stilson"	heavy duty monkey wrench
llenar	to fill
lleno	full
lona	tarp
losa	concrete slab
macho	male (as in a male plug)
macizo	solid
madera	wood
máistro or **mái** for short	a master mason capable of building a home or a small building (corrupted from **maestro**); also used to refer to a bona fide plumber, electrician, auto mechanic, etc.
malla	grille
mampara	any temporary arrangement or structure intended to protect from falling material ; a screen or partition
mancha	stain
manchado	stained
mango	handle
manguera	hose
manija	handle
mano (de pintura)	coat of paint, varnish, etc. (see **capa**)
mano de obra	labor
marco	frame

Latin American Construction Vocabulary

Spanish	English
mármol	marble
martelinado	poured concrete that has been chipped on the surface to make it look like natural stone
martelinar	to chip poured concrete to make it look like natural stone
martillo	hammer
matar	to reduce the sharpness of a wooden or concrete edge by planning, sanding, chipping, etc.
mate	matt; not shiny
material	refers to all material used in construction
mecapal	an age-old method of carrying a heavy load, where the load is in a basket on the back of a person, with ropes leading up and attached to a cloth placed across the forehead, which distributes the weight
metro; flexómetro	a meter; a measuring tape
mezcla	any mixture; cement/sand/gravel/water mixture ready to pour
mojado(a)	wet
mojar	to wet
moldura	molding
mosaico	tile
muebles	furniture
muebles de baño	bathroom fixtures
muro	wall (stucco, concrete, brick, stone)
muro de carga	weight-bearing wall
niple	nipple
nivel	level; mason's level
obra negra	the finished construction before any plastering, windows, doors, finishings, etc., are put in (referring to concrete or brick buildings)
oculto	hidden; unseen
oficial de albañilería	a certified mason; a master mason
orilla	edge; border
oscuro	dark
pala	shovel; spade
palapa	a grass or thatched roof
pandeado(a)	warped (usually referring to wood)
pandear	to warp (usually referring to wood)
pantalla	screen
pared	wall (of any kind) in a house or building, not freestanding, which is a **muro**
parejo	even (not bumpy or wavy); evenly
pasador	a bolt (on a door)
pata	foot (bed, table, etc)
patio	inner court yard (not used as a patio in English, which would be a **terraza** in Spanish)
patrón	a pattern; the boss; the employer
pecho paloma	ornamental carving at the end of a wooden beam
pegar	to stick (with glue, cement, etc.)
pegazulejo	cement for laying tile (Mastik)
peldaño	the height of a step in a staircase
peralte	the height of a step in a staircase
perfil	a metal bar of different thicknesses, calibers and forms used in making metal stairs, doorframes, etc.

Latin American Construction Vocabulary

Spanish	English
perico	monkey wrench (not as heavy as the **llave "stilson"**)
perno	bolt (on which you screw a nut, although the word **tornillo** is also used)
persianas	blinds
pichancha	strainer (a device at the end of a pipe in a cistern through which water is pumped to a tank)
pico	pick (as in pick and shovel)
pie	foot
pija	screw
pilote	pile (a cylindrical support, not a pile of (for example) sand)
pino	pine
pintura	paint
pinzas	tongs or pliers
piscina; alberca	swimming pool
piso	floor
plano(a)	flat (adj.)
plano(s)	drawings or blueprints
plegadizo	folding, like chairs or doors
plomada	the plumb string and bob
plomería	plumbing
plomero	plumber
pluma	boom
polea	pulley
polín	four by four
poroso	porous
portón	gate
prensar	to press
presupuesto	quotation
profundidad	depth
profundo(a)	deep
protección	protection; iron bars on windows and doors
proyecto	project
prueba	test
ptr	a formed metal length used in making stairs, etc.
puerta	door
puertas corredizas	sliding doors
puertas plegadizas	folding doors
pulgada	inch
rampa	ramp
rastrillo	rake
(la) raya	weekly wages
rebajar	to thin (paint); to reduce (price)
recámara	bedroom
rechazar	to reject
redondear	to make round or rounder; to round out
redondo	round
reforzado	reinforced
reforzar	to strengthen or reinforce
regadera	a shower or showerhead
reja	the front gate (usually metal, iron or steel)

Latin American Construction Vocabulary